DR. C. G. JUNG

" PSYCHOLOGY OF THE UNCONSCIOUS "

PSYCHOLOGY OF THE UNCONSCIOUS

*A Study of the Transformations
and Symbolisms of the Libido*

A Contribution to the History of the Evolution of Thought

BY

Dr. C. G. JUNG

Of the University of Zurich

AUTHORIZED TRANSLATION, WITH INTRODUCTION, BY

BEATRICE M. HINKLE, M.D.

Of the Neurological Department of Cornell University Medical
School and of the New York Post Graduate Medical School

ISBN: 978-1-63923-114-0

Printed: March 2023

Published and Distributed By:
Lushena Books
607 Country Club Drive, Unit E
Bensenville, IL 60106
www.lushenabks.com

ISBN: 978-1-63923-114-0

TRANSLATOR'S NOTE

THAT humanity is seeking a new message, a new light upon the meaning of life, and something tangible, as it were, with which it can work towards a larger understanding of itself and its relation to the universe, is a fact I think none will gainsay. Therefore, it has seemed to me particularly timely to introduce to the English-speaking world Dr. Jung's remarkable book, " Wandlungen und Symbole der Libido." In this work he has plunged boldly into the treacherous sea of mythology and folklore, the productions of the ancient mind and that of the common people, and turned upon this vast material the same scientific and painstaking method of psychologic analysis that is applied to the modern mind, in order to reveal the common bond of desire and longing which unites all humanity, and thus bridge the gaps presumed to exist between ancient and widely separated peoples and those of our modern time. The discovery of this undercurrent affecting and influencing ancient peoples as well as modern serves as a foundation or platform from which he proceeds to hold aloft a new ideal, a new goal of attainment possible of achievement and which can be intellectually satisfying, as well as emotionally appealing: the goal of *moral autonomy*.

This book, remarkable for its erudition and the tremendous labor expended upon it, as well as for the new

light which it sheds upon human life, its motives, its
needs and its possibilities, is not one for desultory reading or superficial examination. Such an approach will
prevent the reader from gaining anything of its real
value; but for those who can bring a serious interest and
willingness to give a careful study to it the work will
prove to be a veritable mine capable of yielding the
greatest riches.

The difficulties in translating a book such as this are
almost insuperable, but I have tried faithfully to express
Dr. Jung's thought, keeping as close to the original text
as possible and, at the same time, rendering the difficult
material and complicated German phrasing as simply and
clearly as the subject-matter would allow. In all this
work I owe much to Miss Helen I. Brayton, without
whose faithful assistance the work would never have been
completed. I wish to acknowledge my gratitude to Mr.
Louis Untermeyer, whose help in rendering the poetic
quotations into English verse has been invaluable, and to
express as well my gratitude to other friends who have
assisted me in various ways from time to time.

B. M. H.

New York, 1915.

AN INTRODUCTION TO PSYCHOANALYSIS AND ANALYTIC PSYCHOLOGY

WHEN Professor Freud of Vienna made his early discoveries in the realm of the neuroses, and announced that the basis and origin of the various symptoms grouped under the terms hysteria and neuroses lay in unfulfilled desires and wishes, unexpressed and unknown to the patient for the most part, and concerned chiefly with the sexual instinct, it was not realized what far-reaching influence this unpopular and bitterly attacked theory would exert on the understanding of human life in general.

For this theory has so widened in its scope that its application has now extended beyond a particular group of pathologic states. It has in fact led to a new evaluation of the whole conduct of human life; a new comprehension has developed which explains those things which formerly were unexplained, and there is offered an understanding not only of the symptoms of a neurosis and the phenomena of conduct but the product of the mind as expressed in myths and religions.

This amazing growth has proceeded steadily in an ever-widening fashion despite opposition as violent as any of which we have knowledge in the past. The criticism originally directed towards the little understood and much disliked sexual conception now includes the further teachings of a psychology which by the application to it of such damning phrases as mystical, metaphysical and sacrilegious, is condemned as unscientific.

To add to the general confusion and misundertanding surrounding this new school of thought there has arisen a division amongst the leaders themselves, so that there now exist two schools led respectively by Professor Sigmund Freud of Vienna and Dr. Carl Jung of Zurich, referred to in the literature as the Vienna School and the Zurich School.

It is very easy to understand that criticism and opposition should develop against a psychology so difficult of comprehension, and so disturbing to the ideas which have been held by humanity for ages; a psychology which furthermore requires a special technique as well as an observer trained to recognize and appreciate in psychologic phenomena a verification of the statement that there is no such thing as chance, and that every act and every expression has its own meaning, determined by the inner feelings and wishes of the individual.

It is not a simple matter to come out boldly and state that every individual is to a large extent the determiner of his own destiny, for only by poets and philosophers has this idea been put forth—not by science; and it is a brave act to make this statement with full consciousness of all its meaning, and to stand ready to prove it by scientific reasoning and procedure.

Developed entirely through empirical investigation and through an analysis of individual cases, Freudian psychology seems particularly to belong to that conception of Max Müller's that " An empirical acquaintance with facts rises to a scientific knowledge of facts as soon as the mind discovers beneath the multiplicity of single productions the unity of an organic system." *

Psychoanalysis is the name given to the method developed for reaching down into the hidden depths of the individual to bring to light the underlying motives and determinants of his symptoms and attitudes, and to reveal the unconscious tendencies which lie behind actions and reactions and which influence development and determine the relations of life itself. The result of digging down into the hidden psyche has been to produce a mass of material from below the threshold of consciousness, so astonishing and disturbing and out of relation with the previously held values, as to arouse in any one unfamiliar with the process the strongest antagonism and criticism.

Although originally studied only as a therapeutic method for the sick it was soon realized through an analysis of normal people how slight were the differences in the content of the unconscious of the sick and of the normal. The differences observed were seen to be rather in the reactions to life and to the conflicts produced by contending forces in the individual.

These conflicts, usually not fully perceived by the individual, and having to do with objectionable desires and wishes that are not in keeping with the conscious idea of self, produce marked effects which are expressed either in certain opinions, prejudices, attitudes of conduct,

* " Science of Language," first series, p. 25.

faulty actions, or in some definite pathologic symptom. As Dr. Jung says, he who remains healthy has to struggle with the same complexes that cause the neurotic to fall ill.

In a valuable book called " The Neighbor," written by the late Professor N. Shaler of Harvard University, there occurs this very far-reaching statement: " It is hardly too much to say that all the important errors of conduct, all the burdens of men or of societies are caused by the inadequacies in the association of the primal animal emotions with those mental powers which have been so rapidly developed in mankind."

This statement, reached by a process of reasoning and a method of thought and study entirely different from psychoanalysis, nevertheless so completely expresses in brief form the very basis of the postulates developed through psychoanalysis that I quote it here. Such a statement made in the course of a general examination of human relations does not arouse opposition nor seem to be so difficult of acceptance. It appears to be the individual application of these conceptions that has roused such bitter antagonism and violent denunciations.

Rightly understood and used, psychoanalysis may be compared to surgery, for psychoanalysis stands in the same relation to the personality as surgery does to the body, and they aim at parallel results.

It is well recognized that in the last analysis nature is the real physician, the healer of wounds; but prior to the development of our modern asepsis and surgical technique the healing produced by nature was most often of a very faulty and imperfect type—hideous scars, distorted and crippled limbs, with functions impaired or incapacitated, resulted from the wounds, or else nature was unable to cope with the hurt and the injured one succumbed.

Science has been steadily working for centuries with the aim of understanding nature and finding means to aid and co-operate with her so that healing could take place with the least possible loss of function or permanent injury to the individual. Marvelous results have rewarded these persistent efforts, as the brilliant achievements of surgery plainly indicate.

Meantime, however, little thought was given to the possibility of any scientific method being available to help man overcome the wounds and conflicts taking place in his soul, hurts which retarded his development and progress as a personality, and which frequently in the struggle resulted in physical pains and symptoms of the most varied character. That was left solely to religion and metaphysics. Now, however, this same assistance that surgery has given to the physical body, psychoanalysis attempts to give to the personality. That it cannot always succeed is as much to be expected, and more, than that surgery does not always succeed, for the analytic work requires much of the individual. No real result can be attained if he has not already developed a certain quality of character and intelligence which makes it possible for him to submit himself to a facing of his naked soul, and to the pain and suffering which this often entails. Here, as in no other relation in life, an absolute truth and an absolute honesty are the only basis of action, since deception of any kind deceives no one but the individual himself and acts as a boomerang, defeating his own aims.

Such deep searching and penetrating into the soul is not something to be undertaken lightly nor to be considered a trivial or simple matter, and the fact is that where a strong compulsion is lacking, such as sickness or a situation too difficult to meet, much courage is required to undertake it.

In order to understand this psychology which is pervading all realms of thought and seems destined to be a new psychological-philosophical system for the understanding and practical advancement of human life, it will be necessary to go somewhat into detail regarding its development and present status. For in this new direction lies its greatest value and its greatest danger.

The beginnings of this work were first published in 1895 in a book entitled "Studien über Hysterie," and contained the joint investigations into hysteria of Dr. Breuer of Vienna and his pupil Dr. Sigmund Freud. The results of their investigations seemed to show that the various symptoms grouped under the title of hysteria were the result of emotionally colored reminiscences which, all unknown to the conscious waking self, were really actively expressing themselves through the surrogate form of symptoms and that these experiences, although forgotten by the patient, could be reproduced and the emotional content discharged.

Hypnosis was the means used to enable the physician to penetrate deeply into the forgotten memories, for it was found through hypnosis that these lost incidents and circumstances were not really lost at all but only dropped from consciousness, and were capable of being revived when given the proper stimuli. The astonishing part about it was that with the revival of these memories and their accompanying painful and disturbing emotions, the symptoms disappeared. This led naturally to the conclusion that these symptoms were dependent upon some emotional disturbance or psychic trauma which had been inadequately expressed, and that in order to cure the patient one merely had to establish the connection between the memory and the emotions which properly belonged to it, letting the emotion work itself out through a reproduction of the forgotten scene.

With further investigation Freud found that hypnosis was unnecessary for the revival of the forgotten experiences, and that it was possible to obtain the lost emotional material in the conscious and normal state. For this purpose the patient was encouraged to assume a passive, non-critical attitude and simply let his thoughts flow, speaking of whatever came into his mind, holding nothing back. During this free and easy discussion of his life and conditions, directed by the law of association of ideas, reference was invariably made to the experiences or thoughts which were the most affective and disturbing elements. It was seen to be quite impossible to avoid this indirect revelation because of the strength of the emotions surrounding these ideas and the effect of the conscious wish to repress unpleasant feelings. This important group of ideas or impressions, with the feelings and emotions clustered around them which are betrayed through this process, was called by Jung a *complex*.

However, with the touching of the *complex* which always contains feelings and emotions so painful or unpleasant as to be unacceptable to consciousness, and which are therefore repressed and hidden, great difficulties appeared, for very often the patient came to a sudden stop and could apparently recall nothing more. Memory gaps were frequent, relations twisted, etc. Evidently some force banished these memories so that the person was quite honest in saying that he could remember nothing or that there was nothing to tell. This kind of forgetfulness was called *repression,* and is the normal mechanism by which nature protects the individual from such painful feelings as are caused by unpleasant and unacceptable experiences and thoughts, the recognition of his egoistic nature, and the often quite unbearable conflict of his weaknesses with his feelings of idealism.

At this early time great attention was given towards developing a technique which would render more easy the reproduction of these forgotten memories, for with the abandonment of hypnosis it was seen that some unknown active force was at work which not only banished painful memories and feelings, but also prevented their return; this was called *resistance.* This resistance was found to be the important mechanism which interfered with a free flow of thought and produced the greatest difficulty in the further conduct of the analysis. It appeared under various guises and frequently manifested itself in intellectual objections based on reasoning ground, in criticism directed towards the analyst, or in criticism of the method itself, and finally, often in a complete blocking of expression, so that until the resistance was broken nothing more could be produced.

It was necessary then to find some aid by which these resistances could be overcome and the repressed memories and feelings revived and set free. For it was proven again and again that even though the person was not at all aware of concealing within himself some emotionally disturbing feeling or experience with which his symptoms were associated, yet such was the fact, and that under proper conditions this material could be brought into consciousness. This realm where these unknown but disturbing emotions were hidden was called the " Unconscious "—the " Unconscious " also being a name used arbitrarily to indicate all that material of which the person is not aware at the given time—the not-conscious.

This term is used very loosely in Freudian psychology and is not intended to provoke any academic discussion but to conform strictly to the dictionary classification of a " negative concept which can neither be described nor defined." To say that an idea or feeling is unconscious merely means to indicate that the individual is unaware at that time of its existence, or that all the material of which he is unaware at a given time is unconscious.

With the discovery of the significance in relation to hysteria of these varied experiences and forgotten memories which always led into the erotic realm and usually were carried far back into early childhood, the theory of an infantile sexual trauma as a cause of this neurosis developed. Contrary to the usual belief that children have no sexuality and that only at puberty does it suddenly arise, it was definitely shown that there was a very marked kind of sexuality among children of the most tender years, entirely instinctive and capable of producing a grave effect on the entire later life.

However, further investigations carried into the lives of normal people disclosed quite as many psychic and sexual traumas in their early childhood as in the lives of the patients; therefore, the conception of the " infantile sexual trauma " as the etiological factor was abandoned in favor of " the infantilism of sexuality " itself. In other words, it was soon realized that many of the sexual traumas which were placed in their early childhood by these patients, did not really exist except in their own phantasies and probably were produced as a defence against the memories of their own childish sexual activities. These experiences led to a deep investigation into the nature of the child's sexuality and developed the ideas which Freud incorporated in a work called " Three Contributions to the Sexual Theory." He found so many variations and manifestations of sexual activity even among young children that he realized that this activity was the normal, although entirely unconscious, expression of the child's developing life, and while not comparable to the adult sexuality, nevertheless produced a very definite influence and effect on the child's life.

These childish expressions of this instinct he called " polymorphous perverse," because in many ways they resembled the various abnormalities called perversions when found among adults under certain conditions.

In the light of these additional investigations Freud was led to change his formulation, for instead of the symptoms of the neurotic patient being due to definite sexual experiences, they seemed to be determined by his reactions towards his own sexual constitution and the kind of repression to which these instincts were subjected.

Perhaps one of the greatest sources of misunderstanding and difficulty in this whole subject lies in the term sexuality, for Freud's conception of this is entirely different from that of the popular sense. He conceives sexuality to be practically synonymous with the word *love* and to include under this term all those tender feelings and emotions which have had their origin in a primitive erotic source, even if now their primary aim is entirely lost and another substituted for it. It must also be borne in mind that Freud strictly emphasizes the psychic side of sexuality and its importance, as well as the somatic expression.

Therefore, to understand Freud's theories, his very broad conception of the term sexual must never be forgotten.

Through this careful investigation of the psychic life of the individual, the tremendous influence and importance of phantasy-making for the fate was definitely shown. It was discovered that the indulgence in daydreams and phantasies was practically universal not only among children but among adults, that even whole lives were being lived out in a phantastic world created by the dreamer, a world wherein he could fulfil all those wishes and desires which were found to be too difficult or impossible to satisfy in the world of reality.

Much of this phantasy thinking was seen to be scarcely conscious, but arose from unrealized wishes, desires and strivings which could only express themselves through veiled symbols in the form of phantastic structures not understood, nor fully recognized. Indeed, it is perhaps one of the most common human experiences to find "queer thoughts," undesired ideas and images, forcing themselves upon one's attention to such an extent that the will has to be employed to push them out of mind. It is not unusual to discover long-forgotten impressions of childhood assuming a phantastic shape in memory, and dwelt upon as though they were still of importance.

This material afforded a rich field for the searchers into the soul, for through the operation of the law of association of ideas these phantastic products, traced back to their origin, revealed the fact that instead of being meaningless or foolish, they were produced by a definite process, and arose from distinct wishes and desires which unconsciously veiled themselves in these mysterious forms and pictures.

It is conceded that the most completely unconscious product of an individual is his dream, and therefore Professor Freud turned his attention from phantasies and day-dreams to the investigation of the nightly dreams of his patients to discover whether they would throw light upon the painful feelings and ideas repressed out of consciousness, and therefore inaccessible to direct revelation.

This brilliant idea soon led to a rich fruiting, for it became evident that contrary to the usual conception that the dream is a phantastic and absurd jumble of heterogeneous fragments, having no real relation to the life of the individual, it is full of meaning. In fact, it is usually concerned with the problem of life most pressing at the time, which expresses itself not directly, but in symbolic form so as to be unrecognized. In this way the individual gains an expression and fulfilment of his unrealized wish or desire.

This discovery of the symbolic nature of the dream and the phantasy was brought about entirely through the associative method and developed empirically through investigations of the dreams of many people. In this manner it became evident that certain ideas and objects which recurred again and again in the dreams and phantasies of different people were definitely associated with certain unconscious or unrecognized wishes and desires, and were repeatedly used by the mind to express these meanings where a direct form was repressed and unallowed. Thus certain dream expressions and figures were in a general way considered to be rather definite symbols of these repressed ideas and feelings found in the unconscious. Through a comparative and parallel study it soon appeared that there was a similiar mechanism at work in myths and fairy tales and that the relationship between the dreams and phantasies of an individual and the myths and folk tales of a people was so close that Abraham could say that the myth is a fragment of the infantile soul life of the race and the dream is the myth of the individual.

Thus through relating his dreams the patient himself furnished the most important means of gaining access to the unconscious and disturbing complexes with which his symptoms were connected.

Besides the dream analysis the patient furnished other means of revelation of his complexes—his mannerisms and unconscious acts, his opening remarks to his physician, his emotional reactions to certain ideas; in short the whole behavior and verbal expressions of the individual reveal his inner nature and problems.

Through all this work it became clear that in the emotional nature lay the origin not only of the various nervous illnesses themselves, but also of the isolated symptoms and individual idiosyncrasies and peculiarities which are the part of all humanity and that the pathogenic cause of the disturbances lies not in the ignorance of individuals, but in those inner resistances which are the underlying basis of this ignorance.

Therefore the aim of the therapy became not merely the relief of the ignorance but the searching out and combating of these resistances.

It becomes evident from even this brief description of the analytic procedure that we are dealing with a very complex and delicate material, and with a technique which needs to make definite use of all influences available for the help of the patient. It has long been recognized that the relation established between physician and patient has a great effect upon the medical assistance which he is able to render—in other words, if a confidence and personal regard developed in the patient towards the physician, the latter's advice was just so much more efficacious. This personal feeling has been frankly recognized and made of distinct service in psychoanalytic treatment under the name of *transference*. It is through the aid of this definite relationship which must be established in the one being analyzed towards the analyst that it is possible to deal with the unconscious and organized resistances which so easily blind the individual and render the acceptance of the new valuations very difficult to the raw and sensitive soul.

Freud's emphasis upon the rôle of the sexual instinct in the production of the neurosis and also in its determining power upon the personality of the normal individual does not imply that he does not also recognize other determinants at the root of human conduct, as for instance, the instinct for preservation of life and the ego principle itself. But these motives are not so violently forbidden and repressed as the sexual impulse, and therefore, because of that repressive force and the strength of the impulse he considers this primary in its influence upon the human being.

The importance of this instinct upon human life is clearly revealed by the great place given to it under the name of love in art, literature, poetry, romance and all beauty from the beginning of recorded time. Viewed in this light it cannot seem extraordinary that a difficulty or disturbance in this emotional field should produce such far-reaching consequences for the individual. The sexual impulse is often compared with that of hunger, and this craving and need lying in all humanity is called by Freud *libido*.

THE OEDIPUS PROBLEM

With further investigations into the nature of the repressed complexes a very astonishing situation was revealed. The parental influence on children is something so well recognized and understood that to call attention to it sounds much like a banality. However, here an extraordinary discovery was made, for in tracing out the feelings and emotions of adults it became evident that this influence was paramount not only for children but for adults as well; that the entire direction of lives was largely determined quite unconsciously by the parental associations, and that, although adults, the emotional side of their nature was still infantile in type and demanded unconsciously the infantile or childish relations.

Freud traces out the commencement of the infantile attachment for the parents in this wise.

In the beginning the child derives its first satisfaction and pleasure from the mother in the form of nutrition and care for its wants. In this first act of suckling Freud sees already a kind of sexual pleasure, for he apparently identifies the pleasure principle and the sexual instinct and considers that the former is primarily rooted in the latter. At this early time commence such various infantile actions unconnected with nutrition as thumbsucking, various movements of the body as rubbing, boring, pulling and other manifestations of a definite interest in its own body, a delight in nakedness, the pleasure exhibited in inflicting pain on some object and its opposite, the pleasure from receiving pain. All of these afford the child pleasure and satisfaction, and because they seem analogous to certain perversions in adults they are called by Freud the "polymorphous perverse sexuality" of childhood. The character of these instinctive actions which have nothing to do with any other person, and through which the child attains pleasure from its own body, caused Freud to term this phase of life as auto-erotic after Havelock Ellis. However, with the growth of the child there is a parallel development of the psychic elements of its sexual nature and now the mother, the original object of its love, primarily determined by its helplessness and need, acquires a new valuation. The beginnings of the need for a love object to satisfy the craving or libido of the child are early in evidence and, following along sex lines in general, the little son prefers the mother and the daughter the father after the usual preference of the parents.

At this early time children feel deeply the enormous importance of their parents and their entire world is bounded by the family circle. All the elements of the ego which the child possesses have now become manifest; love, jealousy, curiosity, hate, etc., and those instincts are directed in the greatest degree towards the objects of their libido, namely the parents. With the growing ego of the child there is a development of strong wishes and desires demanding satisfaction which can only be gratified by the mother; therefore there is aroused in the small son the feeling of jealousy and anger towards the father in whom he sees a rival for the affection of the mother and whom he would like to replace. This desire in the soul of the child Freud calls the *Oedipus complex* in recognition of its analogy to the tragedy of King Oedipus who was drawn by his fate to kill his father and win his mother for a wife. Freud presents this as the *nuclear complex* of every neurosis.

At the basis of this complex, some trace of which can be found in every person, Freud sees a definite incest wish towards the mother which only lacks the quality of consciousness. Because of moral reactions this wish is quickly subjected to repression through the operation of the " incest barrier," a postulate he compares to the incest taboo found among inferior peoples. At this time the child is beginning to develop its typical sexual curiosity expressed by the question, " Where do I come from?" The interest and investigation of the child into this problem, aided by observations and deductions from various actions and attitudes of the parents, who have no idea of the watchfulness of the child, lead him, because of his imperfect knowledge and immature development, into many false theories and ideas of birth. These infantile sexual theories are held by Freud to be determinative in the development of the child's character and also for the contents of the unconscious as expressed in a future neurosis.

These various reactions of the child and his sexual curiosity are entirely normal and unavoidable, and if his development proceeds in an orderly fashion then, at the time of definite object choice he will pass smoothly over from the limitations of the family attachment out into the world and find therein his independent existence.

However, if the libido remains fixed on the first chosen object so that the growing individual is unable to tear himself loose from these familial ties, then the incestuous bond is deepened with the developing sexual instinct and its accompanying need of a love object, and the entire future of the young personality endangered. For with the development of the incestuous bond the natural repressions deepen because the moral censor cannot allow these disturbing relations to become clear to the individual. Therefore, the whole matter is repressed more deeply into the unconscious, and even a feeling of positive enmity and repulsion towards the parents is often developed in order to conceal and over-compensate for the impossible situation actually present.

This persistence of the attachment of the libido to the original object, and the inability to find in this a suitable satisfaction for the adult need, interferes with the normal development of the psycho-sexual character, and it is due to this that the adult retains that " infantilism of sexuality " which plays so great a rôle in determining the instability of the emotional life which so frequently leads into the definite neuroses.

These were the conclusions reached and the ground on which Freudian psychology rested, regarding the etiology of the neurosis, and the tendencies underlying normal human mechanisms, when Dr. Carl Jung, the most prominent of Freud's disciples, and the leader of the Zurich school, found himself no longer able to agree with Freud's findings in certain particulars, although the phenomena which Freud observed and the technique of psychoanalysis developed by Freud were the material on which Jung worked and the value of which he clearly emphasizes. The differences which have developed lay in his understanding and interpretation of the phenomena observed.

Beginning with the conception of libido itself as a term used to connote sexual hunger and craving, albeit the meaning of the word sexual was extended by Freud to embrace a much wider significance than common usage has assigned it, Jung was unable to confine himself to this limitation. He conceived this longing, this urge or push of life as something extending beyond sexuality even in its wider sense. He saw in the term libido a concept of unknown nature, comparable to Bergson's élan vital, a hypothetical energy of life, which occupies itself not only in sexuality but in various physiological and psychological manifestations such as growth, development, hunger, and all the human activities and interests. This cosmic energy or urge manifested in the human being he calls libido and compares it with the energy of physics. Although recognizing, in common with Freud as well as with many others, the primal instinct of reproduction as the basis of many functions and present-day activities of mankind no longer sexual in character he repudiates the idea of still calling them sexual, even though their development was a growth originally out of the sexual. Sexuality and its various manifestations Jung sees as most important channels occupied by libido, but not the exclusive ones through which libido flows.

This is an energic concept of life; and from this viewpoint this hypothetical energy of life or libido is a living power used instinctively by man in all the automatic processes of his functioning; such very processes being but different manifestations of this energy. By virtue of its quality of mobility and change man, through his understanding and intelligence, has the power consciously to direct and use his libido in definite and desired ways.

In this conception of Jung will be seen an analogy to Bergson, who speaks of " this change, this movement and becoming, this self-creation, call it what you will, as the very stuff and reality of our being." *

In developing the energic conception of libido and separating it from Freud's sexual definition, Jung makes possible the explanation of interest in general, and provides a working concept by which not only the specifically sexual, but the general activities and reactions of man can be understood.

If a person complains of no longer having interest in his work or of losing interest in his surroundings, then one understands that his libido is withdrawn from this object and that in consequence the object itself seems no longer attractive, whereas, as a matter of fact, the object itself is exactly the same as formerly. In other words, it is

* " Creative Evolution."

the libido that we bestow upon an object that makes it attractive and interesting.

The causes for the withdrawal of libido may be various and are usually quite different from those that the persons offer in explanation. It is the task of psychoanalysis to discover the real reasons, which are usually hidden and unknown. On the other hand, when an individual exhibits an exaggerated interest or places an over-emphasis upon an idea or situation, then we know there is too much libido here and that we may find as a consequence a corresponding depletion elsewhere.

This leads directly into the second point of difference between Jung's views and those of Freud. This is concerned with those practically universal childish manifestations of sexuality called by Freud " polymorphous perverse " because of their similarity to those abnormalities of sexuality which occur in adults and are called perversions.

Jung takes exception to this viewpoint. He sees in the various manifestations of childhood the precursors or forerunners of the later fully developed sexuality, and instead of considering them perverse he considers them preliminary expressions of sexual coloring. He divides human life into three stages. The first stage up to about the third or fourth year, generally speaking, he calls the presexual stage, for there he sees the libido or life energy occupied chiefly in the functions of nutrition and growth, and he draws an analogy between this period and that of the caterpillar stage of the butterfly.

The second stage includes the years from this time

until puberty, and this he speaks of as the prepubertal stage.

The third period is that from puberty onward and can be considered the time of maturity.

It is in the earliest stage, the period of which varies greatly in different individuals, that are fully inaugurated those various manifestations which have so marked a sexual coloring that there can be no question of their relationship, although at that time sexuality in the adult meaning of the word does not exist.

Jung explains the polymorphism of these phenomena as arising from a gradual movement of the libido from exclusive service in the function of nutrition into new avenues which successively open up with the development of the child until the final inauguration of the sexual function proper at puberty. Normally these childish bad habits are gradually relinquished until the libido is entirely withdrawn from these immature phases and with the ushering in of puberty for the first time " appears in the form of an undifferentiated sexual primitive power, clearly forcing the individual towards division, budding, etc."

However, if in the course of its movement from the function of nutrition to the sexual function the libido is arrested or retarded at any phase, then a *fixation* may result, creating a disturbance in the harmony of the normal development. For, although the libido is retarded and remains clinging to some childish manifestation, time goes on and the physical growth of the child does not stand still. Soon a great contrast is created between the infantile manifestations of the emotional life and the needs of the more adult individual, and the foundation is thus prepared for either the development of a definite neurosis or else for those weaknesses of character or symptomatic disturbances which are not sufficiently serious to be called a neurosis.

One of the most active and important forms of childish libido occupation is in phantasy making. The child's world is one of imagery and make-believe where he can create for himself that satisfaction and enjoyment which the world of reality so often denies. As the child grows and real demands of life are made upon him it becomes increasingly necessary that his libido be taken away from his phantastic world and used for the required adaptation to reality needed by his age and condition, until finally for the adult the freedom of the whole libido is necessary to meet the biological and cultural demands of life.

Instead of thus employing the libido in the real world, however, certain people never relinquish the seeking for satisfaction in the shadowy world of phantasy and even though they make certain attempts at adaptation they are halted and discouraged by every difficulty and obstacle in the path of life and are easily pulled back into their inner psychic world. This condition is called a state of *introversion*. It is concerned with the past and the reminiscences which belong thereto. Situations and experiences which should have been completed and finished long ago are still dwelt upon and lived with. Images and matters which were once important but which normally have no significance for their later age are still actively influencing their present lives. The nature and character of these phantasy products are legion, and are easily recognized in the emotional attitudes and pretensions, the childish illusions and exaggerations, the prejudices and inconsistencies which people express in manifold forms. The actual situation is inadequately faced; small matters are reacted towards in an exaggerated manner; or else a frivolous attitude is maintained where real seriousness is demanded. In other words, there is clearly manifested an inadequate psychic adaptation towards reality which is quite to be expected from the child, but which is very discordant in the adult.

The most important of these past influences is that of the parents. Because they are the first objects of the developing childish love, and afford the first satisfaction and pleasure to the child, they become the models for all succeeding efforts, as Freud has worked out. This he called the *nuclear* or *root complex* because this influence was so powerful it seemed to be the determining factor in all later difficulties in the life of the individual.

In this phase of the problem lies the third great difference between Jung's interpretation of the observed phenomena and that of Freud.

Jung definitely recognizes that there are many neurotic persons who clearly exhibited in their childhood the same neurotic tendencies that are later exaggerated. Also that an almost overwhelming effect on the destiny of these children is exercised by the influence of the parents, the frequent over-anxiety or tenderness, the lack of sympathy or understanding, in other words, the complexes of the parent reacting upon the child and producing in him love, admiration, fear, distrust, hate, revolt. The greater the sensitiveness and impressionability of the child, the more he will be stamped with the familial environment, and the more he will unconsciously seek to find again in the world of reality the model of his own small world with all the pleasures and satisfactions, or disappointments and unhappinesses with which it was filled.

This condition to be sure is not a recognized or a conscious one, for the individual may think himself perfectly free from this past influence because he is living in the real world, and because actually there is a great difference between the present conditions and that of his childish past. He sees all this, intellectually, but there is a wide gap between the intellectual grasp of a situation and the emotional development, and it is the latter realm wherein lies the disharmony. However, although many ideas and feelings are connected with the parents, analysis reveals very often that they are only subjective and that in reality they bear little resemblance to the actual past situation. Therefore, Jung speaks no longer of the real father and mother but uses the term imago or image to represent the father or mother, because the feelings and phantasies frequently do not deal with the real parents but with the distorted and subjective image created by the imagination of the individual.

Following this distinction Jung sees in the Oedipus complex of Freud only a symbol for the " childish desire towards the parents and for the conflict which this craving evokes," and cannot accept the theory that in this early stage of childhood the mother has any real sexual significance for the child.

The demands of the child upon the mother, the jealousy so often exhibited, are at first connected with the rôle of the mother as protector, caretaker and supplier of nutritive wants, and only later, with the germinating eroticism, does the child's love become admixed with the developing sexual quality. The chief love objects are still the parents and he naturally continues to seek and to find in them satisfaction for all his desires. In this way the typical conflict is developed which in the son is directed towards the father and in the daughter towards the mother. This jealousy of the daughter towards the mother is called the *Electra complex* from the myth of Electra who took revenge on her mother for the murder of the husband because she was in this way deprived of her father.

Normally as puberty is attained the child gradually becomes more or less freed from his parents, and upon the degree in which this is accomplished depends his health and future well-being.

This demand of nature upon the young individual to free himself from the bonds of his childish dependency and to find in the world of reality his independent existence is so imperious and dominating that it frequently produces in the child the greatest struggles and severest conflicts, the period being characterized symbolically as a *self-sacrifice* by Jung.

It frequently happens that the young person is so closely bound in the family relations that it is only with the greatest difficulty that he can attain any measure of freedom and then only very imperfectly, so that the libido sexualis can only express itself in certain feelings and phantasies which clearly reveal the existence of the complex until then entirely hidden and unrealized. Now commences the secondary struggle against the unfilial and immoral feelings with a consequent development of intense resistances expressing themselves in irritation, anger, revolt and antagonism against the parents, or else in an especially tender, submissive and yielding attitude which over-compensates for the rebellion and reaction held within.

This struggle and conflict gives rise to the unconscious phantasy of self-sacrifice which really means the sacrificing of the childish tendencies and love type in order to free libido; for his nature demands that he attain the capacity for the accomplishment of his own personal fulfilment, the satisfaction of which belongs to the developed man and woman.

This conception has been worked out in detail by Jung in the book which is herein presented to English readers.

We now come to the most important of Jung's conceptions in that it bears practically upon the treatment of certain types of the neuroses and stands theoretically in direct opposition to Freud's hypothesis. While recognizing fully the influence of the parents and of the sexual constitution of the child, Jung refuses to see in this infantile past the real cause for the later development of the illness. He definitely places the cause of the pathogenic conflict *in the present moment* and considers that in seeking for the cause in the distant past one is only following the desire of the patient, which is to withdraw himself as much as possible from the present important period.

The conflict is produced by some important task or duty which is essential biologically and practically for the fulfilment of the ego of the individual, but before which an obstacle arises from which he shrinks, and thus halted cannot go on. With this interference in the path of progression libido is stored up and a *regression* takes place whereby there occurs a reanimation of past ways of libido occupation which were entirely normal to the child, but which for the adult are no longer of value. These regressive infantile desires and phantasies now alive and striving for satisfaction are converted into symptoms, and in these surrogate forms obtain a certain gratification, thus creating the external manifestations of the neurosis. Therefore Jung does not ask from what psychic experience or point of fixation in childhood the patient is suffering, but what is the present duty or task he is avoiding, or what obstacle in his life's path he is unable to overcome? What is the cause of his regression to past psychic experiences?

Following this theory Jung expresses the view that the elaborate phantasies and dreams produced by these patients are really forms of compensation or artificial substitutes for the unfulfilled adaptation to reality. The sexual content of these phantasies and dreams is only apparently and not actually expressive of a real sexual desire or incest wish, but is a regressive employment of sexual forms to symbolically express a present-day need when the attainment of the present ego demand seems too difficult or impossible, and no adaptation is made to what is possible for the individual's capability.*

With this statement Jung throws a new light on the work of analytic psychology and on the conception of the neurotic symptoms, and renders possible of understanding the many apparent incongruities and conflicting observations which have been so disturbing to the critics.

It now becomes proper to ask what has been established by all this mass of investigation into the soul, and what is its value not only as a therapeutic measure for the neurotic sufferer, but also for the normal human being?

First and perhaps most important is the recognition of a definite psychological determinism. Instead of human life being filled with foolish, meaningless or purposeless actions, errors and thoughts, it can be demonstrated that no expression or manifestation of the psyche, however trifling or inconsistent in appearance, is really lawless or unmotivated. Only a possession of the technique is necessary in order to reveal, to any one desirous of knowing, the existence of the unconscious determinants of his mannerisms, trivial expressions, acts and behavior, their purpose and significance.

---

* For a more complete presentation of Jung's views consult his " Theory of Psychoanalysis " in the Nervous and Mental Disease Monograph Series, No. 19.

This leads into the second fundamental conception, which is perhaps even less considered than the foregoing, and that is the relative value of the conscious mind and thought. It is the general attitude of people to judge themselves by their surface motives, to satisfy themselves by saying or thinking " this is what I want to do or say " or " I intended to do thus and so," but somehow what one thought, one intended to say or expected to do is very often the contrary of what actually is said or done. Every one has had these experiences when the gap between the conscious thought and action was gross enough to be observed. It is also a well known experience to consciously desire something very much and when it is obtained to discover that this in no wise satisfied or lessened the desire, which was then transferred to some other object. Thus one became cognizant of the fact that the feeling and idea presented by consciousness as the desire was an error. What is the difficulty in these conditions? Evidently some other directing force than that of which we are aware is at work.

Dr. G. Stanley Hall uses a very striking symbol when he compares the mind to an iceberg floating in the ocean with one-eighth visible above the water and seven-eighths below—the one-eighth above being that part called conscious and the seven-eighths below that which we call the unconscious. The influence and controlling power of the unconscious desires over our thoughts and acts are in this relative proportion. Faint glimmers of other motives and interests than those we accept or which we believe, often flit into consciousness. These indications, if studied or valued accurately, would lead to the realization that consciousness is but a single stage and but one form of expression of mind. Therefore its dictum is but one, often untrustworthy, approach to the great question as to what is man's actual psychic accomplishment, and as to what in particular is the actual soul development of the individual.

A further contribution of equal importance has been the empiric development of a dynamic theory of life; the conception that life is in a state of flux—movement—leading either to construction or destruction. Through the development man has reached he has attained the power by means of his intelligence and understanding of definitely directing to a certain extent this life energy or libido into avenues which serve his interest and bring a real satisfaction for the present day.

When man through ignorance and certain inherent tendencies fails to recognize his needs or his power to fulfil them, or to adapt himself to the conditions of reality of the present time, there is then produced that reanimation of infantile paths by which an attempt is made to gain fulfilment or satisfaction through the production of symptoms or attitudes.

The acceptance of these statements demands the recognition of the existence of an infantile sexuality and the large part played by it in the later life of the individual. Because of the power and imperious influence exerted by the parents upon the child, and because of the unconscious attachment of his libido to the original object, the mother, and the perseverance of this first love model in the psyche, he finds it very difficult, on reaching the stage of adult development and the time for seeking a love object outside of the family, to gain a satisfactory model.

It is exceedingly important for parents and teachers to recognize the requirements of nature, which, beginning with puberty, imperiously demand of the young individual a separation of himself from the parent stem and the development of an independent existence. In our complex modern civilization this demand of nature is difficult enough of achievement for the child who has the heartiest and most intelligent co-operation of his parents and environment—but for the one who has not only to contend with his own inner struggle for his freedom but has in addition the resistance of his parents who would hold him in his childhood at any cost, because they cannot endure the thought of his separation from them, the task becomes one of the greatest magnitude. It is during this period when the struggle between the childish inertia and nature's urge becomes so keen, that there occur the striking manifestations of jealousy, criticism, irritability all usually directed against the parents, of defiance of parental authority, of runaways and various other psychic and nervous disorders known to all.

This struggle, which is the first great task of mankind and the one which requires the greatest effort, is that which is expressed by Jung as the self-sacrifice motive—the sacrifice of the childish feelings and demands, and of the irresponsibility of this period, and the assumption of the duties and tasks of an individual existence.

It is this great theme which Jung sees as the real

motive lying hidden in the myths and religions of man
from the beginning, as well as in the literature and
artistic creations of both ancient and modern time,
and which he works out with the greatest wealth of
detail and painstaking effort in the book herewith presented.

This necessitates a recognition and revaluation of the
enormous importance and influence of the ego and the
sexual instinct upon the thought and reaction of man,
and also predicates a displacement of the psychological
point of gravity from the will and intellect to the realm
of the emotions and feelings. The desired end is a
synthesis of these two paths or the use of the intellect
constructively in the service of the emotions in order to
gain for the best interest of the individual some sort of
co-operative reaction between the two.

No one dealing with analytic psychology can fail to
be struck by the tremendous and unnecessary burdens
which man has placed upon himself, and how greatly
he has increased the difficulties of adaptation by his rigid
intellectual views and moral formulas, and by his inability
to admit to himself that he is actually just a human being
imperfect, and containing within himself all manner of
tendencies, good and bad, all striving for some satisfactory goal. Further, that the refusal to see himself in
this light instead of as an ideal person in no way alters
the actual condition, and that in fact, through the cheap
pretense of being able only to consider himself as a very
virtuous person, or as shocked and hurt when observing
the " sins " of others, he actually is prevented from de-

veloping his own character and bringing his own capacities to their fullest expressions.

There is frequently expressed among people the idea of how fortunate it is that we cannot see each other's thoughts, and how disturbing it would be if our real feelings could be read. But what is so shameful in these secrets of the soul? They are in reality our own egoistic desires all striving, longing, wishing for satisfaction, for happiness; those desires which instinctively crave their own gratification but which can only be really fulfilled by adapting them to the real world and to the social group.

Why is it that it is so painful for man to admit that the prime influence in all human endeavor is found in the ego itself, in its desires, wishes, needs and satisfactions, in short, in its need for self-expression and self-perpetuation, the evolutionary impetus in life?

The basis for the unpleasantness of this idea may perhaps be found in an inner resistance in nature itself which forces man to include others in his scheme, lest his own greedy desires should serve to destroy him. But even with this inner demand and all the ethical and moral teachings of centuries it is everywhere evident that man has only very imperfectly learned that it is to his own interest to consider his neighbor and that it is impossible for him to ignore the needs of the body social of which he is a part. Externally, the recognition of the strength of the ego impulse is objectionable because of the ideal conception that self-striving and so-called selfish seeking are unworthy, ignoble and incompatible with a desirable character and must be ignored at all cost.

The futility of this attitude is to be clearly seen in the failure after all these centuries to even approximate it, as evidenced in our human relations and institutions, and is quite as ineffectual in this realm as in that of sexuality where the effort to overcome this imperious domination has been attempted by lowering the instinct, and seeing in it something vile or unclean, something unspeakable and unholy. Instead of destroying the power of sexuality this struggle has only warped and distorted, injured and mutilated the expression; for not without destruction of the individual can these fundamental instincts be destroyed. Life itself has needs and imperiously demands expression through the forms created. All nature answers to this freely and simply except man. His failure to recognize himself as an instrument through which the life energy is coursing and the demands of which must be obeyed, is the cause of his misery. Despite his possession of intellect and self-consciousness, he cannot without disaster to himself refuse the tasks of life and the fulfilment of his own needs. Man's great task is the adaptation of himself to reality and the recognition of himself as an instrument for the expression of life according to his individual possibilities.

It is in his privilege as a self-creator that his highest purpose is found.

The value of self-consciousness lies in the fact that man is enabled to reflect upon himself and learn to understand the true origin and significance of his actions and opinions, that he may adequately value the real level of his development and avoid being self-deceived and therefore inhibited from finding his biological adaptation. He need no longer be unconscious of the motives underlying his actions or hide himself behind a changed exterior, in other words, be merely a series of reactions to stimuli as the mechanists have it, but he may to a certain extent become a self-creating and self-determining being.

Indeed, there seems to be an impulse towards adaptation quite as Bergson sees it, and it would seem to be a task of the highest order to use intelligence to assist one's self to work with this impulse.

Through the investigation of these different avenues leading into the hidden depths of the human being and through the revelation of the motives and influences at work there, although astonishing to the uninitiated, a very clear and definite conception of the actual human relationship—brotherhood—of all mankind is obtained. It is this recognition of these common factors basically inherent in humanity from the beginning and still active, which is at once both the most hopeful and the most feared and disliked part of psychoanalysis.

It is disliked by those individuals who have prided themselves upon their superiority and the distinction between their reactions and motives and those of ordinary mankind. In other words, they attempt to become personalities through elevating themselves and lowering others, and it is a distinct blow to discover that beneath these pretensions lie the very ordinary elements shared in common by all. On the other hand, to those who have been able to recognize their own weaknesses and have suffered in the privacy of their own souls, the knowledge that these things have not set them apart from others, but that they are the common property of all and that no one can point the finger of scorn at his fellow, is one of the greatest experiences of life and is productive of the greatest relief.

It is feared by many who realize that in these painfully acquired repressions and symptoms lie their safety and their protection from directly facing and dealing with tendencies and characteristics with which they feel unable to cope. The repression and the accompanying symptoms indicate a difficulty and a struggle, and in this way are a sort of compromise or substitute formation which permit, although only in a wasteful and futile manner, the activity of the repressed tendencies. Nevertheless, to analyze the individual back to his original tendencies and reveal to him the meaning of these substitute formations would be a useless procedure in which truly " the last state of that man would be worse than the first " if the work ceased there. The aim is not to destroy those barriers upon which civilized man has so painfully climbed and to reduce him to his primitive state, but, where these have failed or imperfectly succeeded, to help him to attain his greatest possibilities with less expenditure of energy, by less wasteful methods than nature provides. In this achievement lies the hopeful and valuable side of this method—the development of the synthesis. It is hopeful because now a way is opened to deal with these primitive tendencies constructively, and render their effects not only harmless but useful, by utilizing them in higher aims, socially and individually valuable and satisfactory.

This is what has occurred normally in those individuals who seem capable and constructive personalities; in those creative minds that give so much to the race. They have converted certain psychological tendencies which could have produced useless symptoms or destructive actions into valuable productions. Indeed it is not uncommon for strong, capable persons to state themselves that they knew they could have been equally capable of a wasteful or destructive life. This utilization of the energy or libido freed by removing the repressions and the lifting of infantile tendencies and desires into higher purposes and directions suitable for the individual at his present status is called *sublimation*.

It must not be understood by this discussion that geniuses or wonderful personalities can be created through analysis, for this is not the aim of the procedure. Its purpose is to remove the inhibitions and restrictions which interfere with the full development of the personality, to help individuals attain to that level where they really belong, and to prepare people to better understand and meet life whether they are neurotic sufferers or so-called " normal people " with the difficulties and peculiarities which belong to all.

This reasoning and method of procedure is only new when the application is made to the human being. In all improvements of plants and animals these general principles have been recognized and their teachings constructively utilized.

Luther Burbank, that plant wizard whose work is known to all the world, says, " A knowledge of the battle of the tendencies within a plant is the very basis of all plant improvement," and " it is not that the work of plant improvement brings with it, incidentally, as people mistakenly think, a knowledge of these forces, it is the knowledge of these forces, rather, which makes plant improvement possible."

Has this not been also the mistake of man regarding himself, and the cause, partly at least, of his failure to succeed in actually reaching a more advanced and stable development?

This recognition of man's biological relationship to all life and the practical utilization of this recognition, necessitates a readjustment of thought and asks for an examination and reconsideration of the facts of human conduct which are observable by any thoughtful person. A quiet and progressive upheaval of old ideas has taken place and is still going on. Analytic psychology attempts to unify and value all of the various phenomena of man which have been observed and noted at different times by isolated investigators of isolated manifestations and thus bring some orderly sequence into the whole. It offers a method whereby the relations of the human being biologically to all other living forms can be established, the actual achievement of man himself adequately valued, and opens a vista of the possibilities of improvement in health, happiness and accomplishment for the human being.

BEATRICE M. HINKLE.

10 Gramercy Park.

AUTHOR'S NOTE

My task in this work has been to investigate an individual phantasy system, and in the doing of it problems of such magnitude have been uncovered, that my endeavor to grasp them in their entirety has necessarily meant only a superficial orientation toward those paths, the opening and exploration of which may possibly crown the work of future investigators with success.

I am not in sympathy with the attitude which favors the repression of certain possible working hypotheses because they are perhaps erroneous, and so may possess no lasting value. Certainly I endeavored as far as possible to guard myself from error, which might indeed become especially dangerous upon these dizzy heights, for I am entirely aware of the risks of these investigations. However, I do not consider scientific work as a dogmatic contest, but rather as a work done for the increase and deepening of knowledge.

This contribution is addressed to those having similar ideas concerning science.

In conclusion, I must render thanks to those who have assisted my endeavors with valuable aid, especially my dear wife and my friends, to whose disinterested assistance I am deeply indebted.

C. G. JUNG.

ZURICH.

CONTENTS

xlix

CONTENTS

PART II

CONTENTS

"*Therefore theory, which gives to facts their value and significance, is often very useful, even if it is partially false, for it throws light on phenomena which no one observed, it forces an examination, from many angles, of facts which no one had hitherto studied, and it gives the impulse for more extended and more productive researches.*

"*It is, therefore, a moral duty for the man of science to expose himself to the risk of committing error and to submit to criticism, in order that science may continue to progress. A writer has attacked the author for this very severely, saying, here is a scientific ideal very limited and very paltry. But those who are endowed with a mind sufficiently serious and impersonal as not to believe that all that they write is the expression of truth absolute and eternal, approve of this theory which places the aims of science well above the miserable vanity and paltry 'amour propre' of the scientist.*"—GUGLIELMO FERRERO.

Les Lois Psychologiques du Symbolisme—1895. Preface, p. viii.

PART I

INTRODUCTION

ANY ONE who can read Freud's " Interpretation of the Dream " without scientific rebellion at the newness and apparently unjustified daring of its analytical presentation, and without moral indignation at the astonishing nudity of the dream interpretation, and who can allow this unusual array of facts to influence his mind calmly and without prejudice, will surely be deeply impressed at that place where Freud calls to mind the fact that an individual psychologic conflict, namely, the Incest Phantasy, is the essential root of that powerful ancient dramatic material, the Oedipus legend. The impression made by this simple reference may be likened to that wholly peculiar feeling which arises in us if, for example, in the noise and tumult of a modern street we should come across an ancient relic—the Corinthian capital of a walled-in column, or a fragment of inscription. Just a moment ago we were given over to the noisy ephemeral life of the present, when something very far away and strange appears to us, which turns our attention to things of another order; a glimpse away from the incoherent multiplicity of the present to a higher coherence in history. Very likely it would suddenly occur to us that on this spot where we now run busily to and fro a similar life and activity prevailed two thousand years ago in

3

somewhat other forms; similar passions moved mankind, and man was likewise convinced of the uniqueness of his existence. I would liken the impression which the first acquaintance with the monuments of antiquity so easily leaves behind to that impression which Freud's reference to the Oedipus legend makes—for while we are still engaged with the confusing impressions of the variability of the Individual Soul, suddenly there is opened a revelation of the simple greatness of the Oedipus tragedy—that never extinguished light of the Grecian theatre.

This breadth of outlook carries in itself something of revelation. For us, the ancient psychology has long since been buried among the shadows of the past; in the school-room one could scarcely repress a sceptical smile when one indiscreetly reckoned the comfortable matronly age of Penelope and the age of Jocasta, and comically compared the result of the reckoning with the tragic-erotic struggles in the legend and drama. We did not know at that time (and who knows even today?) that the mother can be the all-consuming passion of the son, which perhaps undermines his whole life and tragically destroys it, so that not even the magnitude of the Oedipus Fate seems one jot overdrawn. Rare and pathologically understood cases like Ninon de Lenclos and her son [1] lie too far removed from most of us to give a living impression. But when we follow the paths traced out by Freud, we arrive at a recognition of the present existence of such possibilities, which, although they are too weak to enforce incest, are still strong enough to cause disturbances of considerable magnitude in the soul. The admission of such possibilities to one's self does not occur without a great burst of moral revulsion. Resistances arise which only too easily dazzle the intellect, and, through that, make knowledge of self impossible. Whenever we succeed, however, in stripping feelings from more scientific knowledge, then that abyss which separates our age from the antique is bridged, and, with astonishment, we see that Oedipus is still a living thing for us. The importance of such an impression should not be undervalued. We are taught by this insight that there is an identity of elementary human conflicts existing independent of time and place. That which affected the Greeks with horror still remains true, but it is true for us only when we give up a vain illusion that we are different—that is to say, more moral, than the ancients. We of the present day have nearly succeeded in forgetting that an indissoluble common bond binds us to the people of antiquity. With this truth a path is opened to the understanding of the ancient mind; an understanding which so far has not existed, and, on one side, leads to an inner sympathy, and, on the other side, to an intellectual comprehension. Through buried strata of the individual soul we come indirectly into possession of the living mind of the ancient culture, and, just precisely through that, do we win that stable point of view outside our own culture, from which, for the first time, an objective understanding of their mechanisms would be possible. At least that is the hope which we get from the rediscovery of the Oedipus problem.

The enquiry made possible by Freud's work has al-

ready resulted fruitfully; we are indebted to this stimulation for some bold attacks upon the territory of the
history of the human mind. There are the works of
Riklin,[2] Abraham,[3] Rank,[4] Maeder,[5] Jones,[6]—recently
Silberer has joined their ranks with a beautiful investigation entitled "Phantasie und Mythus."[7] We are indebted to Pfister[8] for a comprehensive work which
cannot be overlooked here, and which is of much importance for Christian religious psychology. The leading
purpose of these works is the unlocking of historical
problems through the application of psychoanalytic
knowledge; that is to say, knowledge drawn from the
activity of the modern unconscious mind concerning specific historical material.

I must refer the reader entirely to the specified works,
in order that he may gain information concerning the
extent and the kind of insight which has already been
obtained. The explanations are in many cases dubious
in particulars; nevertheless, this detracts in no way from
the total result.   It would be significant enough if only
the far-reaching analogy between the psychologic structure of the historical relics and the structure of the recent
individual psychologic products alone were demonstrated.
This proof is possible of attainment for every intelligent
person through the work done up to this time. The
analogy prevails especially in symbolism, as Riklin, Rank,
Maeder, and Abraham have pointed out with illuminating examples; it is also shown in the individual mechanisms of unconscious work, that is to say in repression,
condensation, etc., as Abraham explicitly shows.

Up to the present time the psychoanalytic investigator has turned his interest chiefly to the analysis of the individual psychologic problems. It seems to me, however, that in the present state of affairs there is a more or less imperative demand for the psychoanalyst to broaden the analysis of the individual problems by a comparative study of historical material relating to them, just as Freud has already done in a masterly manner in his book on "Leonardo da Vinci." [9] For, just as the psychoanalytic conceptions promote understanding of the historic psychologic creations, so reversedly historical materials can shed new light upon individual psychologic problems. These and similar considerations have caused me to turn my attention somewhat more to the historical, in the hope that, out of this, new insight into the foundations of individual psychology might be won.

CHAPTER I

CONCERNING THE TWO KINDS OF THINKING

IT is a well-known fact that one of the principles of analytic psychology is that the dream images are to be understood symbolically; that is to say, that they are not to be taken literally just as they are presented in sleep, but that behind them a hidden meaning has to be surmised. It is this ancient idea of a dream symbolism which has challenged not only criticism, but, in addition to that, the strongest opposition. That dreams may be full of import, and, therefore, something to be interpreted, is certainly neither a strange nor an extraordinary idea. This has been familiar to mankind for thousands of years, and, therefore, seems much like a banal truth. The dream interpretations of the Egyptians and Chaldeans, and the story of Joseph who interpreted Pharaoh's dreams, are known to every one, and the dream book of Artemidorus is also familiar. From countless inscribed monuments of all times and peoples we learn of foreboding dreams, of significant, of prophetic and also of curative dreams which the Deity sent to the sick, sleeping in the temple. We know the dream of the mother of Augustus, who dreamt she was to be with child by the Deity transformed into a snake. We will not heap up references and examples to bear witness to the existence of a belief

8

in the symbolism of dreams. When an idea is so old, and is so generally believed, it is probably true in some way, and, indeed, as is mostly the case, *is not literally true, but is true psychologically*. In this distinction lies the reason why the old fogies of science have from time to time thrown away an inherited piece of ancient truth; because it was not literal but psychologic truth. For such discrimination this type of person has at no time had any comprehension.

From our experience, it is hardly conceivable that a God existing outside of ourselves causes dreams, or that the dream, eo ipso, foresees the future prophetically. When we translate this into the psychologic, however, then the ancient theories sound much more reconcilable, namely, *the dream arises from a part of the mind unknown to us, but none the less important, and is concerned with the desires for the approaching day*. This psychologic formula derived from the ancient superstitious conception of dreams, is, so to speak, exactly identified with the Freudian psychology, which assumes a rising wish from the unconscious to be the source of the dream.

As the old belief teaches, the Deity or the Demon speaks in symbolic speech to the sleeper, and the dream interpreter has the riddle to solve. In modern speech we say this means that the dream is a *series of images, which are apparently contradictory and nonsensical, but arise in reality from psychologic material which yields a clear meaning*.

Were I to suppose among my readers a far-reaching

ignorance of dream analysis, then I should be obliged to illustrate this statement with numerous examples. Today, however, these things are quite well known, so that one must proceed carefully with every-day dream material, out of consideration for a public educated in these matters. It is a special inconvenience that no dream can be recounted without being obliged to add to it half a life's history which affords the individual foundations of the dream, but there are some few typical dreams which can be told without too great a ballast. One of these is the dream of the sexual assault, which is especially prevalent among women. A girl sleeping after an evening happily spent in dancing, dreams that a robber breaks open her door noisily and stabs through her body with a lance. This theme, which explains itself, has countless variations, some simple, some complicated. Instead of the lance it is a sword, a dagger, a revolver, a gun, a cannon, a hydrant, a watering pot; or the assault is a burglary, a pursuit, a robbery, or it is some one hidden in the closet or under the bed. Or the danger may be illustrated by wild animals; for instance, a horse which throws the dreamer to the ground and kicks her in the body with his hind foot; lions, tigers, elephants with threatening trunks, and finally snakes in endless variety. Sometimes the snake creeps into the mouth, sometimes it bites the breast like Cleopatra's legendary asp, sometimes it comes in the rôle of the paradisical snake, or in the variations of Franz Stuck, whose pictures of snakes bear the significant titles " Vice," " Sin," " Lust." The mixture of lust and anxiety is expressed incomparably in the very atmosphere of these pictures, and far more brutally, indeed, than in Mörike's charming poem.

The Maiden's First Love Song

What's in the net?
　　Behold,
But I am afraid,
Do I grasp a sweet eel,
Do I seize a snake?
　　Love is a blind
　　Fisherwoman;
　　Tell the child
　　Where to seize.
Already it leaps in my hands.

Oh, Pity, or delight!
With nestlings and turnings
　　It coils on my breast,
　　It bites me, oh, wonder!
　　Boldly through the skin,
　　It darts under my heart.
Oh, Love, I shudder!

What can I do, what can I begin?
　　That shuddering thing;
　　There it crackles within
　　And coils in a ring.
　　It must be poisoned.
　　Here it crawls around.
　　Blissfully I feel as it worms
　　Itself into my soul
　　And kills me finally.

All these things are simple, and need no explanation to be intelligible. Somewhat more complicated, but still unmistakable, is the dream of a woman; she sees the triumphal arch of Constantine. A cannon stands before it, to the right of it a bird, to the left a man. A shot flashes out of the tube; the projectile hits her; it goes into her pocket, into her purse. There it remains, and she holds her purse as if something very precious were in it. The image disappears, and she continues to see only the stock of the cannon, and over that Constantine's motto, " In hoc signo vinces."

These few references to the symbolic nature of dreams are perhaps sufficient. For whomsoever the proof may appear insufficient, and it is certainly insufficient for a beginner, further evidence may be found in the fundamental work of Freud, and in the works of Stekel and Rank which are fuller in certain particulars. We must assume here that the dream symbolism is an established fact, in order to bring to our study a mind suitably prepared for an appreciation of this work. We would not be successful if we, on the contrary, were to be astonished at the idea that an intellectual image can be projected into our conscious psychic activity; an image which apparently obeys such wholly other laws and purposes than those governing the conscious psychic product.

Why are dreams symbolic? Every " why " in psychology is divided into two separate questions: first, *for what purpose are dreams symbolic?* We will answer this question only to abandon it at once. Dreams are symbolic in order that they can not be understood; in order that the wish, which is the source of the dream, may remain unknown. The question why this is so and not otherwise, leads us out into the far-reaching experiences and trains of thought of the Freudian psychology.

Here the second question interests us, viz., *How is it that dreams are symbolic?* That is to say, from where does this capacity for symbolic representation come, of which we, in our conscious daily life, can discover apparently no traces?

Let us examine this more closely. Can we really discover nothing symbolic in our every-day thought? Let us follow our trains of thought; let us take an example. We think of the war of 1870 and 1871. We think about a series of bloody battles, the siege of Strassburg, Belfort, Paris, the Treaty of Peace, the foundation of the German Empire, and so on. How have we been thinking? We start with an idea, or super-idea, as it is also called, and without thinking of it, but each time merely guided by a feeling of direction, we think about individual reminiscences of the war. In this we can find nothing symbolic, and our whole conscious thinking proceeds according to this type.[1]

If we observe our thinking very narrowly, and follow an intensive train of thought, as, for example, the solution of a difficult problem, then suddenly we notice that we are thinking in words, that in wholly intensive thinking we begin to speak to ourselves, or that we occasionally write down the problem, or make a drawing of it so as to be absolutely clear. It must certainly have happened to any one who has lived for some time in a foreign country, that after a certain period he has begun to think in the language of the country. A very intensive train

of thinking works itself out more or less in *word form;*
that is, if one wants to express it, to teach it, or to convince any one of it.   Evidently it directs itself wholly to
the outside world.   To this extent, this directed or logical
thinking is a reality thinking,[2] having a real existence for
us; that is to say, a thinking which adjusts itself to actual
conditions,[3] where we, expressed in other words, imitate
the succession of objectively real things, so that the
images in our mind follow after each other in the same
strictly causal succession as the historical events outside
of our mind.[4]

We call this thinking, thinking with directed attention.
It has, in addition, the peculiarity that one is tired by it,
and that, on this account, it is set into action only for a
time.   Our whole vital accomplishment, which is so ex-
pensive, is adaptation to environment; a part of it is the
directed thinking, which, biologically expressed, is nothing but a process of psychic assimilation, which, as in
every vital accomplishment, leaves behind a corresponding exhaustion.

The material with which we think is *language and
speech concept,* a thing which has been used from time
immemorial as something external, a bridge for thought,
and which has a single purpose—that of communication.
As long as we think directedly, we think for others and
speak to others.[5]

Speech is originally a system of emotional and imita-
tive sounds—sounds which express terror, fear, anger,
love; and sounds which imitate the noises of the elements,
the rushing and gurgling of water, the rolling of thunder,

the tumults of the winds, the tones of the animal world, and so on; and, finally, those which represent a combination of the sounds of perception and of affective reaction.[6] Likewise in the more or less modern languages, large quantities of onomatopoetic relics are retained; for example, sounds for the movement of water,—

Rauschen, risseln, rûschen, rinnen, rennen, to rush, ruscello, ruisseau, river, Rhein.

Wasser, wissen, wissern, pissen, piscis, fisch.

Thus language is orginally and essentially nothing but a system of signs or symbols, which denote real occurrences, or their echo in the human soul.

Therefore one must decidedly agree with Anatole France,[7] when he says,

"What is thought, and how do we think? We think with words; that alone is sensual and brings us back to nature. Think of it! The metaphysician has only the perfected cry of monkeys and dogs with which to construct the system of the world. That which he calls profound speculation and transcendent method is to put end to end in an arbitrary order the natural sounds which cry out hunger, fear, and love in the primitive forests, and to which were attached little by little the meanings which one believed to be abstract, when they were only crude.

"Do not fear that the succession of small cries, feeble and stifled, which compose a book of philosophy, will teach us so much regarding the universe, that we can live in it no longer."

Thus is our directed thinking, and even if we were the loneliest and furthest removed from our fellows, this thinking is nothing but the first notes of a long-drawn-out call to our companions that water had been found, that we had killed the bear, that a storm was approaching, or that wolves were prowling around the camp. A striking paradox of Abélard's which expresses in a very intuitive way the whole human limitation of our complicated thinking process, reads,—"*Sermo generatur ab intellectu et generat intellectum.*" *

Any system of philosophy, no matter how abstract, represents in means and purpose nothing more than an extremely cleverly developed combination of original nature sounds.[8] Hence arises the desire of a Schopenhauer or a Nietzsche for recognition and understanding, and the despair and bitterness of their loneliness. One might expect, perhaps, that a man full of genius could pasture in the greatness of his own thoughts, and renounce the cheap approbation of the crowd which he despises; yet he succumbs to the more powerful impulse of the herd instinct. His searching and his finding, his call, belong to the herd.

When I said just now that directed thinking is properly a thinking with words, and quoted that clever testimony of Anatole France as drastic proof of it, a misunderstanding might easily arise, namely, that directed thinking is really only " word." That certainly would go too far. Language should, however, be comprehended in a wider sense than that of speech, which is in itself only the expression of the formulated thought which is capable of being communicated in the widest sense. Otherwise, the deaf mute would be limited to the utmost in his capacity for thinking, which is not the case in reality. Without

* Speech is generated by the intellect and in turn generates intellect.

any knowledge of the spoken word, he has his "language." This language, considered from the standpoint of history, or in other words, directed thinking, is here a descendant of the primitive words, as, for instance, Wundt [9] expresses it.

"A further important result of that co-operation of sound and sign interchange consists in the fact that very many words gradually lose altogether their original concrete thought meaning, and turn into signs for general ideas and for the expression of the apperceptive functions of relation and comparison and their products. In this manner abstract thought develops, which, because it would not be possible without the change of meaning lying at the root of it, is indeed a production of that psychic and psychophysical reciprocal action out of which the development of language takes place."

Jodl [10] denies the identity of language and thought, because, for one reason, one and the same psychic fact might be expressed in different languages in different ways. From that he draws the conclusion that a "super-language thinking" exists. Certainly there is such a thing, whether with Erdmann one considers it "hypologisch," or with Jodl as "super-language." Only this is not logical thinking. My conception of it agrees with the noteworthy contribution made by Baldwin, which I will quote here word for word. [11]

"The transmission from pre-judgmental to judgmental meaning is just that from knowledge which has social confirmation to that which gets along without it. The meanings utilized for judgment are those already developed in their presuppositions and applications through the confirmation of social intercourse. Thus, the personal judgment, trained in the methods of social rendering, and disciplined by the interaction of its social world, projects its content into that world again.   In other words, the platform for all movement into the assertion of individual judgment—the level from which new experience is utilized—is already and always socialized; and it is just this movement that we find reflected in the actual results as the sense of the ' appropriateness ' or synomic character of the meaning rendered.

" Now the development of thought, as we are to see in more detail, is by a method essentially of trial and error, of experimentation, of the use of meanings as worth more than they are as yet recognized to be worth.   The individual must use his own thoughts, his established knowledges, his grounded judgments, for the embodiment of his new inventive constructions.   He erects his thought as we say ' schematically '—in logic terms, ' problematically,' conditionally, disjunctively; projecting into the world an opinion still peculiar to himself, as if it were true.   *Thus all discovery proceeds.*   But this is, from the linguistic point of view, still to use the current language, still to work by meanings already embodied in social and conventional usage.

" Language grows, therefore, just as thought does, by never losing its synomic or dual reference; its meaning is both personal and social.

" It is the register of tradition, the record of racial conquest, the deposit of all the gains made by the genius of individuals . . . The social copy-system, thus established, reflects the judgmental processes of the race, and in turn becomes the training school of the judgment of new generations.

" Most of the training of the self, whereby the vagaries of personal reaction to fact and image are reduced to the basis of sound judgment, comes through the use of speech.   When the child speaks, he lays before the world his suggestion for a general or common meaning.   The reception he gets confirms or refutes him.   In either case he is instructed.   His next venture is now from a platform of knowledge on which the newer item is more nearly convertible into the common coin of effective intercourse. The point to notice here is not so much the exact mechanism of the exchange—secondary conversion—by which this gain is made, as the training in judgment that the constant use of it affords. In each case, effective judgment is the common judgment.

" Here the object is to point out that it is secured by the development of a function *whose rise is directly ad hoc,* directly for the social experimentation by which growth in personal competence is advanced as well—*the function of speech.*

" In language, therefore, to sum up the foregoing, we have the tangible—the actual—the historical—instrument of the development and conservation of psychic meaning. It is the material evidence and proof of the *concurrence of social and personal judgment.* In it synomic meaning, judged as ' appropriate,' becomes ' social ' meaning, held as socially generalized and acknowledged."

These arguments of Baldwin abundantly emphasize the wide-reaching limitations of thinking caused by language.[12] These limitations are of the greatest significance, both subjectively and objectively; at least their meaning is great enough to force one to ask one's self if, after all, in regard to independence of thought, Franz Mauthner, thoroughly sceptical, is not really correct in his view that thinking is speech and nothing more. Baldwin expresses himself more cautiously and reservedly; nevertheless, his inner meaning is plainly in favor of the primacy of speech (naturally not in the sense of the spoken word) ; the directed thinking, or as we might perhaps call it, the thinking in internal speech, is the manifest instrument of culture, and we do not go astray when we say that the powerful work of education which the centuries have given to directed thinking has produced, just through the peculiar development of thinking from the individual subjective into the social objective, a practical application of the human mind to which we owe

modern empiricism and technic, and which occurs for absolutely the first time in the history of the world. Inquisi-
tive minds have often tormented themselves with the
question why the undoubtedly extraordinary knowledge
of mathematics and principles and material facts
united with the unexampled art of the human hand in
antiquity never arrived at the point of developing those
known technical statements of fact, for instance, the
principles of simple machines, beyond the realm of the
amusing and curious to a real technic in the modern sense.
There is necessarily only one answer to this; the ancients
almost entirely, with the exception of a few extraordinary
minds, lacked the capacity to allow their interest to
follow the transformations of inanimate matter to the
extent necessary for them to be able to reproduce the
process of nature, creatively and through their own art,
by means of which alone they could have succeeded in
putting themselves in possession of the force of nature.
That which they lacked was training in directed thinking,
or, to express it psychoanalytically, the ancients did not
succeed in tearing loose the libido which might be sublimated, from the other natural relations, and did not
turn voluntarily to anthropomorphism. The secret of
the development of culture lies in the *mobility of the
libido,* and in its capacity for transference. It is, therefore, to be assumed that the directed thinking of our time
is a more or less modern acquisition, which was lacking
in earlier times.

But with that we come to a further question, viz., what
happens if we do not think directedly? Then our thinking

lacks the major idea, and the feeling of direction which emanates from that.[13]   We no longer compel our thoughts along a definite track, but let them float, sink and mount according to their own gravity.   According to Kulpe [14] thinking is a kind of inner will action, the absence of which necessarily leads to an automatic play of ideas.   James understands the non-directed thinking, or " merely associative " thinking, as the ordinary one. He expresses himself about that in the following manner :

" Our thought consists for the great part of a series of images, one of which produces the other; *a sort of passive dream-state of which the higher animals are also capable.*   This sort of thinking leads, nevertheless, to reasonable conclusions of a practical as well as of a theoretical nature.

" As a rule, the links of this sort of irresponsible thinking, which are accidentally bound together, are empirically concrete things, not abstractions."

We can, in the following manner, complete these definitions of William James.   This sort of thinking does not tire us; it quickly leads us away from reality into phantasies of the past and future.   Here, thinking in the form of speech ceases, image crowds upon image, feeling upon feeling; more and more clearly one sees a tendency which creates and makes believe, not as it truly is, but as one indeed might wish it to be.[15]   The material of these thoughts which turns away from reality, can naturally be only the past with its thousand memory pictures.   The customary speech calls this kind of thinking " dreaming."

Whoever attentively observes himself will find the general custom of speech very striking, for almost every day we can see for ourselves how, when falling asleep, phantasies are woven into our dreams, so that between the dreams of day and night there is not so great a difference.   Thus we have two forms of thinking— *directed thinking* and *dream or phantasy thinking*.   The first, working for communication with speech elements, is troublesome and exhausting; the latter, on the contrary, goes on without trouble, working spontaneously, so to speak, with reminiscences.   The first creates innovations, adaptations, imitates reality and seeks to act upon it. The latter, on the contrary, turns away from reality, sets free subjective wishes, and is, in regard to adaptation, wholly unproductive.[16]

Let us leave aside the query as to why we possess these two different ways of thinking, and turn back to the second proposition, namely, how comes it that we have two different ways of thinking?   I have intimated above that history shows us that directed thinking was not always as developed as it is at present.   In this age the most beautiful expression of directed thinking is science, and the technic fostered by it.   Both things are indebted for their existence simply to an energetic education in directed thinking.   At the time, however, when a few forerunners of the present culture, like the poet Petrarch, first began to appreciate Nature understandingly [17] there was already in existence an equivalent for our science, to wit, scholasticism.[18]   This took its objects from the phantasies of the past, and it gave to the mind a dialectic training in directed thinking. The only success which beckoned the thinker was rhetorical victory in disputation, and not a visible transformation of reality.

The subjects of thinking were often astonishingly phantastical; for example, questions were discussed, such as how many angels could have a place on the point of a needle? Whether Christ could have done his work of redemption equally well if he had come into the world as a pea? The possibility of such problems, to which belong the metaphysical problems in general, viz., to be able to know the unknowable, shows us of what peculiar kind that mind must have been which created such things which to us are the height of absurdity. Nietzsche had guessed, however, at the biological background of this phenomenon when he spoke of the " beautiful tension " of the Germanic mind which the Middle Ages created. Taken historically, scholasticism, in the spirit of which persons of towering intellectual powers, such as Thomas of Aquinas, Duns Scotus, Abélard, William of Occam and others, have labored, is the mother of the modern scientific attitude, and a later time will see clearly how and in what scholasticism still furnishes living undercurrents to the science of today. Its whole nature lies in dialectic gymnastics which have raised the symbol of speech, the word, to an almost absolute meaning, so that it finally attained to that substantiality which expiring antiquity could lend to its *logos* only temporarily, through attributes of mystical valuation. The great work of scholasticism, however, appears to be the foundation of firmly knitted intellectual sublimation, the *conditio sine qua non* of the modern scientific and technical spirit.

Should we go further back into history, we shall find that which today we call science, dissolved into an indistinct cloud. The modern culture-creating mind is incessantly occupied in stripping off all subjectivity from experience, and in finding those formulas which bring Nature and her forces to the best and most fitting expression. It would be an absurd and entirely unjustified self-glorification if we were to assume that we are more energetic or more intelligent than the ancients—our materials for knowledge have increased, but not our intellectual capacity. For this reason, we become immediately as obstinate and insusceptible in regard to new ideas as people in the darkest times of antiquity. Our knowledge has increased but not our wisdom. The main point of our interest is displaced wholly into material reality; antiquity preferred a mode of thought which was more closely related to a phantastic type. Except for a sensitive perspicuity towards works of art, not attained since then, we seek in vain in antiquity for that precise and concrete manner of thinking characteristic of modern science. We see the antique spirit create not science but mythology. Unfortunately, we acquire in school only a very paltry conception of the richness and immense power of life of Grecian mythology.

Therefore, at first glance, it does not seem possible for us to assume that that energy and interest which today we put into science and technic, the man of antiquity gave in great part to his mythology. That, nevertheless, gives the explanation for the bewildering changes, the kaleido-scopic transformations and new syncretistic groupings, and the continued rejuvenation of the myths in the Grecian sphere of culture. Here, we move in a world of phantasies, which, little concerned with the outer course of things, flows from an inner source, and, con-stantly changing, creates now plastic, now shadowy shapes. This phantastical activity of the ancient mind created artistically *par excellence.* The object of the in-terest does not seem to have been to grasp hold of the " how " of the real world as objectively and exactly as possibly, but to æsthetically adapt subjective phantasies and expectations. There was very little place among ancient people for the coldness and disillusion which Giordano Bruno's thoughts on eternity and Kepler's dis-coveries brought to modern humanity. The naïve man of antiquity saw in the sun the great Father of the heaven and the earth, and in the moon the fruitful good Mother. Everything had its demons; they animated equally a human being and his brother, the animal. Everything was considered according to its anthropomorphic or theriomorphic attributes, as human being or animal. Even the disc of the sun was given wings or four feet, in order to illustrate its movement. Thus arose an idea of the universe which was not only very far from reality, but was one which corresponded wholly to subjective phantasies.

We know, from our own experience, this state of mind. It is an infantile stage. To a child the moon is a man or a face or a shepherd of the stars. The clouds in the sky seem like little sheep; the dolls drink, eat and sleep; the child places a letter at the window for the Christ-child; he calls to the stork to bring him a little brother or sister; the cow is the wife of the horse, and the dog the husband of the cat. We know, too, that lower races, like the negroes, look upon the locomotive as an animal, and call the drawers of the table the child of the table.

As we learn through Freud, the dream shows a similar type. Since the dream is unconcerned with the real condition of things, it brings the most heterogeneous matter together, and a world of impossibilities takes the place of realities. Freud finds progression characteristic of thinking when awake; that is to say, the advancement of the thought excitation from the system of the inner or outer perception through the " endopsychic " work of association, conscious and unconscious, to the motor end; that is to say, towards innervation. In the dream he finds the reverse, namely, regression of the thought excitation from the pre-conscious or unconscious to the system of perception, by the means of which the dream receives its ordinary impression of sensuous distinctness, which can rise to an almost hallucinating clearness. The dream thinking moves in a retrograde manner towards the raw material of memory. " The structure of the dream thoughts is dissolved during the progress of regression into its raw material." The reanimation of the original perception is, however, only one side of regression. The other side is regression to the infantile memory material, which might also be understood as regression to the original perception, but which deserves especial mention on account of its independent importance. This regression might, indeed, be considered as " historical." The dream, according to this conception, might also be described as *the substitute of the infantile scene, changed through transference into the recent scene.*

The infantile scene cannot carry through its revival; it must be satisfied with its return as a dream. From this conception of the historical side of regression, it follows consequently that the modes of conclusion of the dream, in so far as one may speak of them, must show at the same time an analogous and infantile character. This is truly the case, as experience has abundantly shown, so that today every one who is familiar with the subject of dream analysis confirms Freud's proposition that *dreams are a piece of the conquered life of the childish soul.* Inasmuch as the childish psychic life is undeniably of an archaic type, this characteristic belongs to the dream in quite an unusual degree. Freud calls our attention to this especially.

" The dream, which fulfils its wishes by a short, regressive path, affords us only an example of the primary method of working of the psychic apparatus, which has been abandoned by us as unsuitable. That which once ruled in the waking state, when the psychical life was still young and impotent, appears to be banished to the dream life, in somewhat the same way as the bow and arrow, those discarded, primitive weapons of adult humanity, have been relegated to the nursery." [19]

All this experience suggests to us that we draw a parallel between the phantastical, mythological thinking of antiquity and the similar thinking of children, between the lower human races and dreams.[20]   This train of thought is not a strange one for us, but quite familiar through our knowledge of comparative anatomy and the history of development, which show us how the structure and function of the human body are the results of a series of embryonic changes which correspond to similar changes in the history of the race.   Therefore, the supposition is justified that ontogenesis corresponds in psychology to phylogenesis.   Consequently, it would be true, as well, that the state of infantile thinking in the child's psychic life, as well as in dreams, is nothing but a re-echo of the prehistoric and the ancient.[21]

In regard to this, Nietzsche takes a very broad and remarkable standpoint.[22]

" In our sleep and in our dreams we pass through the whole thought of earlier humanity.   I mean, in the same way that man reasons in his dreams, he reasoned when in the waking state many thousands of years.   The first *causa* which occurred to his mind in reference to anything that needed explanation, satisfied him and passed for truth.   In the dream this atavistic relic of humanity manifests its existence within us, for it is the foundation upon which the higher rational faculty developed, and which is still developing in every individual.   The dream carries us back into earlier states of human culture, and affords us a means of understanding it better.   The dream thought is so easy to us now, because we are so thoroughly trained to it through the interminable stages of evolution during which this phantastic and facile form of theorizing has prevailed.   To a certain extent the dream is a restorative for the brain, which during the day is called upon to meet the severe demands for trained thought, made by the conditions of a higher civilization.

" From these facts, we can understand how lately more acute logical thinking, the taking seriously of cause and effect, has been developed; when our functions of reason and intelligence still reach back involuntarily to those primitive forms of conclusion, and we live about half our lives in this condition."

We have already seen that Freud, independently of Nietzsche, has reached a similar standpoint from the basis of dream analysis. The step from this established proposition to the perception of the myths as familiar dream images is no longer a great one. Freud has formulated this conclusion himself.[23]

" The investigation of this folk-psychologic formation, myths, etc., is by no means finished at present. To take an example of this, however, it is probable that the myths correspond to the distorted residue of wish phantasies of whole nations, the secularized dreams of young humanity."

Rank [24] understands the myths in a similiar manner, as a mass dream of the people.[25]   Riklin [26] has insisted rightly upon the dream mechanism of the fables, and Abraham [27] has done the same for the myths. He says:

" The myth is a fragment of the infantile soul-life of the people."

and

" Thus the myth is a *sustained, still remaining* fragment from the infantile soul-life of the people, and the dream is the myth of the individual."

An unprejudiced reading of the above-mentioned authors will certainly allay all doubts concerning the intimate connection between dream psychology and myth psychology. The conclusion results almost from itself, that the age which created the myths thought childishly—

that is to say, phantastically, as in our age is still done, to a very great extent (associatively or analogically) in dreams. The beginnings of myth formations (in the child), the taking of phantasies for realities, which is partly in accord with the historical, may easily be discovered among children.

One might raise the objection that the mythological inclinations of children are implanted by education. The objection is futile. Has humanity at all ever broken loose from the myths? Every man has eyes and all his senses to perceive that the world is dead, cold and unending, and he has never yet seen a God, nor brought to light the existence of such from empirical necessity. On the contrary, there was need of a phantastic, indestructible optimism, and one far removed from all sense of reality, in order, for example, to discover in the shameful death of Christ really the highest salvation and the redemption of the world. Thus one can indeed withhold from a child the substance of earlier myths but not take from him the need for mythology. One can say, that should it happen that all traditions in the world were cut off with a single blow, then with the succeeding generation, the whole mythology and history of religion would start over again. Only a few individuals succeed in throwing off mythology in a time of a certain intellectual supremacy—the mass never frees itself. Explanations are of no avail; they merely destroy a transitory form of manifestation, but not the creating impulse.

Let us again take up our earlier train of thought.

We spoke of the ontogenetic re-echo of the phylogenetic psychology among children, we saw that phantastic thinking is a characteristic of antiquity, of the child, and of the lower races; but now we know also that our modern and adult man is given over in large part to this same phantastic thinking, which enters as soon as the directed thinking ceases. A lessening of the interest, a slight fatigue, is sufficient to put an end to the directed thinking, the exact psychological adaptation to the real world, and to replace it with phantasies. We digress from the theme and give way to our own trains of thought; if the slackening of the attention increases, then we lose by degrees the consciousness of the present, and the phantasy enters into possession of the field.

Here the important question obtrudes itself: How are phantasies created? From the pôets we learn much about it; from science we learn little. The psychoanalytic method, presented to science by Freud, shed light upon this for the first time. It showed us that there are typical cycles. The stutterer imagines he is a great orator. The truth of this, Demosthenes, thanks to his energy, has proven. The poor man imagines himself to be a millionaire, the child an adult. The conquered fight out victorious battles with the conquerer; the unfit torments or delights himself with ambitious plans. We imagine that which we lack. The interesting question of the " why " of all this we must here leave unanswered, while we return to the historic problem: From what source do the phantasies draw their materials? [28] We chose, as an example, a typical phantasy of puberty. A child in that stage before whom the whole frightening uncertainty of the future fate opens, puts back the uncertainty into the past, through his phantasy, and says, "If only I were not the child of my ordinary parents, but the child of a rich and fashionable count, and had been merely passed over to my parents, then some day a golden coach would come, and the count would take his child back with him to his wonderful castle," and so it goes on, as in Grimm's Fairy Tales which the mother tells to her children.[29] With a normal child, it stops with the fugitive, quickly-passing idea which is soon covered over and forgotten. However, at one time, and that was in the ancient world of culture, the phantasy was an openly acknowledged institution. The heroes,—I recall Romulus and Remus, Semiramis, Moses and many others,— have been separated from their real parents.[30] Others are directly sons of gods, and the noble races derive their family trees from heroes and gods. As one sees by this example, the phantasy of modern humanity is nothing but a re-echo of an old-folk-belief, which was very widespread originally.[31] The ambitious phantasy chooses, among others, a form which is classic, and which once had a true meaning. The same thing holds good in regard to the sexual phantasy. In the preamble we have spoken of dreams of sexual assault: the robber who breaks into the house and commits a dangerous act. That, too, is a mythological theme, and in the prehistoric era was certainly a reality too.[32] Wholly apart from the fact that the capture of women was something general in the lawless prehistoric times, it was also a subject of mythology in cultivated epochs. I recall the capture of

Proserpina, Deianira, Europa, the Sabine women, etc. We must not forget that, even today, marriage customs exist in various regions which recall the ancient custom of marriage by capture.

The symbolism of the instrument of coitus was an inexhaustible material for ancient phantasy. It furnished a widespread cult that was designated phallic, the object of reverence of which was the phallus. The companion of Dionysus was Phales, a personification of the phallus proceeding from the phallic Herme of Dionysus. The phallic symbols were countless. Among the Sabines, the custom existed for the bridegroom to part the bride's hair with a lance. The bird, the fish and the snake were phallic symbols. In addition, there existed in enormous quantities theriomorphic representations of the sexual instinct, in connection with which the bull, the he-goat, the ram, the boar and the ass were frequently used. An undercurrent to this choice of symbol was furnished by the sodomitic inclination of humanity. When in the dream phantasy of modern man, the feared man is replaced by an animal, there is recurring in the ontogenetic re-echo the same thing which was openly represented by the ancients countless times. There were he-goats which pursued nymphs, satyrs with she-goats; in still older times in Egypt there even existed a shrine of a goat god, which the Greeks called Pan, where the Hierodules prostituted themselves with goats.[33] It is well known that this worship has not died out, but continues to live as a special custom in South Italy and Greece.[34]

Today we feel for such a thing nothing but the deepest

abhorrence, and never would admit it still slumbered in our souls. Nevertheless, just as truly as the idea of the sexual assault is there, so are these things there too; which we should contemplate still more closely,—not through moral eye-glasses, with horror, but with interest as a natural science, since these things are venerable relics of past culture periods. We have, even today, a clause in our penal code against sodomy. But that which was once so strong as to give rise to a worship among a highly developed people has probably not wholly disappeared from the human soul during the course of a few generations. We may not forget that since the symposium of Plato, in which homo-sexuality faces us on the same level with the so-called "normal sexuality," only ·eighty generations have passed. And what are eighty generations? They shrink to an imperceptible period of· time when compared with the space of time which separates us from the homo-Neandertalensis or Heidelbergensis. I might call to mind, in this connection, some choice thoughts of the great historian Guglielmo Ferrero: [35]

"It is a very common belief that the further man is separated from the present by time, the more does he differ from us in his thoughts and feelings; that the psychology of humanity changes from century to century, like fashions of literature. Therefore, no sooner do we find in past history an institution, a custom, a law or a belief a little different from those with which we are familiar, than we immediately search for some complex meanings, which frequently resolve themselves into phrases of doubtful significance.

"Indeed, man does not change so quickly; his psychology at bottom remains the same, and even if his culture varies much from one epoch to another, it does not change the functioning of his mind. The fundamental laws of the mind remain the same, at least during the short historical period of which we have knowledge, and all phenomena, even the most strange, must be capable of explanation by those common laws of the mind which we can recognize in ourselves."

The psychologist should accept this viewpoint without reservation as peculiarly applicable to himself. Today, indeed, in our civilization the phallic processions, the Dionysian mysteries of classical Athens, the barefaced Phallic emblems, have disappeared from our coins, houses, temples and streets; so also have the theriomorphic representations of the Deity been reduced to small remnants, like the Dove of the Holy Ghost, the Lamb of God and the Cock of Peter adorning our church towers. In the same way, the capture and violation of women have shrunken away to crimes. Yet all of this does not affect the fact that we, in childhood, go through a period in which the impulses toward these archaic inclinations appear again and again, and that through all our life we possess, side by side with the newly recruited, directed and adapted thought, a phantastic thought which corresponds to the thought of the centuries of antiquity and barbarism. Just as our bodies still keep the reminders of old functions and conditions in many old-fashioned organs, so our minds, too, which apparently have outgrown those archaic tendencies, nevertheless bear the marks of the evolution passed through, and the very ancient re-echoes, at least dreamily, in phantasies.

The symbolism which Freud has discovered, is revealed as an expression of a thinking and of an impulse limited to the dream, to wrong conduct, and to derangements of the mind, which form of thinking and impulse at one time ruled as the mightiest influence in past culture epochs.

The question of *whence* comes the inclination and ability which enables the mind to express itself symbolically, brings us to the distinction between the two kinds of thinking—the directed and adapted on one hand, and the subjective, fed by our own egotistic wishes, on the other. The latter form of thinking, presupposing that it were not constantly corrected by the adapted thinking, must necessarily produce an overwhelmingly subjectively distorted idea of the world. We regard this state of mind as infantile. It lies in our individual past, and in the past of mankind.

With this we affirm the important fact that man in his phantastic thinking has kept a condensation of the psychic history of his development. An extraordinarily important task, which even today is hardly possible, is to give a systematic description of phantastic thinking. One may, at the most, sketch it. While directed thinking is a phenomenon conscious throughout,[36] the same cannot be asserted of phantastic thinking. Doubtless, a great part of it still falls entirely in the realm of the conscious, but, at least, just as much goes along in half shadows, and generally an undetermined amount in the unconscious; and this can, therefore, be disclosed only indirectly.[37] By means of phantastic thinking, directed thinking is connected with the oldest foundations of the human mind, which have been for a long time beneath the threshold of the consciousness. The products of this phantastic thinking arising directly from the consciousness are, first, waking dreams, or day-dreams, to which Freud, Flournoy, Pick and others have given special attention; then the dreams which offer to the consciousness, at first, a mysterious exterior, and win meaning only through the indirectly inferred unconscious contents. Lastly, there is a so-called wholly unconscious phantasy system in the split-off complex, which exhibits a pronounced tendency towards the production of a dissociated personality.[38]

Our foregoing explanations show wherein the products arising from the unconscious are related to the mythical. From all these signs it may be concluded that the soul possesses in some degree historical strata, the oldest stratum of which would correspond to the unconscious. The result of that must be that an introversion occurring in later life, according to the Freudian teaching, seizes upon regressive infantile reminiscences taken from the individual past. That first points out the way; then, with stronger introversion and regression (strong repressions, introversion psychoses), there come to light pronounced traits of an archaic mental kind which, under certain circumstances, might go as far as the re-echo of a once manifest, archaic mental product.

This problem deserves to be more thoroughly discussed. As a concrete example, let us take the history of the pious Abbé Oegger which Anatole France has communicated to us.[39] This priest was a hypercritical man, and much given to phantasies, especially in regard to one question, viz., the fate of Judas; whether he was really damned, as the teaching of the church asserts, to everlasting punishment, or whether God had pardoned him after all. Oegger sided with the intelligent point of view that God, in his all-wisdom, had chosen Judas as an instrument, in order to bring about the highest point of the work of redemption by Christ.[40] This necessary instrument, without the help of which the human race would not have been a sharer in salvation, could not possibly be damned by the all-good God. In order to put an end to his doubts, Oegger went one night to the church, and made supplication for a sign that Judas was saved. Then he felt a heavenly touch upon his shoulder. Following this, Oegger told the Archbishop of his resolution to go out into the world to preach God's unending mercy.

Here we have a richly developed phantasy system before us. It is concerned with the subtle and perpetually undecided question as to whether the legendary figure of Judas is damned or not. The Judas legend is, in itself, mythical material, viz., the malicious betrayal of a hero. I recall Siegfried and Hagen, Balder and Loki. Siegfried and Balder were murdered by a faithless traitor from among their closest associates. This myth is moving and tragic—it is not honorable battle which kills the noble, but evil treachery. It is, too, an occurrence which is historical over and over again. One thinks of Cæsar and Brutus. Since the myth of such a deed is very old, and still the subject of teaching and repetition, it is the expression of a psychological fact, that envy does not allow humanity to sleep, and that all of us carry, in a hidden recess of our heart, a deadly wish towards the hero. This rule can be applied generally to mythical tradition. *It does not set forth any account of the old events, but rather acts in such a way that it always reveals a thought common to humanity, and once more rejuvenated.* Thus, for example, the lives and deeds of the founders of old religions are the purest condensations of typical, contemporaneous myths, behind which the individual figure entirely disappears.[41]

But why does our pious Abbé torment himself with the old Judas legend? He first went into the world to preach the gospel of mercy, and then, after some time, he separated from the Catholic church and became a Swedenborgian. Now we understand his Judas phantasy. *He was the Judas* who betrayed his Lord. Therefore, first of all, he had to make sure of the divine mercy, in order to be Judas in peace.

This case throws a light upon the mechanism of the phantasies in general. The known, conscious phantasy may be of mythical or other material; it is not to be taken seriously as such, for it has an indirect meaning. If we take it, however, as important.per se, then the thing is not understandable, and makes one despair of the efficiency of the mind. But we saw, in the case of Abbé Oegger, that his doubts and his hopes did not turn upon the historical problem of Judas, but upon his own personality, which wished to win a way to freedom for itself through the solution of the Judas problem.

The conscious phantasies tell us of mythical or other material of undeveloped or no longer recognized wish tendencies in the soul. As is easily to be understood, an innate tendency, an acknowledgment of which one refuses to make, and which one treats as non-existent, can hardly contain a thing that may be in accord with our conscious character. It concerns the tendencies which are considered immoral, and as generally impossible, and the strongest resentment is felt towards bringing them into the consciousness. What would Oegger have said had he been told confidentially that he was preparing himself for the Judas rôle? And what in ourselves do we consider immoral and non-existent, or which we at least wish were non-existent? It is that which in antiquity lay widespread on the surface, viz., sexuality in all its various manifestations. Therefore, we need not wonder in the least when we find this at the base of most of our phantasies, even if the phantasies have a different appearance. Because Oegger found the damnation of Judas incompatible with God's goodness, he thought about the conflict in that way; that is the conscious sequence. Along with this is the unconscious sequence; because Oegger himself wished to be a Judas, he first made sure of the goodness of God. To Oegger, Judas was the symbol of his own unconscious tendency, and he made use of this symbol in order to be able to meditate over his unconscious wish. The direct coming into consciousness of the Judas wish would have been too painful for him. *Thus, there must be typical myths which are really the instruments of a folk-psychological complex treatment.* Jacob Burckhardt seems to have suspected this when he once said that every Greek of the classical era carried in himself a fragment of the Oedipus, just as every German carries a fragment of Faust.[42]

The problem which the simple story of the Abbé Oegger has brought clearly before us confronts us again when we prepare to examine phantasies which owe their existence this time to an exclusively unconscious work. We are indebted for the material which we will use in the following chapters to the useful publication of an American woman, Miss Frank Miller, who has given to the world some poetical unconsciously formed phantasies under the title, " Quelque faits d'imagination créatrice subconsciente."—*Vol. V., Archives de Psychologie, 1906.*[43]

CHAPTER II

THE MILLER PHANTASIES

WE know, from much psychoanalytic experience, that whenever one recounts his phantasies or his dreams, he deals not only with the most important and intimate of his problems, but with the one the most painful at that moment.[1]

Since in the case of Miss Miller we have to do with a complicated system, we must give our attention carefully to the particulars which I will discuss, following as best. I can Miss Miller's presentation.

In the first chapter, " Phénomènes de suggestion passagère ou d'autosuggestion instantanée," Miss Miller gives a list of examples of her unusual suggestibility, which she herself considers as a symptom of her nervous temperament; for example, she is excessively fond of caviar, whereas some of her relatives loathe it. However, as soon as any one expresses his loathing, she herself feels momentarily the same loathing. I do not need to emphasize especially the fact that such examples are very important in individual psychology; that caviar is a food for which nervous women frequently have an especial predilection, is a fact well known to the psychoanalysist.

Miss Miller has an extraordinary faculty for taking

other people's feelings upon herself, and of identification; for example, she identifies herself to such a degree
in " Cyrano " with the wounded Christian de Neuvillette,
that she feels in her own breast a truly piercing pain at
that place where Christian received the deadly blow.

From the viewpoint of analytic psychology, the theatre,
aside from any esthetic value, may be considered as an
institution for the treatment of the mass complex. The
enjoyment of the comedy, or of the dramatic plot ending
happily is produced by an unreserved identification of
one's own complexes with the play. The enjoyment of
tragedy lies in the thrilling yet satisfactory feeling that
something which might occur to one's self is happening
to another. The sympathy of our author with the dying
Christian means that there is in her a complex awaiting
a similar solution, which whispers softly to her " hodie
tibi, cras mihi," and that one may know exactly what is
considered the effectual moment Miss Miller adds that
she felt a pain in her breast, " Lorsque Sarah Bernhardt
se précipite sur lui pour étancher le sang de sa blessure."
Therefore the effectual moment is when the love between
Christian and Roxane comes to a sudden end.

If we glance over the whole of Rostand's play, we
come upon certain moments, the effect of which one cannot easily escape and which we will emphasize here because they have meaning for all that follows. Cyrano de
Bergerac, with the long ugly nose, on account of which
he undertakes countless duels, loves Roxane, who, for
her part unaware of it, loves Christian, because of the
beautiful verses which really originate from Cyrano's

pen, but which apparently come from Christian. Cyrano is the misunderstood one, whose passionate love and noble soul no one suspects; the hero who sacrifices himself for others, and, dying, just in the evening of life, reads to her once more Christian's last letter, the verses which he himself had composed.

> " Roxane, adieu, je vais mourir!
> C'est pour ce soir, je crois, ma bien-aimée!
> J'ai l'âme lourde encore d'amour inexprimé.
> Et je meurs! Jamais plus, jamais mes yeux grisés,
> Mes regards dont c'était les frémissantes fêtes,
> Ne baiseront au vol les gestes que vous faites;
> J'en revois un petit qui vous est familier
> Pour toucher votre front et je voudrais crier—.
>   Et je crie:
> Adieu!—Ma chère, ma chérie,
> Mon trésor—mon amour!
> Mon coeur ne vous quitta jamais une seconde,
> Et je suis et je serai jusque dans l'autre monde
> Celui qui vous aime sans mesure, celui—"

Whereupon Roxane recognizes in him the real loved one. It is already too late; death comes; and in agonized delirium, Cyrano raises himself, and draws his sword:

> " Je crois, qu'elle regarde. . . .
> Qu'elle ose regarder mon nez, la camarde!
>   (Il lève son épée.)
> Que dites-vous? . . . C'est inutile!
>   Je le sais!
> Mais on ne se bat pas dans l'espoir du succès!
> Non! Non! C'est bien plus beau, lorsque c'est inutile!
> —Qu'est-ce que c'est que tous ceux-là?—Vous êtes mille?
> Ah! je vous reconnais, tous mes vieux ennemis!
> Le mensonge!
>   (Il frappe de son épée le vide.)

Tiens, tiens, ha! ha! les Compromis,
Les Préjugés, les Lâchetés! . . .

                         (Il frappe.)

      Que je pactise?

Jamais, jamais!—Ah, te voilà, toi, la Sottise!
—Je sais bien qu'à la fin vous me mettrez à bas;
N'importe: je me bats! je me bats! je me bats!
Oui, vous m'arrachez tout, le laurier et la rose!
Arrachez! Il y a malgré vous quelque chose
Que j'emporte, et ce soir, quand j'entrerai chez Dieu,
Mon salut balaiera largement le seuil bleu.
Quelque chose que sans un pli, sans une tache,
J'emporte malgré vous, et c'est—mon panache."

Cyrano, who under the hateful exterior of his body hid a soul so much more beautiful, is a yearner and one misunderstood, and his last triumph is that he departs, at least, with a clean shield—" Sans un pli et sans une tache." The identification of the author with the dying Christian, who in himself is a figure but little impressive and sympathetic, expresses clearly that a sudden end is destined for her love just as for Christian's love. The tragic intermezzo with Christian, however, is played as we have seen upon a background of much wider significance, viz., the misunderstood love of Cyrano for Roxane. Therefore, the identification with Christian has only the significance of a substitute memory (" deckerinnerung "), and is really intended for Cyrano. That this is just what we might expect will be seen in the further course of our analysis.

Besides this story of identification with Christian, there follows as a further example an extraordinarily plastic memory of the sea, evoked by the sight of a photograph of a steamboat on the high seas. (" Je sentis les pulsations des machines, le soulèvement des vagues, le balancement du navire.")

We may mention here the supposition that there are connected with sea journeys particularly impressive and strong memories which penetrate deeply into the soul and give an especially strong character to the surface memories through unconscious harmony. To what extent the memories assumed here agree with the above mentioned problem we shall see in the following pages.

This example, following at this time, is singular: Once, while in bathing, Miss Miller wound a towel around her hair, in order to protect it from a wetting. At the same moment she had the following strong impression:

" Il me sembla que j'étais sur un piédéstal, une véritable statue égyptienne, avec tous ses détails: membres raides, un pied en avant, la main tenant des insignes," and so on.

Miss Miller identified herself, therefore, with an Egyptian statue, and naturally the foundation for this was a subjective pretension. That is to say, " I am like an Egyptian statue, just as stiff, wooden, sublime and impassive," qualities for which the Egyptian statue is proverbial. One does not make such an assertion to one's self without an inner compulsion, and the correct formula might just as well be, " as stiff, wooden, etc., as an Egyptian statue I might indeed be." The sight of one's own unclothed body in a bath has undeniable effects for the phantasy, which can be set at rest by the above formula.[2]

The example which follows this, emphasizes the author's personal influence upon an artist:

" J'ai réussi à lui faire rendre des paysages, comme ceux du lac Léman, où il n'a jamais été, et il prétendait que je pouvais lui faire rendre des choses qu'il n'avait jamais vues, et lui donner la sensation d'une atmosphère ambiante qu'il n'avait jamais sentie; bref que je me servais de lui comme lui-même se servait de son crayon, c'est à dire comme d'un simple instrument."

This observation stands in abrupt contrast to the phantasy of the Egyptian statue. Miss Miller had here the unspoken need of emphasizing her almost magic effect upon another person. This could not have happened, either, without an unconscious need, which is particularly felt by one who does not often succeed in making an emotional impression upon a fellow being.

With that, the list of examples which are to picture Miss Miller's autosuggestibility and suggestive effect, is exhausted. In this respect, the examples are neither especially striking nor interesting. From an analytical viewpoint, on the contrary, they are much more important, since they afford us a glance into the soul of the writer. Ferenczi[3] has taught us in an excellent work what is to be thought about suggestibility, that is to say, that these phenomena win new aspects in the light of the Freudian libido theory, in so much as their effects become clear through " Libido-besetzungen." This was already indicated above in the discussion of the examples, and in the greatest detail regarding the identification with Christian. The identification becomes effective by its receiving an influx of energy from the strongly accentuated thought and emotional feeling underlying the Christian motif. Just the reverse is the suggestive effect of the individual in an especial capacity for concentrating interest (that is to say, libido) upon another person, by which the other is unconsciously compelled to reaction (the same or opposed). The majority of the examples concern cases where Miss Miller is put under the effects of suggestion; that is to say, when the libido has spontaneously gained possession of certain impressions, and this is impossible if the libido is dammed up to an unusual degree by the lack of application to reality. Miss Miller's observations about suggestibility inform us, therefore, of the fact that the author is pleased to tell us in her following phantasies something of the history of her love.

CHAPTER III

THE HYMN OF CREATION

THE second chapter in Miss Miller's work is entitled, "Gloire à Dieu. Poème onirique."

When twenty years of age, Miss Miller took a long journey through Europe. We leave the description of it to her:

"After a long and rough journey from New York to Stockholm, from there to Petersburg and Odessa, I found it a true pleasure [1] to leave the world of inhabited cities—and to enter the world of waves, sky and silence—I stayed hours long on deck to dream, stretched out in a reclining chair. The histories, legends and myths of the different countries which I saw in the distance, came back to me indistinctly blended together in a sort of luminous mist, in which things lost their reality, while the dreams and thoughts alone took on somewhat the appearance of reality. At first, I even avoided all company and kept to myself, lost wholly in my dreams, where all that I knew of great, beautiful and good came back into my consciousness with new strength and new life. I also employed a great part of my time writing to my distant friends, reading and sketching out short poems about the regions visited. Some of these poems were of a very serious character."

It may seem superfluous, perhaps, to enter intimately into all these details. If we recall, however, the remark made above,—that when people let their unconscious speak, they always tell us the most important things of

49

their intimate selves—then even the smallest detail appears to have meaning. Valuable personalities invariably tell us, through their unconscious, things that are generally valuable, so that patient interest is rewarded.

Miss Miller describes here a state of " introversion." After the life of the cities with their many impressions had been absorbing her interest (with that already discussed strength of suggestion which powerfully enforced the impression) she breathed freely upon the ocean, and after so many external impressions, became engrossed wholly in the internal with intentional abstraction from the surroundings, so that things lost their reality and dreams became truth. We know from psychopathology that certain mental disturbances [2] exist which are first manifested by the individuals shutting themselves off slowly, more and more, from reality and sinking into, their phantasies, during which process, in proportion as the reality loses its hold, the inner world gains in reality and determining power.[3] This process leads to a certain point (which varies with the individual) when the patients suddenly become more or less conscious of their separation from reality. The event which then enters is the pathological excitation: that is to say, the patients begin to turn towards the environment, with diseased views (to be sure) which, however, still represent the compensating, although unsuccessful, attempt at transference.[4] The methods of reaction are, naturally, very different. I will not concern myself more closely about this here.

This type appears to be generally a psychological rule

which holds good for all neuroses and, therefore, also for the normal in a much less degree. We might, therefore, expect that Miss Miller, after this energetic and persevering introversion, which had even encroached for a time upon the feeling of reality, would succumb anew to an impression of the real world and also to just as suggestive and energetic an influence as that of her dreams. Let us proceed with the narrative:

" But as the journey drew to an end, the ship's officers outdid themselves in kindness (tout ce qu'il y a de plus empressé et de plus aimable) and I passed many amusing hours teaching them English. On the Sicilian coast, in the harbor of Catania, I wrote a sailor's song which was very similar to a song well known on the sea, (Brine, wine and damsels fine). The Italians in general all sing very well, and one of the officers who sang on deck during night watch, had made a great impression upon me and had given me the idea of writing some words adapted to his melody. Soon after that, I was very nearly obliged to reverse the well-known saying, ' Veder Napoli e poi morir,'—that is to say, suddenly I became very ill, although not dangerously so. I recovered to such an extent, however, that I could go on land to visit the sights of the city in a carriage. This day tired me very much, and since we had planned to see Pisa the following day, I went on board early in the evening and soon lay down to sleep without thinking of anything more serious than the beauty of the officers and the ugliness of the Italian beggars."

One is somewhat disappointed at meeting here, instead of the expected impression of reality, rather a small intermezzo, a flirtation. Nevertheless, one of the officers, the singer, had made a great impression (il m'avait fait beaucoup d'impression). The remark at the close of the description, " sans songer à rien de plus sérieux qu'à la beauté des officiers,' and so on, diminishes the seriousness of the impression, it is true. The assumption, however, that the impression openly influenced the mood very much, is supported by the fact that a poem upon a subject of such an erotic character came forth immediately, " Brine, wine and damsels fine," and in the singer's honor. One is only too easily inclined to take such an impression lightly, and one admits so gladly the statements of the participators when they represent everything as simple and not at all serious. I dwell upon this impression at length, because it is important to know that an erotic impression after such an introversion, has a deep effect and is undervalued, possibly, by Miss Miller. The suddenly passing sickness is obscure and needs a psychologic interpretation which cannot be touched upon here because of lack of data. The phenomena now to be described can only be explained as arising from a disturbance which reaches to the very depths of her being.

" From Naples to Livorno, the ship travelled for a night, during which I slept more or less well,—my sleep, however, is seldom deep or dreamless. It seemed to me as if my mother's voice wakened me, just at the end of the following dream. At first I had a vague conception of the words, ' When the morning stars sang together,' which were the praeludium of a certain confused representation of creation and of the mighty chorals resounding through the universe. In spite of the strange, contradictory and confused character which is peculiar to the dream, there was mingled in it the chorus of an oratorio which has been given by one of the foremost musical societies of New York, and with that were also memories of Milton's ' Paradise Lost.' Then from out of this whirl, there slowly emerged certain words, which arranged themselves into three strophes and, indeed, they seemed to be in my own handwriting on ordinary blue-lined writing paper on a page of my old poetry book which I always carried around with me; in short, they appeared to me exactly as some minutes later they were in reality in my book."

Miss Miller now wrote down the following poem, which she rearranged somewhat a few months later, to make it more nearly, in her opinion, like the dream original.

> " When the Eternal first made Sound
> A myriad ears sprang out to hear,
> And throughout all the Universe
> There rolled an echo deep and clear:
> All glory to the God of Sound!
>
> " When the Eternal first made Light
> A myriad eyes sprang out to look,
> And hearing ears and seeing eyes
> Once more a mighty choral took:
> All glory to the God of Light!
>
> " When the Eternal first gave Love
> A myriad hearts sprang into life;
> Ears filled with music, eyes with light;
> Pealed forth with hearts with love all rife:
> All glory to the God of Love! "

Before we enter upon Miss Miller's attempt to bring to light through her suppositions [5] the root of this subliminal creation, we will attempt a short analytic survey of the material already in our possession. The impression on the ship has already been properly emphasized, so that we need have no further difficulty in gaining possession of the dynamic process which brought about this poetical revelation. It was made clear in the preceding paragraphs that Miss Miller possibly had not inconsiderably undervalued the importance of the erotic impression. This assumption gains in probability through experience, which shows that, very generally, relatively weak erotic impressions are greatly undervalued. One can see this best in cases where those concerned, either from social or moral grounds, consider an erotic relation as something quite impossible; for example, parents and children, brothers and sisters, relations (homosexual) between older and younger men, and so on. If the impression is relatively slight, then it does not exist at all for the participators; if the impression is strong, then a tragic dependence arises, which may result in some great nonsense, or be carried to any extent. This lack of understanding can go unbelievably far; mothers, who see the first erections of the small son in their own bed, a sister who half-playfully embraces her brother, a twenty-year-old daughter who still seats herself on her father's lap, and then has " strange " sensations in her " abdomen." They are all morally indignant to the highest degree if one speaks of " sexuality." Finally, our whole education is carried on with the tacit agreement to know as little as possible of the erotic, and to spread abroad the deepest ignorance in regard to it. It is no wonder, therefore, that the judgment, *in puncto,* of the importance of an erotic impression is generally unsafe and inadequate.

Miss Miller was under the influence of a deep erotic impression, as we have seen. Because of the sum-total of the feelings aroused by this, it does not seem that this impression was more than dimly realized, for the dream had to contain a powerful repetition. From analytic experience, one knows that the early dreams which patients bring for analysis are none the less of especial interest, because of the fact that they bring out criticisms and valuations of the physician's personality, which previously, would have been asked for directly in vain. They enrich the conscious impression which the patient had of his physician, and often concerning very important points. They are naturally erotic observations which the unconscious was forced to make, just because of the quite universal undervaluation and uncertain judgment of the relatively weak erotic impression. In the drastic and hyperbolic manner of expression of the dream, the impression often appears in almost unintelligible form on account of the immeasurable dimension of the symbol. A further peculiarity which seems to rest upon the historic strata of the unconscious, is this—that an erotic impression, to which conscious acknowledgment is denied, usurps an earlier and discarded transference and expresses itself in that. Therefore, it frequently happens, for example, that among young girls at the time of their first love, remarkable difficulties develop in the capacity for erotic expression, which may be reduced analytically to disturbances through a regressive attempt at resuscitation of the father image, or the " Father-Imago." [6]

Indeed, one might presume something similar in Miss Miller's case, for the idea of the masculine creative deity is a derivation, analytically and historically psychologic, of the " Father-Imago," [7] and aims, above all, to replace the discarded infantile father transference in such a way that for the individual the passing from the narrow circle of the family into the wider circle of human society may be simpler or made easier.

In the light of this reflection, we can see, in the poem and its " Praeludium," the religious, poetically formed product of an introversion depending upon the surrogate of the " Father-Imago." In spite of the incomplete apperception of the effectual impression, essential component parts of this are included in the idea of compensation, as marks, so to speak, of its origin. (Pfister has coined for this the striking expression, " Law of the Return of the Complex.") The effectual impression was that of the officer singing in the night watch, " When the morning stars sang together." The idea of this opened a new world to the girl. (Creation.)

This creator has created tone, then light, and then love. That the first to be created should have been tone, can be made clear only individually, for there is no cosmogony except the Gnosis of Hermes, a generally quite unknown system, which would have such tendencies. But now we might venture a conjecture, which is already apparent, and which soon will be proven thoroughly, viz., the following chain of associations: the singer—the singing morning stars—the God of tone—the Creator—the God of Light—(of the sun)—(of the fire)—and of Love.

The links of this chain are proven by the material, with the exception of sun and fire, which I put in parentheses, but which, however, will be proven through what follows in the further course of the analysis. All of these expres‧ sions, with one exception, belong to erotic speech. (" My

God, star, light; my sun, fire of love, fiery love," etc.)
" Creator " appears indistinct at first, but becomes understandable through the reference to the undertone of Eros,
to the vibrating chord of Nature, which attempts to renew
itself in every pair of lovers, and awaits the wonder of
creation.

Miss Miller had taken pains to disclose the unconscious
creation of her mind to her understanding, and, indeed
through a procedure which agrees in principle with
psychoanalysis, and, therefore, leads to the same results
as psychoanalysis. But, as usually happens with laymen
and beginners, Miss Miller, because she had no knowledge of psychoanalysis, left off at the thoughts which
necessarily bring the deep complex lying at the bottom
of it to light in an indirect, that is to say, censored manner. More than this, a simple method, merely the carrying out of the thought to its conclusion, is sufficient to discover the meaning. Miss Miller finds it astonishing that
her unconscious phantasy does not, following the Mosaic
account of creation, put light in the first place, instead of
tone.

Now follows an explanation, theoretically constructed
and correct ad hoc, the hollowness of which is, however,
characteristic of all similar attempts at explanation. She
says:

" It is perhaps interesting to recall that Anaxagoras also had
the Cosmos arise out of chaos through a sort of whirlwind, which
does not happen usually without producing sound.[8] But at this
time I had studied no philosophy, and knew nothing either of
Anaxagoras or of his theories about the 'νοῦς,' which I, unconsciously, was openly following. At that time, also, I was equally

in complete ignorance of Leibnitz, and, therefore, knew nothing of his doctrine ' dum Deus calculat, fit mundus.' "

Miss Miller's references to Anaxagoras and to Leibnitz both refer to creation by means of thought; that is to say, that divine thought alone could bring forth a new material reality, a reference at first not intelligible, but which will soon, however, be more easily understood.

We now come to those fancies from which Miss Miller principally drew her unconscious creation.

" In the first place, there is the ' Paradise Lost ' by Milton, which we had at home in the edition illustrated by Doré, and which had often delighted me from childhood. Then the ' Book of Job,' which had been read aloud to me since the time of my earliest recollection. Moreover, if one compares the first words of ' Paradise Lost ' with my first verse, one notices that there is the same verse measure.

" ' Of man's first disobedience . . .

" ' When the Eternal first made sound.'

" My poem also recalls various passages in Job, and one or two places in Handel's Oratorio ' The Creation,' which came out very indistinctly in the first part of the dream." [9]

The " Lost Paradise " which, as is well known, is so closely connected with the beginning of the world, is made more clearly evident by the verse—

" Of man's first disobedience "

which is concerned evidently with the fall, the meaning of which need not be shown any further. I know the objection which every one unacquainted with psychoanalysis will raise, viz., that Miss Miller might just as well have chosen any other verse as an example, and that, accidentally, she had taken the first one that happened to appear which had this content, also accidentally. As is well known, the criticism which we hear equally from our medical colleagues, and from our patients, is generally based on such arguments. This misunderstanding arises from the fact that the law of causation in the psychical sphere is not taken seriously enough; that is to say, there are no accidents, no " just as wells." It is so, and there is, therefore, a sufficient reason at hand why it is so. It is moreover true that Miss Miller's poem is connected with the fall, wherein just that erotic component comes forth, the existence of which we have surmised above.

Miss Miller neglects to tell which passages in Job occurred to her mind. These, unfortunately, are therefore only general suppositions. Take first, the analogy to the Lost Paradise. Job lost all that he had, and this was due to an act of Satan, who wished to incite him against God. In the same way mankind, through the temptation of the serpent, lost Paradise, and was plunged into earth's torments. The idea, or rather the mood which is expressed by the reference to the Lost Paradise, is Miss Miller's feeling that she had lost something which was connected with satanic temptation. To her it happened, just as to Job, that she suffered innocently, for she did not fall a victim to temptation. Job's sufferings are not understood by his friends; [10] no one knows that Satan has taken a hand in the game, and that Job is truly innocent. Job never tires of avowing his innocence. Is there a hint in that? We know that certain neurotic and especially mentally diseased people continually defend their innocence against non-existent attacks; however, one discovers at a closer examination that the patient, while he apparently defends his innocence without reason, fulfils with that a " Deckhandlung," the energy for which arises from just those impulses, whose sinful character is revealed by the contents of the pretended reproach and calumny.[11]

Job suffered doubly, on one side through the loss of his fortune, on the other through the lack of understanding in his friends; the latter can be seen throughout the book. The suffering of the misunderstôod recalls the figure of Cyrano de Bergerac—he too suffered doubly, on one side through hopeless love, on the other side through misunderstanding. He falls, as we have seen, in the last hopeless battle against " Le Mensonge, les Compromis, les Préjugés, les Lâchetés et la Sottise.—Oui, Vous m'arrachez tout le laurier et la rose! "

Job laments

" God delivereth me to the ungodly,
  And casteth me into the hands of the wicked,
  I was at ease, and he brake me asunder;
  Yea, he hath taken me by the neck, and dashed me to pieces:

" *He hath also set me up for his mark.*
  His archers compass me round about;
  He cleaveth my reins asunder, and doth not spare;
  He poureth out my gall upon the ground.
  He breaketh me with breach upon breach;
  He runneth upon me like a giant."—*Job* xvi: 11-15.

The analogy of feeling lies in the suffering of the hopeless struggle against the more powerful. It is as if this conflict were accompanied from afar by the sounds of

" creation,'" which brings up a beautiful and mysterious image belonging to the unconscious, and which has not yet forced its way up to the light of the upper world. We surmise, rather than know, that this battle has really something to do with creation, with the struggles between negations and affirmations. The references to Rostand's " Cyrano " through the identification with Christian, to Milton's " Paradise Lost,'' to the sorrows of Job, misunderstood by his friends, betray plainly that in the soul of the poet something was identified with these ideas. She also has suffered like Cyrano and Job, has lost paradise, and dreams of " creation,"—creation by means of thought —fruition through the whirlwind of Anaxagoras.[12]

We once more submit ourselves to Miss Miller's guidance:

" I remember that when fifteen years old, I was once very much stirred up over an article, read aloud to me by my mother, concerning the idea which spontaneously produced its object. I was so excited that I could not sleep all night because of thinking over and over again what that could mean.

" From the age of nine to sixteen, I went every Sunday to a Presbyterian Church, in charge of which, at that time, was a very cultured minister. In one of the earliest memories which I have retained of him, I see myself as a very small girl sitting in a very large pew, continually endeavoring to keep myself awake and pay attention, without in the least being able to understand what he meant when he spoke to us of Chaos, Cosmos and the Gift of Love (don d'amour)."

There are also rather early memories of the awakening of puberty (nine to sixteen) which have connected the idea of the cosmos springing from chaos with the

" don d'amour." The medium in which these associations occur is the memory of a certain very much honored ecclesiastic who spoke those dark words. From the same period of time comes the remembrance of that excitement about the idea of the " creative thought " which from itself " produced its object." Here are two ways of creation intimated: the creative thought, and the mysterious reference to the " don d'amour."

At the time when I had not yet understood the nature of psychoanalysis, I had a fortunate opportunity of winning through continual observation a deep insight into the soul of a fifteen-year-old girl. Then I discovered, with astonishment, what the contents of the unconscious phantasies are, and how far removed they are from those which a girl of that age shows outwardly. There are wide-reaching phantasies of truly mythical fruitfulness. The girl was, in the split-off phantasy, the race-mother of uncounted peoples.[13] If we deduct the poetically spoken phantasy of the girl, elements are left which at that age are common to all girls, for the unconscious content is to an infinitely greater degree common to all mankind than the content of the individual consciousness. For it is the condensation of that which is historically the average and ordinary.

Miss Miller's problem at this age was the common human problem: " How am I to be creative? " Nature knows but one answer to that: " Through the child (don d'amour!)." " But how is the child attained? " Here the terrifying problem emerges, which, as our analytic experience shows, is connected with the father,[14] where it cannot be solved; because the original sin of incest weighs heavily for all time upon the human race. The strong and natural love which binds the child to the father, turns away in those years during which the humanity of the father would be all too plainly recognized, to the higher forms of the father, to the " Fathers " of the church, and to the Father God,[15] visibly represented by them, and in that there lies still less possibility of solving the problem. However, mythology is not lacking in consolations. Has not the *logos* become flesh too? Has not the divine *pneuma*, even the *logos*, entered the Virgin's womb and lived among us as the son of man? That whirlwind of Anaxagoras was precisely the divine νοῦς which from out of itself has become the world. Why do we cherish the image of the Virgin Mother even to this day? Because it is always comforting and says without speech or noisy sermon to the one seeking comfort, "I too have become a mother,"— through the "idea which spontaneously produces its object."

I believe that there is foundation enough at hand for a sleepless night, if those phantasies peculiar to the age of puberty were to become possessed of this idea—the results would be immeasurable! All that is psychologic has an under and an over meaning, as is expressed in the profound remark of the old mystic: οὐρανὸς ἄνω, οὐρανὸς κάτω, αἰθέρα ἄνω, αἰθέρα κάτω, πᾶν τοῦτο ἄνω, πᾶν τοῦτο κάτω, τοῦτο λαβὲ καὶ εὐτύχει*—

---

* The heaven above, the heaven below, the sky above, the sky below, all things above, all things below, decline and rise.

We would show but slight justice, however, to the intellectual originality of our author, if we were satisfied to trace back the commotion of that sleepless night absolutely and entirely to the sexual problem in a narrow sense. That would be but one-half, and truly, to make use of the mystic's expression, only the under half. The other half is the intellectual sublimation, which strives to make true in its own way the ambiguous expression of " the idea which produces its object spontaneously,"— *ideal creation in place of the real.*

In such an intellectual accomplishment of an evidently very capable personality, the prospect of a spiritual fruitfulness is something which is worthy of the highest aspiration, since for many it will become a necessity of life. Also this side of the phantasy explains, to a great extent, the excitement, for it is a thought with a presentiment of the future; one of those thoughts which arise, to use one of Maeterlinck's expressions,[16] from the " inconscient supérieur," that " prospective potency " of subliminal combinations.[17]

I have had the opportunity of observing certain cases of neuroses of years' duration, in which, at the time of the beginning of the illness or shortly before, a dream occurred, often of visionary clarity. This impressed itself inextinguishably upon the memory, and in analysis revealed a hidden meaning to the patient which anticipated the subsequent events of life; that is to say, their psychologic meaning.[18] I am inclined to grant this meaning to the commotion of that restless night, because the resulting events of life, in so far as Miss Miller consciously and unconsciously unveils them to us, are entirely of a nature to confirm the supposition that that moment is to be considered as the inception and presentiment of a sublimated aim in life.

Miss Miller concludes the list of her fancies with the following remarks:

"The dream seemed to me to come from a mixture of the representation of 'Paradise Lost,' 'Job,' and 'Creation,' with ideas such as 'thought which spontaneously produces its object': 'the gift of love,' 'chaos, and cosmos.'"

In the same way as colored splinters of glass are combined in a kaleidoscope, in her mind fragments of philosophy, æsthetics and religion would seem to be combined—

"under the stimulating influence of the journey, and the countries hurriedly seen, combined with the great silence and the indescribable charm of the sea. 'Ce ne fut que cela et rien de plus.' 'Only this, and nothing more!'"

With these words, Miss Miller shows us out, politely and energetically. Her parting words in her negation, confirmed over again in English, leave behind a curiosity; viz., what position is to be negated by these words? "Ce ne fut que cela et rien de plus"—that is to say, really, only "le charme impalpable de la mer"—and the young man who sang melodiously during the night watch is long since forgotten, and no one is to know, least of all the dreamer, that he was a morning star, who came before the creation of a new day.[19] One should take care lest he satisfy himself and the reader with a sentence such as "ce ne fut que cela." Otherwise, it might immediately happen that one would become disturbed again. This occurs to Miss Miller too, since she allowed an English quotation to follow,—" Only this, and nothing more," without giving the source, it is true. The quotation comes from an unusually effective poem, " The Raven " by Poe. The line referred to occurs in the following:

" While I nodded, nearly napping, suddenly there came a tapping
　As of some one gently rapping, rapping at my chamber door—
　' 'Tis some visitor,' I muttered, ' tapping at my chamber door '—
　　　Only this, and nothing more."

The spectral raven knocks nightly at his door and reminds the poet of his irrevocably lost " Lenore." The raven's name is " Nevermore," and as a refrain to every verse he croaks his horrible " Nevermore." Old memories come back tormentingly, and the spectre repeats inexorably " Nevermore." The poet seeks in vain to frighten away the dismal guest; he calls to the raven:

" ' Be that word our sign of parting, bird or fiend,' I shrieked, upstarting—
　' Get thee back into the tempest and the night's Plutonian shore!
　Leave no black plume as a token of that lie thy soul hath spoken!
　Leave my loneliness unbroken, quit the bust above my door!
　Take thy beak from out my heart, and take thy form from off my door!'
　　　Quoth the raven, ' Nevermore.' "

That quotation, which, apparently, skips lightly over the situation, " Only this, and nothing more," comes from a text which depicts in an affecting manner the despair over the lost Lenore. That quotation also misleads our poet in the most striking manner. Therefore, she undervalues the erotic impression and the wide-reaching effect of the commotion caused by it. It is this undervaluation, which Freud has formulated more precisely as " repression," which is the reason why the erotic problem does not attain directly conscious treatment, and from this there arise " these psychologic riddles." The erotic impression works in the unconscious, and, in its stead, pushes symbols forth into consciousness. Thus, one plays hide-and-seek with one's self. First, it is " the morning stars which sing together "; then " Paradise Lost "; then the erotic yearning clothes itself in an ecclesiastical dress and utters dark words about " World Creation " and finally rises into a religious hymn to find there, at last, a way out into freedom, a way against which the censor of the moral personality can oppose nothing more. The hymn contains in its own peculiar character the marks of its origin. It thus has fulfilled itself—the " Law of the Return of the Complex." The night singer, in this circuitous manner of the old transference to the Father-Priest, has become the " Eternal," the " Creator," the *God of Tone, of Light, of Love.*

The indirect course of the libido seems to be a way of sorrow; at least " Paradise Lost " and the parallel reference to Job lead one to that conclusion. If we take, in addition to this, the introductory intimation of the identification with Christian, which we see concludes with Cyrano, then we are furnished with material which pictures the indirect course of the libido as truly a way of sorrow. It is the same as when mankind, after the sinful fall, had the burden of the earthly life to bear, or like

the tortures of Job, who suffered under the power of
Satan and of God, and who himself, without suspecting it,
became a plaything of the superhuman forces which we
no longer consider as metaphysical, but as metapsycho-
logical.   Faust also offers us the same exhibition of
God's wager.

Mephistopheles:
    What will you bet?   There's still a chance to gain him
    If unto me full leave you give
    Gently upon my road to train him!

Satan:
    But put forth thine hand now, and touch all that he hath,
and he will curse thee to thy face.—*Job* i: 11.

While in Job the two great tendencies are characterized simply as good and bad, the problem in Faust is a
pronouncedly erotic one; viz., the battle between sublimation and eros, in which the Devil is strikingly characterized through the fitting rôle of the erotic tempter.   The
erotic is lacking in Job; at the same time Job is not conscious of the conflict within his own soul; he even continuously disputes the arguments of his friends who wish
to convince him of evil in his own heart.   To this extent,
one might say that Faust is considerably more honorable since he openly confesses to the torments of his
soul.

Miss Miller acts like Job; she says nothing, and lets
the evil and the good come from the other world, from
the metapsychologic.   Therefore, the identification with
Job is also significant in this respect.   A wider, and, in-

deed, a very important analogy remains to be mentioned. The creative power, which love really is, rightly considered from the natural standpoint, remains as the real attribute of the Divinity, sublimated from the erotic impression; therefore, in the poem God is praised throughout as Creator.

Job offers the same illustration. Satan is the destroyer of Job's fruitfulness. God is the fruitful one himself, therefore, at the end of the book, he gives forth, as an expression of his own creative power, this hymn, filled with lofty poetic beauty. In this hymn, strangely enough, two unsympathetic representatives of the animal kingdom, behemoth and the leviathan, both expressive of the crudest force conceivable in nature, are given chief consideration; the behemoth being really the phallic attribute of the God of Creation.

" Behold now behemoth, which I made as well as thee;
He eateth grass as an ox.
Lo, now; his strength is in his loins,
And his force is in the muscles of his belly.
He moveth his tail like a cedar:
The sinews of his thighs are knit together.
His bones are as tubes of brass;
His limbs are like bars of iron.
He is the chief of the ways of God:
He only that made him giveth him his sword. . . .
Behold, if a river overflow, he trembleth not;
He is confident though a Jordan swell even to his mouth.
Shall any take him when he is on the watch.
Or pierce through his nose with a snare?
Canst thou draw leviathan with a fish-hook?
Or press down his tongue with a cord? . . .

Lay thy hand upon him;
Remember the battle and do no more.
None is so fierce that dare stir him up:
Who then is he that can stand before me?
Who hath first given unto me, that I should repay him?
Whatsoever is under the whole heaven is mine."   .
                              —*Job* xl: 15-20, 23-24; xli: 1, 8, 10-11.

God says this in order to bring his power and omnipotence impressively before Job's eyes.   God is like the behemoth and the leviathan; the fruitful nature giving forth abundance,—the untamable wildness and boundlessness of nature,—and the overwhelming danger of the unchained power.[20]

But what has destroyed Job's earthly paradise?   The unchained power of nature.   As the poet lets it be seen here, God has simply turned his other side outwards for once; the side which man calls the devil, and which lets loose all the torments of nature on Job, naturally for the purpose of discipline and training.   The God who created such monstrosities, before whom the poor weak man stiffens with anxiety, truly must hide qualities within himself which are food for thought.   This God lives in the heart, in the unconscious, in the realm of metapsychology. There is the source of the anxiety before the unspeakably horrible, and of the strength to withstand the horrors. The person, that is to say his conscious " I," is like a plaything, like a feather which is whirled around by different currents of air; sometimes the sacrifice and sometimes the sacrificer, and he cannot hinder either.   The Book of Job shows us God at work both as creator and destroyer. Who is this God?   A thought which humanity in every part of the world and in all ages has brought forth from itself and always again anew in similar forms; a power in the other world to which man gives praise, a power which creates as well as destroys, an idea necessary to life. Since, psychologically understood, the divinity is nothing else than a projected complex of representation which is accentuated in feeling according to the degree of religiousness of the individual, so God is to be considered as the representative of a certain sum of energy (libido). This energy, therefore, appears projected (metaphysically) because it works from the unconscious outwards, when it is dislodged from there, as psychoanalysis shows. As I have earlier made apparent in the " Bedeutung des Vaters," the religious instinct feeds upon the incestuous libido of the infantile period. In the principal forms of religion which now exist, the father transference seems to be at least the moulding influence; in older religions, it seems to be the influence of the mother transference which creates the attributes of the divinity. The attributes of the divinity are omnipotence, a sternly persecuting paternalism ruling through fear (Old Testament) and a loving paternalism (New Testament). These are the attributes of the libido in that wide sense in which Freud has conceived this idea empirically. In certain pagan and also in certain Christian attributes of divinity the maternal stands out strongly, and in the former the animal also comes into the greatest prominence.[21] Likewise, the infantile, so closely interwoven with religious phantasies, and from time to time breaking forth so violently, is nowhere lacking.[22] All this points to the sources

of the dynamic states of religious activity. These are
those impulses which in childhood are withdrawn from
incestuous application through the intervention of the
incest barrier and which, especially at the time of puberty,
as a result of affluxes of libido coming from the still incompletely employed sexuality, are aroused to their own
peculiar activity. As is easily understood, that which is
valuable in the God-creating idea is not the form but
the power, the libido. The primitive power which Job's
Hymn of Creation vindicates, the unconditional and inexorable, the unjust and the superhuman, are truly and
rightly attributes of libido, which " lead us unto life,"
which " let the poor be guilty," and against which struggle is in vain. Nothing remains for mankind but to work
in harmony with this will. Nietzsche's " Zarathustra "
teaches us this impressively.

We see that in Miss Miller the religious hymn arising
from the unconscious is the compensating amend for the
erotic; it takes a great part of its materials from the
infantile reminiscences which she re-awakened into life
by the introversion of the libido. Had this religious creation not succeeded (and also had another sublimated
application been eliminated) then Miss Miller would
have yielded to the erotic impression, either to its natural
consequence or to a negative issue, which would have
replaced the lost success in love by a correspondingly
strong sorrow. It is well known that opinions are much
divided concerning the worth of this issue of an erotic
conflict, such as Miss Miller has presented to us. It is
thought to be much more beautiful to solve unnoticed an

erotic tension, in the elevated feelings of religious poetry, in which perhaps many other people can find joy and consolation. One is wrong to storm against this conception from the radical standpoint of fanaticism for truth.

I think that one should view with philosophic admiration the strange paths of the libido and should investigate the purposes of its circuitous ways.

It is not too much to say that we have herewith dug up the erotic root, and yet the problem remains unsolved. Were there not bound up with that a mysterious purpose, probably of the greatest biological meaning, then certainly twenty centuries would not have yearned for it with such intense longing. Doubtless, this sort of libidian current moves in the same direction as, taken in the widest sense, did that ecstatic ideal of the Middle Ages and of the ancient mystery cults, one of which became the later Christianity. There is to be seen biologically in this ideal an exercise of psychologic projection (of the paranoidian mechanism, as Freud would express it).[23] The projection consists in the repressing of the conflict into the unconscious and the setting forth of the repressed contents into seeming objectivity, which is also the formula of paranoia. The repression serves, as is well known, for the freeing from a painful complex from which one must escape by all means because its compelling and oppressing power is feared. The repression can lead to an apparent complete suppression which corresponds to a strong self-control. Unfortunately, however, self-control has limits which are only too narrowly drawn.

Closer observation of people shows, it is true, that calm is maintained at the critical moment, but certain results occur which fall into two categories.

First, the suppressed effect comes to the surface immediately afterwards; seldom directly, it is true, but ordinarily in the form of a displacement to another object (e. g. a person is, in official relations, polite, submissive, patient, and so on, and turns his whole anger loose upon his wife or his subordinates).

Second, the suppressed effect creates compensations elsewhere. For example, people who strive for excessive ethics, who try always to think, feel, and act altruistically and ideally, avenge themselves, because of the impossibility of carrying out their ideals, by subtle maliciousness, which naturally does not come into their own consciousness as such, but which leads to misunderstandings and unhappy situations. Apparently, then, all of these are only " especially unfortunate circumstances," or they are the guilt and malice of other people, or they are tragic complications.

One is, indeed, freed of the conscious conflict, nevertheless it lies invisible at one's feet, and is stumbled over at every step. The technic of the apparent suppressing and forgetting is inadequate because it is not possible of achievement in the last analysis—it is in reality a mere makeshift. The religious projection offers a much more effectual help. In this one keeps the conflict in sight (care, pain, anxiety, and so on) and gives it over to a personality standing outside of one's self, the Divinity. The evangelical command teaches us this:

"Cast all your anxiety upon him, because he careth for you."—*I Peter* v: 7.

"In nothing be anxious; but in every thing by prayer and supplication . . . let your requests be made known unto God."—*Phil.* iv: 6.

One must give the burdening complex of the soul consciously over to the Deity; that is to say, associate it with a definite representation complex which is set up as objectively real, as a person who answers those questions, for us unanswerable. To this inner demand belongs the candid avowal of sin and the Christian humility presuming such an avowal. Both are for the purpose of making it possible for one to examine one's self and to know one's self.[24] One may consider the mutual avowal of sins as the most powerful support to this work of education ("Confess, therefore, your sins one to another."—James v: 16). These measures aim at a conscious recognition of the conflicts, thoroughly psychoanalytic, which is also a *conditio sine qua non* of the psychoanalytic condition of recovery. Just as psychoanalysis in the hands of the physician, a secular method, sets up the real object of transference as the one to take over the conflicts of the oppressed and to solve them, so the Christian religion sets up the Saviour, considered as real; "In whom we have redemption through his blood, the forgiveness of sins. . . ." (Eph. i: 7 and Col. i: 14.)[25] He is the deliverer and redeemer of our guilt, a God who stands above sin, "who did no sin, neither was guile found in his mouth" (Pet. ii: 22). "Who his own self bare our sins in his body upon the tree" (Pet. ii: 24). "Therefore Christ has been sacrificed once to take away the sins of many" (Heb. ix:28). The God, thus thought of, is distinguished as innocent in himself and as the self-sacrificer. (These qualities are true also for that amount of energy—libido—which belongs to the representation complex designated the Redeemer.) The conscious projection towards which the Christian education aims, offers, therefore, a double benefit: first, one is kept conscious of the conflict (sins) of two opposing tendencies mutually resistant, and through this one prevents a known trouble from becoming, by means of repressing and forgetting, an unknown and therefore so much more tormenting sorrow. Secondly, one lightens one's burden by surrendering it to him to whom all solutions are known. One must not forget that the individual psychologic roots of the Deity, set up as real by the pious, are concealed from him, and that he, although unaware of this, still bears the burden alone and is still alone with his conflict. This delusion would lead infallibly to the speedy breaking up of the system, for Nature cannot indefinitely be deceived, but the powerful institution of Christianity meets this situation. The command in the book of James is the best expression of the psychologic significance of this: " Bear ye one another's burdens." [26]

This is emphasized as especially important in order to preserve society upright through mutual love (Transference); the Pauline writings leave no doubt about this:

" Through love be servants one to another."—*Gal.* v: 13.

" Let love of the brethren continue."—*Heb.* xiii: 1.

" And let us consider one another to provoke unto love and

good works. Not forgetting our own assembling together as is the custom of some, but exhorting one another."—*Heb.* x: 24-25.

We might say that the real transference taught in the Christian community is the condition absolutely necessary for the efficacy of the miracle of redemption; the first letter of John comes out frankly with this:

" He that loveth his brother abideth in the light."—*I John* ii: 10.
" If we love one another, God abideth in us."—*I John* iv: 12.

The Deity continues to be efficacious in the Christian religion only upon the foundation of brotherly love. Consequently, here too the mystery of redemption is the unresisting real transference.[27] One may properly ask one's self, for what then is the Deity useful, if his efficacy consists only in the *real transference?* To this also the evangelical message has a striking answer:

" Men are all brothers in Christ."
" So Christ also, having been once offered to bear the sins of many, shall appear a second time apart from sin to them that wait for him unto salvation."—*Heb.* ix: 28.

The condition of transference among brothers is to be such as between man and Christ, a spiritual one. As the history of ancient cults and certain Christian sects shows, this explanation of the Christian religion is an especially important one biologically, for the psychologic intimacy creates certain shortened ways between men which lead only too easily to that from which Christianity seeks to release them, namely to the sexual relation with all those consequences and necessities under which the really already highly civilized man had to suffer at the beginning of our Christian era. For just as the ancient religious experience was regarded distinctly as a bodily union with the Deity,[28] just so was worship permeated with sexuality of every kind. Sexuality lay only too close to the relations of people with each other. The moral degeneracy of the first Christian century produced a moral reaction arising out of the darkness of the lowest strata of society which was expressed in the second and third centuries at its purest in the two antagonistic religions, Christianity on the one side, and Mithracism on the other. These religions strove after precisely that higher form of social intercourse symbolic of a projected " become flesh " idea (logos), whereby all those strongest impulsive energies of the archaic man, formerly plunging him from one passion into another,[29] and which seemed to the ancients like the compulsion of the evil constellations, as εἰμαρμένη,* and which in the sense of later ages might be translated as the driving force of the libido,[30] the δύναμις κινητική† of Zeno, could be made use of for social preservation.[31]

It may be assumed most certainly that the domestication of humanity has cost the greatest sacrifices. An age which produced the stoical ideal must certainly have known why and against what it was created. The age of Nero serves to set off effectually the famous extracts from the forty-first letter of Seneca to Lucilius:

* Destiny.
† Power for putting in motion.

"One drags the other into error, and how can we attain to salvation when no one bids us halt, when all the world drives us in deeper?"

"Do you ever come across a man unafraid in danger, untouched by desires, happy in misfortune, peaceful in the midst of a storm, elevated above ordinary mortals, on the same plane as the gods, does not reverence seize you? Are you not compelled to say, 'Such an exalted being is certainly something different from the miserable body which he inhabits'? A divine strength rules there, such an excellent mind, full of moderation, raised above all trivialities, which smiles at that which we others fear or strive after: a heavenly power animates such a person, a thing of this kind does not exist without the coöperation of a deity. The largest part of such a being belongs to the region from which he came. Just as the sun's rays touch the earth in reality and yet are at home only there from whence they come, so an eminent holy man associates with us. He is sent to us that we may learn to know the divine better, and although with us, still really belongs to his original home. He looks thither and reaches towards it; among us he walks as an exalted being."

The people of this age had grown ripe for identification with the λόγος (word) "become flesh," for the founding of a new fellowship, united by one idea,[32] in the name of which people could love each other and call each other brothers.[33] The old vague idea of a μεσίτης (Messiah), of a mediator in whose name new ways of love would be created, became a fact, and with that humanity made an immense step forward. This had not been brought about by a speculative, completely sophisticated philosophy, but by an elementary need in the mass of people vegetating in spiritual darkness. The profoundest necessities had evidently driven them towards that, since humanity did not thrive in a state of dissoluteness.[34] The meaning of those cults—I speak of Christianity and Mithracism—is clear; it is a moral restraint of animal impulses.[35] The dynamic appearance of both religions betrays something of that enormous feeling of redemption which animated the first disciples and which we to-day scarcely know how to appreciate, for these old truths are empty to us. Most certainly we should still understand it, had our customs even a breath of ancient brutality, for we can hardly realize in this day the whirlwinds of the unchained libido which roared through the ancient Rome of the Cæsars. The civilized man of the present day seems very far removed from that. He has become merely neurotic. So for us the necessities which brought forth Christianity have actually been lost, since we no longer understand their meaning. We do not know against what it had to protect us.[36] For enlightened people, the so-called religiousness has already approached very close to a neurosis. In the past two thousand years Christianity has done its work and has erected barriers of repression, which protect us from the sight of our own " sinfulness." The elementary emotions of the libido have come to be unknown to us, for they are carried on in the unconscious; therefore, the belief which combats them has become hollow and empty. Let whoever does not believe that a mask covers our religion, obtain an impression for himself from the appearance of our modern churches, from which style and art have long since fled.

With this we turn back to the question from which we digressed, namely, whether or not Miss Miller has created something valuable with her poem. If we bear in mind under what psychologic or moral conditions Christianity came into existence; that is to say, at a time when fierce brutality was an every-day spectacle, then we understand the religious seizure of the whole personality and the worth of that religion which defended the people of the Roman culture against the visible storms of wickedness. It was not difficult for those people to remain conscious of sin, for they saw it every day spread out before their eyes. The religious product was at that time the accomplishment of the total personality. Miss Miller not only undervalues her " sins," but the connection between the " depressing and unrelenting need " and her religious product has even escaped her. Thus her poetical creation completely loses the living value of a religious product. It is not much more than a sentimental transformation of the erotic which is secretly carried out close to consciousness and principally possesses the same worth as the manifest content of the dream [37] with its uncertain and delusive perishableness. Thus the poem is properly only a dream become audible.

To the degree that the modern consciousness is eagerly busied with things of a wholly other sort than religion, religion and its object, original sin, have stepped into the background; that is to say, into the unconscious in great part. Therefore, today man believes neither in the one nor in the other. Consequently the Freudian school is accused of an impure phantasy, and yet one might convince one's self very easily with a rather fleeting glance at the history of ancient religions and morals as to what kind of demons are harbored in the human soul. With this disbelief in the crudeness of human nature is bound up the disbelief in the power of religion. The phenomenon, well known to every psychoanalyst, of the unconscious transformation of an erotic conflict into religious activity is something *ethically wholly worthless* and nothing but an hysterical production. Whoever, on the other hand, to his conscious sin just as consciously places religion in opposition, does something the greatness of which cannot be denied. This can be verified by a backward glance over history. Such a procedure is sound religion. *The unconscious recasting of the erotic into something religious lays itself open to the reproach of a sentimental and ethically worthless pose.*

By means of the secular practice of the naïve projection which is, as we have seen, nothing else than a veiled or indirect real-transference (through the spiritual, through the logos), Christian training has produced a widespread weakening of the animal nature so that a great part of the strength of the impulses could be set free for the work of social preservation and fruitfulness.[38] This abundance of libido, to make use of this singular expression, pursues with a budding renaissance (for example Petrarch) a course which outgoing antiquity had already sketched out as religious; viz., the way of the transference to nature.[39] The transformation of this libidinous interest is in great part due to the Mithraic worship, which was a nature religion in the best sense of the word;[40] while the primitive Christians exhibited throughout an antagonistic attitude to the beauties of this world.[41] I remember the passage of St. Augustine mentioned by J. Burkhardt:

" Men draw thither to admire the heights of the mountains and the powerful waves of the sea—and to turn away from themselves."

The foremost authority on the Mithraic cult, Franz Cumont,[42] says as follows:

" The gods were everywhere and mingled in all the events of daily life. The fire which cooked the means of nourishment for the believers and which warmed them; the water which quenched their thirst and cleansed them; also the air which they breathed, and the day which shone for them, were the objects of their homage. Perhaps no religion has given to its adherents in so large a degree as Mithracism opportunity for prayer and motive for devotion. When the initiated betook himself in the evening to the sacred grotto concealed in the solitude of the forest, at every step new sensations awakened in his heart some mystical emotion. The stars that shone in the sky, the wind that whispered in the foliage, the spring or brook which hastened murmuring to the valley, even the earth which he trod under his feet, were in his eyes divine; and all surrounding nature a worshipful fear of the infinite forces that swayed the universe."

These fundamental thoughts of Mithracism, which, like so much else of the ancient spiritual life, arose again from their grave during the renaissance are to be found in the beautiful words of Seneca:[43]

" When you enter a grove peopled with ancient trees, higher than the ordinary, and whose boughs are so closely interwoven that the sky cannot be seen, the stately shadows of the wood, the privacy of the place, and the awful gloom cannot but strike you, as with the presence of a deity, or when we see some cave at the foot of a mountain penetrating the rocks, not made by human

hands, but hollowed out to great depths by nature; it fills the
mind with a religious fear; we venerate the fountain-heads of
great rivers; the sudden eruption of a vast body of water from
the secret places of the earth, obtains an altar: we adore likewise
the springs of warm baths, and either the opaque quality or
immense depths, hath made some lakes sacred."

All this disappeared in the transitory world of the
Christian, only to break forth much later when the
thought of mankind had achieved that *independence of
the idea* which could resist the æsthetic impression, so that
thought was no longer fettered by the emotional effects
of the impression, but could rise to reflective observation.
Thus man entered into a new and independent relation to
nature whereby the foundation was laid for natural science
and technique. With that, however, there entered in for
the first time a displacement of the weight of interest;
there arose again real-transference which has reached its
greatest development in our time. Materialistic interest
has everywhere become paramount. Therefore, the
realms of the spirit, where earlier the greatest conflicts
and developments took place, lie deserted and fallow; the
world has not only lost its God as the sentimentalists of
the nineteenth century bewail, but also to some extent has
lost its soul as well. One, therefore, cannot wonder that
the discoveries and doctrines of the Freudian school, with
their wholly psychologic views, meet with an almost universal disapproval. Through the change of the centre of
interest from the inner to the outer world, the knowledge
of nature has increased enormously in comparison with
that of earlier times. By this the anthropomorphic conception of the religious dogmas has been definitely thrown

open to question; therefore, the present-day religions can only with the greatest difficulty close their eyes to this fact; for not only has the intense interest been diverted from the Christian religion, but criticism and the necessary correction have increased correspondingly. The Christian religion seems to have fulfilled its great biological purpose, in so far as we are able to judge. It has led human thought to independence, and has lost its significance, therefore, to a yet undetermined extent; in any case its dogmatic contents have become related to Mithracism. In consideration of the fact that this religion has rendered, nevertheless, inconceivable service to education, one cannot reject it " eo ipso " today. It seems to me that we might still make use in some way of its form of thought, and especially of its great wisdom of life, which for two thousand years has been proven to be particularly efficacious. The stumbling block is the *unhappy combination of religion and morality.* That must be overcome. There still remain traces of this strife in the soul, the lack of which in a human being is reluctantly felt. It is hard to say in what such things consist; for this, ideas as well as words are lacking. If, in spite of that, I attempt to say something about it, I do it parabolically, using Seneca's words: [44]

" Nothing can be more commendable and beneficial if you persevere in the pursuit of wisdom. It is what would be ridiculous to wish for when it is in your power to attain it. There is no need to lift up your hands to Heaven, or to pray the servant of the temple to admit you to the ear of the idol that your prayers may be heard the better. God is near thee; he is with thee. Yes, Lucilius, a holy spirit resides within us, the observer of

good and evil, and our constant guardian. And as we treat
him, he treats us; no good man is without a God. Could any one
ever rise above the power of fortune without his assistance? It
is he that inspires us with thoughts, upright, just and pure. We
do not, indeed, pretend to say what God; but that a God dwells
in the breast of every good man is certain."

CHAPTER IV

THE SONG OF THE MOTH

A LITTLE later Miss Miller travelled from Geneva to Paris. She says:

" My weariness on the railway was so great that I could hardly sleep an hour. It was terrifically hot in the ladies' carriage."

At four o'clock in the morning she noticed a moth that flew against the light in her compartment. She then tried to go to sleep again. Suddenly the following poem took possession of her mind.

The Moth to the Sun

" I longed for thee when first I crawled to consciousness.
My dreams were all of thee when in the chrysalis I lay.
Oft myriads of my kind beat out their lives
Against some feeble spark once caught from thee.
And one hour more—and my poor life is gone;
Yet my last effort, as my first desire, shall be
But to approach thy glory; then, having gained
One raptured glance, I'll die content.
For I, the source of beauty, warmth and life
Have in his perfect splendor once beheld."

Before we go into the material which Miss Miller offers us for the understanding of the poem, we will again cast a glance over the psychologic situation in which the poem originated. Some months or weeks appear to have elapsed since the last direct manifestation of the unconscious that Miss Miller reported to us; about this period we have had no information. We learn nothing about the moods and phantasies of this time. If one might draw a conclusion from this silence it would be presumably that in the time which elapsed between the two poems, really nothing of importance had happened, and that, therefore, this poem is again but a voiced fragment of the unconscious working of the complex stretching out over months and years. It is highly probable that it is concerned with the same complex as before.[1] The earlier product, a hymn of creation full of hope, has, however, but little similarity to the present poem. The poem lying before us has a truly hopeless, melancholy character; moth and sun, two things which never meet. One must in fairness ask, is a moth really expected to rise to the sun? We know indeed the proverbial saying about the moth that flew into the light and singed its wings, but not the legend of the moth that strove towards the sun. Plainly, here, two things are connected in her thoughts that do not belong together; first, the moth which fluttered around the light so long that it burnt itself; and then, the idea of a small ephemeral being, something like the day fly, which, in lamentable contrast to the eternity of the stars, longs for an imperishable daylight. This idea reminds one of Faust:

" Mark how, beneath the evening sunlight's glow
    The green-embosomed houses glitter;
    The glow retreats, done is the day of toil,
    It yonder hastes, new fields of life exploring;

Ah, that no wing can lift me from the soil
Upon its track to follow, follow soaring!
Then would I see eternal Evening gild
The silent world beneath me glowing. . . .
Yet, finally, the weary god is sinking;
The new-born impulse fires my mind,—
I hasten on, his beams eternal drinking,
The day before me and the night behind,
Above me heaven unfurled, the floor of waves beneath me,—
A glorious dream! though now the glories fade.
Alas! the wings that lift the mind no aid
Of wings to lift the body can bequeath me."

Not long afterwards, Faust sees " the black dog roving there through cornfields and stubble," the dog who is the same as the devil, the tempter, in whose hellish fires Faust has singed his wings. When he believed that he was expressing his great longing for the beauty of the sun and the earth, " he went astray thereover " and fell into the hands of " the Evil One."

" Yes, resolute to reach some brighter distance,
On earth's fair sun I turn my back."

This is what Faust had said shortly before, in true recognition of the state of affairs. The honoring of the beauty of nature led the Christian of the Middle Ages to pagan thoughts which lay in an antagonistic relation to his conscious religion, just as once Mithracism was in threatening competition with Christianity, for Satan often disguises himself as an angel of light.[2]

The longing of Faust became his ruin. The longing for the Beyond had brought as a consequence a loathing for life, and he stood on the brink of self-destruction.[3]

The longing for the beauty of this world led him anew to ruin, into doubt and pain, even to Marguerite's tragic death. His mistake was that he followed after both worlds with no check to the driving force of his libido, like a man of violent passion. Faust portrays once more the folk-psychologic conflict of the beginning of the Christian era, but what is noteworthy, in a reversed order.

Against what fearful powers of seduction Christ had to defend himself by means of his hope of the absolute world beyond, may be seen in the example of Alypius in Augustine. If any of us had been living in that period of antiquity, he would have seen clearly that that culture must inevitably collapse because humanity revolted against it. It is well known that even before the spread of Christianity a remarkable expectation of redemption had taken possession of mankind. The following eclogue of Virgil might well be a result of this mood:

> " Ultima Cumæi venit jam carminis ætas; *
> Magnus ab integro Sæclorum nascitur ordo,
> Jam redit et Virgo,⁴ redeunt Saturnia regna;

* " The last age of Cumean prophecy has come already!
  Over again the great series of the ages commences:
  Now too returns the Virgin, return the Saturnian kingdoms;
  Now at length a new progeny is sent down from high Heaven.
  Only, chaste Lucina, to the boy at his birth be propitious,
  In whose time first the age of iron shall discontinue,
  And in the whole world a golden age arise: now rules thy Apollo.

  Under thy guidance, if any traces of our guilt continue,
  Rendered harmless, they shall set the earth free from fear forever,
  He shall partake of the life of the gods, and he shall see
  Heroes mingled with gods, and he too shall be seen by them.
  And he shall rule a peaceful world with his father's virtues."

Jam nova progenies cælo demittitur alto.
Tu modo nascenti puero, quo ferrea primum
Desinet ac toto surget gens aurea mundo,
Casta fave Lucina: tuus jam regnat Apollo.

"Te duce, si qua manent sceleris vestigia nostri,
Inrita perpetua solvent formidine terras.
Ille deum vitam accipiet divisque videbit
Permixtos heroas et ipse videbitur illis,
Pacatumque reget patriis virtutibus orbem." [5]

The turning to asceticism resulting from the general expansion of Christianity brought about a new misfortune to many: monasticism and the life of the anchorite.[6]

Faust takes the reverse course; for him the ascetic ideal means death. He struggles for freedom and wins life, at the same time giving himself over to the Evil One; but through this he becomes the bringer of death to her whom he loves most, Marguerite. He tears himself away from pain and sacrifices his life in unceasing useful work, through which he saves many lives.[7] His double mission as saviour and destroyer has already been hinted in a preliminary manner:

Wagner:
With what a feeling, thou great man, must thou
Receive the people's honest veneration!

Faust:
Thus we, our hellish boluses compounding,
Among these vales and hills surrounding,
Worse than the pestilence, have passed.
Thousands were done to death from poison of my giving;
And I must hear, by all the living,
The shameless murderers praised at last!

A parallel to this double rôle is that text in the Gospel of Matthew which has become historically significant:

" I came not to send peace, but a sword."—*Matt.* x: 34.

Just this constitutes the deep significance of Goethe's Faust, that he clothes in words a problem of modern man which has been turning in restless slumber since the Renaissance, just as was done by the drama of Oedipus for the Hellenic sphere of culture. What is to be the way out between the Scylla of renunciation of the world and the Charybdis of the acceptance of the world?

The hopeful tone, voiced in the " Hymn to the God of Creation," cannot continue very long with our author. The pose simply promises, but does not fulfil. The old longing will come again, for it is a peculiarity of all complexes worked over merely in the unconscious [8] that they lose nothing of their original amount of affect. Meanwhile, their outward manifestations can change almost endlessly. One might therefore consider the first poem as an unconscious longing to solve the conflict through positive religiousness, somewhat in the same manner as they of the earlier centuries decided their conscious conflicts by opposing to them the religious standpoint. This wish does not succeed. Now with the second poem there follows a second attempt which turns out in a decidedly more material way; its thought is unequivocal. Only once " having gained one raptured glance . . ." and then—to die.

From the realms of the religious world, the attention, just as in Faust,[9] turns towards the sun of this world, and already there is something mingled with it which has another sense, that is to say, *the moth which fluttered so long around the light that it burnt its wings.*

We now pass to that which Miss Miller offers for the better understanding of the poem. She says:

"This small poem made a profound impression upon me. I could not, of course, find immediately a sufficiently clear and direct explanation for it. However, a few days later when I once more read a certain philosophical work, which I had read in Berlin the previous winter, and which I had enjoyed very much, (I was reading it aloud to a friend), I came across the following words: 'La même aspiration passionnée de la mite vers l'étoile, de l'homme vers Dieu.' (The same passionate longing of the moth for the star, of man for God.) I had forgotten this sentence entirely, but it seemed very clear to me that precisely these words had reappeared in my hypnagogic poem. In addition to that it occurred to me that a play seen some years previously, 'La Mite et La Flamme,' was a further possible cause of the poem. It is easy to see how often the word 'moth' had been impressed upon me."

The deep impression made by the poem upon the author shows that she put into it a large amount of love. In the expression "aspiration passionnée" we meet the passionate longing of the moth for the star, of man for God, and indeed, the moth is Miss Miller herself. Her last observation that the word "moth" was often impressed upon her shows how often she had noticed the word "moth" as applicable to herself. *Her longing for God resembles the longing of the moth for the " star."* The reader will recall that this expression has already had a place in the earlier material, " when the morning stars sang together," that is to say, the ship's officer who sings on deck in the night watch. The passionate longing for God is the same as that longing for the singing morning stars. It was pointed out at great length in the foregoing chapter that this analogy is to be expected: " Sic parvis componere magna solebam."

It is shameful or exalted just as one chooses, that the divine longing of humanity, which is really the first thing to make it human, should be brought into connection with an erotic phantasy. Such a comparison jars upon the finer feelings. Therefore, one is inclined in spite of the undeniable facts to dispute the connection. An Italian steersman with brown hair and black moustache, and the loftiest, dearest conception of humanity! These two things cannot be brought together; against this not only our religious feelings revolt, but our taste also rebels.

It would certainly be unjust to make a comparison of the two objects as concrete things since they are so heterogeneous. One loves a Beethoven sonata but one loves caviar also. It would not occur to any one to liken the sonata to caviar. It is a common error for one to judge the longing according to the quality of the object. The appetite of the gourmand which is only satisfied with goose liver and quail is no more distinguished than the appetite of the laboring man for corned beef and cabbage. The longing is the same; the object changes. Nature is beautiful only by virtue of the longing and love given her by man. The æsthetic attributes emanating from that has influence primarily on the libido, which alone constitutes the beauty of nature. The dream recognizes this well when it depicts a strong and beautiful feeling by means of a representation of a beautiful landscape. Whenever one moves in the territory of the erotic it becomes altogether clear how little the object and how much the love means. The " sexual object " is as a rule overrated far too much and that only on account of the extreme degree to which libido is devoted to the object.

Apparently Miss Miller had but little left over for the officer, which is humanly very intelligible. But in spite of that a deep and lasting effect emanates from this connection which places divinity on a par with the erotic object. The moods which apparently are produced by these objects do not, however, spring from them, but are manifestations of her strong love. When Miss Miller praises either God or the sun she means her love, that deepest and strongest impulse of the human and animal being.

The reader will recall that in the preceding chapter the following chain of synonyms was adduced: the singer— God of sound—singing morning star—creator—God of Light—sun—fire—God of Love.

At that time we had placed sun and fire in parentheses. Now they are entitled to their right place in the chain of synonyms. With the changing of the erotic impression from the affirmative to the negative the symbols of light occur as the paramount object. In the second poem where the longing is clearly exposed it is by no means the ter- restrial sun. Since the longing has been turned away from the real object, its object has become, first of all, a sub- jective one, namely, God. Psychologically, however, God is the name of a representation-complex which is grouped around a strong feeling (the sum of libido). Properly, the feeling is what gives character and reality to the complex.[10] *The attributes and symbols of the divinity must belong in a consistent manner to the feeling (longing, love, libido, and so on).* If one honors God, the sun or the fire, then one honors one's own vital force, the libido. It is as Seneca says: " God is near you, he is with you, in you." God is our own longing to which we pay divine honors.[11] If it were not known how tremendously significant religion was, and is, this marvellous play with one's self would appear absurd. There must be something more than this, however, because, notwithstanding its absurdity, it is, in a certain sense, conformable to the purpose in the highest degree. To bear a God within one's self signifies a great deal; it is a guarantee of happiness, of power, indeed even of omnipotence, as far as these attributes belong to the Deity. To bear a God within one's self signifies just as much as to be God one's self. In Christianity, where, it is true, the grossly sensual representations and symbols are weeded out as carefully as possible, which seems to be a continuation of the poverty of symbols of the Jewish cult, there are to be found plain traces of this psychology. There are even plainer traces, to be sure, in the " becoming-one with God " in those mysteries closely related to the Christian, where the mystic himself is lifted up to divine adoration through initiatory rites. At the close of the consecration into the Isis mysteries the mystic was crowned with the palm crown,[12] he was placed on a pedestal and worshipped as Helios.[13] In the magic papyrus of the Mithraic liturgy published by Dieterich there is the ἱερος λόγος* of the consecrated one:

Ἐγώ εἰμι σύμπλανος ὑμῖν ἀστὴρ καὶ ἐκ τοῦ βάθους ἀναλάμπων.†

The mystic in religious ecstasies put himself on a plane with the stars, just as a saint of the Middle Ages put himself by means of the stigmata on a level with Christ. St. Francis of Assisi expressed this in a truly pagan manner,[14] even as far as a close relationship with the brother sun and the sister moon. These representations of " becoming-one with God " are very ancient. The old belief removed the becoming-one with God until the time after death; the mysteries, however, suggest this as taking place already in this world. A very old text brings most beautifully before one this unity with God; it is the song of triumph of the ascending soul.[15]

> " I am the God Atum, I who alone was.
> I am the God Rê at his first splendor.
> I am the great God, self-created, God of Gods,
> To whom no other God compares."

" I was yesterday and know tomorrow; the battle-ground of Gods was made when I spoke. I know the name of that great God who tarries therein.

" I am that great Phoenix who is in Heliopolis, who there keeps account of all there is, of all that exists.

" I am the God Min, at his coming forth, who placed the feathers upon my head.[16]

" I am in my country, I come into my city. Daily I am together with my father Atum.[17]

---

* Sacred word.

† I am a star wandering about with you, and flaming up from the depths.

" My impurity is driven away, and the sin which was in me
is overcome.　I washed myself in those two great pools of water
which are in Heracleopolis,· in which is purified the sacrifice of
mankind for that great God who abideth there.

" I go on my way to where I wash my head in the sea of the
righteous.　I arrive at this land of the glorified, and enter
through the splendid portal.

" Thou, who standest before me, stretch out to me thy hands,
it is I, I am become one of thee.　Daily am I together with my
Father Atum."

The identification with God necessarily has as a result
the enhancing of the meaning and power of the individual.[18]　That seems, first of all, to have been really its
purpose: a strengthening of the individual against his
all too great weakness and insecurity in real life.　This
great megalomania thus has a genuinely pitiable background.　The strengthening of the consciousness of
power is, however, only an external result of the " becoming-one with God."　Of much more significance are the
deeper-lying disturbances in the realm of feeling.　*Whoever introverts libido—that is to say, whoever takes it
away from a real object without putting in its place a real
compensation—is overtaken by the inevitable results of
introversion.*　The libido, which is turned inward into the
subject, awakens again from among the sleeping remembrances one which contains the path upon which earlier
the libido once had come to the real object.　At the
very first and in foremost position it was father and
mother who were the objects of the childish love.　They
are unequalled and imperishable.　Not many difficulties
are needed in an adult's life to cause those memories to

reawaken and to become effectual. *In religion the regressive reanimation of the father-and-mother imago is organized into a system.* The benefits of religion are the benefits of parental hands; its protection and its peace are the results of parental care upon the child; its mystic feelings are the unconscious memories of the tender emotions of the first childhood, just as the hymn expresses it:

"I am in my country, I come into my city. Daily am I together with my father Atum." [19]

The visible father of the world is, however, the sun, the heavenly fire; therefore, Father, God, Sun, Fire are mythologically synonymous. The well-known fact that in the sun's strength the great generative power of nature is honored shows plainly, very plainly, to any one to whom as yet it may not be clear that in the Deity man honors his own libido, and naturally in the form of the image or symbol of the present object of transference. This symbol faces us in an especially marked manner in the third Logos of the Dieterich papyrus. After the second prayer [20] stars come from the disc of the sun to the mystic, " five-pointed, in quantities, filling the whole air. If the sun's disc has expanded, you will see an immeasurable circle, and fiery gates which are shut off." The mystic utters the following prayer:

Ἐπακουσόν μου, ἀκουσόν μου—ὁ συνδήσας πνεύματι τὰ πύρινα κλεῖθρα τοῦ οὐρανοῦ, δισώματος πυρίπολε, φωτὸς κτίστα—πυρίπνοε, πυρίθυμε, πνευματόφως, πυρι-χαρῆ, καλλίφως, φωτοκράτωρ, πυρισώματε, φωτοδότα, πυρισπόρε, πυρικλόνε, φωτόβιε, πυριδῖνα, φωτοκινῆτα, κεραυνοκλόνε, φωτὸς κλέος, αὐξησίφως, ἐνπυρισχησίφως, ἀστροδάμα.*

The invocation is, as one sees, almost inexhaustible in light and fire attributes, and can be likened in its extravagance only to the synonymous attributes of love of the mystic of the Middle Ages. Among the innumerable texts which might be used as an illustration of this, I select a passage from the writings of Mechtild von Magdeburg (1212-1277):

"O Lord, love me excessively and love me often and long; the oftener you love me, so much the purer do I become; the more excessively you love me, the more beautiful I become; the longer you love me, the more holy will I become here upon earth."

God answered: "That I love you often, that I have from my nature, for I myself am love. That I love you excessively, that I have from my desire, for I too desire that men love me excessively. That I love you long, that I have from my everlastingness, for I am without end." [21]

The religious regression makes use indeed of the parent image without, however, consciously making it an object of transference, for the incest horror [22] forbids that. It remains rather as a synonym, for example, of the father or of God, or of the more or less personified symbol of the sun and fire. [23] Sun and fire—that is to say,

---

* Hear me, grant me my prayer—Binding together the fiery bolts of heaven with spirit, two-bodied fiery sky, creator of humanity, fire-breathing, fiery-spirited, spiritual being rejoicing in fire, beauty of humanity, ruler of humanity of fiery body, light-giver to men, fire-scattering, fire-agitated, life of humanity, fire-whirled, mover of men who confounds with thunder, famed among men, increasing the human race, enlightening humanity, conqueror of stars.

the fructifying strength and heat—are attributes of the libido. In Mysticism the inwardly perceived, divine vision is often merely sun or light, and is very little, or not at all, personified. In the Mithraic liturgy there is found, for example, a significant quotation:

Ἡ δὲ πορεία τῶν ὁρωμένων θεῶν διὰ τοῦ δίσκου, πατρός μου, θεοῦ φανήσεται.*

Hildegarde von Bingen (1100-1178) expresses herself in the following manner: [24]

"But the light I see is not local, but far off, and brighter than the cloud which supports the sun. I can in no way know the form of this light since I cannot entirely see the sun's disc. But within this light I see at times, and infrequently, another light which is called by me the living light, but when and in what manner I see this I do not know how to say, and when I see it all weariness and need is lifted from me, then too, I feel like a simple girl and not like an old woman."

Symeon, the New Theologian (970-1040), says the following:

"My tongue lacks words, and what happens in me my spirit sees clearly but does not explain. It sees the invisible, that emptiness of all forms, simple throughout, not complex, and in extent infinite. For it sees no beginning, and it sees no end. It is entirely unconscious of the meanings, and does not know what to call that which it sees. Something complete appears, it seems to me, not indeed through the being itself, but through a participation. For you enkindle fire from fire, and you receive the whole fire; but this remains undiminished and undivided, as before. Similarly, that which is divided separates itself from the first; and like something corporeal spreads itself into several lights. This,

* The path of the visible Gods will appear through the sun, the God my father.

however, is something spiritual, immeasurable, indivisible, and inexhaustible. For it is not separated when it becomes many, but remains undivided and is in me, and enters within my poor heart like a sun or circular disc of the sun, similar to the light, for it is a light." [25]

That that thing, perceived as inner light, as the sun of the other world, is longing, is clearly shown by Symeon's words: [26]

" And following It my spirit demanded to embrace the splendor beheld, but it found It not as creature and did not succeed in coming out from among created beings, so that it might embrace that uncreated and uncomprehended splendor. Nevertheless it wandered everywhere, and strove to behold It. *It penetrated the air, it wandered over the Heavens, it crossed over the abysses, it searched, as it seemed to it, the ends of the world.*" But in all of that it found nothing, for all was created. And I lamented and was sorrowful, and my breast burned, and I lived as one distraught in mind. But It came, as It would, and descending like a luminous mystic cloud, It seemed to envelop my whole head so that dismayed I cried out. But flying away again It left me alone. And when I, troubled, sought for It, I realized suddenly *that It was in me, myself, and in the midst of my heart It appeared as the light of a spherical sun.*"

In Nietzsche's " Glory and Eternity " we meet with an essentially similar symbol:

" Hush! I see vastness!—and of vasty things
Shall man be done, unless he can enshrine
Them with his words? Then take the night which brings
The heart upon thy tongue, charmed wisdom mine!

" I look above, there rolls the star-strewn sea.
O night, mute silence, voiceless cry of stars!
And lo! A sign! The heaven its verge unbars—
A shining constellation falls towards me." *

* Translated by Dr. T. G. Wrench.

It is not astonishing if Nietzsche's great inner loneliness calls again into existence certain forms of thought which the mystic ecstasy of the old cults has elevated to ritual representation. In the visions of the Mithraic liturgy we have to deal with many similar representations which we can now understand without difficulty as the ecstatic symbol of the libido:

Μετὰ δὲ τὸ εἰπεῖν σε τὸν δεύτερον λόγον, ὅπου σιγὴ δὶς καὶ τὰ ἀκόλουθα, σύρισον δὶς καὶ πόππυσον δὶς καὶ εὐθέως ὄψει ἀπὸ τοῦ δίσκου ἀστέρας προσερχομένους πεν-ταδακτυλιαίους πλείστους καὶ πιπλῶντας ὅλον τὸν αέρα. Σὺ δὲ πάλιν λέγε: σιγή, σιγή. Καὶ τοῦ δίσκου ἀνοιγέντος ὄψει ἄπειρον κύκλωμα καὶ θύρας πυρίνας ἀποκεκλεισ-μένας. *

Silence is commanded, then the vision of light is revealed. The similarity of the mystic's condition and Nietzsche's poetical vision is surprising. Nietzsche says "constellation." It is well known that constellations are chiefly therio- or anthropo-morphic symbols.

The papyrus says, ἀστέρας πενταδακτυλιαίους† (similar to the "rosy-fingered" Eos), which is nothing else than an anthropomorphic image. Accordingly, one may expect from that, that by long gazing a living being would be formed out of the "flame image," a "star constellation" of therio- or anthropo-morphic nature, for the symbolism of the libido does not end with sun, light

---

* After you have said the second prayer, when silence is twice commanded; then whistle twice and snap twice,[28] and straightway you will see many five-pointed stars coming down from the sun and filling the whole lower air. But say once again—Silence! Silence! and you, Neophyte, will see the Circle and fiery doors cut off from the opening disc of the sun.

† Five-fingered stars.

and fire, but makes use of wholly other means of expression. I yield precedence to Nietzsche:

The Beacon *

"Here, where the island grew amid the seas,
A sacrificial rock high-towering,
Here under darkling heavens,
Zarathustra lights his mountain-fires.

"These flames with grey-white belly,
In cold distances sparkle their desire,
Stretches its neck towards ever purer heights—
A snake upreared in impatience:

"This signal I set up there before me.
This flame is mine own soul,
Insatiable for new distances,
Speeding upward, upward its silent heat.

"At all lonely ones I now throw my fishing rod.
Give answer to the flame's impatience,
Let me, the fisher on high mountains,
Catch my seventh, last solitude!"

Here libido becomes fire, flame and snake. The Egyptian symbol of the "living disc of the sun," the disc with the two entwining snakes, contains the combination of both the libido analogies. The disc of the sun with its fructifying warmth is analogous to the fructifying warmth of love. The comparison of the libido with sun and fire is in reality analogous.

There is also a "causative" element in it, for sun and fire as beneficent powers are objects of human love; for example, the sun-hero Mithra is called the "well-

---

* "Ecce Homo," translated by A. M. Ludovici.

beloved." In Nietzsche's poem the comparison is also a causative one, but this time in a reversed sense. The comparison with the snake is unequivocally phallic, corresponding completely with the tendency in antiquity, which was to see in the symbol of the phallus the quintessence of life and fruitfulness. *The phallus is the source of life and libido, the great creator and worker of miracles,* and as such it received reverence everywhere. We have, therefore, three designating symbols of the libido: First, the *comparison by analogy,* as sun and fire. Second, the *comparisons based on causative relations,* as A: Object comparison. The libido is designated by its object, for example, the beneficent sun. B: *The subject comparison,* in which the libido is designated by its place of origin or by analogies of this, for example, by phallus or (analogous) snake.

To these two fundamental forms of comparison still a third is added, in which the " tertium comparationis " is *the activity;* for example, the libido is dangerous when fecundating like the bull—through the power of its passion—like the lion, like the raging boar when in heat, like the ever-rutting ass, and so on.

This activity comparison can belong equally well to the category of the analogous or to the category of the causative comparisons. *The possibilities of comparison mean just as many possibilities for symbolic expression,* and from this basis all the infinitely varied symbols, so far as they are libido images, may properly be reduced to a very simple root, that is, just to *libido and its fixed primitive qualities.* This psychologic reduction and simplification is in accordance with the historic efforts of civilization to unify and simplify, to syncretize, the endless number of the gods. We come across this desire as far back as the old Egyptians, where the unlimited polytheism as exemplified in the numerous demons of places finally necessitated simplification. All the various local gods, Amon of Thebes, Horus of Edfu, Horus of the East, Chnum of Elephantine, Atum of Heliopolis, and others,[29] became identified with the sun God Ré. In the hymns to the sun the composite being Amon-Ré-Harmachis-Atum was invoked as " the only god which truly lives." [30]

Amenhotep IV (XVIII dynasty) went the furthest in this direction. He replaced all former gods by the " living great disc of the sun," the official title reading:

" The sun ruling both horizons, triumphant in the horizon in his name; the glittering splendor which is in the sun's disc."

" And, indeed," Erman adds,[31] " the sun, as a God, should not be honored, but the sun itself as a planet which imparts through its rays [32] the infinite life which is in it to all living creatures."

Amenhotep IV by his reform completed a work which is psychologically important. He united all the bull,[33] ram,[34] crocodile [35] and pile-dwelling [36] gods into the disc of the sun, and made it clear that their various attributes were compatible with the sun's attributes.[37] A similar fate overtook the Hellenic and Roman polytheism through the syncretistic efforts of later centuries. The beautiful prayer of Lucius [38] to the queen of the Heavens furnishes an important proof of this:

"Queen of Heaven, whether thou art the genial Ceres, the prime parent of fruits;—or whether thou art celestial Venus;—or whether thou art the sister of Phœbus;—or whether thou art Proserpina, terrific with midnight howlings—with that feminine brightness of thine illuminating the walls of every city." [39]

This attempt to gather again into a few units the religious thoughts which were divided into countless variations and personified in individual gods according to their polytheistic distribution and separation makes clear the fact that already at an earlier time analogies had formally arisen. Herodotus is rich in just such references, not to mention the systems of the Hellenic-Roman world. Opposed to the endeavor to form a unity there stands a still stronger endeavor to create again and again a multiplicity, so that even in the so-called severe monotheistic religions, as Christianity, for example, the polytheistic tendency is irrepressible. The Deity is divided into three parts at least, to which is added the feminine Deity of Mary and the numerous company of the lesser gods, the angels and saints, respectively. These two tendencies are in constant warfare. There is only one God with countless attributes, or else there are many gods who are then simply known differently, according to locality, and personify sometimes this, sometimes that attribute of the fundamental thought, an example of which we have seen above in the Egyptian gods.

With this we turn once more to Nietzsche's poem, "The Beacon." We found the flame there used as an image of the libido, theriomorphically represented as a snake (also as an image of the soul: [40] "This flame is

mine own soul "). We saw that the snake is to be taken
as a phallic image of the libido (upreared in impatience),
and that this image, also an attribute of the conception of
the sun (the Egyptian sun idol), is an image of the
libido in the combination of sun and phallus. It is not
a wholly strange conception, therefore, that the sun's
disc is represented with a penis, as well as with hands and
feet. We find proof for this idea in a peculiar part of
the Mithraic liturgy: ὁμοίως δὲ καὶ ὁ καλούμενος αὐλός,
ἡ ἀρχὴ τοῦ λειτουργοῦντος ἀνέμου. Ὄψει γὰρ ἀπὸ τοῦ
δίσκου ὡς αὐλὸν κρεμάμενον.*

This extremely important vision of a tube hanging
down from the sun would produce in a religious text, such
as that of the Mithraic liturgy, a strange and at the same
time meaningless effect if it did not have the phallic meaning. The tube is the place of origin of the wind. The
phallic meaning seems very faint in this idea, but one
must remember that the wind, as well as the sun, is a
fructifier and creator. This has already been pointed out
in a footnote.⁴¹ There is a picture by a Germanic painter
of the Middle Ages of the " conceptio immaculata "
which deserves mention here. The conception is represented by a tube or pipe coming down from heaven and
passing beneath the skirt of Mary. Into this flies the
Holy Ghost in the form of a dove for the impregnation
of the Mother of God.⁴²

Honegger discovered the following hallucination in an
insane man (paranoid dement) : The patient sees in the

---

* In like manner the so-called tube, the origin of the ministering wind,
will become visible. For it will appear to you as a tube hanging down
from the 'sun.

sun an " upright tail " similar to an erected penis. When he moves his head back and forth, then, too, the sun's penis sways back and forth in a like manner, and out of that the wind arises. This strange hallucination remained unintelligible to us for a long time until I became acquainted with the Mithraic liturgy and its visions. This hallucination threw an illuminating light, as it appears to me, upon a very obscure place in the text which immediately follows the passage previously cited:

εἰς δὲ τὰ μέρη τὰ πρὸς λίβα ἀπέραντον οἷον ἀπηλιώτην. Ἐὰν ᾖ κεκληρώμενος εἰς δὲ τὰ μέρη τοῦ ἀπηλιώτου ὁ ἕτερος, ὁμοίως εἰς τὰ μέρη τὰ ἐκείνου ὄψει τὴν ἀποφορὰν τοῦ ὁράματος.

Mead translates this very clearly: [43]

"And towards the regions westward, as though it were an infinite Eastwind. But if the other wind, towards the regions of the East, should be in service, in the like fashion shalt thou see towards the regions of that side the converse of the sight."

In the original ὅραμα is the vision, the thing seen. ἀποφορά means properly the carrying away. The sense of the text, according to this, might be: the thing seen may be carried or turned sometimes here, sometimes there, according to the direction of the wind. The ὅραμα is the tube, "the place of origin of the wind," which turns sometimes to the east, sometimes to the west, and, one might add, generates the corresponding wind. The vision of the insane man coincides astonishingly with this description of the movement of the tube. [44]

The various attributes of the sun, separated into a series, appear one after the other in the Mithraic liturgy. According to the vision of Helios, seven maidens appear with the heads of snakes, and seven gods with the heads of black bulls.

It is easy to understand the maiden as a symbol of the libido used in the sense of causative comparison. The snake in Paradise is usually considered as feminine, as the seductive principle in woman, and is represented as feminine by the old artists, although properly the snake has a phallic meaning. Through a similar change of meaning the snake in antiquity becomes the symbol of the earth, which on its side is always considered feminine. The bull is the well-known symbol for the fruitfulness of the sun. The bull gods in the Mithraic liturgy were called κνωθακοφύλακες, " guardians of the axis of the earth,'" by whom the axle of the orb of the heavens was turned. The divine man, Mithra, also had the same attributes; he is sometimes called the "Sol invictus " itself, sometimes the mighty companion and ruler of Helios; he holds in his right hand the "bear constellation, which moves and turns the heavens." The bull-headed gods, equally ἱεροὶ καὶ ἄλκιμοι νεανίαι with Mithra himself, to whom the attribute νεώτερος, "young one," "the new-comer," is given, are merely attributive components of the same divinity. The chief god of the Mithraic liturgy is himself subdivided into Mithra and Helios; the attributes of each of these are closely related to the other. Of Helios it is said: ὄψει θεὸν νεώτερον εὐειδῆ πυρινό-

τρίχα ἐν χιτῶνι λευκῷ καὶ χλαμύδι κοκκίνῃ, ἔχοντα
πύρινον στέφανον.*

Of Mithra it is said: ὄψει θεὸν ὑπερμεγέθη, φωτινὴν
ἔχοντα τὴν ὄψιν, νεώτερον, χρυσοκόμαν, ἐν χιτῶνι λευκῷ
καὶ χρυσῷ στεφάνῳ καὶ ἀναξυρίσι, κατέχοντα τῇ δεξιᾷ
χειρὶ μόσχου ὠμόν χρύσεον, ὅς ἐστιν ἄρκτος ἡ κινοῦσα
καὶ ἀντιστρέφουσα τὸν οὐρανόν, κατὰ ὥραν ἀναπολεύ-
ουσα καὶ καταπολεύουσα.   ἔπειτα ὄψει αὐτοῦ ἐκ τῶν
ὀμμάτων ἀστραπὰς καὶ ἐκ τοῦ σώματος ἀστέρας ἁλλομέ-
νους. †

If we place fire and gold as essentially similar, then a
great accord is found in the attributes of the two gods.
To these mystical pagan ideas there deserve to be added
the probably almost contemporaneous vision of Revelation:

"And being turned, I saw seven golden candlesticks. And
in the midst of the candlesticks [45] one like unto the son of man,
clothed with a garment down to the foot, and girt about at the
breasts with a golden girdle. And his head and his hair were
white as white wool, white as snow, and his eyes were as a flame
of fire. And his feet like unto burnished brass, as if it had been
refined in a furnace; and his voice as the sound of many waters.
And he had in his right hand seven stars,[46] and out of his mouth
proceeded a sharp two-edged sword,[47] and his countenance was
as the sun shineth in his strength."—Rev. i: 12 ff.

"And I looked, and beheld a white cloud, and upon the cloud

* "You will see the god youthful, graceful, with glowing locks, in a
white garment and a scarlet cloak, with a fiery helmet."

† "You will see a god very powerful, with a shining countenance,
young, with golden hair, clothed in white vestments, with a golden
crown, holding in his right hand a bullock's golden shoulder, that is, the
bear constellation, which wandering hourly up and down, moves and
turns the heavens: then out of his eyes you will see lightning spring forth
and from his body, stars."

I saw one sitting like unto the son of man, having on his head a golden crown, and in his hand a sharp sickle." [48]—*Rev.* xiv: 14.

" And his eyes were as a flame of fire, and upon his head were many diadems. And he was arrayed in a garment [49] sprinkled with blood. . . . And the armies which were in heaven followed him upon white horses, clothed in fine linen, [50] white and pure. And out of his mouth proceeded a sharp sword."—*Rev.* xix: 12-15.

One need not assume that there is a direct dependency between the Apocalypse and the Mithraic liturgy. The visionary images of both texts are developed from a source, not limited to one place, but found in the soul of many divers people, because the symbols which arise from it are too typical for it to belong to one individual only. I put these images here to show how the primitive symbolism of light gradually developed, with the increasing depth of the vision, into the idea of the sun-hero, the " well-beloved." [51] The development of the symbol of light is thoroughly typical. In addition to this, perhaps I might call to mind the fact that I have previously pointed out this course with numerous examples, [52] and, therefore, I can spare myself the trouble of returning to this subject. [53] These visionary occurrences are the psychological roots of the sun-coronations in the mysteries. Its rite is religious hallucination congealed into liturgical form, which, on account of its great regularity, could become a generally accepted outer form. After all this, it is easily understood how the ancient Christian Church, on one side, stood in an especial bond to Christ as " sol novus," and, on the other side, had a certain difficulty in freeing itself from the earthly symbols of Christ. Indeed

Philo of Alexandria saw in the sun the image of the divine logos or of the Deity especially (" De Somniis," 1 : 85). In an Ambrosian hymn Christ is invoked by " O sol salutis," and so on. At the time of Marcus Aurelius, Meliton, in his work,[54] περὶ λούτρου, called Christ the Ἥλιος ἀνατολῆς . . . μόνος ἥλιος οὗτος ἀνέτειλεν ἀπ᾽ οὐρανοῦ.*

Still more important is a passage from Pseudo-Cyprian: [55]

"O quam præclara providentia ut illo die quo factus est sol, in ipso die nasceretur Christus, v. Kal. Apr. feria IV, et ideo de ipso ad plebem dicebat Malachias propheta: 'Orietur vobis sol iustitiæ et curatio est in pennis ejus,' hic est sol iustitiæ cuis in pennis curatio præostendebatur." † [56]

In a work nominally attributed to John Chrysostomus, " De Solstitiis et Aequinoctiis," [57] occurs this passage:

"Sed et dominus nascitur mense Decembri hiemis tempore, VIII. Kal. Januarias, quando oleæ maturæ præmuntur ut unctio, id est Chrisma, nascatur—sed et Invicti natalem appellant. Quis utique tam invictus nisi dominus noster qui mortem subactam devicit? Vel quod dicant Solis esse natalem, ipse est sol iustitiæ, de quo Malachias propheta dixit: 'Dominus lucis ac noctis conditor et discretor qui a phopheta Sol iustitiæ cognominatus est.' " ‡

* Helios, the rising sun—the only sun rising from heaven!

† " O, how remarkable a providence that Christ should be born on the same day on which the sun moves onward, V. Kal. of April the fourth holiday, and for this reason the prophet Malachi spoke to the people concerning Christ: 'Unto you shall the sun of righteousness arise with healing in his wings, this is the sun of righteousness in whose wings healing shall be displayed.'"

‡ Moreover the Lord is born in the month of December in the winter on the 8th Kal. of January when the ripe olives are gathered, so that the oil, that is the chrism, may be produced, moreover they call it the birthday of the Unconquered One. Who in any case is as unconquered as our Lord, who conquered death itself? Or why should they call it the birthday of

According to the testimony of Eusebius of Alexandria, the Christians also shared in the worship of the rising sun, which lasted into the fifth century:

οὐαῖ τοῖς προσκυνοῦσι τὸν ἥλιον καὶ τὴν σελήνην καὶ τοὺς ἀστέρας. Πολλοὺς γὰρ οἶδα τοὺς προσκυνοῦντας καὶ εὐχομένους εἰς τὸν ἥλιον. Ἤδη γὰρ ἀνατείλαντος τοῦ ἡλίου, προσεύχονται καὶ λέγουσιν "Ἐλέησον ἡμᾶς" καὶ οὐ μόνον Ἡλιογνῶσται καὶ αἱρετικοὶ τοῦτο ποιοῦσιν ἀλλὰ καὶ χριστιανοὶ καὶ ἀφέντες τὴν πίστιν τοῖς αἱρετικοῖς συναμίγνυνται.*

Augustine preached emphatically to the Christians:

" Non est Dominus Sol factus sed per quem Sol factus est—ne quis carnaliter sapiens Solem istum (Christum) intelligendum putaret."

Art has preserved much of the remnants of sun-worship,[58] thus the nimbus around the head of Christ and the halo of the saints in general. The Christian legends also attribute many fire and light symbols to the saints.[59] The twelve apostles, for example, are likened to the twelve signs of the zodiac, and are represented, therefore, with a star over the head.[60]

It is not to be wondered at that the heathen, as Tertullian avows, considered the sun as the Christian God.

the sun; he himself is the sun of righteousness, concerning whom Malachi, the prophet, spoke: 'The Lord is the author of light and of darkness, he is the judge spoken of by the prophet as the Sun of righteousness.'"

* "Ah! woe to the worshippers of the sun and the moon and the stars. For I know many worshippers and prayer sayers to the sun. For now at the rising of the sun, they worship and say, 'Have mercy on us,' and not only the sun-gnostics and the heretics do this, but also Christians who leave their faith and mix with the heretics."

Among the Manichæans God was really the sun. One
of the most remarkable works extant, where the Pagan,
Asiatic, Hellenic and Christian intermingle, is the
Ἐξήγησις περὶ τῶν ἐν Περσίδι πραχθέντων, edited by
Wirth.[61] This is a book of fables, but, nevertheless, a
mine for near-Christian phantasies, which gives a profound insight into Christian symbolism. In this is found
the following magical dedication: Διὶ Ἡλίῳ θεῷ μεγάλῳ
βασιλεῖ Ἰησοῦ—* In certain parts of Armenia the
rising sun is still worshipped by Christians, that " it
may let its foot rest upon the faces of the worshippers." [62] The foot occurs as an anthropomorphic attribute, and we have already met the theriomorphic
attribute in the feathers and the sun phallus. Other comparisons of the sun's ray, as knife, sword, arrow, and so
on, have also, as we have learned from the psychology
of the dream, a phallic meaning at bottom. This meaning is attached to the foot as I here point out,[63] and also
to the feathers, or hair, of the sun, which signify the
power or strength of the sun. I refer to the story of
Samson, and to that of the Apocalypse of Baruch, concerning the phœnix bird, which, flying before the sun, loses
its feathers, and, exhausted, is strengthened again in an
ocean bath at evening.

Under the symbol of " moth and sun " we have dug
down into the historic depths of the soul, and in doing
this we have uncovered an old buried idol, the youthful,
beautiful, fire-encircled and halo-crowned sun-hero, who,
forever unattainable to the mortal, wanders upon the

* " To Zeus, the Great Sun God, the King, the Saviour."

earth, causing night to follow day; winter, summer; death, life; and who returns again in rejuvenated splendor and gives light to new generations. The longing of the dreamer concealed behind the moth stands for him.

The ancient pre-Asiatic civilizations were acquainted with a sun-worship having the idea of a God dying and rising again (Osiris, Tammuz, Attis-Adonis),[64] Christ, Mithra and his bull,[65] Phœnix and so on. The beneficent power as well as the destroying power was worshipped in fire. The forces of nature always have two sides, as we have already seen in the God of Job. This reciprocal bond brings us back once more to Miss Miller's poem. Her reminiscences support our previous supposition, that the symbol of moth and sun is a condensation of two ideas, about one of which we have just spoken; the other is the moth and the flame. As the title of a play, about the contents of which the author tells us absolutely nothing, " Moth and Flame " may easily have the well-known erotic meaning of flying around the flame of passion until one's wings are burned. The passionate longing, that is to say, the libido, has its two sides; it is power which beautifies everything, and which under other circumstances destroys everything. It often appears as if one could not accurately understand in what the destroying quality of the creative power consists. A woman who gives herself up to passion, particularly under the present-day condition of culture, experiences the destructive side only too soon. One has only to imagine one's self a little away from the every-day moral conditions in order to understand what feelings of extreme insecurity overwhelm the individual who gives himself unconditionally over to Fate.

To be fruitful means, indeed, to destroy one's self, because with the rise of the succeeding generation the previous one has passed beyond its highest point; thus our descendants are our most dangerous enemies, whom we cannot overcome, for they will outlive us, and, therefore, without fail, will take the power from our enfeebled hands. The anxiety in the face of the erotic fate is wholly understandable, for there is something immeasurable therein. Fate usually hides unknown dangers, and the perpetual hesitation of the neurotic to venture upon life is easily explained by his desire to be allowed to stand still, so as not to take part in the dangerous battle of life.[66] *Whoever renounces the chance to experience must stifle in himself the wish for it, and, therefore, commits a sort of self-murder.* From this the death phantasies which readily accompany the renunciation of the erotic wish are made clear. In the poem *Miss Miller has voiced these phantasies.*

She adds further to the material with the following:

"I had been reading a selection from one of Byron's poems which pleased me very much and made a deep and lasting impression. Moreover, the rhythm of my last two verses, 'For I the source, etc.,' and the two lines of Byron's are very similar.

'Now let me die as I have lived in faith,
Nor tremble though the universe should quake.'"

This reminiscence with which the series of ideas is closed confirms the death phantasies which follow from

renunciation of the erotic wish. The quotation comes—
which Miss Miller did not mention—from an uncompleted
poem of Byron's called " Heaven and Earth." [67]   The
whole verse follows:

> " Still blessed be the Lord,
>   For what is passed,
>   For that which is;
>   For all are His,
>   From first to last—
>   Time—Space—Eternity—Life—Death—
>   The vast known and immeasurable unknown
>   He made and can unmake,
>   And shall I for a little gasp of breath
>   Blaspheme and groan?
>   No, let me die as I have lived in faith,
>   Nor quiver though the universe may quake! "

The words are included in a kind of praise or prayer,
spoken by a " mortal " who is in hopeless flight before
the mounting deluge. Miss Miller puts herself in the
same situation in her quotation; that is to say, she readily
lets it be seen that her feeling is similar to the despond-
ency of the unhappy ones who find themselves hard
pressed by the threatening mounting waters of the deluge.
With this the writer allows us a deep look into the dark
abyss of her longing for the sun-hero. We see that her
longing is in vain; she is a mortal, only for a short time
borne upwards into the light by means of the highest
longing, and then sinking to death, or, much more, urged
upwards by the fear of death, like the people before the
deluge, and in spite of the desperate conflict, irretriev-
ably given over to destruction. This is a mood which re-

calls vividly the closing scene in " Cyrano de Bergerac ": [68]

Cyrano:
> Oh, mais . . . puisqu'elle est en chemin,
> Je l'attendrai debout . . . et l'épée à la main.
>
> Que dites-vous? . . . C'est inutile? Je le sais.
> Mais on ne se bat pas dans l'espoir du succès.
> Non, non. C'est bien plus beau lorsque c'est inutile.
>
> Je sais bien qu'à la fin vous me mettrez à bas. . . .

We already know sufficiently well what longing and
what impulse it is that attempts to clear a way for itself
to the light, but that it may be realized quite clearly and
irrevocably, it is shown plainly in the quotation " No, let
me die," which confirms and completes all earlier remarks.
The divine, the " much-beloved," who is honored in the
image of the sun, is also the goal of the longing of our
poet.

Byron's " Heaven and Earth " is a mystery founded on
the following passage from Genesis, chapter vi: 2:
" And it came to pass . . . that the sons of God saw the
daughters of men that they were fair, and they took
them wives of all that they chose." Byron offers as a
further motif for his poem the following passage from
Coleridge: *" And woman wailing for her Demon lover."*
Byron's poem is concerned with two great events, one
psychologic and one telluric; the passion which throws
down all barriers; and all the terrors of the unchained
powers of nature: a parallel which has already been introduced into our earlier discussion. The angels Samiasa

and Azaziel burn with sinful love for the beautiful daughters of Cain, Anah and Aholibama, and force a way through the barrier which is placed between mortal and immortal. They revolt as Lucifer once did against God, and the archangel Raphael raises his voice warningly:

> " But man hath listened to his voice
> And ye to woman's—beautiful she is,
> The serpent's voice less subtle than her kiss.
> The snake but vanquished dust; but she will draw
> A second host from heaven to break heaven's law."

The power of God is threatened by the seduction of passion; a second fall of angels menaces heaven. Let us translate this mythologic projection back into the psychologic, from whence it originated. Then it would read: the power of the good and reasonable ruling the world wisely is threatened by the chaotic primitive power of passion; therefore passion must be exterminated; that is to say, projected into mythology. The race of Cain and the whole sinful world must be destroyed from the roots by the deluge. It is the inevitable result of that sinful passion which has broken through all barriers. Its counterpart is the sea and the waters of the deep and the floods of rain,[69] the generating, fructifying and " maternal waters," as the Indian mythology refers to them. Now they leave their natural bounds and surge over the mountain tops, engulfing all living things; for passion destroys itself. The libido is God and Devil. With the destruction of the sinfulness of the libido an essential portion of the libido would be destroyed. Through the loss of the Devil, God himself suffered a considerable loss, somewhat like an amputation upon the body of the Divinity. The mysterious hint in Raphael's lament concerning the two rebels, Samiasa and Azaziel, suggests this.

> ". . . . Why,
> Cannot this earth be made, or be destroyed,
> Without involving ever some vast void
> In the immortal ranks? . . ."

Love raises man, not only above himself, but also above the bounds of his mortality and earthliness, up to divinity itself, and in the very act of raising him it destroys him. Mythologically, this self-presumption finds its striking expression in the building of the heaven-high tower of Babel, which brings confusion to mankind.[70] In Byron's poem it is the sinful ambition of the race of Cain, for love of which it makes even the stars subservient and leads away the sons of God themselves. If, indeed, longing for the highest things—if I may speak so—is legitimate, then it lies in the circumstances that it leaves its human boundaries, that of sinfulness, and, therefore, destruction. The longing of the moth for the star is not absolutely pure and transparent, but glows in sultry mist, for man continues to be man. Through the excess of his longing he draws down the divine into the corruption of his passion;[71] therefore, he seems to raise himself to the Divine; but with that his humanity is destroyed. Thus the love of Anah and Aholibama for their angels becomes the ruin of gods and men. The invocation with which Cain's daughters implore their angels is psychologically an exact parallel to Miss Miller's poem.

Anah:[72]
Seraph!
From thy sphere!
Whatever star[73] contains thy glory.

In the eternal depths of heaven
Albeit thou watchest with the ' seven,'
Though through space infinite and hoary
Before thy bright wings worlds will be driven,

      Yet hear!
Oh! think of her who holds thee dear!

And though she nothing is to thee,
Yet think that thou art all to her.

  .   .   .   .   .

Eternity is in thy years,
Unborn, undying beauty in thine eyes;
With me thou canst not sympathize,
Except in love, and there thou must
Acknowledge that more loving dust
Ne'er wept beneath the skies.
Thou walkest thy many worlds,[74] thou seest
The face of him who made thee great,
As he hath made of me the least
Of those cast out from Eden's gate;

Yet, Seraph, dear!
      Oh hear!
For thou hast loved me, and I would not die
Until I know what I must die in knowing,
That thou forgettest in thine eternity
Her whose heart death could not keep from o'erflowing
For thee, immortal essence as thou art,[75]
Great is their love who love in sin and fear;
And such, I feel, are waging in my heart
A war unworthy: to an Adamite

Forgive, my Seraph! that such thoughts appear.
For sorrow is our element. . . .

.   .   .   .

   The hour is near
Which tells me we are not abandoned quite.
   Appear! Appear!
   Seraph!
My own Azaziel! be but here,
And leave the stars to their own light.

Aholibama:
   I call thee, I await thee and I love thee.

.   .   .   .   .

Though I be formed of clay,
And thou of beams [76]
More bright than those of day on Eden's streams,
Thine immortality cannot repay
With love more warm than mine
My love. There is a ray [77]
In me, which though forbidden yet to shine,
I feel was lighted at thy God's and mine. [78]
It may be hidden long: death and decay
Our mother Eve bequeathed us—but my heart
Defies it: though this life must pass away,
Is that a cause for thee and me to part?

.   .   .   .   .

I can share all things, even immortal sorrow;
For thou hast ventured to share life with me,
And shall I shrink from thine eternity?
No, though the serpent's sting [79] should pierce me through,
And thou thyself wert like the serpent, coil
Around me still. [80] And I will smile
And curse thee not, but hold
Thee in as warm a fold
As—but descend and prove
A mortal's love
For an immortal. . . .

The apparition of both angels which follows the invocation is, as always, a shining vision of light.

> *Aholibama:*
> The clouds from off their pinions flinging
> As though they bore to-morrow's light.
>
> *Anah:*
> But if our father see the sight!
>
> *Aholibama:*
> He would but deem it was the moon
> Rising unto some sorcerer's tune
> An hour too soon.
>
> .   .   .
>
> *Anah:*
> Lo! They have kindled all the west,
> Like a returning sunset. . . .
> On Ararat's late secret crest
> A wild and many colored bow,
> The remnant of their flashing path,
> Now shines! . . .

At the sight of this many-colored vision of light, where both women are entirely filled with desire and expectation, Anah makes use of a simile full of presentiment, which suddenly allows us to look down once more into the dismal dark depths, out of which for a moment the terrible animal nature of the mild god of light emerges.

> " . . . and now, behold! it hath
> Returned to night, as rippling foam,
> Which the leviathan hath lashed
> From his unfathomable home,
> When sporting on the face of the calm deep,
> Subsides soon after he again hath dash'd
> Down, down to where the ocean's fountains sleep."

Thus like the leviathan! We recall this overpowering weight in the scale of God's justice in regard to the man Job. There, where the deep sources of the ocean are, the leviathan lives; from there the all-destroying flood ascends, the all-engulfing flood of animal passion. That stifling, compressing feeling [81] of the onward-surging impulse is projected mythologically as a flood which, rising up and over all, destroys all that exists, in order to allow a new and better creation to come forth from this destruction.

Japhet:
    The eternal will
    Shall deign to expound this dream
    Of good and evil; and redeem
    Unto himself all times, all things;

    And, gather'd under his almighty wings,
    Abolish hell!
    And to the expiated Earth
    Restore the beauty of her birth.

Spirits:
    And when shall take effect this wondrous spell?

Japhet:
    When the Redeemer cometh; first in pain
    And then in glory.

Spirits:
    New times, new climes, new arts, new men, but still
    The same old tears, old crimes, and oldest ill,
    Shall be amongst your race in different forms;
    But the same mortal storms
    Shall oversweep the future, as the waves
    In a few hours the glorious giants' graves.

The prophetic visions of Japhet have almost prophetic meaning for our poetess; with the death of the moth in the light, evil is once more laid aside; the complex has once again, even if in a censored form, expressed itself. With that, however, the problem is not solved; all sorrow and every longing begins again from the beginning, but there is " Promise in the Air "—the premonition of the Redeemer, of the " Well-beloved," of the Sun-hero, who again mounts to the height of the sun and again descends to the coldness of the winter, who is the light of hope from race to race, the image of the libido.

PART II

CHAPTER I

ASPECTS OF THE LIBIDO

BEFORE I enter upon the contents of this second part, it seems necessary to cast a backward glance over the singular train of thought which the analysis of the poem "The Moth to the Sun" has produced. Although this poem is very different from the foregoing Hymn of Creation, closer investigation of the "longing for the sun" has carried us into the realm of the fundamental ideas of religion and astral mythology, which ideas are closely related to those considered in the first poem. The creative God of the first poem, whose dual nature, moral and physical, was shown especially clearly to us by Job, has in the second poem a new qualification of astral-mythological, or, to express it better, of astrological character. The God becomes the sun, and in this finds an adequate natural expression quite apart from the moral division of the God idea into the heavenly father and the devil. The sun is, as Renan remarked, really the only rational representation of God, whether we take the point of view of the barbarians of other ages or that of the modern physical sciences. In both cases the sun is the parent God, mythologically predominantly the Father God, from whom all living things draw life; He is the fructifier and creator of all that lives, the source of energy of our world. The discord into which the soul of man has fallen through the action of moral laws [1] can be resolved into complete harmony through the sun as the natural object which obeys no human moral law. The sun is not only beneficial, but also destructive; therefore the zodiacal representation of the August heat is the herd-devouring lion whom the Jewish hero Samson [2] killed in order to free the parched earth from this plague. Yet it is the harmonious and inherent nature of the sun to scorch, and its scorching power seems natural to men. It shines equally on the just and on the unjust, and allows useful living objects to flourish as well as harmful ones. Therefore, the sun is adapted as is nothing else to represent the visible God of this world. That is to say, that driving strength of our own soul, which we call libido, and whose nature it is to allow the useful and injurious, the good and the bad to proceed. That this comparison is no mere play of words is taught us by the mystics. When by looking inwards (introversion) and going down into the depths of their own being they find " in their heart " the image of the Sun, they find their own love or libido, which with reason, I might say with physical reason, is called the Sun; for our source of energy and life is the Sun. Thus our life substance, as an energic process, is entirely Sun. Of what special sort this " Sun energy " seen inwardly by the mystic is, is shown by an example taken from the Hindoo mythology. [3] From the explanation of Part III of the " Shvetâshvataropanishad " we take the following quotation, which relates to the Rudra : [4]

(2) "Yea, the one Rudra who all these worlds with ruling power doth rule, stands not for any second. Behind those that are born he stands; at ending time ingathers all the worlds he hath evolved, protector (he).

(3) "He hath eyes on all sides, on all sides surely hath faces, arms surely on all sides, on all sides feet. With arms, with wings he tricks them out, creating heaven and earth, the only God.

(4) "Who of the gods is both the source and growth, the Lord of all, the Rudra. Mighty seer; who brought the shining germ of old into existence—may he with reason pure conjoin us." [5]

These attributes allow us clearly to discern the all-creator and in him the Sun, which has wings and with a thousand eyes scans the world. [6]

The following passages confirm the text and join to it the idea most important for us, that God is also contained in the individual creature:

(7) "Beyond this (world) the Brahman beyond, the mighty one, in every creature hid according to its form, the one encircling Lord of all, Him having known, immortal they become.

(8) "I know this mighty man, Sun-like, beyond the darkness, Him (and him) only knowing, one crosseth over death; no other path (at all) is there to go.

(11) ". . . spread over the universe is He the Lord therefore as all-pervader, He's benign."

The powerful God, the equal of the Sun, is in that one, and whoever knows him is immortal. [7] Going on further with the text, we come upon a new attribute, which informs us in what form and manner Rudra lived in men.

(12) "The mighty monarch, He, the man, the one who doth the essence start towards that peace of perfect stainlessness, lordly, exhaustless light.

(13) "The Man, the size of a thumb, the inner self, sits ever in the heart of all that's born, by mind, mind ruling in the heart, is He revealed. That they who know, immortal they become.

(14) "The Man of the thousands of heads (and) thousands of eyes (and) thousands of feet, covering the earth on all sides, He stands beyond, ten finger-breadths.

(15) "The Man is verily this all, (both) what has been and what will be, Lord (too) of deathlessness which far all else surpasses."

Important parallel quotations are to be found in the " Kathopanishad," section 2, part 4.

(12) "The Man of the size of a thumb, resides in the midst within the self, of the past and the future, the Lord.

(13) "The Man of the size of a thumb like flame free from smoke, of past and of future the Lord, the same is to-day, to-morrow the same will He be."

Who this Tom-Thumb is can easily be divined—the phallic symbol of the libido. The phallus is this hero dwarf, who performs great deeds; he, this ugly god in homely form, who is the great doer of wonders, since he is the visible expression of the creative strength incarnate in man. This extraordinary contrast is also very striking in " Faust " (the mother scene) :

> *Mephistopheles:*
> I'll praise thee ere we separate: I see
> Thou knowest the devil thoroughly:
> Here take this key.
>
> *Faust:*
> That little thing!
>
> *Mephistopheles:*
> Take hold of it, not undervaluing!

Faust:
  It glows, it shines, increases in my hand!

Mephistopheles:
  How much it is worth, thou soon shalt understand,
  The key will scent the true place from all others!
  Follow it down!—'twill lead thee to the Mothers! *

Here the devil again puts into Faust's hand the marvellous tool, a phallic symbol of the libido, as once before in the beginning the devil, in the form of the black dog, accompanied Faust, when he introduced himself with the words:

  " Part of that power, not understood,
Which always wills the bad and always creates the good."

United to this strength, Faust succeeded in accomplishing his real life task, at first through evil adventure and then for the benefit of humanity, for without the evil there is no creative power. Here in the mysterious mother scene, where the poet unveils the last mystery of the creative power to the initiated, Faust has need of the phallic magic wand (in the magic strength of which he has at first no confidence), in order to perform the greatest of wonders, namely, the creation of Paris and Helen. With that Faust attains the divine power of working miracles, and, indeed, only by means of this small, insignificant instrument. This paradoxical impression seems to be very ancient, for even the Upanishads could say the following of the dwarf god:

* Bayard Taylor's translation of " Faust " is used throughout this book. —TRANSLATOR.

(19) "Without hands, without feet, He moveth, He graspeth: Eyeless He seeth, (and) earless He heareth: He knoweth what is to be known, yet is there no knower of Him. Him call the first, mighty the Man.

(20) "Smaller than small, (yet) greater than great in the heart of this creature the self doth repose . . . etc."

The phallus is the being, which moves without limbs, which sees without eyes, which knows the future; and as symbolic representative of the universal creative power existent everywhere immortality is vindicated in it. It is always thought of as entirely independent, an idea current not only in antiquity, but also apparent in the pornographic drawings of our children and artists. It is a seer, an artist and a worker of wonders; therefore it should not surprise us when certain phallic characteristics are found again in the mythological seer, artist and sorcerer. Hephaestus, Wieland the smith, and Mani, the founder of Manicheism, whose followers were also famous, have crippled feet. The ancient seer Melampus possessed a suggestive name (Blackfoot),[8] and it seems also to be typical for seers to be blind. Dwarfed stature, ugliness and deformity have become especially typical for those mysterious chthonian gods, the sons of Hephaestus, the Cabiri,[9] to whom great power to perform miracles was ascribed. The name signifies "powerful," and the Samothracian cult is most intimately united with that of the ithyphallic Hermes, who, according to the account of Herodotus, was brought to Attica by the Pelasgians. They are also called $\mu\varepsilon\gamma\acute{\alpha}\lambda o\iota$ $\theta\varepsilon o\acute{\iota}$, the great gods. Their near relations are the "Idaean dactyli" (finger or Idaean thumb),[10] to whom the mother of the gods had taught the blacksmith's art. ("The key will scent the true place from all others! follow it down!—'t will lead thee to the Mothers!") They were the first leaders, the teachers of Orpheus, and invented the Ephesian magic formulas and the musical rhythms.[11] The characteristic disparity which is shown above in the Upanishad text, and in "Faust," is also found here, since the gigantic Hercules passed as an Idaean dactyl.

The colossal Phrygians, the skilled servants of Rhea,[12] were also Dactyli. The Babylonian teacher of wisdom, Oannes,[13] was represented in a phallic fish form.[14] The two sun heroes, the Dioscuri, stand in relation to the Cabiri;[15] they also wear the remarkable pointed head-covering (Pileus) which is peculiar to these mysterious gods,[16] and which is perpetuated from that time on as a secret mark of identification. Attis (the elder brother of Christ) wears the pointed cap, just as does Mithra. It has also become traditional for our present-day chthonian infantile gods,[17] the brownies (Penates), and all the typical kind of dwarfs. Freud[18] has already called our attention to the phallic meaning of the hat in modern phantasies. A further significance is that probably the pointed cap represents the foreskin. In order not to go too far afield from my theme, I must be satisfied here merely to present the suggestion. But at a later opportunity I shall return to this point with detailed proof.

The dwarf form leads to the figure of the divine boy, the *puer eternus,* the young Dionysus, Jupiter Anxurus, Tages,[19] and so on. In the vase painting of Thebes,

already mentioned, a bearded Dionysus is represented
as *KABEIPOΣ*, together with a figure of a boy as *Παῖς*,
followed by a caricatured boy's figure designated as
ΠΡΑΤΟΛΑΟΣ and then again a caricatured man, which
is represented as *MITOΣ*.[20] *Μίτος* really means thread,
but in orphic speech it stands for semen. It was con-
jectured that this collection corresponded to a group of
statuary in the sanctuary of a cult. This supposition is
supported by the history of the cult as far as it is known;
it is an original Phenician cult of father and son;[21] of
an old and young Cabir who were more or less assimilated with the Grecian gods. The double figures of the
adult and the child Dionysus lend themselves particularly
to this assimilation. One might also call this the cult
of the large and small man. Now, under various aspects,
Dionysus is a phallic god in whose worship the phallus
held an important place; for example, in the cult of the
Argivian Bull—Dionysus. Moreover, the phallic herme
of the god has given occasion for a personification of the
phallus of Dionysus, in the form of the god Phales,
who is nothing else but a Priapus. He is called *ἑταῖρος*
or *σύγκωμος Βάκχου**.[22] Corresponding to this state
of affairs, one cannot very well fail to recognize in the previously mentioned Cabiric representation, and in the
added boy's figure, the picture of man and his penis.[23] The
previously mentioned paradox in the Upanishad text
of large and small, of giant and dwarf, is expressed more
mildly here by man and boy, or father and son.[24] The
motive of deformity which is used constantly by the

* Comrade—fellow-reveller.

Cabiric cult is present also in the vase picture, while the parallel figures to Dionysus and Παῖς are the caricatured Μίτος and Πρατόλαος. Just as formerly the difference in size gave occasion for division, so does the deformity here.[25]

Without first bringing further proof to bear, I may remark that from this knowledge especially strong sidelights are thrown upon the original psychologic meaning of the religious heroes. Dionysus stands in an intimate relation with the psychology of the early Asiatic God who died and rose again from the dead and whose manifold manifestations have been brought together in the figure of Christ into a firm personality enduring for centuries. We gain from our premise the knowledge that these heroes, as well as their typical fates, are personifications of the human libido and its typical fates. They are imagery, like the figures of our nightly dreams—the actors and interpreters of our secret thoughts. And since we, in the present day, have the power to decipher the symbolism of dreams and thereby surmise the mysterious psychologic history of development of the individual, so a way is here opened to the understanding of the secret springs of impulse beneath the psychologic development of races. Our previous trains of thought, which demonstrate the phallic side of the symbolism of the libido, also show how thoroughly justified is the term " libido." [26] Originally taken from the sexual sphere, this word has become the most frequent technical expression of psychoanalysis, for the simple reason that its significance is wide enough to cover all the unknown and countless manifestations of the Will in the sense of Schopenhauer. It is sufficiently comprehensive and rich in meaning to characterize the real nature of the psychical entity which it includes. The exact classical significance of the word libido qualifies it as an entirely appropriate term. Libido is taken in a very wide sense in Cicero:[27]

"(Volunt ex duobus opinatis) bonis (nasci) Libidinem et Lætitiam; ut sit lætitia præsentium bonorum: libido futurorum. —Lætitia autem et Libido in bonorum opinione versantur, cum Libido ad id, quod videtur bonum, illecta et inflammata rapiatur. —Natura enim omnes ea, quae bona videntur, sequuntur, fugiuntque contraria. Quamobrem simul objecta species cuiuspiam est, quod bonum videatur, ad id adipiscendum impellit ipsa natura. Id cum constanter prudenterque fit, ejusmodi appetitionem stoici βούλησιν appellant, nos appellamus voluntatem; eam illi putant in solo esse sapiente, quam sic definiunt; voluntas est quæ quid cum ratione desiderat: quæ autem ratione adversa incitata est vehementius, ea libido est, vel cupiditas effrenata, quæ in omnibus stultis invenitur." *

The meaning of libido here is " to wish," and in the stoical distinction of will, dissolute desire. Cicero[28] used " libido " in a corresponding sense:

* From the good proceed desire and joy—joy having reference to some present good, and desire to some future one—but joy and desire depend upon the opinion of good; as desire being inflamed and provoked is carried on eagerly toward what has the appearance of good, and joy is transported and exults on obtaining what was desired: for we naturally pursue those things that have the appearance of good, and avoid the contrary—wherefore as soon as anything that has the appearance of good presents itself, nature incites us to endeavor to obtain it. Now where this strong desire is consistent and founded on prudence, it is by the stoics called Bulesis and the name which we give it is volition, and this they allow to none but their wise men, and define it thus; volition is a reasonable desire; but whatever is incited too violently in opposition to reason, that is a lust or an unbridled desire which is discoverable in all fools. —*The Tusculan Disputation,* Cicero, page 403.

"Agere rem aliquam libidine, non ratione." *

In the same sense Sallust says :

"Iracundia pars est libidinis."

In another place in a milder and more general sense, which completely approaches the analytical use:

"Magisque in decoris armis et militaribus equis, quam in scortis et conviviis libidinem habebant." *

Also:

"Quod si tibi bona libido fuerit patriæ, etc."

The use of libido is so general that the phrase "libido est scire" merely had the significance of "I will, it pleases me." In the phrase "aliquam libido urinæ lacessit" libido had the meaning of urgency. The significance of sexual desire is also present in the classics.

This general classical application of the conception agrees with the corresponding etymological context of the word, *libido* or *lubido* (with *libet,* more ancient *lubet*), it pleases me, and *libens* or *lubens* = gladly, willingly. Sanskrit, *lúbhyati* = to experience violent longing, *lôbhayati* = excites longing, *lubdha-h* = eager, *lôbha-h* = longing, eagerness. Gothic = *liufs,* and Old High German *liob* = love. Moreover, in Gothic, *lubains* was represented as hope; and Old High German, *lobôn* = to praise, *lob* = commendation, praise, glory; Old Bulgarian, *ljubiti* = to love, *ljuby* = love; Lithuanian, *liáup-*

---

* Libido is used for arms and military horses rather than for dissipations and banquets.

sinti = to praise.[29]   It can be said that the conception of libido as developed in the new work of Freud and of his school has functionally the same significance in the biological territory as has the conception of energy since the time of Robert Mayer in the physical realm.[30]   It may not be superfluous to say something more at this point concerning the conception of libido after we have followed the formation of its symbol to its highest expression in the human form of the religious hero.

CHAPTER II

THE CONCEPTION AND THE GENETIC THEORY OF LIBIDO

THE chief source of the history of the analytic conception of libido is Freud's "Three Contributions to the Sexual Theory." There the term libido is conceived by him in the original narrow sense of sexual impulse, sexual need. Experience forces us to the assumption of a capacity for displacement of the libido, because functions or localizations of non-sexual force are undoubtedly capable of taking up a certain amount of libidinous sexual impetus, a libidinous afflux.[1] Functions or objects could, therefore, obtain sexual value, which under normal circumstances really have nothing to do with sexuality.[2] From this fact results the Freudian comparison of the libido with a stream, which is divisible, which can be dammed up, which overflows into branches, and so on.[3] Freud's original conception does not interpret "everything sexual," although this has been asserted by critics, but recognizes the existence of certain forces, the nature of which are not well known; to which Freud, however, compelled by the notorious facts which are evident to any layman, grants the capacity to receive "affluxes of libido." The hypothetical idea at the basis is the symbol of the "Triebbündel"[4] (bundle of impulses), wherein the sexual impulse figures as a partial impulse of the whole system, and its encroachment into the other realms of impulse is a fact of experience. The theory of Freud, branching off from this interpretation, according to which the motor forces of a neurotic system correspond precisely to their libidinous additions to other (non-sexual) functional impulses, has been sufficiently proven as correct, it seems to me, by the work of Freud and his school.[5] Since the appearance of the " Three Contributions," in 1905, a change has taken place [6] in the libido conception; its field of application has been widened. An extremely clear example of this amplification is this present work. However, I must state that Freud, as well as myself, saw the need of widening the conception of libido. It was paranoia, so closely related to dementia præcox, which seemed to compel Freud to enlarge the earlier limits of the conception. The passage in question, which I will quote here, word for word, reads: [7]

" A third consideration which presents itself, in regard to the views developed here, starts the query as to whether we should accept as sufficiently effectual the universal receding of the libido from the outer world, in order to interpret from that, the end of the world: or whether in this case, the firmly rooted possession of the ' I ' must not suffice to uphold the rapport with the outer world. Then one must either let that which we call possession of the libido (interest from erotic sources) coincide with interest in general, or else take into consideration the possibility that great disturbance in the disposition of the libido can also induce a corresponding disturbance in the possession of the ' I.' Now, these are the problems, which we are still absolutely helpless and unfitted to answer. Things would be different could we proceed from a safe fund of knowledge of instinct. But the truth is, we have nothing of that kind at our disposal. We understand instinct as the resultant of the reaction of the somatic and the psychic.

We see in it the psychical representation of organic forces and take the popular distinction between the ' I ' impulse and the sexual impulse, which appears to us to be in accord with the biological double rôle of the individual being who aspires to his own preservation as well as to the preservation of the species. But anything beyond this is a structure, which we set up, and also willingly let fall again in order to orient ourselves in the confusion of the dark processes of the soul; we expect particularly, from the psychoanalytic investigations into diseased soul processes, to have certain decisions forced upon us in regard to questions of the theory of instinct. This expectation has not yet been fulfilled on account of the still immature and limited investigations in these fields. At present the possibility of the reaction of libido disturbance upon the possession of the ' I ' can be shown as little as the reverse; the secondary or induced disturbances of the libido processes through abnormal changes in the ' I.' It is probable that processes of this sort form the distinctive character of the psychoses. The conclusions arising from this, in relation to paranoia, are at present uncertain. One cannot assert that the paranoiac has completely withdrawn his interest from the outer world, nor withdrawn into the heights of repression, as one sometimes sees in certain other forms of hallucinatory psychoses. He takes notice of the outer world, he takes account of its changes, he is stirred to explanations by their influence, and therefore I consider it highly probable that the changed relation to the world is to be explained, wholly or in great part, by the deficiency of the libido interest."

In this passage Freud plainly touches upon the question whether the well-known longing for reality of the paranoic dement (and the dementia præcox patients),[8] to whom I have especially called attention in my book, "The Psychology of Dementia Præcox,"[9] is to be traced back to the withdrawal of the "libidinous affluxes" alone, or whether this coincides with the so-called objective interest in general. It is hardly to be assumed

that the normal " fonction du réel " ('Janet) [10] is maintained only through affluxes of libido or erotic interest.
The fact is that in very many cases reality disappears
entirely, so that not a trace of psychological adaptation
or orientation can be recognized. Reality is repressed
under these circumstances and replaced by the contents
of the complex. One must of necessity say that not only
the erotic interest but the interest in general has disappeared, that is to say, the whole adaptation to reality has
ceased. To this category belong the stuporose and catatonic automatons.

I have previously made use of the expression " psychic
energy " in my " Psychology of Dementia Præcox " because I was unable to establish the theory of this psychosis upon the conception of the displacement of the
affluxes of libido. My experience, at that time chiefly
psychiatric, did not enable me to understand this theory.
However, the correctness of this theory in regard to
neuroses, strictly speaking the transference neuroses, was
proven to me later after increased experience in the field
of hysteria and compulsion neuroses. In the territory
of these neuroses it is mainly a question whether any
portion of the libido which is spared through the specific
repression becomes introverted and regressive into
earlier paths of transference; for example, the path of
the parental transference.[11] With that, however, the
former non-sexual psychologic adaptation to the environment remains preserved so far as it does not concern the
erotic and its secondary positions (symptoms). The
reality which is lacking to the patients is just that portion

of the libido to be found in the neurosis. In dementia
præcox, on the contrary, not merely that portion of libido
which is saved in the well-known specific sexual repression
is lacking for reality, but much more than one could write
down to the account of sexuality in a strict sense. The
function of reality is lacking to such a degree that even
the motive power must be encroached upon in the loss.
The sexual character of this must be disputed absolutely,[12]
for reality is not understood to be a sexual function.
Moreover, if that were so, the introversion of the libido
in the strict sense must have as a result a loss of reality
in the neuroses, and, indeed, a loss which could be compared with that of dementia præcox. These facts have
rendered it impossible for me to transfer Freud's theory
of libido to dementia præcox, and, therefore, I am of
the opinion that Abraham's investigation [13] is hardly ten-
able theoretically, from the standpoint of the Freudian
theory of libido. If Abraham believes that through the
withdrawal of the libido from the outer world the paranoid system or the schizophrenic symptomatology results,
then this assumption is not justified from the standpoint
of the knowledge of that time, because a mere libido introversion and regression leads, speedily, as Freud has
clearly shown, into the neuroses, and, strictly speaking,
into the transference neuroses, and not into dementia
præcox. Therefore, the transference of the libido theory
to dementia præcox is impossible, because this illness
produces a loss of reality which cannot be explained by
the deficiency of the libido defined in this narrow sense.

It affords me especial satisfaction that our teacher also,

when he laid his hand on the delicate material of the paranoic psychology, was forced to doubt the applicability of
the conception of libido held by him at that time. The
sexual definition of this did not permit me to understand
those disturbances of function, which affect the vague territory of the hunger instinct just as much as that of the
sexual instinct. For a long time the theory of libido
seemed to me inapplicable to dementia præcox. With
increasing experience in analytical work, however, I became aware of a gradual change in my conception of
libido. In place of the descriptive definition of the
" Three Contributions " there gradually grew up a genetic
definition of the libido, which rendered it possible for me
to replace the expression " psychic energy " by the term
" libido." I was forced to ask myself whether indeed the
function of reality to-day does not consist only in its
smaller part of libido sexualis and in the greater part of
other impulses? It is still a very important question
whether phylogenetically the function of reality is not, at
least in great part, of sexual origin. To answer this question directly in regard to the function of reality is not
possible, but we shall attempt to come to an understanding indirectly.

A fleeting glance at the history of evolution is sufficient
to teach us that countless complicated functions to which
to-day must be denied any sexual character were originally pure derivations from the general impulse of
propagation. During the ascent through the animal kingdom an important displacement in the fundamentals of
the procreative instinct has taken place. The mass of

the reproductive products with the uncertainty of fertilization has more and more been replaced by a controlled
impregnation and an effective protection of the offspring.
In this way part of the energy required in the production
of eggs and sperma has been transposed into the creation
of mechanisms for allurement and for protection of the
young.   Thus we discover the first instincts of art in animals used in the service of the impulse of creation, and
limited to the breeding season.   The original sexual character of these biological institutions became lost in their
organic fixation and functional independence.   Even if
there can be no doubt about the sexual origin of music,
still it would be a poor, unæsthetic generalization if one
were to include music in the category of sexuality.   A
similar nomenclature would then lead us to classify the
cathedral of Cologne as mineralogy because it is built
of stones.   It can be a surprise only to those to whom the
history of evolution is unknown to find how few things
there really are in human life which cannot be reduced in
the last analysis to the instinct of procreation.   It includes
very nearly everything, I think, which is beloved and dear
to us.   We spoke just now of libido as the creative impulse and at the same time we allied ourselves with the
conception which opposes libido to hunger in the same way
that the instinct of the preservation of the species is
opposed to the instinct of self-preservation.   In nature,
this artificial distinction does not exist.   Here we see only
a continuous life impulse, a will to live which will attain
the creation of the whole species through the preservation
of the individual.   Thus far this conception coincides with

the idea of the Will in Schopenhauer, for we can conceive Will objectively, only as a manifestation of an internal desire. This throwing of psychological perceptions into material reality is characterized philosophically as "introjection." (Ferenczi's conception of "introjection" denoted the reverse, that is, the taking of the outer world into the inner world.) [14] Naturally, the conception of the world was distorted by introjection. Freud's conception of the principle of desire is a voluntary formulation of the idea of introjection, while his once more voluntarily conceived "principle of reality" corresponds functionally to that which I designate as "corrective of reality," and R. Avenarius [15] designates as "empiriokritische Prinzipial-koordination." The conception of power owes its existence to this very introjection; this has already been said expressively by Galileo in his remark that its origin is to be sought in the subjective perception of the muscular power of the individual. Because we have already arrived at the daring assumption that the libido, which was employed originally in the exclusive service of egg and seed production, now appears firmly organized in the function of nest-building, and can no longer be employed otherwise; similarly this conception forces us to relate it to every desire, including hunger. For now we can no longer make any essential distinction between the will to build a nest and the will to eat. This view brings us to a conception of libido, which extends over the boundaries of the physical sciences into a philosophical aspect—to a conception of the will in general. I must give this bit of psychological "Voluntarismus" into the hands of the

philosophers for them to manage. For the rest I refer
to the words of Schopenhauer [16] relating to this. In con-
nection with the psychology of this conception (by which
I understand neither metapsychology nor metaphysics) I
am reminded here of the cosmogenic meaning of Eros in
Plato and Hesiod,[17] and also of the orphic figure of
Phanes, the "*shining one,*" the first created, the "father
of Eros." Phanes has also orphically the significance of
Priapus; he is a god of love, bisexual and similar to the
Theban Dionysus Lysios.[18] The orphic meaning of
Phanes is similar to that of the Indian Kâma, the god of
love, which is also the cosmogenic principle. To Plotinus,
of the Neo-Platonic school, the world-soul is the energy
of the intellect.[19] Plotinus compares "The One," the creative primal principle, with light in general; the intellect
with the Sun (☉), the world-soul with the moon (♀).
In another comparison Plotinus compares "The One"
with the Father, the intellect with the Son.[20] The "One"
designated as Uranus is transcendent. The son as Kronos
has dominion over the visible world. The world-soul
(designated as Zeus) appears as subordinate to him. The
"One," or the Usia of the whole existence is designated
by Plotinus as hypostatic, also as the three forms of emanation, also μία οὐσία ἐν τρισὶν ὑποστάσεσιν.* As Drews
observed, this is also the formula of the Christian
Trinity (God the Father, God the Son, and God the Holy
Ghost) as it was decided upon at the councils of Nicea
and Constantinople.[21] It may also be noticed that certain
early Christian sectarians attributed a maternal signifi-

* One substance in three forms.

cance to the Holy Ghost (world-soul, moon). (See what
follows concerning Chi of Timæus.) According to Plotinus, the world-soul has a tendency toward a divided
existence and towards divisibility, the *conditio sine qua
non* of all change, creation and procreation (also a maternal quality). It is an "unending all of life" and
wholly energy; it is a living organism of ideas, which
attain in it effectiveness and reality.[22] The intellect is
its procreator, its father, which, having conceived it,
brings it to development in thought.[23]

"What lies enclosed in the intellect, comes to development in
the world-soul as logos, fills it with meaning and makes it as if
intoxicated with nectar." [24]

Nectar is analogous to soma, the drink of fertility and
of life, also to sperma. The soul is fructified by the
intellect; as oversoul it is called heavenly Aphrodite, as
the undersoul the earthly Aphrodite. " It knows the birth
pangs," [25] and so on. The bird of Aphrodite, the dove,
is not without good cause the symbol of the Holy Ghost.

This fragment of the history of philosophy, which may
easily be enlarged, shows the significance of the endopsychic perception of the libido and of its symbolism in
human thought.

In the diversity of natural phenomena we see the desire, the libido, in the most diverse applications and forms.
We see the libido in the stage of childhood almost wholly
occupied in the instinct of nutrition, which takes care of
the upbuilding of the body. With the development of the
body there are successively opened new spheres of appli-

cation for the libido. The last sphere of application, and surpassing all the others in its functional significance, is sexuality, which seems at first almost bound up with the function of nutrition. (Compare with this the influence on procreation of the conditions of nutrition in lower animals and plants.) In the territory of sexuality, the libido wins that formation, the enormous importance of which has justified us in the use of the term libido in general. Here the libido appears very properly as an impulse of procreation, and almost in the form of an undifferentiated sexual primal libido, as an energy of growth, which clearly forces the individual towards division, budding, etc. (The clearest distinction between the two forms of libido is to be found among those animals in whom the stage of nutrition is separated from the sexual stage by a chrysalis stage.)

From that sexual primal libido which produced millions of eggs and seeds from one small creature derivatives have been developed with the great limitation of the fecundity; derivatives in which the functions are maintained by a special differentiated libido. This differentiated libido is henceforth desexualized because it is dissociated from its original function of egg and sperma production; nor is there any possibility of restoring it to its original function. Thus, in general, the process of development consists in an increasing transformation of the primal libido which only produced products of generation to the secondary functions of allurement and protection of the young. This now presupposes a very different and very complicated relation to reality, a true function of reality, which, functionally inseparable, is bound up with the needs of procreation. Thus the altered mode of procreation carries with it as a correlate a correspondingly heightened adaptation to reality.[26]

In this way we attain an insight into certain primitive conditions of the function of reality. It would be radically wrong to say that its compelling power is a sexual one. It was a sexual one to a large extent. The process of transformation of the primal libido into secondary impulses always took place in the form of affluxes of sexual libido, that is to say, sexuality became deflected from its original destination and a portion of it turned, little by little, increasing in amount, into the phylogenetic impulse of the mechanisms of allurement and of protection of the young. This diversion of the sexual libido from the sexual territory into associated functions is still taking place.[27] Where this operation succeeds without injury to the adaptation of the individual it is called *sublimation.* Where the attempt does not succeed it is called *repression.*

The descriptive standpoint of psychology accepts the multiplicity of instincts, among which is the sexual instinct, as a special phenomenon; moreover, it recognizes certain affluxes of libido to non-sexual instincts.

Quite otherwise is the genetic standpoint. It regards the multiplicity of instincts as issuing from a relative unity, the primal libido;[28] it recognizes that definite amounts of the primal libido are split off, as it were, associated with the newly formed functions and finally merged in them. As a result of this it is impossible, from the genetic standpoint, to hold to the strictly limited conception of libido of the descriptive standpoint; it leads inevitably to a broadening of the conception. With this we come to the theory of libido that I have surreptitiously introduced into the first part of this work for the purpose of making this genetic conception familiar to the reader. The explanation of this harmless deceit I have saved until the second part.

For the first time, through this genetic idea of libido, which in every way surpasses the descriptive sexual, the transference was made possible of the Freudian libido theory into the psychology of mental disease. The passage quoted above shows how the present Freudian conception of libido collides with the problem of the psychoses.[29] Therefore, when I speak of libido, I associate with it the genetic conception which contains not only the immediate sexual but also an amount of desexualized primal libido. When I say a sick person takes his libido away from the outer world, in order to take possession of the inner world with it, I do not mean that he takes away merely the affluxes from the function of reality, but he takes energy away, according to my view, from those desexualized instincts which regularly and properly support the function of reality.

With this alteration in the libido conception, certain parts of our terminology need revision as well. As we know, Abraham has undertaken the experiment of transferring the Freudian libido theory to dementia præcox and has conceived the characteristic lack of rapport and the cessation of the function of reality as autoerotism. This conception needs revision. Hysterical introversion of the libido leads to autoerotism, since the patient's erotic afflux of libido designed for the function of adaptation is introverted, whereby his ego is occupied by the corresponding amount of erotic libido. The schizophrenic, however, shuns reality far more than merely the erotic afflux would account for; therefore, his inner condition is very different from that of the hysteric. He is more than autoerotic, he builds up an intra-psychic equivalent for reality, for which purpose he has necessarily to employ other dynamics than that afforded by the erotic afflux. Therefore, I must grant to Bleuler the right to reject the conception of autoerotism, taken from the study of hysterical neuroses, and there legitimate, and to replace it by the conception of autismus.[30] I am forced to say that this term is better fitted to facts than autoerotism. With this I acknowledge my earlier idea of the identity of autismus (Bleuler) and autoerotism (Freud) as unjustified, and, therefore, retract it.[31] This thorough revision of the conception of libido has compelled me to this.

From these considerations it follows necessarily that the descriptive psychologic conception of libido must be given up in order for the libido theory to be applied to dementia præcox. That it is there applicable is best shown in Freud's brilliant investigation of Schreber's phantasies. The question now is whether this genetic conception of libido proposed by me is suitable for the neuroses. I believe that this question may be answered affirmatively. " Natura non fecit saltum "—it is not merely to be expected but it is also probable that at least temporary functional disturbances of various degrees appear in the neuroses, which transcend the boundaries of the immediate sexual; in any case, this occurs in psychotic episodes. I consider the broadening of the conception of libido which has developed through the most recent analytic work as a real advance which will prove of especial advantage in the important field of the introversion psychoses. Proofs of the correctness of my assumption are already at hand. It has become apparent through a series of researches of the Zurich School, which are now published in part,[32] that the phantastic substitution products which take the place of the disturbed function of reality bear unmistakable traces of archaic thought. This confirmation is parallel to the postulate asserted above, according to which reality is deprived, not merely of an immediate (individual) amount of libido, but also of an already differentiated or desexualized quantity of libido, which, among normal people, has belonged to the function of reality ever since prehistoric times. *A dropping away of the last acquisition of the function of reality (or adaptation) must of necessity be replaced by an earlier mode of adaptation.* We find this principle already in the doctrines of the neuroses, that is, that a repression resulting from the failure of the recent transference is replaced by an old way of transference, namely, through a regressive revival of the parent imago. In the transference neurosis (hysterical), where merely a part of the *immediate sexual* libido is taken away from reality by the specific sexual repression, the substituted product is a phantasy of individual origin and significance, with only a trace of those archaic traits found in the phantasies of those

mental disorders in which a portion of the general human
function of reality organized since antiquity has broken
off. This portion can be replaced only by a generally
valid archaic surrogate. We owe a simple and clear example of this proposition to the investigation of Honegger.[33] A paranoic of good intelligence who has a clear
idea of the spherical form of the earth and its rotation
around the sun replaces the modern astronomical views
by a system worked out in great detail, which one must
call archaic, in which the earth is a flat disc over which
the sun travels.[34] (I am reminded of the sun-phallus
mentioned in the first part of this book, for which we are
also indebted to Honegger.) Spielrein has likewise furnished some very interesting examples of archaic definitions which begin in certain illnesses to overlay the real
meanings of the modern word. For example, Spielrein's
patient had correctly discovered the mythological significance of alcohol, the intoxicating drink, to be " an effusion
of seed." [35] She also had a symbolism of boiling which I
must place parallel to the especially important alchemistic
vision of Zosimos,[36] who found people in boiling water
within the cavity of the altar.[37] This patient used earth
in place of mother, and also water to express mother.[38] I
refrain from further examples because future work of the
Zurich School will furnish abundant evidence of this sort.

My foregoing proposition of the replacement of the
disturbed function of reality by an archaic surrogate is
supported by an excellent paradox of Spielrein's. She
says: " I often had the illusion that these patients might

be simply victims of a folk superstition." As a matter of fact, patients substitute phantasies for reality, phantasies similar to the actually incorrect mental products of the past, which, however, were once the view of reality. As the Zosimos vision shows, the old superstitions were symbols [39] which permitted transitions to the most remote territory. This must have been very expedient for certain archaic periods, for by this means convenient bridges were offered to lead a partial amount of libido over into the mental realm. Evidently Spielrein thinks of a similar biological meaning of the symbols when she says: [40]

" Thus a symbol seems to me to owe its origin in general to the tendency of a complex for dissolution in the common totality of thought. . . . The complex is robbed by that of the personal element. . . . This tendency towards dissolution (transformation) of every individual complex is the motive for poetry, painting, for every sort of art."

When here we replace the formal conception " complex " by the conception of the quantity of libido (the total effect of the complex), which, from the standpoint of the libido theory, is a justified measure, then does Spielrein's view easily agree with mine. When primitive man understands in general what an act of generation is, then, according to the principle of the path of least resistance, he never can arrive at the idea of replacing the generative organs by a sword-blade or a shuttle; but this is the case with certain Indians, who explain the origin of mankind by the union of the two transference symbols. He then must be compelled to devise an analogous thing in order to bring a manifest sexual interest upon an asexual expression. The propelling motive of this transition of the *immediate sexual* libido to the non-sexual representation can, in my opinion, be found only in a *resistance which opposes primitive sexuality*.

It appears as if, by this means of phantastic analogy formation, more libido would gradually become desexualized, because increasingly more phantasy correlates were put in the place of the primitive achievement of the sexual libido. With this an enormous broadening of the world idea was gradually developed because new objects were always assimilated as sexual symbols. It is a question whether the human consciousness has not been brought to its present state entirely or in great part in this manner. It is evident, in any case, that an important significance in the development of the human mind is due to the impulse towards the discovery of analogy. We must agree thoroughly with Steinthal when he says that an absolutely overweening importance must be granted to the little phrase " Gleich wie " (even as) in the history of the development of thought. It is easy to believe that the carryover of the libido to a phantastic correlate has led primitive man to a number of the most important discoveries.

CHAPTER III

THE TRANSFORMATION OF THE LIBIDO. A POSSIBLE SOURCE OF PRIMITIVE HUMAN DISCOVERIES

In the following pages I will endeavor to picture a concrete example of the transition of the libido. I once treated a patient who suffered from a depressive catatonic condition. The case was one of only a slight introversion psychosis; therefore, the existence of many hysterical features was not surprising. In the beginning of the analytic treatment, while telling of a very painful occurrence she fell into a hysterical-dreamy state, in which she showed all signs of sexual excitement. For obvious reasons she lost the knowledge of my presence during this condition. The excitement led to a masturbative act (frictio femorum). This act was accompanied by a peculiar gesture. She made a very *violent rotary motion* with the forefinger of the left hand on the left temple, as if she were boring a hole there. Afterwards there was complete amnesia for what had happened, and there was nothing to be learned about the queer gesture with her hand. Although this act can easily be likened to a boring into the mouth, nose or ear, now transferred to the temple, it belongs in the territory of infantile ludus sexualis [1]—to the preliminary exercise preparatory to sexual activity. Without really understanding it, this gesture,

nevertheless, seemed very important to me. Many weeks
later I had an opportunity to speak to the patient's
mother, and from her I learned that her daughter had
been a very exceptional child. When only two years old
she would sit with her back to an open cupboard door for
hours and rhythmically beat her head against the door [2]—
to the distraction of the household. A little later, instead
of playing as other children, she began to bore a hole with
her finger in the plaster of the wall of the house. She
did this with little turning and scraping movements, and
kept herself busy at this occupation for hours. She was
a complete puzzle to her parents. From her fourth year
she practised onanism. It is evident that in this early
infantile activity the preliminary stage of the later trouble
may be found. The especially remarkable features in this
case are, first, that the child did not carry out the action
on its own body, and, secondly, the assiduity with which
it carried on the action.[3] One is tempted to bring these
two facts into a causal relationship and to say, because the
child does not accomplish this action on her own body,
perhaps that is the reason of the assiduity, for by boring
into the wall she never arrives at the same satisfaction as
if she executed the activity onanistically on her own body.

The very evident onanistic boring of the patient can be
traced back to a very early stage of childhood, which is
prior to the period of local onanism. That time is still
psychologically very obscure, because individual reproductions and memories are lacking to a great extent, the same
as among animals. The race characteristics (manner of
life) predominate during the entire life of the animal,

whereas among men the individual character asserts itself over the race type. Granting the correctness of this remark, we are struck with the apparently wholly incomprehensible individual activity of this child at this early age. We learn from her later life history that her development, which is, as is always the case, intimately interwoven with parallel external events, has led to that mental disturbance which is especially well known on account of its individuality and the originality of its productions, i. e. dementia præcox. The peculiarity of this disturbance, as we have pointed out above, depends upon the predominance of the phantastic form of thought—of the infantile in general. From this type of thinking proceed all those numerous contacts with mythological products, and that which we consider as original and wholly individual creations are very often creations which are comparable with nothing but those of antiquity. I believe that this comparison can be applied to all formations of this remarkable illness, and perhaps also to this special symptom of boring. We have already seen that the onanistic boring of the patient dated from a very early stage of childhood, that is to say, it was reproduced from that period of the past. The sick woman fell back for the first time into the early onanism only after she had been married many years, and following the death of her child, with whom she had identified herself through an overindulgent love. When the child died the still healthy mother was overcome by early infantile symptoms in the form of scarcely concealed fits of masturbation, which were associated with this very act of boring. As already observed, the primary boring appeared at a time which preceded the infantile onanism localized in the genitals. This fact is of significance in so far as this boring differs thereby from a similar later practice which appeared after the genital onanism. The later bad habits represent, as a rule, a substitution for repressed genital masturbation, or for an attempt in this direction. As such these habits (finger-sucking, biting the nails, picking at things, boring into the ears and nose, etc.) may persist far into adult life as regular symptoms of a repressed amount of libido.

As has already been shown above, the libido in youthful individuals at first manifests itself in the nutritional zone, when food is taken in the act of suckling with rhythmic movements and with every sign of satisfaction. With the growth of the individual and the development of his organs the libido creates for itself new avenues to supply its need of activity and satisfaction. The primary model of rhythmic activity, producing pleasure and satisfaction, must now be transferred to the zone of other functions, with sexuality as its final goal. A considerable part of the " hunger libido " is transferred into the " sexual libido." This transition does not take place suddenly at the time of puberty, as is generally supposed, but very gradually in the course of the greater part of childhood. The libido can free itself only with difficulty and very slowly from that which is peculiar to the function of nutrition, in order to enter into the peculiarity of the sexual function. Two periods are to be distinguished in this state of transition, so far as I can judge—*the epoch of suckling and the epoch of the displaced rhythmic activity.*

Suckling still belongs to the function of nutrition, but passes beyond it, however, in that it is no longer the function of nutrition, but rhythmic activity, with pleasure and satisfaction as a goal, without the taking of nourishment. Here the hand enters as an auxiliary organ. In the period of the displaced rhythmic activity the hand appears still more clearly as an auxiliary organ; the gaining of pleasure leaves the mouth zone and turns to other regions. The possibilities are now many. As a rule, other openings of the body become the objects of the libido interest; then the skin, and special portions of that. The activity expressed in these parts, which can appear as rubbing, boring, picking, and so on, follows a certain rhythm and serves to produce pleasure. After longer or shorter tarryings of the libido at these stations, it passes onward until it reaches the sexual zone, and there, for the first time, can be occasion for the beginning of onanistic attempts. In its migration the libido takes more than a little of the function of nutrition with it into the sexual zone, which readily accounts for the numerous and innate correlations between the functions of nutrition and sexuality. If, after the occupation of the sexual zone, an obstacle arises against the present form of application of the libido, then there occurs, according to the well-known laws, a regression to the nearest station lying behind, to the two abovementioned periods. It is now of special importance that the epoch of the displaced rhythmic activity coincides in a general way with the time of the development of the mind and of speech. I might designate the period from birth until the occupation of the sexual zone as the pre-

sexual stage of development. This generally occurs between the third and fifth year, and is comparable to the
chrysalis stage in butterflies. It is distinguished by the
irregular commingling of the elements of nutrition and of
sexual functions. Certain regressions follow directly back
to the presexual stage, and, judging from my experience,
this seems to be the rule in the regression of dementia
præcox. I will give two brief examples. One case concerns a young girl who developed a catatonic state during
her engagement. When she saw me for the first time, she
came up suddenly, embraced me, and said, " Papa, give
me something to eat." The other case concerns a young
maidservant who complained that people pursued her
with electricity and that this caused a queer feeling in her
genitals, " as if it ate and drank down there."

These regressive phenomena show that even from the
distance of the modern mind those early stages of the
libido can be regressively reached. One may assume,
therefore, that in the earliest states of human development this road was much more easily travelled than it is
to-day. It becomes then a matter of great interest to
learn whether traces of this have been preserved in
history.

We owe our knowledge of the ethnologic phantasy of
boring to the valuable work of Abraham,[4] who also refers
us to the writings of Adalbert Kuhn.[5] Through this investigation we learn that Prometheus, the fire-bringer,
may be a brother of the Hindoo Pramantha, that is to
say, of the masculine fire-rubbing piece of wood. The
Hindoo fire-bringer is called Mâtariçvan, and the activity

of the fire preparation is always designated in the hieratic text by the verb " manthâmi," [6] which means *shaking, rubbing, bringing forth by rubbing.* Kuhn has put this verb in connection with the Greek μανθάνω, which means " to learn," and has explained this conceptual relationship.[7] The " tertium comparationis " might lie in the rhythm, the movement to and fro in the mind. According to Kuhn, the root " manth" or " math " must be traced. from μανθάνω (μάθημα, μάθησις) to προ-μηθέομαι to Προμηθεύς,* who is the Greek fire-robber. Through an unauthorized Sanskrit word " pramâthyus," which comes by way of " pramantha," and which possesses the double meaning of " Rubber " and " Robber," the transition to Prometheus was effected. With that, however, the prefix " pra " caused special difficulty, so that the whole derivation was doubted by a series of authors, and was held, in part, as erroneous. On the other hand, it was pointed out that as the Thuric Zeus bore the especially interesting cognomen Προ-μανθεύς, thus Προ-μηθεύς might not be an original Indo-Germanic stem word that was related to the Sanskrit " pramantha," but might represent only a cognomen. This interpretation is supported by a gloss of Hesychius, Ἰθάς: ὁ τῶν Τιτάνων κήρυξ Προμηθεύς.† Another gloss of Hesychius explains ἰθαίνομαι (ἰαίνω) as θερμαίνομαι, through which Ἰθάς attains the meaning of " the flaming one," analogous to Αἴθων or Φλεγύας.[8] The relation of Prometheus to

---

*I learn (that which is learned, knowledge; the act of learning), to take thought beforehand, to Prometheus (forethought).

† Prometheus, the herald of the Titans.

pramantha could scarcely be so direct as Kuhn conjectures. The question of an indirect relation is not decided with that. Above all, Προμηθεύς is of great significance as a surname for Ἰθάς, since the " flaming one " is the " fore-thinker." (Pramati = precaution is also an attribute of Agni, although pramati is of another derivation.) Prometheus, however, belongs to the line of Phlegians which was placed by Kuhn in uncontested relationship to the Indian priest family of Bhrgu.⁹ The Bhrgu are like Mâtariçvan (the " one swelling in the mother "), also fire-bringers. Kuhn quotes a passage, according to which Bhrgu also arises from the flame like Agni. (" In the flame Bhrgu originated. Bhrgu roasted, but did not burn.") This view leads to a root related to Bhrgu, that is to say, to the Sanskrit bhrây = to light, Latin fulgeo and Greek φλέγω (Sanskrit bhargas = splendor, Latin fulgur). Bhrgu appears, therefore, as " the shining one." Φλεγύας means a certain species of eagle, on account of its burnished gold color. The connection with φλέγειν, which signifies " to burn," is clear. The Phlegians are also the fire eagles.¹⁰ Prometheus also belongs to the Phlegians. The path from Pramantha to Prometheus passes not through the word, but through the idea, and, therefore, we should adopt this same meaning for Prometheus as that which Pramantha attains from the Hindoo fire symbolism.¹¹

The Pramantha, as the tool of Manthana (the fire sacrifice), is considered purely sexual in the Hindoo; the Pramantha as phallus, or man; the bored wood underneath as vulva, or woman.¹² The resulting fire is the child, the divine son Agni. The two pieces of wood are called in the cult Purûravas and Urvaçî, and were thought of personified as man and woman. The fire was born from the genitals of the woman.[13] An especially interesting representation of fire production, as a religious ceremony (manthana), is given by Weber:[14]

" A certain sacrificial fire was lit by the rubbing together of two sticks; one piece of wood is taken up with the words: ' Thou art the birthplace of the fire,' and two blades of grass are placed upon it; ' Ye are the two testicles,' to the ' adhârarani ' (the underlying wood) : ' Thou art Urvaçî '; then the utarârani (that which is placed on top) is anointed with butter. ' Thou art Power.' This is then placed on the adhârarani. ' Thou art Purûravas ' and both are rubbed three times. ' I rub thee with the Gâyatrîmetrum: I rub thee with the Trishtubhmetrum: I rub thee with the Jagatîmetrum.' "

The sexual symbolism of this fire production is unmistakable. We see here also the rhythm, the metre in its original place as sexual rhythm, rising above the mating call into music. A song of the Rigveda [15] conveys the same interpretation and symbolism :

" Here is the gear for function, here tinder made ready for the spark.
Bring thou the matron: [16] we will rub Agni in ancient fashion forth.
In the two fire-sticks Jâtavedas lieth, even as the well-formed germ in pregnant women;
Agni who day by day must be exalted by men who watch and worship with oblations;
Lay this with care on that which lies extended: straight hath she borne the steer when made prolific.

With his red pillar—radiant in his splendor—in our skilled
task is born the son of Ilâ." [17]—*Book III.* xxix: 1-3.

Side by side with the unequivocal coitus symbolism we
see that the Pramantha is also Agni, the created son.
The Phallus is the son, or the son is the Phallus. Therefore, Agni in the Vedic mythology has the threefold character. With this we are once more connected with the
above-mentioned Cabiric Father-Son-Cult. In the modern
German language we have preserved echoes of the primitive symbols. A boy is designated as "bengel" (short,
thick piece of wood). In Hessian as "stift" or "bol-
zen" (arrow,[18] wooden peg or stump). The Artemisia
Abrotanum, which is called in German "Stabwurz"
(stick root), is called in English "Boy's Love." (The
vulgar designation of the penis as "boy" was remarked
even by Grimm and others.) The ceremonial production
of fire was retained in Europe as late as the nineteenth
century as a superstitious custom. Kuhn mentions such a
case even in the year 1828, which occurred in Germany.
The solemn, magic ceremony was called the "Nodfyr"
—"The fire of need" [19]—and the charm was chiefly used
against cattle epidemics. Kuhn cites from the chronicle
of Lanercost of the year 1268 an especially noteworthy
case of the "Nodfyr,"[20] the ceremonies of which plainly
reveal the fundamental phallic meaning:

"Pro fidei divinæ integritate servanda recolat lector, quod cum
hoc anno in Laodonia pestis grassaretur in pecudes armenti, quam
vocant usetati Lungessouht, quidam bestiales, habitu claustrales
non animo, docebant idiotas patriæ ignem confrictione de lignis
educere et simulacrum Priapi statuere, et per haec bestiis succur-

rere. Quod cum unus laicus Cisterciensis apud Fentone fecisset ante atrium aulæ, ac intinctis testiculis canis in aquam benedictam super animalis sparsisset, etc." *

These examples, which allow us to recognize a clear sexual symbolism in the generation of fire, prove, therefore, since they originate from different times and different peoples, the existence of a universal tendency to credit to fire production not only a magical but also a sexual significance. This ceremonial or magic repetition of this very ancient, long-outlived observance shows how insistently the human mind clings to the old forms, and how deeply rooted is this very ancient reminiscence of fire boring. One might almost be inclined to see in the sexual symbolism of fire production a relatively late addition to the priestly lore. This may, indeed, be true for the ceremonial elaboration of the fire mysteries, but whether originally the generation of fire was in general a sexual action, that is to say, a " coitus-play," is still a question. That similar things occur among very primitive people we learn from the Australian tribe of the Watschandies,[21] who in the spring perform the following magic ceremonies of fertilization: They dig a hole in the ground, so formed and surrounded with bushes as to

* Instead of preserving the divine faith in its purity, the reader will call to mind the fact that in this year when the plague, usually called Lung sickness, attacked the herds of cattle in Laodonia, certain bestial men, monks in dress but not in spirit, taught the ignorant people of their country to make fire by rubbing wood together and to set up a statue of Priapus, and by that method to succor the cattle. After a Cistercian lay brother had done this near Fentone, in front of the entrance of the " Court," he sprinkled the animals with holy water and with the preserved testicles of a dog, etc.

counterfeit a woman's genitals. They dance the night long around this hole; in connection with this they hold spears in front of themselves in a manner to recall the penis in erection. They dance around the hole and thrust their spears into the ditch, while they cry to it, " Pulli nira, pulli nira, wataka! " (non fossa, non fossa, sed cunnus!) Such obscene dances appear among other primitive races as well.[22]

In this spring incantation are contained the elements of the coitus play.[23] This play is nothing but a coitus game, that is to say, originally this play was simply a coitus in the form of sacramental mating, which for a long time was a mysterious element among certain cults, and reappeared in sects.[24] In the ceremonies of Zinzendorf's followers echoes of the coitus sacrament may be recognized; also in other sects.

One can easily think that just as the above-mentioned Australian bushmen perform the coitus play in this manner the same performance could be enacted in another manner, and, indeed, in the form of fire production. Instead of through two selected human beings, the coitus was represented by two substitutes, by Purûravas and Urvaçi, by Phallus and Vulva, by borer and opening. Just as the primitive thought behind other customs is really the sacramental coition so here the primal tendency is really the act itself. For the act of fertilization is the climax—the true festival of life, and well worthy to become the nucleus of a religious mystery. If we are justified in concluding that the symbolism of the hole in the earth used by the Watschandies for the fertilization of

the earth takes the place of the coitus, then the generation of fire could be considered in the same way as a
substitute for coitus; and, indeed, it might be further concluded as a consequence of this reasoning that the invention of fire-making is also due to the need of supplying a
symbol for the sexual act.[25]

Let us return, for a moment, to the infantile symptom
of boring. Let us imagine a strong adult man carrying
on the boring with two pieces of wood with the same perseverance and the energy corresponding to that of this
child. He may very easily create fire by this play. But
of greatest significance in this work is the rhythm.[26] This
hypothesis seems to me psychologically possible, although
it should not be said with this that only in this way could
the discovery of fire occur. It can result just as well by
the striking together of flints. It is scarcely possible that
fire was created in only one way. All I want to establish
here is merely the psychologic process, the symbolic indications of which point to the possibility that in such a
way was fire invented or prepared.

The existence of the primitive coitus play or rite seems
to me sufficiently proven. The only thing that is obscure
is the energy and emphasis of the ritual play. It is well
known that those primitive rites were often of very bloody
seriousness, and were performed with an extraordinary
display of energy, which appears as a great contrast to
the well-known indolence of primitive humanity. Therefore, the ritual activity entirely loses the character of play,
and wins that of purposeful effort. If certain Negro
races can dance the whole night long to three tones in

the most monotonous manner, then, according to our idea, there is in this an absolute lack of the character of play pastime; it approaches nearer to exercise. There seems to exist a sort of compulsion to transfer the libido into such ritual activity. If the basis of the ritual activity is the sexual act, we may assume that it is really the underlying thought and object of the exercise. Under these circumstances, the question arises why the primitive man endeavors to represent the sexual act symbolically and with effort, or, if this wording appears to be too hypothetical, why does he exert energy to such a degree only to accomplish practically useless things, which apparently do not especially amuse him? [27] It may be assumed that the sexual act is more desirable to primitive man than such absurd and, moreover, fatiguing exercises. It is hardly possible but that a certain compulsion conducts the energy away from the original object and real purpose, inducing the production of surrogates. The existence of a phallic or orgiastic cult does not indicate *eo ipso* a particularly lascivious life any more than the ascetic symbolism of Christianity means an especially moral life. One honors that which one does not possess or that which one is not. This compulsion, to speak in the nomenclature formulated above, removes a certain amount of libido from the real sexual activity, and creates a symbolic and practically valid substitute for what is lost. This psychology is confirmed by the above-mentioned Watschandie ceremony; during the entire ceremony none of the men may look at a woman. This detail again informs us from whence the libido is to be diverted. But this gives rise to the pressing question, Whence comes this compulsion? We have already suggested above that the primitive sexuality encounters a resistance which leads to a side-tracking of the libido on to substitution actions (analogy, symbolism, etc.). It is unthinkable that it is a question of any outer opposition whatsoever, or of a real obstacle, since it occurs to no savage to catch his elusive quarry with ritual charms; but it is a question of an internal resistance; will opposes will; libido opposes libido, since a psychologic resistance as an energic phenomenon corresponds to a certain amount of libido. The psychologic compulsion for the transformation of the libido is based on an original division of the will. I will return to this primal splitting of the libido in another place. Here let us concern ourselves only with the problem of the transition of the libido. The transition takes place, as has been repeatedly suggested by means of shifting to an analogy. The libido is taken away from its proper place and transferred to another substratum.

The resistance against sexuality aims, therefore, at preventing the sexual act; it also seeks to crowd the libido away from the sexual function. We see, for example, in hysteria, how the specific repression blocks the real path of transference; therefore, the libido is obliged to take another path, and that an earlier one, namely, the incestuous road which ultimately leads to the parents. Let us speak, however, of the incest prohibition, which hindered the very first sexual transference. Then the situation changes in so far that no earlier way of transference is left, except that of the presexual stage of development,

where the libido was still partly in the function of nutrition. By a regression to the presexual material the libido
becomes quasi-desexualized. But as the incest prohibition
signifies only a temporary and conditional restriction of
the sexuality, thus only that part of the libido which is
best designated as the incestuous component is now
pushed back to the presexual stage. The repression,
therefore, concerns only that part of the sexual libido
which wishes to fix itself permanently upon the parents.
The sexual libido is only withdrawn from the incestuous
component, repressed upon the presexual stage, and
there, if the operation is successful, desexualized, by
which this amount of libido is prepared for an asexual
application. However, it is to be assumed that this operation is accomplished only with difficulty, because the
incestuous libido, so to speak, must be artificially separated from the sexual libido, with which, for ages, through
the whole animal kingdom, it was indistinguishably united.
The regression of the incestuous component must, therefore, take place, not only with great difficulty, but also
carry with it into the presexual stage a considerable
sexual character. The consequence of this is that the resulting phenomena, although stamped with the character
of the sexual act, are, nevertheless, not really sexual acts
de facto; they are derived from the presexual stage, and
are maintained by the repressed sexual libido, therefore
possess a double significance. Thus the fire boring is a
coitus (and, to be sure, an incestuous one), but a desexualized one, which has lost its immediate sexual worth, and
is, therefore, indirectly useful to the propagation of the

species. The presexual stage is characterized by count-less possibilities of application, because the libido has not yet formed definite localizations. It therefore appears intelligible that an amount of libido which reaches this stage through regression is confronted with manifold pos-sibilities of application. Above all, it is met with the possibility of a purely onanistic activity. But as the mat-ter in question in the regressive component of libido is sexual libido, the ultimate object of which is propagation, therefore it goes to the external object (Parents); it will also introvert with this destination as its essential char-acter. The result, therefore, is that the purely onanistic activity turns out to be insufficient, and another object must be sought for, which takes the place of the incest object. The nurturing mother earth represents the ideal example of such an object. The psychology of the pre-sexual stage contributes the nutrition component; the sexual libido the coitus idea. From this the ancient sym-bols of agriculture arise. In the work of agriculture hunger and incest intermingle. The ancient cults of mother earth and all the superstitions founded thereon saw in the cultivation of the earth the fertilization of the mother. The aim of the action is desexualized, however, for it is the fruit of the field and the nourishment con-tained therein. The regression resulting from the incest prohibition leads, in this case, to the new valuation of the mother; this time, however, not as a sexual object, but as a nourisher.

The discovery of fire seems to be due to a very similar regression to the pre-sexual stage, more particularly to the nearest stage of the displaced rhythmic manifestation. The libido, introverted from the incest prohibition (with the more detailed designation of the motor components of coitus), when it reaches the presexual stage, meets the related infantile boring, to which it now gives, in accordance with its realistic destination, an actual material. (Therefore the material is fittingly called " materia," as the object is the mother as above.) As I sought to show above, the action of the infantile boring requires only the strength and perseverance of an adult man and suitable " material " in order to generate fire. If this is so, it may be expected that analogous to our foregoing case of onanistic boring the generation of fire originally occurred as such an act of quasi-onanistic activity, objectively expressed. The demonstration of this can never be actually furnished, but it is thinkable that somewhere traces of this original onanistic preliminary exercise of fire production have been preserved. I have succeeded in finding a passage in a very old monument of Hindoo literature which contains this transition of the sexual libido through the onanistic phase in the preparation of fire. This passage is found in Brihadâranyaka-Upanishad: [28]

" In truth, he (Âtman) [29] was as large as a woman and a man, when they embrace each other. This, his own self, he divided into two parts, out of which husband and wife were formed. [30] With her, he copulated; from this humanity sprang. She, however, pondered: ' How may he unite with me after he has created me from himself? Now I shall hide! ' Then she became a cow; he, however, became a bull and mated with her. From that sprang the horned cattle. Then she became a mare; he, however, became a stallion; she became a she-ass; he, an ass, and mated with her. From these sprang the whole-hoofed animals. She became a goat; he became a buck; she became an ewe; he became a ram, and mated with her. Thus were created goats and sheep. Thus it happened that all that mates, even down to the ants, he created —then he perceived: 'Truly I myself am Creation, for I have created the whole world!' Thereupon he rubbed his hands (held before the mouth) so that he brought forth fire from his mouth, as from the mother womb, and from his hands."

We meet here a peculiar myth of creation which requires a psychologic interpretation. In the beginning the libido was undifferentiated and bisexual;[31] this was followed by differentiation into a male and a female component. From then on man knows what he is. Now follows a gap in the coherence of the thought where belongs that very resistance which we have postulated above for the explanation of the urge for sublimation. Next follows the onanistic act of rubbing or boring (here finger-sucking) transferred from the sexual zone, from which proceeds the production of fire.[32] The libido here leaves its characteristic manifestation as sexual function and regresses to the presexual stage, where, in conformity with the above explanation, it occupies one of the preliminary stages of sexuality, thereby producing, in the view expressed in the Upanishad, the first human art, and from there, as suggested by Kuhn's idea of the root "manth," perhaps the higher intellectual activity in general. This course of development is not strange to the psychiatrist, for it is a well-known psychopathological fact that onanism and excessive activity of phantasy are very closely related. (The sexualizing-autonomizing of the

mind through autoerotism [33] is so familiar a fact that
examples of that are superfluous.)   The course of the
libido, as we may conclude from these studies, originally
proceeded in a similar manner as in the child, only in a
reversed sequence.   The sexual act was pushed out of its
proper zone and was transferred into the analogous
mouth zone [34]—the mouth receiving the significance of the
female genitals; the hand and the fingers, respectively, receiving the phallic meaning. [35]   In this manner the regressively reoccupied activity of the presexual stage is invested
with the sexual significance, which, indeed, it already
possessed, in part, before, but in a wholly different sense.
Certain functions of the presexual stage are found to be
permanently suitable, and, therefore, are retained later
on as sexual functions.   Thus, for example, the mouth
zone is retained as of erotic importance, meaning that its
valuation is permanently fixed.   Concerning the mouth,
we know that it also has a sexual meaning among animals,
inasmuch as, for example, stallions bite mares in the sexual
act; also, cats, cocks, etc.   A second significance of the
mouth is as an instrument of speech, it serves essentially
in the production of the mating call, which mostly represents the developed tones of the animal kingdom.   As to
the hand, we know that it has the important significance
of the contrectation organ (for example, among frogs).
The frequent erotic use of the hand among monkeys is
well known.   If there exists a resistance against the real
sexuality, then the accumulated libido is most likely to
cause a hyperfunction of those collaterals which are most
adapted to compensate for the resistance, that is to say,

the nearest functions which serve for the introduction of the act;[36] on one side the function of the hand, on the other that of the mouth. The sexual act, however, against which the opposition is directed is replaced by a similar act of the presexual stage, the classic case being either finger-sucking or boring. Just as among apes the foot can on occasions take the place of the hand, so the child is often uncertain in the choice of the object to suck, and puts the big toe in the mouth instead of the finger. This last movement belongs to a Hindoo rite, only the big toe was not put in the mouth, but held against the eye.[37] Through the sexual significance of the hand and mouth these organs, which in the presexual stage served to obtain pleasure, are invested with a procreating power which is identical with the above-mentioned destination, which aims at the external object, because it concerns the sexual or creating libido. When, through the actual preparation of fire, the sexual character of the libido employed in that is fulfilled, then the mouth zone remains without adequate expression; only the hand has now reached its real, purely human goal in its first art.

The mouth has, as we saw, a further important function, which has just as much sexual relation to the object as the hand, that is to say, the production of the mating call. In opening up the autoerotic ring (hand-mouth),[38] where the phallic hand became the fire-producing tool, the libido which was directed to the mouth zone was obliged to seek another path of functioning, which naturally was found in the already existing love call. The excess of libido entering here must have had the usual results, namely, the stimulation of the newly possessed function; hence an elaboration of the mating call.

We know that from the primitive sounds human speech has developed. Corresponding to the psychological situation, it might be assumed that language owes its real origin to this moment, when the impulse, repressed into the presexual stage, turns to the external in order to find an equivalent object there. The real thought as a conscious activity is, as we saw in the first part of this book, a thinking with positive determination towards the external world, that is to say, a " speech thinking." This sort of thinking seems to have originated at that moment. It is very remarkable that this view, which was won by the path of reasoning, is again supported by old tradition and other mythological fragments.

In Aitareyopanishad [39] the following quotation is to be found in the doctrine of the development of man: " Being brooded-o'er, his mouth hatched out, like as an egg; from out his mouth (came) speech, from speech, the fire." In Part II, where it is depicted how the newly created objects entered man, it reads: " Fire, speech becoming, entered in the mouth." These quotations allow us to plainly recognize the intimate connection between fire and speech. [40] In Brihadâranyaka-Upanishad is to be found this passage:

" ' Yayñavalkya,' thus he spake, ' when after the death of this man his speech entereth the fire, his breath into the wind, his eye into the sun, etc.' "

A further quotation from the Brihadâranyaka-Upanishad reads:

" But when the sun is set, O Yayñavalkya, and the moon has set, and the fire is extinguished, what then serves man as light? Then speech serves him as light; then, by the light of speech he sits, and moves, he carries on his work, and he returns home. But when the sun is set, O Yayñavalkya, and the moon is set, and the fire extinguished, and the voice is dumb, what then serves man as light? Then he serves himself (Atman) as light; then, by the light of himself, he sits and moves, carries on his work and returns home."

In this passage we notice that fire again stands in the closest relation to speech. Speech itself is called a " light," which, in its turn, is reduced to the " light " of the Atman, the creating psychic force, the libido. Thus the Hindoo metapsychology conceives speech and fire as emanations of the inner light from which we know that it is libido. Speech and fire are its forms of manifestation, the first human arts, which have resulted from its transformation. This common psychologic origin seems also to be indicated by certain results of philology. The Indo-Germanic root *bhâ* designates the idea of " to lighten, to shine." This root is found in Greek, φάω, φαίνω, φάος*; in old Icelandic *bán* = white, in New High German *bohnen* = to make shining. The same root *bhâ* also designates " to speak "; it is found in Sanskrit *bhan* = to speak, Armenian *ban* = word, in New High German *bann* = to banish, Greek φā-μί, ἔφαν, φάτις.† Latin *fâ-ri*, *fânum*.

The root *bhelso*, with the meanings " to ring, to bark," is found in Sanskrit *bhas* = to bark and *bhâs* = to talk,

---

* To shine; to show forth; reveal;—light.
† I said; they said; a saying; an oracle.

to speak; Lithuanian *balsas* = voice, tone. Really *bhel-sô* = to be bright or luminous. Compare Greek φάλος = bright, Lithuanian *bálti* = to become white, Middle High German *blasz* = pale.

The root *lâ*, with the meaning of "to make sound, to bark," is found in Sanskrit *las, lásati* = to resound; and *las, lásati* = to radiate, to shine.

The related root *lesô*, with the meaning "desire," is also found in Sanskrit *las, lásati* = to play; *lash, láshati* = to desire. Greek λάσταυρος = lustful, Gothic *lustus*, New High German *Lust*, Latin *lascivus*.

A further related root, *lásô* = to shine, to radiate, is found in *las, lásati* = to radiate, to shine.

This group unites, as is evident, the meanings of "to desire, to play, to radiate, and to sound." A similar archaic confluence of meanings in the primal libido symbolism (as we are perhaps justified in calling it) is found in that class of Egyptian words which are derived from the closely related roots *ben* and *bel* and the reduplication *benben* and *belbel*. The original significance of these roots is "to burst forth, to emerge, to extrude, to well out," with the associated idea of bubbling, boiling and roundness. *Belbel*, accompanied by the sign of the obelisk, of originally phallic nature, means source of light. The obelisk itself had besides the names of *techenu* and *men* also the name *benben*, more rarely *berber* and *belbel*.[41] The libido symbolism makes clear this connection, it seems to me.

The Indo-Germanic root *vel*, with the meaning "to wave, to undulate" (fire), is found in Sanskrit *ulunka*

= burning, Greek ἀλέα, Attic ἀλέα = warmth of the sun, Gothic *vulan* = to undulate, Old High German and Middle High German *walm* = heat, glow.

The related Indo-Germanic root *vélkô*, with the meaning of "to lighten, to glow," is found in Sanskrit *ulkă* = firebrand, Greek Ϝελχᾶνος = Vulcan. This same root *vel* means also "to sound"; in Sanskrit *vâni* = tone, song, music. Tschech *volati* = to call.

The root *svénô* = to sound, to ring, is found in Sanskrit *svan*, *svánati* = to rustle, to sound; Zend *qanañt*, Latin *sonâre*, Old Iranian *senm*, Cambrian *sain*, Latin *sonus*, Anglo-Saxon *svinsian* = to resound. The related root *svénos* = noise, sound, is found in Vedic *svánas* = noise, Latin *sonor*, *sonorus*. A further related root is *svonós* = tone, noise; in Old Iranian *son* = word.

The root *své* (n), locative *svéni*, dative *sunéi*, means sun; in Zend *qeñg* = sun. (Compare above *svénô*, Zend *qanañt*); Gothic *sun-na*, *sunnô*.[42] Here Goethe has preceded us:

> "The sun orb sings in emulation,
>   'Mid brother-spheres, his ancient round:
>   His path predestined through Creation,
>   He ends with step of thunder sound."
>   —*Faust.* Part I.

> "Hearken! Hark! the hours careering!
>   Sounding loud to spirit-hearing,
>   See the new-born Day appearing!
>   Rocky portals jarring shatter,
>   Phœbus' wheels in rolling clatter,
>   With a crash the Light draws near!
>   Pealing rays and trumpet-blazes,
>   Eye is blinded, ear amazes;

> The Unheard can no one hear!
> Slip within each blossom-bell,
> Deeper, deeper, there to dwell,—
> In the rocks, beneath the leaf!
> If it strikes you, you are deaf."
>
> —*Faust*.   Part II.

We also must not forget the beautiful verse of Hölderlin:

> "Where art thou?   Drunken, my soul dreams
> Of all thy rapture.   Yet even now I hearken
> As full of golden tones the radiant sun youth
> Upon his heavenly lyre plays his even song
> To the echoing woods and hills."

Just as in archaic speech fire and the speech sounds (the mating call, music) appear as forms of emanation of the libido, thus light and sound entering the psyche become one: libido.

Manilius expresses it in his beautiful verses:

> "Quid mirum noscere mundum
> Si possunt homines, quibus est et mundus in ipsis
> Exemplumque dei quisque est in imagine parva?
> An quoquam genitos nisi cælo credere fas est
> Esse homines?
>   Stetit unus in arcem
> Erectus capitis victorque ad sidera mittit sidereos oculos." *

The idea of the Sanskrit *têjas* suggests the fundamental significance of the libido for the conception of the world in general.   I am indebted to Dr. Abegg, in Zurich, a

* Why is it wonderful to understand the universe, if men are able? i.e., men in whose very being the universe exists and each one (of whom) is a representative of God in miniature?   Or is it right to believe that men have sprung in any way except from heaven—He alone stands in the midst of the citadel, a conqueror, his head erect and his shining eyes fixed on the stars.

thorough Sanskrit scholar, for the compilation of the eight meanings of this word.

Têjas signifies:

1. Sharpness, cutting edge.
2. Fire, splendor, light, glow, heat.
3. Healthy appearance, beauty.
4. The fiery and color-producing power of the human organism (thought to be in the bile).
5. Power, energy, vital force.
6. Passionate nature.
7. Mental, also magic, strength; influence, position, dignity.
8. Sperma.

This gives us a dim idea of how, for primitive thought, the so-called objective world was, and had to be, a subjective image. To this thought must be applied the words of the " Chorus Mysticus ":

> " All that is perishable
> Is only an allegory."

The Sanskrit word for fire is *agnis* (the Latin *ignis*) ; [43] the fire personified is the god Agni, the divine mediator, [44] whose symbol has certain points of contact with that of Christ. In Avesta and in the Vedas the fire is the messenger of the gods. In the Christian mythology certain parts are closely related with the myth of Agni. Daniel speaks of the three men in the fiery furnace:

" Then Nebuchadnezar, the King, was astonished, and rose up in haste and spake, and said unto his counsellors: ' Did not we cast three men bound into the midst of the fire? '

" They answered and said: ' True, O King! '

" He answered and said: ' Lo, I see four men loose, walking in the midst of the fire, and they have no hurt; and the form of the fourth is like the Son of God.' "

In regard to that the " Biblia pauperum " observes (according to an old German incunabulum of 1471) :

" One reads in the third chapter of the prophet Daniel that Nebuchadnezar, the King, caused three men to be placed in a glowing furnace and that the king often went there, looked in, and that he saw with the three, a fourth, who was like the Son of God. The three signify for us, the Holy Trinity and the fourth, the unity of the being. Christ, too, in His explanation designated the person of the Trinity and the unity of the being."

According to this mystic interpretation, the legend of the three men in the fiery furnace appears as a magic fire ceremony by means of which the Son of God reveals himself. The Trinity is brought together with the unity, or, in other words, through coitus a child is produced. The glowing furnace (like the glowing tripod in " Faust ") is a mother symbol, where the children are produced.[45] The fourth in the fiery furnace appears as Christ, the Son of God, who has become a visible God in the fire. The mystic trinity and unity are sexual symbols. (Compare with that the many references in Inman: " Ancient Pagan and Modern Christian Symbolism.") It is said of the Saviour of Israel (the Messiah) and of his enemies, Isaiah x: 17:

" And the light of Israel shall be for a fire, and his Holy One for a flame."

In a hymn of the Syrian Ephrem it is said of Christ:

" Thou who art all fire, have mercy upon me."

Agni is the sacrificial flame, the sacrificer, and the sacrificed, as Christ himself. Just as Christ left behind his redeeming blood, φάρμακον ἀθανασίας,* in the stimulating wine, so Agni is the Soma, the holy drink of inspiration, the mead of immortality.[46] Soma and Fire are entirely identical in Hindoo literature, so that in Soma we easily rediscover the libido symbol, through which a series of apparently paradoxical qualities of the Soma are immediately explained. As the old Hindoos recognized in fire an emanation of the inner libido fire, so too they recognized, in the intoxicating drink (Firewater, Soma-Agni, as rain and fire), an emanation of libido. The Vedic definition of Soma as seminal fluid confirms this interpretation.[47] The Soma significance of fire, similar to the significance of the body of Christ in the Last Supper (compare the Passover lamb of the Jews, baked in the form of a cross), is explained by the psychology of the presexual stage, where the libido was still in part the function of nutrition. The "Soma" is the "nourishing drink," the mythological characterization of which runs parallel to fire in its origin; therefore, both are united in Agni. The drink of immortality was stirred by the Hindoo gods like fire. Through the retreat of the libido into the presexual stage it becomes clear why so many gods were either defined sexually or were devoured.

As was shown by our discussion of fire preparation, the fire tool did not receive its sexual significance as a later addition, but the sexual libido was the motor power which led to its discovery, so that the later teachings of the

* A potion of immortality.

priests were nothing but confirmations of its actual origin.
Other primitive discoveries probably have acquired their
sexual symbolism in the same manner, being also derived
from the sexual libido.

In the previous statements, which were based on the
Pramantha of the Agni sacrifice, we have concerned ourselves only with one significance of the word manthâmi
or mathnâmi, that is to say, with that which expresses
the movement of rubbing. As Kuhn shows, however, this
word also possesses the meaning of tearing off, taking
away by violence, robbing.[48] As Kuhn points out, this
significance is already extant in the Vedic text. The
legend of its discovery always expresses the production of
fire as a robbery. (In this far it belongs to the motive
widely spread over the earth of the treasure difficult to
attain.) The fact that in many places and not alone in
India the preparation of fire is represented as having its
origin in robbery, seems to point to a widely spread
thought, according to which the preparation of fire was
something forbidden, something usurped or criminal,
which could be obtained only through stratagem or deeds
of violence (mostly through stratagem).[49] When onanism confronts the physician as a symptom it does so frequently under the symbol of secret pilfering, or crafty
imposition, which always signifies the concealed fulfilment of a forbidden wish.[50] Historically, this train of
thought probably implies that the ritual preparation of
fire was employed with a magic purpose, and, therefore,
was pursued by official religions; then it became a ritual
mystery,[51] guarded by the priests and surrounded with

secrecy.   The ritual laws of the Hindoos threaten with severe punishment him who prepares fire in an incorrect manner.   The fact alone that something is mysterious means the same as something done in concealment; that which must remain secret, which one may not see nor do; also something which is surrounded by severe punishment of body and soul; therefore, presumably, *something forbidden* which has received a license as a religious rite. After all has been said about the genesis of the preparation of fire, it is no longer difficult to guess what is the forbidden thing; *it is onanism.*   When I stated before that it might be lack of satisfaction which breaks up the autoerotic ring of the displaced sexual activity transferred to the body itself, and thus opens wider fields of culture, I did not mention that this loosely closed ring of the displaced onanistic activity could be much more firmly closed, when man makes the other great discovery, that of true onanism.[52]   With that the activity is started in the proper place, and this, under certain circumstances, may mean a satisfaction sufficient for a long time, but at the expense of cheating sexuality of its real purpose.   It is a fraud upon the natural development of things, because all the dynamic forces which can and should serve the development of culture are withdrawn from it through onanism, since, instead of the displacement, a regression to the local sexual takes place, which is precisely the opposite of that which is desirable.   Psychologically, however, onanism is a discovery of a significance not to be undervalued.   One is protected from fate, since no sexual need then has the power to give one up to life.   For with onanism one has the greatest magic in one's hands; one needs only to phantasy, and with that to masturbate, then one possesses all the pleasure of the world, and is no longer compelled to conquer the world of one's desires through hard labor and wrestling with reality.[53] Aladdin rubs his lamp and the obedient genii stand at his bidding; thus the fairy tale expresses the great psychologic advantage of the easy regression to the local sexual satisfaction. Aladdin's symbol subtly confirms the ambiguity of the magic fire preparation.

The close relation of the generation of fire to the onanistic act is illustrated by a case, the knowledge of which I owe to Dr. Schmid, in Cery, that of an imbecile peasant youth who set many incendiary fires. At one of these conflagrations he drew suspicion to himself by his behavior. He stood with his hands in his trouser pockets in the door of an opposite house and gazed with apparent delight at the fire. Under examination in the insane asylum, he described the fire in great detail, and made suspicious movements in his trouser pockets with his hands. The physical examination undertaken at once showed that he had masturbated. Later he confessed that he had masturbated at the time when he had enjoyed the fire which he had enkindled himself.

The preparation of fire in itself is a perfectly ordinary useful custom, employed everywhere for many centuries, which in itself involved nothing more mysterious than eating and drinking. However, there was always a tendency from time to time to prepare fire in a ceremonious and mysterious manner (exactly as with ritual eating and

drinking), which was to be carried out in an exactly pre-
scribed way and from which no one dared differ. This
mysterious tendency associated with the technique is the
second path in the onanistic regression, always present
by the side of culture. The strict rules applied to it,
the zeal of the ceremonial preparations and the religious
awe of the mysteries next originate from this source;
the ceremonial, although apparently irrational, is an extremely ingenious institution from the psychologic standpoint, for it represents a substitute for the possibility of
onanistic regression accurately circumscribed by law.
The law cannot apply to the content of the ceremony, for
it is really quite indifferent for the ritual act, whether it
is carried out in this way or in that way. On the contrary, it is very essential whether the restrained libido is
discharged through a sterile onanism or transposed into
the path of sublimation. These severe measures of protection apply primarily to onanism.[54]

I am indebted to Freud for a further important reference to the onanistic nature of the fire theft, or rather
the motive of *the treasure difficult of attainment* (to
which fire theft belongs). Mythology contains repeated
formulas which read approximately as follows: The
treasure must be plucked or torn off from a taboo tree
(Paradise tree, Hesperides); this is a forbidden and dangerous act. The clearest example of this is the old barbaric custom in the service of Diana of Aricia: only he
can become a priest of the goddess who, in her sacred
grove, dares to tear off ("abzureissen") a bough. The
tearing off has been retained in vulgar speech (besides

" abreiben," rubbing) as a symbol of the act of onanism. Thus " reiben," to rub, is like " reissen," to break off, both of which are contained in manthami and united apparently only through the myth of the fire theft bound up in the act of onanism in a deeper stratum wherein " reiben," properly speaking, " reissen," is employed, but in a transferred sense. Therefore, it might perhaps be anticipated that in the deepest stratum, namely, the incestuous, which precedes the autoerotic stage,[55] the two meanings coincide, which, through lack of mythological tradition, can perhaps be traced through etymology only.

CHAPTER IV

THE UNCONSCIOUS ORIGIN OF THE HERO

PREPARED by the previous chapters, we approach the personification of the libido in the form of a conqueror, a hero or a demon. With this, symbolism leaves the impersonal and neuter realm, which characterizes the astral and meteorologic symbol, and takes human form: the figure of a being changing from sorrow to joy, from joy to sorrow, and which, like the sun, sometimes stands in its zenith, sometimes is plunged in darkest night, and arises from this very night to new splendor.[1] Just as the sun, guided by its own internal laws, ascends from morn till noon, and passing beyond the noon descends towards evening, leaving behind its splendor, and then sinks completely into the all-enveloping night, thus, too, does mankind follow his course according to immutable laws, and also sinks, after his course is completed, into night, in order to rise again in the morning to a new cycle in his children. The symbolic transition from sun to man is easy and practicable. The third and last creation of Miss Miller's also takes this course. She calls this piece " Chiwantopel," a " hypnagogic poem." She gives us the following information about the circumstances surrounding the origin of this phantasy:

" After an evening of care and anxiety, I lay down to sleep at about half past eleven. I felt excited and unable to sleep, although I was very tired. There was no light in the room. I closed my eyes, and then I had the feeling that something was about to happen. The sensation of a general relaxation came over me, and I remained as passive as possible. Lines appeared before my eyes,—sparks and shining spirals, followed by a kaleidoscopic review of recent trivial occurrences."

The reader will regret with me that we cannot know the reason for her cares and anxieties. It would have been of great importance for what follows to have information on this point. This gap in our knowledge is the more to be deplored because, between the first poem in 1898 and the time of the phantasy here discussed (1902), four whole years have passed. All information is lacking regarding this period, during which the great problem surely survived in the unconscious. Perhaps this lack has its advantages in that our interest is not diverted from the universal applicability of the phantasy here produced by sympathy in regard to the personal fate of the author. Therefore, something is obviated which often prevents the analyst in his daily task from looking away from the tedious toil of detail to that wider relation which reveals each neurotic conflict to be involved with human fate as a whole.

The condition depicted by the author here corresponds to such a one as usually precedes an intentional somnambulism [2] often described by spiritualistic mediums. A certain inclination to listen to these low nocturnal voices must be assumed; otherwise such fine and hardly perceptible inner experiences pass unnoticed. We recognize in this listening a current of the libido leading inward and beginning to flow towards a still invisible, mysterious goal. It seems that the libido has suddenly discovered an object in the depths of the unconscious which powerfully attracts it. The life of man, turned wholly to the external by nature, does not ordinarily permit such introversion; there must, therefore, be surmised a certain exceptional condition, that is to say, a lack of external objects, which compels the individual to seek a substitute for them in his own soul. It is, however, difficult to imagine that this rich world has become too poor to offer an object for the love of human atoms; nor can the world and its objects be held accountable for this lack. It offers boundless opportunities for every one. It is rather the *incapacity to love which robs mankind of his possibilities.* This world is empty to him alone who does not understand how to direct his libido towards objects, and to render them alive and beautiful for himself, for Beauty does not indeed lie in things, but in the feeling that we give to them. That which compels us to create a substitute for ourselves is not the external lack of objects, but our incapacity to lovingly include a thing outside of ourselves. Certainly the difficulties of the conditions of life and the adversities of the struggle for existence may oppress us, yet even adverse external situations would not hinder the giving out of the libido; on the contrary, they may spur us on to the greatest exertions, whereby we bring our whole libido into reality. Real difficulties alone will never be able to force the libido back permanently to such a degree as to give rise, for example, to a neurosis. *The conflict, which is the condition of every neu-*

rosis, is lacking. The resistance, which opposes its unwillingness to the will, alone has the power to produce
that pathogenic introversion which is the starting point of
every psychogenic disturbance. The resistance against
loving produces the inability to love. Just as the normal
libido is comparable to a steady stream which pours its
waters broadly into the world of reality, so the resistance,
dynamically considered, is comparable, not so much to a
rock rearing up in the river bed which is flooded over
or surrounded by the stream, as to a backward flow
towards the source. A part of the soul desires the outer
object; another part, however, harks back to the subjective world, where the airy and fragile palaces of
phantasy beckon. One can assume the dualism of the
human will for which Bleuler, from the psychiatric point
of view, has coined the word " ambitendency " [3] as something generally present, bearing in mind that even
the most primitive motor impulse is in opposition; as,
for example, in the act of extension, the flexor muscles
also become innervated. This normal ambitendency,
however, never leads to an inhibition or prevention of the
intended act, but is the indispensable preliminary require-
ment for its perfection and coördination. For a resistance disturbing to this act to arise from this harmony of
finely attuned opposition an abnormal plus or minus
would be needed on one or the other side. The resistance originates from this added third. [4] This applies also
to the duality of the will, from which so many difficulties
arise for mankind. The abnormal third frees the pair
of opposites, which are normally most intimately united,

and causes their manifestation in the form of separate
tendencies; it is only thus that they become willingness
and unwillingness, which interfere with each other.   The
Bhagavad-Gîtâ says, " Be thou free of the pairs of
opposites." [5]   The harmony thus becomes disharmony.
It cannot be my task here to investigate whence the unknown third arises, and what it is.   Taken at the roots
in the case of our patients, the " nuclear complex "
(Freud) reveals itself as the *incest problem*.   The sexual
libido regressing to the parents appears as the incest tendency.   The reason this path is so easily travelled is due
to the enormous indolence of mankind, which will relinquish no object of the past, but will hold it fast forever.
The " sacrilegious backward grasp " of which Nietzsche
speaks reveals itself, stripped of its incest covering,
as an original passive arrest of the libido in its first object
of childhood.   This indolence is also a passion, as La
Rochefoucauld [6] has brilliantly expressed it:

" Of all passions, that which is least known to ourselves is
indolence: it is the most ardent and malignant of them all, although its violence may be insensible, and the injuries it causes
may be hidden; if we will consider its power attentively, we will
see that it makes itself, upon all occasions, mistress of our senti-
ments, of our interests, and of our pleasures; it is the anchor,
which has the power to arrest the largest vessels; it is a calm more
dangerous to the most important affairs than rocks and the worst
tempest.   The repose of indolence is a secret charm of the soul
which suddenly stops the most ardent pursuits and the firmest
resolutions; finally to give the true idea of this passion, one
must say that indolence is like a beatitude of the soul which
consoles it for all its losses and takes the place of all its posses-
sions."

This dangerous passion, belonging above all others to primitive man, appears under the hazardous mask of the incest symbol, from which the incest fear must drive us away, and which must be conquered, in the first place, under the image of the "terrible mother." [7] It is the mother of innumerable evils, not the least of which are neurotic troubles. For, especially from the fogs of the arrested remnants of the libido, arise the harmful phantasmagoria which so veil reality that adaptation becomes almost impossible. However, we will not investigate any further in this place the foundations of the incest phantasies. The preliminary suggestion of my purely psychologic conception of the incest problem may suffice. We are here only concerned with the question whether *resistance* which leads to introversion in our author signifies a conscious external difficulty or not. If it were an external difficulty, then, indeed, the libido would be violently dammed back, and would produce a flood of phantasies, which can best be designated as schemes, that is to say, plans as to how the obstacles could be overcome. They would be very concrete ideas of reality which seek to pave the way for solutions. It would be a strenuous meditation, indeed, which would be more likely to lead to anything rather than to a hypnagogic poem. The passive condition depicted above in no way fits in with a real external obstacle, but, precisely through its passive submission, it indicates a tendency which doubtless scorns real solutions and prefers phantastic substitutes. Ultimately and essentially we are, therefore, dealing with an internal conflict, perhaps after the manner of those earlier conflicts which led to the two first unconscious creations. We, therefore, are forced to conclude that the external object cannot be loved, because a predominant amount of libido prefers a phantastic object, which must be brought up from the depths of the unconscious as a compensation for the missing reality.

The visionary phenomena, produced in the first stages of introversion, are grouped among the well-known phenomena [8] of hypnagogic vision. They form, as I explained in an earlier paper, the foundation of the true visions of the symbolic autorevelations of the libido, as we may now express it.

Miss Miller continues:

"Then I had the impression that some communication was immediately impending. It seemed to me as if there were re-echoed in me the words, ' Speak, O Lord, for Thy servant listens; open Thou mine ears!' "

This passage very clearly describes the intention; the expression "communication" is even a current term in spiritualistic circles. The Biblical words contain a clear invocation or "prayer," that is to say, a wish (libido) directed towards divinity (the unconscious complex). The prayer refers to Samuel, i: 3, where Samuel at night was three times called by God, but believed that it was Eli calling, until the latter informed him that it was God himself who spoke, and that he must answer if his name was called again—"Speak, O Lord, for Thy Servant hears!" The dreamer uses these words really in an inverse sense, namely, in order to produce God with them.

With that she directs her desires, her libido, into the depths of her unconscious.

We know that, although individuals are widely separated by the differences in the contents of their consciousness, they are closely alike in their unconscious psychology. It is a significant impression for one working in practical psychoanalysis when he realizes how uniform are the typical unconscious complexes. Difference first arises from individualization. This fact gives to an essential portion of the Schopenhauer and Hartmann philosophies a deep psychologic justification.[9] The very evident uniformity of the unconscious mechanism serves as a psychologic foundation for these philosophic views. The unconscious contains the differentiated remnants of the earlier psychologic functions overcome by the individual differentiation. The reaction and products of the animal psyche are of a generally diffused uniformity and solidity, which, among men, may be discovered apparently only in traces. Man appears as something extraordinarily individual in contrast with animals.

This might be a tremendous delusion, because we have the appropriate tendency always to recognize only the difference of things. This is demanded by the psychologic adaptation which, without the most minute differentiation of the impressions, would be absolutely impossible. In opposition to this tendency we have ever the greatest difficulty in recognizing in their common relations the things with which we are occupied in everyday life. This recognition becomes much easier with things which are more remote from us. For example, it is almost impossible for a European to differentiate the faces in a Chinese throng, although the Chinese have just as individual facial formations as the Europeans, but the similarity of their strange facial expression is much more evident to the remote onlooker than their individual differences. But when we live among the Chinese then the impression of their uniformity disappears more and more, and finally the Chinese become individuals also. Individuality belongs to those conditional actualities which are greatly overrated theoretically on account of their practical significance. It does not belong to those overwhelmingly clear and therefore universally obtrusive general facts upon which a science must primarily be founded. The individual content of consciousness is, therefore, the most unfavorable object imaginable for psychology, because it has veiled the universally valid until it has become unrecognizable. The essence of consciousness is the process of adaptation which takes place in the most minute details. On the other hand, the unconscious is the generally diffused, which not only binds the individuals among themselves to the race, but also unites them backwards with the peoples of the past and their psychology. Thus the unconscious, surpassing the individual in its generality, is, in the first place, the object of a true psychology, which claims not to be psychophysical.

Man as an individual is a suspicious phenomenon, the right of whose existence from a natural biological standpoint could be seriously contested, because, from this point of view, the individual is only a race atom, and has a significance only as a mass constituent. The ethical

standpoint, however, gives to the human being an individual tendency separating him from the mass, which, in
the course of centuries, led to the development of personality, hand in hand with which developed the hero
cult, and has led to the modern individualistic cult of
personages. The attempts of rationalistic theology to
keep hold of the personal Jesus as the last and most
precious remnant of the divinity which has vanished beyond the power of the imagination corresponds to this
tendency. In this respect the Roman Catholic Church
was more practical, because she met the general need of
the visible, or at least historically believed hero, through
the fact that she placed upon the throne of worship a
small but clearly perceptible god of the world, namely,
the Roman Pope, the Pater patrum, and at the same time
the Pontifex Maximus of the invisible upper or inner God.
The sensuous demonstrability of God naturally supports
the religious process of introversion, because the human
figure essentially facilitates the transference, for it is not
easy to imagine something lovable or venerable in a spiritual being. This tendency, everywhere present, has been
secretly preserved in the rationalistic theology with its
Jesus historically insisted upon. This does not mean that
men loved the visible God; they love him, not as he is,
for he is merely a man, and when the pious wished to
love humanity they could go to their neighbors and their
enemies to love them. Mankind wishes to love in God
only their ideas, that is to say, the ideas which they pro-
ject into God. By that they wish to love their unconscious,
that is, that remnant of ancient humanity and the cen-

turies-old past in all people, namely, the common property left behind from all development which is given to all men, like the sunshine and the air. But in loving this inheritance they love that which is common to all. Thus they turn back to the mother of humanity, that is to say, to the spirit of the race, and regain in this way something of that connection and of that mysterious and irresistible power which is imparted by the feeling of belonging to the herd. It is the problem of Antæus, who preserves his gigantic strength only through contact with mother earth. This temporary withdrawal into one's self, which, as we have already seen, signifies a regression to the childish bond to the parent, seems to act favorably, within certain limits, in its effect upon the psychologic condition of the individual. It is in general to be expected that the two fundamental mechanisms of the psychoses, transference and introversion, are to a wide extent extremely appropriate methods of normal reaction against complexes; transference as a means of escaping from the complex into reality; introversion as a means of detaching one's self from reality through the complex.

After we have informed ourselves about the general purposes of prayer, we are prepared to hear more about the vision of our dreamer. After the prayer, " the head of a sphinx with an Egyptian headdress '" appeared, only to vanish quickly. Here the author was disturbed, so that for a moment she awoke. This vision recalls the previously mentioned phantasy of the Egyptian statue, whose rigid gesture is entirely in place here as a phenomenon of the so-called functional category. The light

stages of the hypnosis are designated technically as
" Engourdissement " (stiffening). The word Sphinx in
the whole civilized world signifies the same as riddle: a
puzzling creature who proposes riddles, like the Sphinx
of Oedipus, standing at the portal of his fate like a
symbolic proclamation of the inevitable. The Sphinx is
a semi-theriomorphic representation of that " mother
image " which may be designated as the " terrible
mother," of whom many traces are found in mythology.
This interpretation is correct for Oedipus. Here the
question is opened. The objection will be raised that
nothing except the word " Sphinx " justifies the allusion
to the Sphinx of Oedipus. On account of the lack of
subjective materials, which in the Miller text are wholly
lacking in regard to this vision, an individual interpretation would also be excluded. The suggestion
of an " Egyptian " phantasy (Part I, Chapter II) is
entirely insufficient to be employed here. Therefore we
are compelled, if we wish to venture at all upon an
understanding of this vision, to direct ourselves—perhaps
in all too daring a manner—to the available ethnographic
material under the assumption that the unconscious of the
present-day man coins its symbols as was done in the most
remote past. The Sphinx, in its traditional form, is a half-
human, half-animal creature, which we must, in part,
interpret in the way that is applicable to such phantastic
products. The reader is directed to the deductions in
the first part of this volume where the theriomorphic representations of the libido were discussed. This manner
of representation is very familiar to the analyst, through

the dreams and phantasies of neurotics (and of normal men). The impulse is readily represented as an animal, as a bull, horse, dog, etc. One of my patients, who had questionable relations with women, and who began the treatment with the fear, so to speak, that I would surely forbid him his sexual adventures, dreamed that I (his physician) very skilfully speared to the wall a strange animal, half pig, half crocodile. Dreams swarm with such theriomorphic representations of the libido. Mixed beings, such as are in this dream, are not rare. A series of very beautiful illustrations, where especially the lower half of the animal was represented theriomorphically, has been furnished by Bertschinger.[10] The libido which was represented theriomorphically is the " animal " sexuality which is in a repressed state. The history of repression, as we have seen, goes back to the incest problem, where the first motives for moral resistance against sexuality display themselves. The objects of the repressed libido are, in the last degree, the images of father and mother; therefore the theriomorphic symbols, in so far as they do not symbolize merely the libido in general, have a tendency to present father and mother (for example, father represented by a bull, mother by a cow). From these roots, as we pointed out earlier, might probably arise the theriomorphic attributes of the Divinity. In as far as the repressed libido manifests itself under certain conditions, as anxiety, these animals are generally of a horrible nature. In consciousness we are attached by all sacred bonds to the mother; in the dream she pursues us as a terrible animal. The Sphinx, mythologically considered, is actually a fear animal, which reveals distinct traits of a mother derivate. In the Oedipus legend the Sphinx is sent by Hera, who hates Thebes on account of the birth of Bacchus; because Oedipus conquers the Sphinx, which is nothing but fear of the mother, he must marry Jocasta, his mother, for the throne and the hand of the widowed queen of Thebes belonged to him who freed the land from the plague of the Sphinx. The genealogy of the Sphinx is rich in allusions to the problem touched upon here. She is a daughter of Echnida, a mixed being; a beautiful maiden above, a hideous serpent below. This double creature corresponds to the picture of the mother; above, the human, lovely and attractive half; below, the horrible animal half, converted into a fear animal through the incest prohibition. Echnida is derived from the All-mother, the mother Earth, Gaea, who, with Tartaros, the personified underworld (the place of horrors), brought her forth. Echnida herself is the mother of all terrors, of the Chimaera, Scylla, Gorgo, of the horrible Cerberus, of the Nemean Lion, and of the eagle who devoured the liver of Prometheus; besides this she gave birth to a number of dragons. One of her sons is Orthrus, the dog of the monstrous Geryon, who was killed by Hercules. With this dog, her son, Echnida, in incestuous intercourse, produced the Sphinx. These materials will suffice to characterize that amount of libido which led to the Sphinx symbol. If, in spite of the lack of subjective material, we may venture to draw an inference from the Sphinx symbol of our author, we must say that the Sphinx represents an original incestuous amount of libido detached from the bond to the mother.   Perhaps·it is better to postpone this conclusion until we have examined the following visions.

After Miss Miller had concentrated herself again, the vision developed further:

" Suddenly an Aztec appeared, absolutely clear in every detail; the hands spread open, with large fingers, the head in profile, armored, headdress similar to the feather ornaments of the American Indian.   The whole was somewhat suggestive of Mexican sculpture."

The ancient Egyptian character of the Sphinx is replaced here by American antiquity—by the Aztec.   The essential idea is neither Egypt nor Mexico, for the two could not be interchanged; but it is the subjective factor which the dreamer produces from her own past.   I have frequently observed in the analysis of Americans that certain unconscious complexes, i.e. repressed sexuality, are represented by the symbol of a Negro or an Indian; for example, when a European tells in his dream, " Then came a ragged, dirty individual," for Americans and for those who live in the tropics it is a Negro.   When with Europeans it is a vagabond or a criminal, with Americans it is a Negro or an Indian which represents the individual's own repressed sexual personality, and the one considered inferior.   It is also desirable to go into the particulars of this vision, as there are various things worthy of notice.   The feather cap, which naturally had to consist of eagles' feathers, is a sort of magic charm. The hero assumes at the same time something of the sunlike character of this bird when he adorns himself with its feathers, just as the courage and strength of the enemy are appropriated in swallowing his heart or taking his scalp. At the same time, the feather crest is a crown which is equivalent to the rays of the sun. The historical importance of the Sun identification has been seen in the first part.[11]

Especial interest attaches to the hand, which is described as " open," and the fingers, which are described as " large." It is significant that it is the hand upon which the distinct emphasis falls. One might rather have expected a description of the facial expression. It is well known that the gesture of the hand is significant; unfortunately, we know nothing about that here. Nevertheless, a parallel phantasy might be mentioned, which also puts the emphasis upon hands. A patient in a hypnagogic condition saw his mother painted on a wall, like a painting in a Byzantine church. She held one hand up, open wide, with fingers spread apart. The fingers were very large, swollen into knobs on the ends, and each surrounded by a small halo. The immediate association with this picture was the fingers of a frog with sucking discs at the ends. Then the similarity to the penis. The ancient setting of this mother picture is also of importance. Evidently the hand had, in this phantasy, a phallic meaning. This interpretation was confirmed by a further very remarkable phantasy of the same patient. He saw something like a " sky-rocket " ascending from his mother's hand, which at a closer survey becomes a shining bird with golden wings, a golden pheasant, as it then occurs to his mind. We have seen in the previous chapter that the hand has actually a phallic, generative meaning, and that this meaning plays a great part in the production of fire. In connection with this phantasy, there is but one observation to make: fire was bored with the hand; therefore it comes from the hand; Agni, the fire, was worshipped as a golden-winged bird.[12] It is extremely significant that it is the mother's hand. I must deny myself the temptation to enter more deeply into this. Let it be sufficient to have pointed out the possible significance of the hand of the Aztec by means of these parallel hand phantasies. We have mentioned the mother suggestively with the Sphinx. The Aztec taking the place of the Sphinx points, through his suggestive hand, to parallel phantasies in which the phallic hand really belongs to the mother. Likewise we encounter an antique setting in parallel phantasies. The significance of the antique, which experience has shown to be the symbol for "infantile," is confirmed by Miss Miller in this connection in the annotation to her phantasies, for she says:

"In my childhood, I took a special interest in the Aztec fragments and in the history of Peru and of the Incas."

Through the two analyses of children which have been published we have attained an insight into the child's small world, and have seen what burning interests and questions secretly surround the parents, and that the parents are, for a long time, the objects of the greatest interest.[13] We are, therefore, justified in suspecting that the antique setting applies to the "ancients," that is to say, the parents, and that consequently this Aztec has something of the father or mother in himself. Up to this time indirect hints point only to the mother, which is nothing remarkable in an American girl, because Americans, as a result of the extreme detachment from the father, are characterized by a most enormous mother complex, which again is connected with the especial social position of woman in the United States. This position brings about a special masculinity among capable women, which easily makes possible the symbolizing into a masculine figure.[14]

After this vision, Miss Miller felt that a name formed itself " bit by bit," which seemed to belong to this Aztec— " the son of an Inca of Peru." The name is " Chi-wan-to-pel." As the author intimated, something similar to this belonged to her childish reminiscences. The act of naming is, like baptism, something exceedingly important for the creation. of a personality, because, since olden times, a magic power has been attributed to the name, with which, for example, the spirit of the dead can be conjured. To know the name of any one means, in mythology, to have power over that one. As a well-known example I mention the fairy tale of " Rumpelstilzchen." In an Egyptian myth, Isis robs the Sun god Ré permanently of his power by compelling him to tell her his real name. Therefore, to give a name means to give power, invest with a definite personality.[15] The author observed, in regard to the name itself, that it reminded her very much of the impressive name Popocatepetl, a name which belongs to unforgettable school memories, and, to the greatest indignation of the patient, very often emerges in an analysis in a dream or phantasy and brings with it that same old joke which one heard in school, told one-self and later again forgot. Although one might hesitate to consider this unhallowed joke as of psychologic im-portance, still one must inquire for the reason of its being. One must also put, as a counter question, Why is it always Popocatepetl and not the neighboring Iztaccihuatl, or the even higher and just as clear Orizaba? The last has certainly the more beautiful and more easily pronounced name. Popocatepetl is impressive because of its onoma-topoetic name. In English the word is " to pop " (pop-gun), which is here considered as onomatopoesy; in Ger-man the words are *Hinterpommern, Pumpernickel; Bombe; Petarde (le pet =* flatus). The frequent German word *Popo* (Podex) does not indeed exist in English, but flatus is designated as " to poop " in childish speech. The act of defecation is often designated as " to pop." A joking name for the posterior part is " the bum." (Poop also means the rear end of a ship.)   In French, *pouf!* is onomatopoetic; *pouffer = platzen* (to explode), *la poupe =* rear end of ship, *le poupard =* the baby in arms, *la poupée =* doll. *Poupon* is a pet name for a chubby-faced child.   In Dutch *pop,* German *Puppe* and Latin *puppis =* doll; in Plautus, however, it is also used jokingly for the posterior part of the body; *pupus* means child; *pupula =* girl, little dollie.   The Greek word ποππύζω designates a cracking, snapping or blowing sound.   It is used of kissing; by Theocritus also of the as-sociated noise of flute blowing.   The etymologic parallels show a remarkable relationship between the part of the body in question and the child. This relationship we will mention here, only to let it drop at once, as this question will claim our attention later.

One of my patients in his childhood had always connected the act of defecation with a phantasy that his posterior was a volcano and a violent eruption took place, explosion of gases and gushings forth of lava. The terms for the elemental occurrences of nature are originally not at all poetical; one thinks, for example, of the beautiful phenomenon of the meteor, which the German language most unpoetically calls " Sternschnuppe " (the smouldering wick of a star). Certain South American Indians call the shooting star the " urine of the stars." According to the principle of the least resistance, expressions are taken from the nearest source available. (For example, the transference of the metonymic expression of urination as *Schiffens*, " to rain.")

Now it seems to be very obscure why the mystical figure of Chiwantopel, whom Miss Miller, in a note, compares to the control spirit of the spiritualistic medium,[16] is found in such a disreputable neighborhood that his nature (name) was brought into relation with this particular part of the body. In order to understand this possibility, we must realize that when we produce from the unconscious the first to be brought forth is the infantile material long lost in memory. One must, therefore, take the point of view of that time in which this infantile material was still on the surface. If now a much-honored object is related in the unconscious to the anus, then one must conclude that something of a high valuation was expressed thereby. The question is only whether this corresponds to the psychology of the child. Before we enter upon this question, it must be stated that the anal region is very closely connected with veneration. One thinks of the traditional fæces of the Great Mogul. An Oriental tale has the same to say of Christian knights, who anointed themselves with the excrement of the pope and cardinals in order to make themselves formidable. A patient who is characterized by a special veneration for her father had a phantasy that she saw her father sitting upon the toilet in a dignified manner, and people going past greeted him effusively.[17] The association of the anal relations by no means excludes high valuation or esteem, as is shown by these examples, and as is easily seen from the intimate connection of fæces and gold.[18] Here the most worthless comes into the closest relation with the most valuable. This also happens in religious valuations. I discovered (at that time to my great astonishment) that a young patient, very religiously trained, represented in a dream the Crucified on the bottom of a blue-flowered chamber pot, namely, in the form of excrements. The contrast is so enormous that one must assume that the valuations of childhood must indeed be very different from ours. This is actually the truth. Children bring to the act of defecation and the products of this an esteem and interest [19] which later on is possible only to the hypochondriac. We do not comprehend this interest until we learn that the child very early connects with it a theory of propagation.[20] The libido afflux probably accounts for the enormous interest in this act. The child sees that this is the way in which something is produced, in which something comes out. The same child whom I reported in the little brochure " Über Konflicte der kindlichen Seele," and who had a well-developed anal theory of birth, like little Hans, whom Freud made known to us, later contracted a habit of staying a long time on the toilet. Once the father grew impatient, went to the toilet and called, " Do come out of there; what are you making?" Whereupon the answer came from within, " A little wagon and two ponies." The child was making a little wagon and two ponies, that is to say, things which at that time she especially wished for. In this way one can make what one wishes, and the thing made is the thing wished for. The child wishes earnestly for a doll or, at heart, for a real child. (That is, the child practised for his future biological task, and in the way in which everything in general is produced he made the doll[21] himself as representative of the child or of the thing wished for in general.[22]) From a patient I have learned a parallel phantasy of her childhood. In the toilet there was a crevice in the wall. She phantasied that from this crevice a fairy would come out and present her with everything for which she wished. The " locus " is known to be the place of dreams where much was wished for and created which later would no longer be suspected of having this place of origin. A pathological phantasy in place here is told us by Lombroso,[23] concerning two insane artists. Each of them considered himself God and the ruler of the world. They created or produced the world by making it come forth from the rectum,

just as the egg of birds originates in the egg canal. One
of these two artists was endowed with a true artistic
sense. He painted a picture in which he was just in the
act of creation; the world came forth from his anus; the
membrum was in full erection; he was naked, surrounded
by women, and with all insignia of his power. The excrement is in a certain sense the thing wished for, and on that
account it receives the corresponding valuation. When I
first understood this connection, an observation made
long ago, and which disturbed me greatly because I never
rightly understood it, became clear to me. It concerned
an educated patient who, under very tragic circumstances,
had to be separated from her husband and child, and was
brought into the insane asylum. She exhibited a typical
apathy and slovenliness which was considered as
affective mental deterioration. Even at that time I
doubted this deterioration, and was inclined to regard
it as a secondary adjustment. I took especial pains to
ascertain how I could discover the existence of the affect
in this case. Finally, after more than three hours' hard
work, I succeeded in finding a train of thought which suddenly brought the patient into a completely adequate and
therefore strongly emotional state. At this moment the
affective connection with her was completely reëstab-
lished. That happened in the forenoon. When I returned at the appointed time in the evening to the ward to
see her she had, for my reception, smeared herself from
head to foot with excrement, and cried laughingly, " Do I
please you so? " She had never done that before; it was
plainly destined for me. The impression which I received

was one of a personal affront and, as a result of this, I was convinced for years after of the affective deterioration of such cases. Now we understand this act as an infantile ceremony of welcome or a declaration of love.

The origin of Chiwantopel, that is to say, an unconscious personality, therefore means, in the sense of the previous explanation, " I make, produce, invent him myself." It is a sort of human creation or birth by the anal route. The first people were made from excrement, potter's earth, or clay. The Latin *lutum,* which really means " moistened earth," also has the transferred meaning of dirt. In Plautus it is even a term of abuse, something like " You scum." The birth from the anus also reminds us of the motive of " throwing behind oneself." A well-known example is the oracular command, which Deucalion and Pyrrha, who were the only survivors from the great flood, received. They were to throw behind them the bones of the great mother. They then threw behind them stones, from which mankind sprang. According to a tradition, the Dactyli in a similar manner sprang from dust, which the nymph Anchiale threw behind her. There is also humorous significance attached to the anal products. The excrements are often considered in popular humor as a monument or memorial (which plays a special part in regard to the criminal in the form of *grumus merdæ);* every one knows the humorous story of the man who, led by the spirit through labyrinthian passages to a hidden treasure, after he had shed all his pieces of clothing, deposited excrement as a last guide post on his road.

In a more distant past a sign of this kind possessed as great a significance as the dung of animals to indicate the direction taken.   Simple monuments ("little stone figures") have taken the place of this perishable mark.

It is noteworthy that Miss Miller quotes another case, where a name suddenly obtruded itself, parallel to the emerging into consciousness of Chiwantopel, namely, A-ha-ma-ra-ma, with the feeling that it dealt with something Assyrian.[24]   As a possible source of this, there occurred to her "Asurabama, who made cuneiform bricks,"[25] those imperishable documents made from clay: the monuments of the most ancient history.   If it were not emphasized that the bricks are "cuneiform," then it might mean ambiguously "wedged-shaped bricks," which is more suggestive of our interpretation than that of the author.

Miss Miller remarks that besides the name "Asurabama" she also thought of "Ahasuerus" or "Ahasverus."   This phantasy leads to a very different aspect of the problem of the unconscious personality.   While the previous materials betrayed to us something of the infantile theory of creation, this phantasy opens up a vista into the dynamics of the unconscious creation of personality. Ahasver is, as is well known, the Wandering Jew; he is characterized by endless and restless wanderings until the end of the world.   The fact that the author has thought of this particular name justifies us in following this trail. The legend of Ahasver, the first literary traces of which belong to the thirteenth century, seems to be of Occidental origin, and belongs to those ideas which possess inde-

structible vital energy. The figure of the Wandering Jew
has undergone more literary elaboration than the figure
of Faust, and nearly all of this work belongs to the last
century. If the figure is not called Ahasver, still it is there
under another name, perhaps as Count of St. Germain,
the mysterious Rosicrucian, whose immortality was assured, and whose temporary residence (the land) was
equally known.[26] Although the stories about Ahasver
cannot be traced back any earlier than the thirteenth century, the oral tradition can reach back considerably
further, and it is not an impossibility that a bridge to the
Orient exists. There is the parallel figure of Chidr, or
" al Chadir," the " ever-youthful Chidher " celebrated in
song by Rueckert. The legend is purely Islamitic. The
peculiar feature, however, is that Chidher is not only a
saint, but in Sufic circles [27] rises even to divine significance.
In view of the severe monotheism of Islam, one is inclined to think of Chidher as a pre-Islamitic Arabian
divinity who would hardly be officially recognized by the
new religion, but might have been tolerated on political
grounds. But there is nothing to prove that. The first
traces of Chidher are found in the commentaries of the
Koran, Buchâri and Tabare and in a commentary to a
noteworthy passage of the eighteenth sura of the Koran.
The eighteenth sura is entitled " the cave," that is, after
the cave of the seven sleepers, who, according to the
legend, slept there for 309 years, and thus escaped persecution, and awoke in a new era. Their legend is recounted in the eighteenth sura, and divers reflections were
associated with it. The wish-fulfilment idea of the legend

is very clear. The mystic material for it is the immutable model of the Sun's course. The Sun sets periodically, but does not die. It hides in the womb of the sea or in a subterranean cave,[28] and in the morning is " born again," complete. The language in which this astronomic occurrence is clothed is one of clear symbolism; the Sun returns into the mother's womb, and after some time is again born. Of course, this event is properly an incestuous act, of which, in mythology, clear traces are still retained, not the least of which is the circumstance that the dying and resurrected gods are the lovers of their own mothers or have generated themselves through their own mothers. Christ as the " God becoming flesh " has generated himself through Mary; Mithra has done the same. These Gods are unmistakable Sun-gods, for the Sun also does this, in order to again renew himself. Naturally, it is not to be assumed that astronomy came first and these conceptions of gods afterwards; the process was, as always, inverted, and it is even true that primitive magic charms of rebirth, baptism, superstitious usages of all sorts, concerning the cure of the sick, etc., were projected into the heavens. These youths were born from the cave (the womb of mother earth), like the Sun-gods, in a new era, and this was the way they vanquished death. In this far they were immortal. It is now interesting to see how the Koran comes, after long ethical contemplations in the course of the same sura, to the following passage, which is of especial significance for the origin of the Chidher myth. For this reason I quote the Koran literally:

" Remember when Moses said to his servant, ' I will not stop till I reach the confluence of the two seas, or for eighty years will I journey on.'

" But when they reached their confluence they forgot their fish, and it took its way in the sea at will.

" And when they had passed on, Moses said to his servant, ' Bring us our morning meal, for now we have incurred weariness from this our journey.'

" He said, ' What thinkest thou? When we repaired to the rock for rest, then verily I forgot the fish; and none but Satan made me forget it, so as not to mention it; and it hath taken its way in the sea in a wondrous sort.'

" He said, ' It is this we were in quest of.' So they both went back retracing their footsteps.

" Then found they one of our servants to whom we had vouch-safed our mercy, and whom we had instructed with our knowl-edge; [29]

" Moses said to him, ' Shall I follow thee that thou teach me, for guidance of that which thou hast been taught? '

" He said, ' Verily, thou canst by no means have patience with me; and how canst thou be patient in matters whose meaning thou comprehendest not? ' "—Trans. Rodwell, page 188.

Moses now accompanies the mysterious servant of God, who does divers things which Moses cannot comprehend; finally, the Unknown takes leave of Moses, and speaks to him as follows:

" They will ask thee of Dhoulkarnein (the two-horned).[30] Say: ' I will recite to you an account of him.'

" Verily, we established his power upon the earth and we gave him a means to accomplish every end, so he followed his way;

" Until when he reached the setting of the sun, he found it to set in a miry forest; and hard by, he found a people. . . ."

Now follows a moral reflection; then the narrative con-tinues:

" Then he followed his course further until he came to the place where the sun rises. . . ."

If now we wish to know who is the unknown servant of God, we are told in this passage *he is Dhulqarnein, Alexander, the Sun; he goes to the place of setting and he goes to the place of rising.* The passage about the unknown servant of God is explained by the commentaries in a well-defined legend. The servant is Chidher, " the verdant one," the never-tiring wanderer, who roams for hundreds and thousands of years over lands and seas, the teacher and counsellor of pious men; the one wise in divine knowledge—the immortal.[31] The authority of the Tabari associates Chidher with Dhulqarnein; Chidher is said to have reached the " stream of life " as a follower of Alexander, and both unwittingly had drunk of it, so that they became immortal. Moreover, *Chidher is identified by the old commentators with Elias,* who also did not die, but *who was taken to Heaven in a fiery chariot.* Elias is *Helios.*[32] It is to be observed that Ahasver also owes his existence to an obscure place in the holy Christian scriptures. This place is to be found in Matthew xvi: 28. First comes the scene where Christ appoints Peter as the rock of his church, and nominates him the governor of his power.[33] After that follows the prophecy of his death, and then comes the passage:

" Verily, I say unto you, there be some standing here, which shall not taste of death till they see the Son of Man coming in his kingdom."

Here follows the scene of the transfiguration:

" And was transfigured before them: and his face did shine as the sun, and his raiment was white as the light.

" And behold there appeared unto them Moses and Elias talking with him.

" Then answered Peter and said unto Jesus, ' Lord, it is good for us to be here; if thou wilt, let us make here three tabernacles; one for thee and one for Moses and one for Elias.' " [34]

From these passages it appears that Christ stands on the same plane as Elias, without being identified with him,[35] although the people consider him as Elias. The ascension places Christ as identical with Elias. The prophecy of Christ shows that there exist aside from himself one or more immortals who shall not die until Parousai. According to John xxi: 22nd verse, the boy John was considered as one of these immortals, and in the legend he is, in fact, not dead but merely sleeping in the ground until Parousai, and breathes so that the dust swirls round his grave.[36] As is evident, there are passable bridges from Christ by way of Elias to Chidher and Ahasuerus. It is said in an account of this legend [37] that Dhulqarnein led his friend Chidher to the " source of life " in order to have him drink of immortality.[38] Alexander also bathed in the stream of life and performed the ritual ablutions. As I previously mentioned in a footnote, according to Matthew xvii: 12th verse, John the Baptist is Elias, therefore primarily identical with Chidher. Now, however, it is to be noted that in the Arabian legend Chidher appears rather as a companion or accompanied (Chidher with Dhulqarnein or with Elias, " like unto them "; or identified with them [39]). There are therefore, two similar figures who resemble each other, but who, nevertheless, are distinct.   The analogous situation in the Christian legend is found in the scene by the Jordan where John leads Christ to the " source of life."   Christ is there, the subordinate, John the superior, similar to Dhulqarnein and Chidher, or Chidher and Moses, also Elias.   The latter relation especially is such that Vollers compares Chidher and Elias, on the one side, with Gilgamesh and his mortal brother Eabani; on the other side, with the Dioscuri, one of whom is immortal, the other mortal.   This relation is also found in Christ and John the Baptist,[40] on the one hand, and Christ and Peter, on the other.   The last-named parallel only finds its explanation through comparison with the Mithraic mysteries, where the esoteric contents are revealed to us through monuments.   Upon the Mithraic marble relief of Klagenfurt [41] it is represented how with a halo Mithra crowns Helios, who either kneels before him or else floats up to him from below.   Mithra is represented on a Mithraic monument of Osterburken as holding in his right hand the shoulder of the mystic ox above Helios, who stands bowed down before him, the left hand resting on a sword hilt.   A crown lies between them on the ground.   Cumont observes about this scene that it probably represents the divine prototype of the ceremony of the initiation into the degree of Miles, in which a sword and a crown were conferred upon the mystic.   Helios is, therefore, appointed the Miles of Mithra.   In a general way, Mithra seems to occupy the rôle of patron to Helios, which reminds us of the boldness of Hercules towards Helios.   Upon his journey towards Geryon, Helios burns too hotly; Hercules, full of anger, threatens him with his never-failing arrows. Therefore, Helios is compelled to yield, and lends to the hero his Sun ship, with which he was accustomed to journey across the sea. Thus Hercules returns to Erythia, to the cattle herds of Geryon.[42] On the monument at Klagenfurt, Mithra is furthermore represented pressing Helios's hand, either in farewell or as a ratification. In a further scene Mithra mounts the Chariot of Helios, either for the ascension or the " Sea Journey."[43] Cumont is of the opinion that Mithra gives to Helios a sort of ceremonious investiture and consecrates him with his divine power by crowning him with his own hands. This relation corresponds to that of Christ to Peter. Peter, through his symbol, the cock, has the character of a sun-god. After the ascension (or sea journey) of Christ, he is the visible pontiff of the divinity; he suffers, therefore, the same death (crucifixion) as Christ, and becomes the great Roman deity (*Sol invictus*), the conquering, triumphant Church itself, embodied in the Pope. In the scene of Malchus he is always shown as the miles of Christ, to whom the sword is granted, and as the rock upon which the Church is founded. The crown[44] is also given to him who possesses the power to bind and to set free. Thus, Christ, like the Sun, is the visible God, whereas the Pope, like the heir of the Roman Cæsars, is *solis invicti comes*. The setting sun appoints a successor whom he invests with the power of the sun.[45] Dhulqarnein gives Chidher eternal life. Chidher communicates his wisdom to Moses.[46] There even exists a report according to which

the forgetful servant of Joshua drinks from the well of
life, whereupon he becomes immortal, and is placed in a
ship by Chidher and Moses, as a punishment, and is cast
out to sea, once more a fragment of a sun myth, the
motive of the " sea journey." [47]

The primitive symbol, which designates that portion
of the Zodiac in which the Sun, with the Winter Solstice,
again enters upon the yearly course, is the goat, fish sign,
the αἰγωκέρως. The Sun mounts like a goat to the
highest mountain, and later goes into the water as a fish.
The fish is the symbol of the child,[48] for the child before
his birth lives in the water like a fish, and the Sun, because
it plunges into the sea, becomes equally child and fish.
The fish, however, is also a phallic symbol,[49] also a symbol for the woman.[50] Briefly stated, the fish is a libido
symbol, and, indeed, as it seems predominately *for the
renewal of the libido.*

The journey of Moses with his servant is a life-journey
(eighty years). They grow old and lose their life force
(libido), that is, they lose the fish which " pursues its
course in a marvellous manner to the sea," which means
the setting of the sun. When the two notice their loss,
they discover at the place where the " source of life " is
found (where the dead fish revived and sprang into the
sea) Chidher wrapped in his mantle,[51] sitting on the
ground. According to another version, he sat on an
island in the sea, or " in the wettest place on earth," that
is, he was just *born from the maternal depths.* Where
the fish vanished Chidher, " the verdant one," was born
as a " son of the deep waters," his head veiled, a Cabir,

a proclaimer of divine wisdom; the old Babylonian
Oannes-Ea, who was represented in the form of a fish,
and daily came from the sea as a fish to teach the people
wisdom.[52] His name was brought into connection with
John's. With the rising of the renewed sun all that lived
in darkness, as water-animal or fish, surrounded by all
terrors of night and death,[53] became as the shining fiery
firmament of the day. Thus the words of John the Baptist [54] gain especial meaning:

" I indeed baptize you with water unto repentance, but he that
cometh after me is mightier than I, whose shoes I am not worthy
to bear; he shall baptize you with the Holy Ghost and with fire."

With Vollers we may also compare Chidher and Elias
(Moses and his servant Joshua) with Gilgamesh and
his brother Eabani. Gilgamesh wandered through the
world, driven by anxiety and longing, to find immortality.
His path led him across the seas to the wise Utnapishtim
(Noah), who knew how to cross the waters of death.
There Gilgamesh had to dive down to the bottom of the
sea for the magical herb which was to lead him back to
the land of men. When he had come again to his native
land a serpent stole the magic plant from him (the fish
again slid into the sea). But on the return from the
land of the blessed an immortal mariner accompanied
him, who, banished by a curse of Utnapishtim, was forbidden to return to the land of the blessed. Gilgamesh's
journey had lost its purpose on account of the loss of the
magic herb; instead he is accompanied by an immortal,
whose fate, indeed, we cannot learn from the fragments

of the epic. This banished immortal is the model for Ahasver, as Jensen [55] aptly remarked.

Again we encounter the motive of the Dioscuri, mortal and immortal, setting and rising sun. This *motive is also represented as if projected from the hero.*

The Sacrificium Mithriacum (the sacrifice of the bull) is in its religious representation very often flanked by the two Dadophores, Cautes and Cautopates, one with a raised and the other with a lowered torch. They represent brothers who reveal their character through the symbolic position of the torch. Cumont connects them, not without meaning, with the sepulchral " erotes " who as genii with the reversed torches have traditional meaning. The one is supposed to stand for death and the other for life. I cannot refrain from mentioning the similarity between the Sacrificium Mithriacum (where the sacrificed bull in the centre is flanked on both sides by Dadophores) to the Christian sacrifice of the lamb (ram). The Crucified is also traditionally flanked by the two thieves, one of whom ascends to Paradise, while the other descends to Hell.[56] The idea of the mortal and the immortal seems to have passed also into the Christian worship. Semitic gods are often represented as flanked by two Paredroi; for example, Baal of Edessa, accompanied by Aziz and Monimoz (Baal as the Sun, accompanied by Mars and Mercury, as expressed in astronomical teachings). According to the Chaldean view, the gods are grouped into triads. In this circle of ideas belongs also the Trinity, the idea of the triune God, in which Christ must be considered in his unity with the

Father and the Holy Ghost. So, too, do the two thieves
belong inwardly to Christ. The two Dadophores are, as
Cumont points out, nothing but offshoots [57] from the chief
figure of Mithra, to whom belongs a mysterious threefold character. According to an account of Dionysus
Areopagita, the magicians celebrated a festival, "τοῦ
τριπλασίου Μίθρου." * [58]   An observation likewise refer-·
ring to the Trinity is made by Plutarch concerning Or-
muzd: τρὶς ἑαυτὸν αὐξήσας ἀπέστησε τοῦ ἡλίου.† The
Trinity, as three different states of the unity, is also a
Christian thought. In the very first place this suggests
a sun myth. An observation by Macrobius 1 : 18 seems to
lend support to this idea:

"Hæ autem ætatum diversitates ad solem referuntur, ut par-
vulus videatur hiemali solstitio, qualem Aegyptii proferunt ex
adyto die certa, . . . æquinoctio vernali figura iuvenis ornatur.
Postea statuitur ætas ejus plenissima effigie barbæ solstitio æstivo
. . . exunde per diminutiones veluti senescenti quarta forma deus
figuratur." ‡ [59]

As Cumont observes, Cautes and Cautapates occasionally carry in their hands the head of a bull, and a scorpion. [60]   Taurus and Scorpio are equinoctial signs, which
clearly indicate that the sacrificial scene refers primarily
to the Sun cycle; the rising Sun, which sacrifices itself at

---

* Of the threefold Mithra.

† Having expanded himself threefold, he departed from the sun.

‡ Now these differences in the seasons refer to the Sun, which seems at
the winter solstice an infant, such as the Egyptians on a certain day bring
out of their sanctuaries; at the vernal equinox it is represented as a youth.
Later, at the summer solstice, its age is represented by a full growth of
beard, while at the last, the god is represented by the gradually diminish-
ing form of an old man.

the summer solstice, and the setting Sun. In the sacrificial scene the symbol of the rising and setting Sun was
not easily represented; therefore, this idea was removed
from the sacrificial image.

We have pointed out above that the Dioscuri represent
a similar idea, although in a somewhat different form;
the one sun is always mortal, the other immortal. As
this entire sun mythology is merely a psychologic projection to the heavens, the fundamental thesis probably is
as follows; just as man consists of a mortal and immortal
part, so the sun is a pair of brothers,[61] one being mortal,
the other immortal. This thought lies at the basis of all
theology in general. Man is, indeed, mortal, but there
are some who are immortal, or there is something in us
which is immortal. Thus the gods, " a Chidher or a St.
Germain," are our immortal part, which, though incomprehensible, dwells among us somewhere.

Comparison with the sun teaches us over and over
again that the gods are libido. It is that part of us
which is immortal, since it represents that bond through
which we feel that in the race we are never extinguished.[62]
It is life from the life of mankind. Its springs, which well
up from the depths of the unconscious, come, as does our
life in general, from the root of the whole of humanity,
since we are indeed only a twig broken off from the
mother and transplanted.

Since the divine in us is the libido,[63] we must not wonder that we have taken along with us in our theology
ancient representations from olden times, which give the
triune figure to the God. We have taken this τριπλάσιον

θεόν* from the phallic symbolism, the originality of
which may well be uncontested.[64] The male genitals are
the basis for this Trinity. It is an anatomical fact that
one testicle is generally placed somewhat higher than
the other, and it is also a very old, but, nevertheless,
still surviving, superstition that one testicle generates a
boy and the other a girl.[65] A late Babylonian bas-relief
from Lajard's [66] collection seems to be in accordance with
this view. In the middle of the image stands an androgynous god (masculine and feminine face [67]); upon the
right, male side, is found a serpent, with a sun halo round
its head; upon the left, female side, there is also a serpent, with the moon above its head. Above the head of
the god there are three stars. This ensemble would seem
to confirm the Trinity [68] of the representation. The Sun
serpent at the right side is male; the serpent at the left
side is female (signified by the moon). This image possesses a symbolic sexual suffix, which makes the sexual
significance of the whole obtrusive. Upon the male side
a rhomb is found—a favorite symbol of the female genitals; upon the female side there is a wheel or felly. A
wheel always refers to the Sun, but the spokes are thick-
ened and enlarged at the ends, which suggests phallic
symbolism. It seems to be a phallic wheel, which was
not unknown in antiquity. There are obscene bas-reliefs
where Cupid turns a wheel of nothing but phalli.[69] It is
not only the serpent which suggests the phallic significance
of the Sun; I quote one especially marked case, from an
abundance of proof. In the antique collection at Verona

* Threefold God.

I discovered a late Roman mystic inscription in which are the following representations:

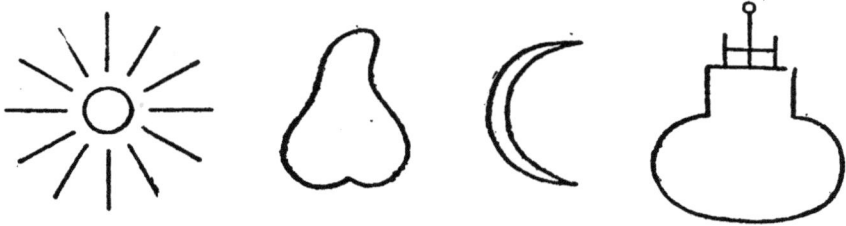

These symbols are easily read: Sun—Phallus, Moon—Vagina (Uterus). This interpretation is confirmed by another figure of the same collection. There the same representation is found, only the vessel [70] is replaced by the figure of a woman. The impressions on coins, where in the middle a palm is seen encoiled by a snake, flanked by two stones (testicles), or else in the middle a stone encircled by a snake; to the right a palm, to the left a shell (female genitals [71]), should be interpreted in a similar manner. In Lajard's " Researches " (" The Cult of Venus ") there is a coin of Perga, where Artemis of Perga is represented by a conical stone (phallic) flanked by a man (claimed to be Men) and by a female figure (claimed to be Artemis). Men (the so-called Lunus) is found upon an Attic bas-relief apparently with the spear but fundamentally a sceptre with a phallic significance, flanked by Pan with a club (phallus) and a female figure.[72] The traditional representation of the Crucified flanked by John and Mary is closely associated with this circle of ideas, precisely as is the Crucified with the thieves. From this we see how, beside the Sun, there emerges again and again the much more primitive com-

parison of the libido with the phallus. An especial trace
still deserves mention here. The Dadophor Cautapates,
who represents Mithra, is also represented with the cock [73]
and the pineapple. But these are the attributes of the
Phrygian god Men, whose cult was widely diffused. Men
was represented with Pileus,[74] the pineapple and the cock,
also in the form of a boy, just as the Dadophores are
boyish figures. (This last-named property relates them
with Men to the Cabiri.) Men has a very close connection with Attis, the son and lover of Cybele. In the time
of the Roman Cæsars, Men and Attis were entirely identified, as stated above. Attis also wears the Pileus like
Men, Mithra and the Dadophores. As the son and lover
of his mother he again leads us to the source of this
religion-creating incest libido, namely, to the mother.
Incest leads logically to ceremonial castration in the
Attic-Cybele cult, for the Hero, driven insane by his
mother, mutilates himself.[75] I must at present forego
entering more deeply into this matter, because the incest
problem is to be discussed at the close. Let this suggestion suffice—that from different directions the analysis
of the libido symbolism always leads back again to the
mother incest. Therefore, we may surmise that the longing of the libido raised to God (repressed into the unconscious) is a primitive, incestuous one which concerns
the mother. Through renouncing the virility to the first
beloved, the mother, the feminine element becomes extremely predominant; hence the strongly androgynous
character of the dying and resurrected Redeemer. That
these heroes are nearly always wanderers [76] is a psycho-

logically clear symbolism. The wandering is a representation of longing,[77] of the ever-restless desire, which
nowhere finds its object, for, unknown to itself, it seeks
the lost mother. The wandering association renders the
Sun comparison easily intelligible; also, under this aspect,
the heroes always resemble the wandering Sun, which
seems to justify the fact that the myth of the hero is a
sun myth. But the myth of the hero, however, is, as it
appears to me, the myth of our own suffering unconscious, which has an unquenchable longing for all the
deepest sources of our own being; for the body of the
mother, and through it for communion with infinite life
in the countless forms of existence. Here I must introduce the words of the Master who has divined the deepest roots of Faustian longings:

" Unwilling, I reveal a loftier mystery.—
   In solitude are throned the Goddesses,
   No Space around them, Place and Time still less:
   Only to speak of them embarrasses.
   They are THE MOTHERS!

" Goddesses unknown to ye,
   The Mortals,—named by us unwillingly.
   Delve in the deepest depths must thou to reach them:
   'Tis thine own fault that we for help beseech them.

" Where is the way?

            " No way! To the Unreachable,
   Ne'er to be trodden! A way to the Unbeseechable,
   Never to be besought! Art thou prepared?
   There are no locks, no latches to be lifted!
   Through endless solitudes shalt thou be drifted!
   Hast thou through solitudes and deserts dared?

And hadst thou swum to farthest verge of ocean
And there the boundless space beheld,
Still hadst thou seen wave after wave in motion,
Even though impending doom thy fear compelled.
Thou hadst seen something—in the beryl dim
Of peace-lulled seas, the sportive dolphins swim;
Hadst seen the flying clouds, sun, moon and star;
Nought shalt thou see in endless Void afar—
Not hear thy footstep fall, nor meet
A stable spot to rest thy feet.

" Here, take this key!
The Key will scent the true place from all others;
Follow it down! 'Twill lead thee to the Mothers.

" Descend then!   I could also say: Ascend!
'Twere all the same. *Escape from the Created*
To shapeless forms in liberated spaces!
Enjoy what long ere this was dissipated!
There whirls the press, like clouds on clouds unfolding;
Then with stretched arm swing high the key thou'rt holding!

" At last a blazing tripod,[78] tells thee this,
That there the utterly deepest bottom is.
Its light to thee will then the Mothers show,
Some in their seats, the others stand or go,
At their own will: Formation, Transformation,
The Eternal Mind's eternal recreation,
Forms of all Creatures,—there are floating free.
They'll see thee not! for only wraiths they see.
So pluck up heart,—the danger then is great.
Go to the tripod ere thou hesitate,
And touch it with the key."

CHAPTER V

SYMBOLISM OF THE MOTHER AND OF REBIRTH

THE vision following the creation of the hero is described by Miss Miller as a " throng of people." This representation is known to us from dream interpretation as being, above all, the symbol of mystery.[1] Freud thinks that this choice of symbol is determined on account of its possibility of representing the idea. The bearer of the mystery is placed in opposition to the multitude of the ignorant. *The possession of the mystery cuts one off from intercourse with the rest of mankind.* For a very complete and smooth rapport with the surroundings is of great importance for the management of the libido and the *possession of a subjectively important secret generally creates a great disturbance.* It may be said that the whole art of life shrinks to the one problem of how the libido may be freed in the most harmless way possible. Therefore, the neurotic derives special benefit in treatment when he can at last rid himself of his various secrets. The symbol of the crowd of people, chiefly the streaming and moving mass, is, as I have often seen, substituted for the great excitement in the unconscious, especially in persons who are outwardly calm.

The vision of the " throng " develops further; horses emerge; a battle is fought. With Silberer, I might accept the significance of this vision as belonging, first of all, in the " functional category," because, fundamentally, the conception of the intermingling crowds is nothing but the symbol of the present onrush of the mass of thought; likewise the battle, and possibly the horses, which illustrate the movement. The deeper significance of the appearance of the horses will be seen for the first time in the further course of our treatment of the mother symbolism. The following vision has a more definite and significantly important character. Miss Miller sees a City of Dreams (" Cité de Rêves "). The picture is similar to one she saw a short time before on the cover of a magazine. Unfortunately, we learn nothing further about it. One can easily imagine under this " Cité de Rêves " a fulfilled wish dream, that is to say, something very beautiful and greatly longed for; a sort of heavenly Jerusalem, as the poet of the Apocalypse has dreamed it. The city is a maternal symbol, a woman who fosters the inhabitants as children. It is, therefore, intelligible that the two mother goddesses, Rhea and Cybele, both wear the wall crown. The Old Testament treats the cities of Jerusalem, Babel, etc., as women (Isaiah xlvii: 1-5) :

" Come down and sit in the dust, O virgin daughter of Babylon, sit on the ground: there is no throne, O daughter of the Chaldeans; for thou shalt no more be called tender and delicate. Take the millstones and grind meal; uncover thy locks, make bare the leg, uncover the thigh, pass over the rivers. That thy nakedness shall be uncovered, yea, thy shame shall be seen; sit thou silent, and get thee into darkness, O daughter of the Chaldeans; for thou shalt no more be called the lady of the kingdoms."

Jeremiah says of Babel (l: 12) :

" Your mother shall be sore confounded; she that bare you shall be ashamed."

Strong, unconquered cities are virgins; colonies are sons and daughters. Cities are also whores. Isaiah says of Tyre (xxiii: 16) :

" Take an harp, go about the city, thou harlot; thou hast been forgotten."

And:

" How does it come to pass that the virtuous city has become an harlot? "

We come across a similar symbolism in the myth of Ogyges, the mythical king who rules in Egyptian Thebes and whose wife was appropriately named Thebe. The Bœotian Thebes founded by Cadmus received on that account a surname, " Ogygian." This surname was also given to the great flood, as it was called " Ogygian " because it occurred under Ogyges. This coincidence will be found later on to be hardly accidental. The fact that the city and the wife of Ogyges bear the same name indicates that somewhere a relation must exist between the city and the woman, which is not difficult to understand, for the city is identical with the woman. We meet a similar idea in Hindoo lore where Indra appears as the husband of Urvara, but Urvara means "the fertile land." In a similar way the occupancy of a country by the king was understood as marriage with the ploughed land. Similar representations must have prevailed in Europe as well. Princes had to guarantee, for example, a good harvest at their accession. The Swedish King Domaldi was actually killed on account of the failure of the harvest (Ynglinga sâga 18). In the Rama sâga the hero Rama marries Sîtâ, the furrow of the field.[2] To the same group of ideas belongs the Chinese custom of the Emperor ploughing a furrow at his ascension to the throne. This idea of the soil being feminine also embraces the idea of continual companionship with the woman, a physical communication. Shiva, the Phallic God, is, like Mahadeva and Parwati, male and female. He has even given one-half of his body to his consort Parwati as a dwelling place.[3] Inman[4] gives us a drawing of a Pundite of Ardanari-Iswara; one-half of the god is masculine, the other half feminine, and the genitals are in continuous cohabitation. The motive of continuous cohabitation is expressed in a well-known lingam symbol, which is to be found everywhere in Indian temples; the base is a female symbol, and within that is the phallus.[5] The symbol approaches very closely the Grecian mystic phallic basket and chests. (Compare with this the Eleusinian mysteries.) The chest or box is here a female symbol, that is, the mother's womb. This is a very well-known conception in the old mythologies.[6] The chest, basket or little basket, with its precious contents, was thought of as floating on the water; a remarkable inversion of the natural fact that the child floats in the amniotic fluid and that this is in the uterus.

This inversion brings about a great advantage for sublimation, for it creates enormous possibilities of application for the myth-weaving phantasy, that is to say, for the annexation to the sun cycle. The Sun floats over the sea like an immortal god, which every evening is immersed in the maternal water and is born again renewed in the morning. Frobenius says:

" Perhaps in connection with the blood-red sunrise, the idea occurs that here a birth takes place, the birth of a young son; the question then arises inevitably, whence comes the paternity? How has the woman become pregnant? And since this woman symbolizes the same idea as the fish, which means the sea, (because we proceed from the assumption that the Sun descends into the sea as well as arises from it) thus the curious primitive answer is that this sea has previously swallowed the old Sun. Consequently the resulting myth is, that the woman (sea) has formerly devoured the Sun and now brings a new Sun into the world, and thus she has become pregnant."

All these sea-going gods are sun symbols. They are enclosed in a chest or an ark for the " night journey on the sea " (Frobenius), often together with a woman (again an inversion of the actual situation, but in support of the motive of continuous cohabitation, which we have met above). During the night journey on the sea the Sun-god is enclosed in the mother's womb, oftentimes threatened by dangers of all kinds. Instead of many individual examples, I will content myself with reproducing the scheme which Frobenius has constructed from numberless myths of this sort:

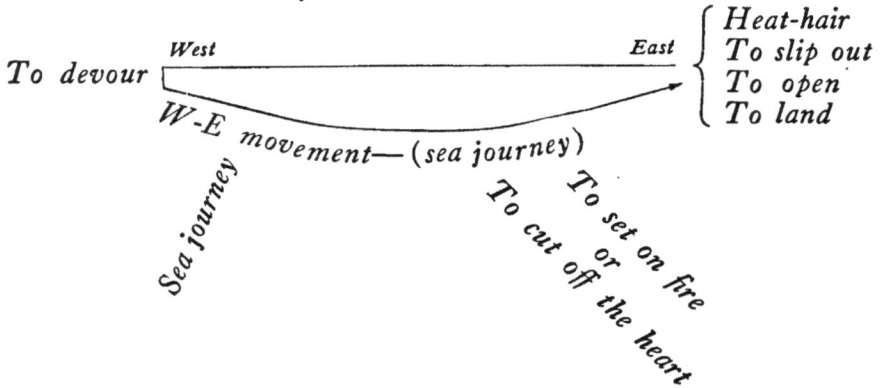

Frobenius gives the following legend to illustrate this:

"A hero is devoured by a water monster in the West (to devour). The animal carries him within him to the East (sea journey). Meanwhile, he kindles a fire in the belly of the monster (to set on fire) and since he feels hungry he cuts off a piece of the hanging heart (to cut off the heart). Soon after he notices that the fish glides upon the dry land (to land); he immediately begins to cut open the animal from within outwards (to open) then he slides out (to slip out). In the fish's belly, it had been so hot, that all his hair had fallen out (heat-hair). The hero frequently frees all who were previously devoured (to devour all) and all now slide out (slip out)."

A very close parallel is Noah's journey during the flood, in which all living creatures die; only he and the life guarded by him are brought to a new birth. In a Mela-polynesian legend (Frobenius) it is told that the hero in the belly of the King Fish took his weapon and cut open the fish's belly. "He slid out and saw a splendor, and he sat down and reflected. 'I wonder where I am,' he said. Then the sun rose with a bound and turned from

one side to the other." The Sun has again slipped out.
Frobenius mentions from the Ramayana the myth of
the ape Hanuman, who represents the Sun-hero. The
sun in which Hanuman hurries through the air throws a
shadow upon the sea. The sea monster notices this and
through this draws Hanuman toward itself; when the latter
sees that the monster is about to devour him, he stretches
out his figure immeasurably; the monster assumes the
same gigantic proportions. As he does that Hanuman
becomes as small as a thumb, slips into the great body
of the monster and comes out on the other side. In another part of the poem it is said that he came out from
the right ear of the monster (like Rabelais' Gargantua,
who also was born from the mother's ear). " Hanuman
thereupon resumes his flight, and finds a new obstacle in
another sea monster, which is the mother of Rahus, the
sun-devouring demon. The latter draws Hanuman's
shadow [7] to her in the same way. Hanuman again has
recourse to the earlier stratagem, becomes small and slips
into her body, but hardly is he there than he grows to a
gigantic mass, swells up, tears her, kills her, and in that
way makes his escape."

Thus we understand why the Indian fire-bringer Ma-
târiçvan is called " the one swelling in the mother "; the
ark (little box, chest, cask, vessel, etc.) is a symbol of
the womb, just as is the sea, into which the Sun sinks
for rebirth. From this circle of ideas we understand the
mythologic statements about Ogyges; he it is who possesses the mother, the City, who is united with the mother;
therefore under him came the great flood, for it is a

typical fragment of the sun myth that the hero, when united with the woman attained with difficulty, is exposed in a cask and thrown into the sea, and then lands for a new life on a distant shore. The middle part, the " night journey on the sea " in the ark, is lacking in the tradition of Ogyges.[8] But the rule in mythology is that the typical parts of a myth can be united in all conceivable variations, which adds greatly to the extraordinary difficulty of the interpretation of a particular myth without knowledge of all the others. The meaning of this cycle of myths mentioned here is clear; it is the longing *to attain rebirth through the return to the mother's womb, that is to say, to become as immortal as the sun.* This longing for the mother is frequently expressed in our holy scriptures.[9] I recall, particularly the place in the epistle to the Galatians, where it is said (iv: 26) :

(26) " But Jerusalem which is above is free, which is the mother of us all.

(27) " For it is written, Rejoice, thou barren that beareth not: break forth and cry, thou that travailest not: for the desolate hath many more children than she which hath an husband.

(28) " Now we, brethren, as Isaac was, are the children of promise.

(29) " But as he that was born after the flesh persecuted him that was born after the spirit, even so it is now.

(30) " Nevertheless, what sayeth the scripture? Cast out the bondwoman and her son; for the son of a bondwoman shall not be heir with the son of a freewoman.

(31) " So, then, brethren, we are not children of the bondwoman, but of the free."

Chapter v:

(1) "Stand fast therefore in the liberty wherewith Christ has made us free."

The Christians are the children of the City Above, a symbol of the mother, not sons of the earthly city-mother, who is to be cast out; for those born after the flesh are opposed to those born after the spirit, who are not born from the mother in the flesh, but from a symbol for the mother. One must again think of the Indians at this point, who say the first people proceeded from the sword-hilt and a shuttle. The religious thought is bound up with the compulsion to call the mother no longer mother, but City, Source, Sea, etc. This compulsion can be derived from the need to manifest an amount of libido bound up with the mother, but in such a way that the mother is represented by or concealed in a symbol. The symbolism of the city we find well-developed in the revelations of John, where two cities play a great part, one of which is insulted and cursed by him, the other greatly desired. We read in Revelation (xvii: 1):

(1) "Come hither: I will shew unto thee the judgment of the great whore that sitteth on many waters.

(2) "With whom the kings of the earth have committed forni-cation and the inhabitants of the earth have been made drunk with the wine of her fornication.

(3) "So he carried me away in the spirit into the wilderness: and I saw a woman sit on a scarlet colored beast, full of the names of blasphemy, and having seven heads and ten horns.

(4) "And the woman was arrayed in purple and scarlet colors, and decked with gold and precious stones and pearls, having a golden cup [10] in her hand full of abominations and filthiness of her fornication.

(5) "And upon her forehead was a name written: *Mystery.*

*Babylon the great. The Mother of Harlots and Abominations
of the Earth.*

(6) " And I saw the woman drunken with the blood of saints,
and with the blood of the martyrs of Jesus: and when I saw her
I wondered with a great admiration.''

Here follows an interpretation of the vision unintelligible to us, from which we can only emphasize the point
that the seven heads [11] of the dragon means the seven
hills upon which the woman sits. This is probably a distinct allusion to Rome, the city whose temporal power
oppressed the world at the time of the Revelation. The
waters upon which the woman " the mother " sits are
" peoples and throngs and nations and tongues." This
also seems to refer to Rome, for she is the mother of
peoples and possessed all lands. Just as in common
speech, for example, colonies are called daughters, so
the people subject to Rome are like members of a family
subject to the mother. In another version of the picture,
the kings of the people, namely, the fathers, commit
fornication with this mother. Revelation continues
(xviii: 2) :

(2) " And he cried mightily with a strong voice, saying, Babylon the Great is fallen, is fallen, and is become the habitation of
devils, and the hold of every foul spirit, and a cage of every
unclean and hateful bird.

(3) " For all nations have drunk of the wine of the wrath
of her fornication.''

Thus this mother does not only become the mother of
all abominations, but also in truth the receptacle of all
that is wicked and unclean. The birds are images of

souls;[12] therefore, this means all souls of the condemned and evil spirits. Thus the mother becomes Hecate, the underworld, the City of the damned itself. We recognize easily in the ancient idea of the woman on the dragon,[13] the above-mentioned representation of Echnida, the mother of the infernal horrors. Babylon is the idea of the "terrible" mother, who seduces all people to whoredom with devilish temptation, and makes them drunk with her wine. The intoxicating drink stands in the closest relation to fornication, for it is also a libido symbol, as we have already seen in the parallel of fire and sun. After the fall and curse of Babylon, we find in Revelation (xix: 6-7) the hymn which leads from the under half to the upper half of the mother, where now everything is possible which would be impossible without the repression of incest:

(6) "Alleluia, the Lord God omnipotent reigneth.

(7) "Let us be glad and rejoice, and give honor to him: for the marriage of the Lamb is come,[14] and his wife hath made herself ready.

(8) "And to her was granted that she should be arrayed in fine linen, clean and white: for the fine linen is the righteousness of saints.

(9) "And he saith unto me, 'Write, Blessed are they which are called unto the marriage supper of the Lamb.' "

The Lamb is the son of man who celebrates his marriage with the "woman." Who the "woman" is remains obscure at first. But Revelation (xxi: 9) shows us which "woman" is the bride, the Lamb's wife:

(9) "Come hither, I will show thee the bride, the Lamb's wife.[15]

(10) "And he carried me away in the spirit to a great and high mountain, and showed me that great city, the holy Jerusalem, descending out of heaven from God, having the glory of God."

It is evident from this quotation, after all that goes before, that the City, the heavenly bride, who is here promised to the Son, is the mother.[16]   In Babylon the impure maid was cast out, according to the Epistle to the Galatians, so that here in heavenly Jerusalem the mother-bride may be attained the more surely.   It bears witness to the most delicate psychologic perception that the fathers of the church who formulated the canons preserved this bit of the symbolic significance of the Christ mystery.   It is a treasure house for the phantasies and myth materials which underlie primitive Christianity.[17] The further attributes which were heaped upon the heavenly Jerusalem make its significance as mother overwhelmingly clear:

(1) "And he shewed me a pure river of water of life, clear as crystal, proceeding out of the throne of God and of the Lamb.

(2) "In the midst of the street of it, and on either side of the river, was there the tree of life, which bare twelve manner of fruits, and yielded her fruit every month, and the leaves of the tree were for the healing of nations.

(3) "And there shall be no more curse."

In this quotation we come upon the symbol of the waters, which we found in the mention of Ogyges in connection with the city.   The maternal significance of water belongs to the clearest symbolism in the realm of mythology,[18] so that the ancients could say: ἡ θάλασσα— τῆς γενέσεως σύμβολον.* From water comes life;[19]

* The sea is the symbol of birth.

therefore, of the two gods which here interest us the most, Christ and Mithra, the latter was born beside a river, according to representations, while Christ experienced his new birth in the Jordan; moreover, he is born from the Πηγή,[20] the "sempiterni fons amoris," the mother of God, who by the heathen-Christian legend was made a nymph of the Spring. The "Spring" is also found in Mithracism. A Pannonian dedication reads, "Fonti perenni." An inscription in Apulia is dedicated to the "Fons Aeterni." In Persia, Ardvîçûra is the well of the water of life. Ardvîçûra-Anahita is a goddess of water and love (just as Aphrodite is born from foam). The neo-Persians designate the Planet Venus and a nubile girl by the name "Nahid." In the temples of Anaitis there existed prostitute Hierodules (harlots). In the Sakaeen (in honor of Anaitis) there occurred ritual combats as in the festival of the Egyptian Ares and his mother. In the Vedas the waters are called Mâtritamâh—the most maternal.[20] All that is living rises as does the sun, from the water, and at evening plunges into the water. Born from the springs, the rivers, the seas, at death man arrives at the waters of the Styx in order to enter upon the "night journey on the sea." The wish is that the black water of death might be the water of life; that death, with its cold embrace, might be the mother's womb, just as the sea devours the sun, but brings it forth again out of the maternal womb (Jonah motive [21]). Life believes not in death.

> "In the flood of life, in the torrent of deeds,
> I toss up and down,

I am blown to and fro!
Cradle and grave,
An eternal sea;
A changing web,
A glowing life."   —*Goethe: Faust.*

That ξύλον ζωῆς, the wood of life, or the tree of life, is a maternal symbol would seem to follow from the previous deductions. The etymologic connection of ὕω, ὕλη, υἱός, in the Indo-Germanic root suggests the blending of the meanings in the underlying symbolism of mother and of generation. The tree of life is probably, first of all, a fruit-bearing genealogical tree, that is, a mother-image. Countless myths prove the derivation of man from trees; many myths show how the hero is enclosed in the maternal tree—thus dead Osiris in the column, Adonis in the myrtle, etc. Numerous female divinities were worshipped as trees, from which resulted the cult of the holy groves and trees. It is of transparent significance when Attis castrates himself under a pine tree, i. e. he does it because of the mother. Goddesses were often worshipped in the form of a tree or of a wood. Thus Juno of Thespiæ was a branch of a tree, Juno of Samos was a board. Juno of Argos was a column. The Carian Diana was an uncut piece of wood. Athene of Lindus was a polished column. Tertullian calls Ceres of Pharos " rudis palus et informe lignum sine effigie." Athenaeus remarks of Latona at Dalos that she is ξύλινον ἄμορφον, a shapeless piece of wood.[22] Tertullian calls an Attic Pallas " crucis stipes," a wooden pale or mast. The wooden pale is phallic, as the name

suggests, φάλης, Pallus. The φαλλός is a pale, a ceremonial lingam carved out of figwood, as are all Roman
statues of Priapus. Φᾶλος means a projection or centre-
piece on the helmet, later called κῶνος, just as ἀνα-
φαλ-αντίασις signifies baldheadedness on the forepart
of the head, and φαλακρός signifies baldheadedness in regard to the φᾶλος-κῶνος of the helmet; a semi-phallic
meaning is given to the upper part of the head as well.[23]
Φάλληνος has, besides φαλλός, the significance of
" wooden "; φαλ-άγγωμα," cylinder ";φάλαγξ," a round
beam." The Macedonian battle array, distinguished by
its powerful impetus, is called φάλαγξ; moreover, the
finger-joint [24] is called φάλαγξ. φάλλαινα or φάλαινα
is a whale. Now φαλός appears with the meaning
" shining, brilliant." The Indo-Germanic root is bhale
= to bulge, to swell.[25] Who does not think of Faust?

" It grows, it shines, increases in my hand! "

That is primitive libido symbolism, which shows how
immediate is the connection between phallic libido and
light. The same relations are found in the Rigveda in
Rudra's utterances.

Rigveda i, 114, 3:
" May we obtain your favor, thou man ruling, Oh urinating
Rudra."

I refer here to the previously mentioned phallic symbolism of Rudra in the Upanishads:

(4) " We call for help below to the flaming Rudra, to the
one bringing the sacrifice; him who encircles and wanders (wandering in the vault of Heaven) to the seer."

2, 33, 5:

"He who opens up the sweet, who listens to our calls, the ruddy one, with the beautiful helmet, may he not give us over to the powers of jealousy.

(6) "I have been rejoiced by the bull connected with Marut, the supplicating one with strong force of life.

(8) "Sound the powerful song of praise to the ruddy bull to the white shining one; worship the flaming one with honor, we sing of the shining being Rudra.

"May Rudra's missile (arrow) not be used on us, may the great displeasure of the shining one pass us by: Unbend the firm (bow or hard arrow?) for the princes, thou who blessest with the waters of thy body (generative strength), be gracious to our children and grandchildren." [26]

In this way we pass from the realm of mother symbolism imperceptibly into the realm of male phallic symbolism. This element also lies in the tree, even in the family tree, as is distinctly shown by the mediæval family trees. From the first ancestor there grows upward, in the place of the "membrum virile," the trunk of the great tree. The bisexual symbolic character of the tree is intimated by the fact that in Latin trees have a masculine termination and a feminine gender.[27] The feminine (especially the maternal) meaning of the forest and the phallic significance of trees in dreams is well known. I mention an example.

It concerns a woman who had always been nervous, and who, after many years of marriage, became ill as a result of the typical retention of the libido. She had the following dream after she had learned to know a young man of many engaging free opinions who was very pleasing to her: She found herself in a garden where stood a remarkable exotic tree with strange red fleshy flowers or fruits. She picked them and ate them. Then, to her horror, she felt that she was poisoned. This dream idea may easily be understood by means of the antique or poetic symbolism, so I can spare information as to the analytic material.

The double significance of the tree is readily explained by the fact that such symbols are not to be understood " anatomically " but psychologically as libido symbols; therefore, it is not permissible to interpret the tree on account of its similar form as directly phallic; it can also be called a woman or the uterus of the mother. The uniformity of the significance lies alone in the similarity to the libido.[28] One loses one's way in one " cul de sac " after another by saying that this is the symbol substituted for the mother and that for the penis. In this realm there is no fixed significance of things. The only reality here is the libido, for which " all that is perishable is merely a symbol." It is not the physical actual mother, but the libido of the son, the object of which was once the mother. We take mythologic symbols much too concretely and wonder at every step about the endless contradictions. These contradictions arise only because we constantly forget that in the realm of phantasy " feeling is all." Whenever we read, therefore, " his mother was a wicked sorcerer," the translation is as follows: The son is in love with her, namely, he is unable to detach his libido from the mother-imago; he therefore suffers from incestuous resistance.

The symbolism of water and trees, which are met with

as further attributes in the symbol of the City, also refer
to that amount of libido which unconsciously is fastened
to the mother-imago.   In certain parts of Revelation
the unconscious psychology of religious longing is revealed, namely, the longing for the *mother*.[29]   The expectation of Revelation ends in the mother: καὶ πᾶν
κατάθεμα οὐκ ἔσται ἔτι. ("and there shall be no more
curse").   There shall be no more sins, no repression, no
disharmony with one's self, no guilt, no fear of death and
no pain of separation.more!

Thus Revelation echoes that same radiant mystical
harmony which was caught again 2,000 years later and
expressed poetically in the last prayer of Dr. Marianus:

> " Penitents, look up, elate,
> Where she beams salvation;
> Gratefully to blessed fate
> Grow, in recreation!
> Be our souls, as they have been,
> Dedicate to thee!
> Virgin Holy, Mother, Queen,
> Goddess, gracious be! "   —*Goethe: Faust.*

One principal question arises at the sight of this beauty
and greatness of feeling, that is, whether the primary
tendency compensated by religion is not too narrowly
understood as incestuous.   I have previously observed in
regard to this that I consider the " resistance opposed to
libido " as in a general way coincident with the incest prohibition.   I must leave open for the present the definition
of the psychological incest conception.   However, I will
here emphasize the point that it is most especially the

totality of the sun myth which proves to us that the fundamental basis of the "incestuous" desire does not aim at cohabitation, but at the special thought of becoming a child again, of turning back to the parent's protection, of coming into the mother once more in order to be born again. But incest stands in the path to this goal, that is to say, the necessity of in some way again gaining entrance into the mother's womb. One of the simplest ways would be to impregnate the mother, and to reproduce one's self identically. But here the incest prohibition interferes; therefore, the myths of the sun or of rebirth teem with all possible proposals as to how incest can be evaded. A very simple method of avoidance is to transform the mother into another being or to rejuvenate [30] her after birth has occurred, to have her disappear again or have her change back. It is not incestuous cohabitation which is desired, but the rebirth, which now is attained most readily through cohabitation. But this is not the only way, although perhaps the original one. The resistance to the incest prohibition makes the phantasy inventive; for example, it was attempted to impregnate the mother by means of a magic charm of fertility (to wish for a child). Attempts in this respect remain in the stage of mythical phantasies; but they have one result, and that is the exercise of the phantasy which gradually produces paths through the creation of phantastic possibilities, in which the libido, taking an active part, can flow off. Thus the libido becomes *spiritualized in an imperceptible manner.* The power "which always wishes evil" thus creates a spiritual life. Therefore, in religions, this course is now raised to a system. On that account it is exceedingly instructive to see how religion takes pains to further these symbolic transferences.[31] The New Testament furnishes us with an excellent example in regard to this. Nicodemus, in the speech regarding rebirth, cannot forbear understanding the matter very realistically.

John iii: 4:
(4) " How can a man be born when he is old? Can he enter a second time into his mother's womb, and be born? "

But Jesus endeavors to raise into purity the sensuous view of Nicodemus's mind moulded in materialistic heaviness, and announces to him—really the same—and yet not the same:

(5) " Verily, verily, I say unto thee, Except a man be born of water and of the spirit, he cannot enter into the kingdom of God.
(6) " That which is born of the flesh is flesh: and that which is born of the spirit is spirit.
(7) " Marvel not that I said unto thee, Ye must be born again.
(8) " The wind bloweth where it listeth, and thou hearest the sound thereof, but canst not tell whence it cometh and whither it goeth; so is everyone that is born of the spirit."

To be born of water means simply to be born from the mother's womb. To be born of the spirit means to be born from the fructifying breath of the wind; this we learn from the Greek text (where spirit and wind are expressed by the same word, $\pi\nu\epsilon\tilde{\upsilon}\mu\alpha$) τὸ γεγεννημένον ἐκ τῆς σαρκὸς σάρξ ἐστιν, καὶ τὸ γεγεννημένον ἐκ τοῦ πνεύματος πνεῦμά ἐστιν.—Τὸ πνεῦμα ὅπου θέλει πνεῖ,* etc.

This symbolism rose from the same need as that which produced the Egyptian legend of the vultures, the mother symbol. They were only females and were fertilized by the wind. One recognizes very clearly the ethical demand as the foundation of these mythologic assertions: *thou must say of the mother that she was not impregnated by a mortal in the ordinary way, but by a spiritual being in an unusual manner.* This demand stands in strict opposition to the real truth; therefore, the myth is a fitting solution. One can say it was a hero who died and was born again in a remarkable manner, and in this way attained immortality. The need which this demand asserts is evidently a prohibition against a definite phantasy concerning the mother. A son may naturally think that a father has generated him in a carnal way, but not that he himself impregnated the mother and so caused himself to be born again into renewed youth. This incestuous phantasy which for some reason possesses an extraordinary strength,[32] and, therefore, appears as a compulsory wish, is repressed and, conforming to the above demand, under certain conditions, expresses itself again, symbolically, concerning the problem of birth, or rather concerning individual rebirth from the mother. In Jesus's challenge to Nicodemus we clearly recognize this tendency: "Think not carnally or thou art carnal, but think symbolically, then art thou spirit." It is evident

* That which is born of the flesh is flesh and that which is born of the spirit is spirit; the spirit bloweth where it listeth.

how extremely educative and developing this compulsion
toward symbolism can be. Nicodemus would remain fixed
in low commonplaces if he did not succeed in raising himself through symbols above this repressed incestuous
desire. As a righteous philistine of culture, he probably
was not very anxious for this effort, because men seem
really to remain satisfied in repressing the incestuous
libido, and at best to express it by some modest religious
exercises. Yet it seems to be important, on the other
side, that man should not merely renounce and repress
and thereby remain firmly fixed in the incestuous bond,
but that he should redeem those dynamic forces which
lie bound up in incest, in order to fulfil himself. For man
needs his whole libido, to fill out the boundaries of his
personality, and then, for the first time, he is in a condition to do his best. The paths by which man may manifest his incestuously fixed libido seem to have been
pointed out by the religious mythologic symbols. On this
account Jesus teaches Nicodemus: "Thou thinkest of
thy incestuous wish for rebirth, but thou must think that
thou art born from the water and that thou art generated
by the breath of the wind,[33] and in this way thou shalt
share in eternal life."

Thus the libido which lies inactive in the incestuous
bond repressed and in fear of the law and the avenging
Father God can be led over into sublimation through the
symbol of baptism (birth from water) and of generation
(spiritual birth) through the symbol of the descent of the
Holy Ghost. Thus man becomes a child [34] again and is
born into a circle of brothers and sisters; but his mother

is the "communion of the saints," the church, and his circle of brothers and sisters is humanity, with whom he is united anew in the common inheritance of the primitive symbol.

It seems that at the time in which Christianity had its origin this process was especially necessary; for that period, as the result of the incredible contrast between slavery and the freedom of the citizens and masters, had entirely lost the consciousness of the common bond of mankind. One of the next and most essential reasons for the energetic regression to the infantile in Christianity, which goes hand in hand with the revival of the incest problem, was probably to be found in the far-reaching depreciation of women. At that time sexuality was so easily attainable that the result could only be a very excessive depreciation of the sexual object. The existence of personal values was first discovered by Christianity, and there are many people who have not discovered it even in the present day. However, the depreciation of the sexual object hinders the outflow of that libido which cannot be satisfied by sexual activity, because it belongs to an already desexualized higher order. (If it were not so, a Don Juan could never be neurotic; but the contrary is the case.) For how might those higher valuations be given to a worthless, despised object? Therefore, the libido, after having seen a " Helen in every woman " for so long a time, sets out on a search for the difficult to obtain, the worshipped, but perhaps unattainable, goal, and which in the unconscious is the mother. Therefore the symbolic needs, based on the incest resist-

ance, arise again in an increased degree, which promptly
transforms the beautiful, sinful world of the Olympian
Gods into incomprehensible, dreamlike, dark mysteries,
which, with their accessions of symbols and obscure mean-
ingful texts, remove us very far from the religious
feelings of that Roman-Græco world. When we see
how much trouble Jesus took to make acceptable to Nicodemus the symbolic perception of things, that is to say,
really a repression and veiling over of the actual facts,
and how important it was for the history of civilization
in general, that people thought and still think in this
way, then we understand the revolt which is raised everywhere against the psychologic discovery of the true background of the neurotic or normal symbolism. Always
and everywhere we encounter the odious realm of sexuality, which represents to all righteous people of to-day
something defiled. However, less than 2,000 years have
passed since the religious cult of sexuality was more or
less openly in full bloom. To be sure, they were heathen
and did not know better, but the nature of religious power
does not change from cycle to cycle. If one has once received an effectual impression of the sexual contents of
the ancient cults, and if one realizes oneself that the religious experience, that is, the union [35] with the God of
antiquity, was understood by antiquity as a more or less
concrete coitus, then truly one can no longer fancy that
the motor forces of a religion have suddenly become
wholly different since the birth of Christ. Exactly the
same thing has occurred as with the hysteric who at first
indulges in some quite unbeautiful, infantile sexual mani-

festations and afterwards develops a hyperæsthetic negation in order to convince every one of his special purity.
*Christianity, with its repression of the manifest sexual, is
the negative of the ancient sexual cult.* The original cult
has changed its tokens.[36] One only needs to realize how
much of the gay paganism, even to the inclusion of un-
seemly Gods, has been taken into the Christian church.
Thus the old indecent Priapus celebrated a gay festival of
resurrection in St. Tychon.[37] Also partly in the physicians
Sts. Kosma and Damien, who graciously condescended to
accept the " membra virilia " in wax at their festival.[38]
St. Phallus of old memories emerges again to be worshipped in country chapels, to say nothing of the rest of
the paganism!

There are those who have not yet learned to recognize
sexuality as a function equivalent to hunger and who,
therefore, consider it as disgraceful that certain taboo
institutions which were considered as asexual refuges are
now recognized as overflowing with sexual symbolism.
Those people are doomed to the painful realization that
such is still the case, in spite of their great revolt. One
must learn to understand that, opposed to the customary
habit of thought, psychoanalytic thinking reduces and
resolves those symbolic structures which have become
more and more complicated through countless elaboration. This means a course of reduction which would
be an intellectual enjoyment if the object were different.
But here it becomes distressing, not only æsthetically, but
apparently also ethically, because the repressions which
are to be overcome have been brought about by our best

intentions. We must commence to overcome our virtuousness with the certain fear of falling into baseness on
the other side. This is certainly true, for virtuousness is
always inwardly compensated by a great tendency towards
baseness; and how many profligates are there who inwardly preserve a mawkish virtue and moral megalomania? Both categories of men turn out to be snobs
when they come in contact with analytic psychology, because the moral man has imagined an objective and cheap
verdict on sexuality and the unmoral man is entirely unaware of the vulgarity of his sexuality and of his incapacity for an unselfish love. One completely forgets that
one can most miserably be carried away, not only by a
vice, but also by a virtue. There is a fanatic orgiastic
self-righteousness which is just as base and which entails
just as much injustice and violence as a vice.

At this time, when a large part of mankind is beginning to discard Christianity, it is worth while to understand clearly why it was originally accepted. It was accepted in order to escape at last from the brutality of
antiquity. As soon as we discard it, licentiousness returns, as impressively exemplified by life in our large
modern cities. This step is not a forward step, but a
backward one. It is as with individuals who have laid
aside one form of transference and have no new one.
Without fail they will occupy regressively the old path
of transference, to their great detriment, because the
world around them has since then essentially changed.
He who is repelled by the historical and philosophical
weakness of the Christian dogmatism and the religious

emptiness of an historical Jesus, of whose person we know nothing and whose religious value is partly Talmudic, partly Hellenic wisdom, and discards Christianity, and therewith Christian morality, is certainly confronted with the ancient problem of licentiousness. Today the individual still feels himself restrained by the public hypocritical opinion, and, therefore, prefers to lead a secret, separate life, but publicly to represent morality. It might be different if men in general all at once found the moral mask too dull, and if they realized how dangerously their beasts lie in wait for each other, and then truly a frenzy of demoralization might sweep over humanity. This is the dream, the wish dream, of the morally limited man of today; he forgets necessity, which strangles men and robs them of their breath, and which with a stern hand interrupts every passion.

It must not be imputed to me that I am wishing to refer the libido back by analytical reduction to the primitive, almost conquered, stages, entirely forgetting the fearful misery this would entail for humanity. Indeed, some individuals would let themselves be transported by the old-time frenzy of sexuality, from which the burden of guilt has been removed, to their own greatest detriment.

But these are the ones who under other circumstances would have prematurely perished in some other way. However, I well know the most effectual and most inexorable regulator of human sexuality. This is necessity. With this leaden weight human lust will never fly too high.

To-day there are countless neurotics who are so simply

because they do not know how to seek happiness in their own manner. They do not even realize where the lack lies. And besides these neurotics there are many more normal people—and precisely people of the higher type— who feel restricted and discontented. For all these re- duction to the sexual elements should be undertaken, in order that they may be reinstated into the possession of their primitive self, and thereby learn to know and value its relation to the entire personality. In this way alone can certain requirements be fulfilled and others be re- pudiated as unfit because of their infantile character. In this way the individual will come to realize that certain things are to be sacrificed, although they are accom- plished, *but in another sphere.* We imagine that we have long renounced, sacrificed and cut off our incest wish, and that nothing of it is left. But it does not occur to us that this is not true, but that we unconsciously commit incest in another territory. In religious symbols, for example, we come across incest.[39] We consider the in- cestuous wish vanished and lost, and then rediscover it in full force in religion. This process or transformation has taken place unconsciously in secular development. Just as in Part I it is shown that a similar unconscious transformation of the libido is an ethically worthless pose, and with which I compared the Christianity of early Roman antiquity, where evidently licentiousness and bru- tality were strongly resisted, so here I must remark in regard to the sublimation of the incestuous libido, that the belief in the religious symbol has ceased to be an ethical ideal; but it is an unconscious transformation of the incest wish into symbolic acts and symbolic concepts which cheat men, as it were, so that heaven appears to them as a father and earth as a mother and the people upon it children and brothers and sisters. Thus man can remain a child for all time and satisfy his incest wish all unawares. This state would doubtless be ideal [40] if it were not infantile and, therefore, merely a one-sided wish, which maintains a childish attitude. *The reverse is anxiety.* Much is said of pious people who remain unshaken in their trust in God and wander unswervingly safe and blessed through the world. I have never seen this Chidher yet. It is probably a wish figure. The rule is great uncertainty among believers, which they drown with fanatical cries among themselves or among others; moreover, they have religious doubts, moral uncertainty, doubts of their own personality, feelings of guilt and, deepest of all, great fear of the opposite aspect of reality, against which the most highly intelligent people struggle with all their force. This other side is the devil, the adversary or, expressed in modern terms, the corrective of reality, of the infantile world picture, which has been made acceptable through the predominating pleasure principle.[41] But the world is not a garden of God, of the Father, but a place of terrors. Not only is heaven no father and earth no mother and the people not brothers nor sisters, but they represent hostile, destroying powers, to which we are abandoned the more surely, the more childishly and thoughtlessly we have entrusted ourselves to the so-called Fatherly hand of God. One should never forget the harsh speech of the first Napoleon, that the good God is always on the side of the heaviest artillery.

The religious myth meets us here as one of the greatest and most significant human institutions which, despite misleading symbols, nevertheless gives man assurance and strength, so that he may not be overwhelmed by the monsters of the universe. The symbol, considered from the standpoint of actual truth, is misleading, indeed, but it is *psychologically true*,[42] because it was and is the bridge to all the greatest achievements of humanity.

But this does not mean to say that this unconscious way of transformation of the incest wish into religious exercises is the only one or the only possible one. There is also a conscious recognition and understanding with which we can take possession of this libido which is bound up in incest and transformed into religious exercises so that we no longer need the stage of religious symbolism for this end. It is thinkable that instead of doing good to our fellow-men, for " the love of Christ," we do it from the knowledge that humanity, even as ourselves, could not exist if, among the herd, the one could not sacrifice himself for the other. *This would be the course of moral autonomy, of perfect freedom, when man could without compulsion wish that which he must do, and this from knowledge, without delusion through belief in the religious symbols.*

It is a positive creed which keeps us infantile and, therefore, ethically inferior. Although of the greatest significance from the cultural point of view and of imperishable beauty from the æsthetic standpoint, this delusion can no longer ethically suffice humanity striving after moral autonomy.

The infantile and moral danger lies in belief in the symbol because through that we guide the libido to an imaginary reality. The simple negation of the symbol changes nothing, for the entire mental disposition remains the same; we merely remove the dangerous object. But the object is not dangerous; the danger is our own infantile mental state, for love of which we have lost something very beautiful and ingenious through the simple abandonment of the religious symbol. I think *belief should be replaced by understanding;* then we would keep the beauty of the symbol, but still remain free from the depressing results of submission to belief. This would be the psychoanalytic cure for belief and disbelief.

The vision following upon that of the city is that of a " strange fir tree with gnarled branches." This vision does not seem extraordinary to us after all that we have learned of the tree of life and its associations with the city and the waters of life. This especial tree seems simply to continue the category of the mother symbols. The attribute " strange " probably signifies, as in dreams, a special emphasis, that is, a special underlying complex material. Unfortunately, the author gives us no individual material for this. As the tree already suggested in the symbolism of the city is particularly emphasized through the further development of Miss Miller's visions here, I find it necessary to discuss at some length the history of the symbolism of the tree.

It is well known that trees have played a large part in the cult myth from the remotest times. The typical myth tree is the tree of paradise or of life which we discover abundantly used in Babylonian and also in Jewish lore; and in prechristian times, the pine tree of Attis, the tree or trees of Mithra; in Germanic mythology, Ygdrasil and so on. The hanging of the Attis image on the pine tree; the hanging of Marsyas, which became a celebrated artistic motive; the hanging of Odin; the Germanic hanging sacrifices—indeed, the whole series of hanged gods—teaches us that the hanging of Christ on the cross is not a unique occurrence in religious mythology, but belongs to the same circle of ideas as others. In this world of imagery the cross of Christ is the tree of life, and equally the wood of death. This contrast is not astounding. Just as the origin of man from trees was a legendary idea, so there were also burial customs, in which people were buried in hollow trees. From that the German language retains even now the expression " Totenbaum " (tree of death) for a coffin. Keeping in mind the fact that the tree is predominantly a mother symbol, then the mystic significance of this manner of burial can be in no way incomprehensible to us. *The dead are delivered back to the mother for rebirth.* We encounter this symbol in the Osiris myth, handed down by Plutarch,[43] which is, in general, typical in various aspects. Rhea is pregnant with Osiris; at the same time also with Isis; Osiris and Isis mate even in the mother's womb (motive of the night

journey on the sea with incest). Their son is Arueris,
later called Horus. It is said of Isis that she was born
" in absolute humidity " (τετάρτη δὲ τῆν Ἴσιν ἐν πανύ-
γροις γενέσθαι*). It is said of Osiris that a certain Pamyles in Thebes heard a voice from the temple of Zeus
while drawing water, which commanded him to proclaim
that Osiris was born μέγας βασιλεὺς εὐεργέτης Ὄσιρις.†
In honor of this the Pamylion were celebrated. They
were similar to the phallophorion. Pamyles is a phallic
demon, similar to the original Dionysus. The myth reduced reads: Osiris and Isis were generated by phallus
from the water (mother womb) in the ordinary manner.
(Kronos had made Rhea pregnant, the relation was
secret, and Rhea was his sister. Helios, however, observed it and cursed the relation.) Osiris was killed in
a crafty manner by the god of the underworld, Typhon,
who locked him in a chest. He was thrown into the Nile,
and so carried out to sea. Osiris, however, mated in the
underworld with his second sister, Nephthys (motive of
the night journey to the sea with incest). One sees here
how the symbolism is developed. In the mother womb,
before the outward existence, Osiris commits incest; in
death, the second intrauterine existence, Osiris again commits incest. Both times with a sister who is simply substituted for the mother as a legal, uncensured symbol,
since the marriage with a sister in early antiquity was not
merely tolerated, but was really commended. Zarathustra also recommended the marriage of kindred. This

---

* In the fourth place Isis was born in absolute humidity.
† The great beneficent king, Osiris.

form of myth would be impossible to-day, because co-habitation with the sister, being incestuous, would be repressed. The wicked Typhon entices Osiris craftily into a box or chest; this distortion of the true state of affairs is transparent. The " original sin " caused men to wish to go back into the mother again, that is, the incestuous desire for the mother, condemned by law, is the ruse supposedly invented by Typhon. The fact is, the ruse is very significant. Man tries to sneak into rebirth through subterfuge in order to become a child again. An early Egyptian hymn [44] even raises an accusation against the mother Isis because she destroys the sun-god Ré by treachery. It was interpreted as the ill-will of the mother towards her son that she banished and betrayed him. The hymn describes how Isis fashioned a snake, put it in the path of Rê, and how the snake wounded the sun-god with a poisonous bite, from which wound he never recovered, so that finally he had to retire on the back of the heavenly cow. But this cow is the cow-headed goddess, just as Osiris is the bull Apis. The mother is accused as if she were the cause of man flying to the mother in order to be cured of the wound which she had herself inflicted. This wound is the prohibition of incest. [45] Man is thus cut off from the hopeful certainty of childhood and early youth, from all the unconscious, instinctive happenings which permit the child to live as an appendage of his parents, unconscious of himself. There must be contained in this many sensitive memories of the animal age, where there was not any " thou shalt " and " thou shalt not," but all was just simple occurrence. Even yet a deep animosity seems to live in man because a brutal law has separated him from the instinctive yielding to his desires and from the great beauty of the harmony of the animal nature. This separation manifested itself, among other things, in the incest prohibition and its correlates (laws of marriage, etc.); therefore pain and anger relate to the mother, as if she were responsible for the domestication of the sons of men. In order not to become conscious of his incest wish (his backward harking to the animal nature), the son throws all the burden of the guilt on the mother, from which arises the idea of the "terrible mother."[46] The mother becomes for him a spectre of anxiety, a nightmare.[47]

After the completed "night journey to the sea," the chest of Osiris was cast ashore by Byblos, and lay in the branches of an Erica, which grew around the coffin and became a splendid tree. The king of the land had the tree placed as a column under his roof.[48] During this period of Osiris's absence (the winter solstice) the lament customary during thousands of years for the dead god and his return occurs, and its εὕρεσις is a feast of joy. A passage from the mournful quest of Isis is especially noteworthy:

"She flutters like a swallow lamenting around the column, which encloses the god sleeping in death."

(This same motive returns in the Kyffhäuser saga.)

Later on Typhon dismembers the corpse and scatters the pieces. We come upon the *motive of dismember-*

ment in countless sun myths,[49] namely, the inversion of
the idea of the composition of the child in the mother's
womb.[50]   In fact, the mother Isis collects the pieces of
the body with the help of the jackal-headed Anubis. (She
finds the corpse with the help of dogs.)   Here the nocturnal devourers of bodies, the dogs and jackals, become
the assistants of the composition, of the reproduction.[51]
The Egyptian vulture owes its symbolic meaning as
mother to this necrophagic habit.   In Persian antiquity the
corpses were thrown out for the dogs to devour, just as
to-day in the Indian funeral pyres the removal of the
carcasses is left to the vultures.   Persia was familiar with
the custom of leading a dog to the bed of one dying,
whereupon the latter had to present the dog with a morsel.[52]   The custom, on its surface, evidently signifies that
the morsel is to belong to the dog, so that he will spare
the body of the dead, precisely as Cerberus was soothed
by the honey-cakes which Hercules gave to him in the
journey to hell.   But when we bear in mind the jackal-
headed Anubis who rendered his good services in the
gathering together of the dismembered Osiris, and the
mother significance of the vulture, then the question arises
whether something deeper was not meant by this ceremony.   Creuzer has also concerned himself with this idea,
and has come to the conclusion that the astral form of
the dog ceremony, that is, the appearance of Sirius, the
dog star, at the period of the sun's highest position, is
related to this in that the introduction of the dog has a
compensatory significance, death being thereby made, re-

FRUCTIFICATION FOLLOWING UPON THE MITHRAIC SACRIFICE

versedly, equal to the sun's highest position. This is quite in conformity with psychologic thought, which results from the very general fact that death is interpreted as entrance into the mother's womb (rebirth). This interpretation would seem to be supported by the otherwise enigmatic function of the dog in the Sacrificium Mithriacum. In the monuments a dog always leaps up upon the bull killed by Mithra. However, this sacrifice is probably to be interpreted through the Persian legend, as well as through the monument, as the moment of the *highest fecundity*. The most beautiful expression of this is seen upon the magnificent Mithra relief of Heddernheim. Upon one side of a large stone slab (formerly probably rotating) is seen the stereotyped overthrowing and sacrifice of the bull, but upon the other side stands Sol, with a bunch of grapes in his hand, Mithra with the cornucopia, the Dadophores with fruits, corresponding to the legend that all fecundity proceeds from the dead bull of the world, fruits from the horns, wine from its blood, grain from the tail, cattle from its sperma, leek from its nose, and so on. Silvanus stands above this scene with the animals of the forest arising from him. The significance suspected by Creuzer might very easily belong to the dog in this connection.[53] Let us now turn back to the myth of Osiris. In spite of the restoration of the corpse accomplished by Isis, the resuscitation succeeds only incompletely in so far as the phallus of Osiris cannot again be produced, because it was eaten by the fishes; the power of life was wanting.[54] Osiris as a phantom once more impregnated Isis, but the fruit is Harpocrates, who was feeble in τοῖς κάτωθεν γυίοις (in the lower limbs), that is, corresponding to the significance of γυῖον (at the feet). (Here, as is plainly evident, foot is used in the phallic meaning.) This incurability of the setting sun corresponds to the incurability of Rê in the above-mentioned older Egyptian sun hymn. Osiris, although only a phantom, now prepares the young sun, his son Horus, for a battle with Typhon, the evil spirit of darkness. Osiris and Horus correspond to the father-son symbolism mentioned in the beginning, which symbolic figure, corresponding again to the above formulation,[55] is flanked by the well-formed and ugly figures of Horus and Harpocrates, the latter appearing mostly as a cripple, often represented distorted to a mere caricature.[56]

He is confused in the tradition very much with Horus, with whom he also has the name in common. Hor-pi-chrud, as his real name [57] reads, is composed from chrud, "child," and Hor, from the adjective hri = up, on top, and signifies the up-coming child, as the rising sun, and opposed to Osiris, who personifies the setting sun—the sun of the west. Thus Osiris and Horpichrud or Horus are one being, both husband and son of the same mother, Hathor-Isis. The Chnum-Ra, the sun god of lower Egypt, represented as a ram, has at his side, as the female divinity of the land, Hatmehit, who wears the fish on her head. She is the mother and wife of Bi-neb-did (Ram, local name of Chnum-Ra). In the hymn of Hibis,[58] Amon-ra was invoked:

"Thy (Chum-Ram) dwells in Mendes, united as the quadruple god Thmuis. He is the phallus, the lord of the gods. The bull of his mother rejoices in the cow (ahet, the mother) and man fructifies through his semen."

In further inscriptions Hatmehit was directly referred to as the "mother of Mendes." (Mendes is the Greek form of Bi-neb-did: ram.) She is also invoked as the "Good," with the additional significance of *ta-nofert*, or "young woman." The cow as symbol of the mother is found in all possible forms and variations of Hathor-Isis, and also in the female Nun (parallel to this is the primitive goddess Nit or Neith), the protoplasm which, related to the Hindoo Atman,[59] is equally of masculine and feminine nature. Nun is, therefore, invoked as Amon,[60] the original water,[61] which is in the beginning. He is also designated as the father of fathers, the mother of mothers. To this corresponds the invocation to the female side of Nun-Amon, of Nit or Neith.

"Nit, the ancient, the mother of god, the mistress of Esne, the father of fathers, the mother of mothers, who is the beetle and the vulture, the being in its beginning.

"Nit, the ancient, the mother who bore the light god, Râ, who bore first of all, when there was nothing which brought forth.

"The cow, the ancient, which bore the sun, and then laid the germ of gods and men."

The word "nun" has the significance of young, fresh, new, also the on-coming waters of the Nile flood. In a transferred sense "nun" was also used for the chaotic primitive waters; in general for the primitive generating matter [62] which was personified by the goddess Nunet. From her Nut sprang, the goddess of heaven, who was represented with a starry body, and also as the heavenly cow with a starry body.

When the sun-god, little by little, retires on the back of the heavenly cow, just as poor Lazarus returns into Abraham's bosom, each has the same significance; they return into the mother, in order to rise as Horus. Thus it can be said that in the morning the goddess is the .mother, at noon the sister-wife and in the evening again the mother, who receives the dying in her lap, reminding us of the Pietà of Michelangelo. As shown by the illustration (from Dideron's " Iconographie Chrétienne "), this thought has been transferred as a whole into Christianity.

Thus the fate of Osiris is explained: he passes into the mother's womb, the chest, the sea, the tree, the column of Astartes; he is dismembered, re-formed, and reappears again in his son, Hor-pi-chrud.

Before entering upon the further mysteries which the beautiful myth reveals to us, there is still much to be said about the symbol of the tree. Osiris lies in the branches of the tree, surrounded by them, as in the mother's womb. The motive of *embracing and entwining* is often found in the sun myths, meaning that it is the *myth of rebirth*. A good example is the Sleeping Beauty, also the legend of the girl who is enclosed between the bark and the trunk, but who is freed by a youth with his horn.[63] The horn is of gold and silver, which hints at the sunbeam in the phallic meaning. (Compare the previous legend of the horn.) An exotic legend tells of the sun-hero, how he must be freed from the plant entwining around him.[64]

A girl dreams of her lover who has fallen into the water; she tries to save him, but first has to pull seaweed and sea-grass from the water; then she catches him. In an African myth the hero, after his act, must first be disentangled from the seaweed. In a Polynesian myth the hero's ship was encoiled by the tentacles of a gigantic polyp. Ré's ship is encoiled by a night serpent on its night journey on the sea. In the poetic rendering of the history of Buddha's birth by Sir Edwin Arnold (" The Light of Asia," p. 5) the motive of an embrace is also found:

> " Queen Maya stood at noon, her days fulfilled,
> Under a Palso in the palace grounds,
> A stately trunk, straight as a temple shaft,
> With crown of glossy leaves and fragrant blooms;
> And knowing the time come—for all things knew—
> The conscious tree bent down its boughs to make
> A bower about Queen Maya's majesty:
> And earth put forth a thousand sudden flowers
> To spread a couch: while ready for the bath
> The rock hard by gave out a limpid stream
> Of crystal flow. So brought she forth the child." [65]

We come across a very similar motive in the cult legend of the Samian Hera. Yearly it was claimed that the image disappeared from the temple, was fastened somewhere on the seashore on a trunk of a Lygos tree and wound about with its branches. There it was " found," and was treated with wedding-cake. This feast is undoubtedly a ἱερὸς γάμος (ritual marriage), because in Samos there was a legend that Zeus had first had a long-continued secret love relation with Hera. In Plataea and Argos, the marriage procession was represented with bridesmaids, marriage feast, and so on. The festival took place in the wedding month "Γαμηλιών" (beginning of February). But in Plataea the image was previously carried into a lonely place in the wood; approximately corresponding to the legend of Plutarch that Zeus had kidnapped Hera and then had hidden her in a cave of Cithaeron. According to our deductions, previously made, we must conclude from this that there is still another train of thought, namely, the magic charm of rejuvenation, which is condensed in the Hierosgamos. The disappearance and hiding in the wood, in the cave, on the seashore, entwined in a willow tree, points to the death of the sun and rebirth. The early springtime Γαμηλιών (the time of Marriage) in February fits in with that very well. In fact, Pausanias informs us that the Argivan Hera *became a maiden again by a yearly bath in the spring of Canathos.* The significance of the bath is emphasized by the information that in the Plataeian cult of Hera Teleia, Tritonian nymphs appeared as water-carriers. In a tale from the Iliad, where the conjugal couch of Zeus upon Mount Ida is described, it is said: [66]

> " The son of Saturn spake, and took his wife
> Into his arms, while underneath the pair,
> The sacred Earth threw up her freshest herbs:
> The dewy lotos, and the crocus-flower,
> And thick and soft the hyacinth. All these
> Upbore them from the ground. Upon this couch
> They lay, while o'er them a bright golden cloud
> Gathered and shed its drops of glistening dew.

So slumbered on the heights of Gargarus
The All-Father overcome by sleep and love,
And held his consort in his arms."

—Trans. by W. C. Bryant.

Drexler recognizes in this description an unmistakable allusion to the garden of the gods on the extreme western shore of the ocean, an idea which might have been taken from a Prehomeric Hierosgamos hymn. This western land is the land of the setting sun, whither Hercules, Gilgamesh, etc., hasten with the sun, in order to find there immortality, where the sun and the maternal sea unite in an eternally rejuvenating intercourse. Our supposition of a condensation of the Hierosgamos with the myth of rebirth is probably confirmed by this. Pausanias mentions a related myth fragment where the statue of Artemis Orthia is also called Lygodesma (chained with willows), because it was found in a willow tree; this tale seems to be related to the general Greek celebration of Hierosgamos with the above-mentioned customs.[67]

The motive of the "devouring" which Frobenius has shown to be a regular constituent of the sun myths is closely related to this (also metaphorically). The "whale dragon" (mother's womb) always "devours" the hero. The devouring may also be partial instead of complete.

A six-year-old girl, who goes to school unwillingly, dreams that her leg is encircled by a large red worm. She had a tender interest for this creature, contrary to what might be expected. An adult patient, who cannot separate from an older friend on account of an extraordinarily strong mother transference, dreams that " she had to get across some deep water (typical idea!) with this friend; her friend fell in (mother transference); she tries to drag her out, and almost succeeds, but a large crab seizes on the dreamer by the foot and tries to pull her in."

Etymology also confirms this conception: There is an Indo-Germanic root *vélu-, vel-*, with the meaning of " encircling, surrounding, turning." From this is derived Sanskrit *val, valati* = to cover, to surround, to encircle, to encoil (symbol of the snake); *vallî* = creeping plant; *ulûta* = boa-constrictor = Latin *volûtus*, Lithuanian *velù, velti* = *wickeln* (to roll up); Church Slavonian *vlina* = Old High German, *wella* = *Welle* (wave or billow). To the root *vélu* also belongs the root *vlvo*, with the meaning " cover, corium, womb." (The serpent on account of its casting its skin is an excellent symbol of rebirth.) Sanskrit *ulva, ulba* has the same meaning; Latin *volva, volvula, vulva.* To *vélu* also belongs the root *ulvorâ*, with the meaning of " fruitful field, covering or husk of plants, sheath." Sanskrit *urvárâ* = sown field. Zend *urvara* = plant. (See the personification of the ploughed furrow.) The same root *vel* has also the meaning of " wallen " (to undulate). Sanskrit *ulmuka* = conflagration. Ϝαλέα, Ϝέλα, Gothic *vulan* = *wallen* (to undulate). Old High German and Middle High German *walm* = heat, glow.[68] It is typical that in the state of " involution " the hair of the sun-hero always falls out from the heat. Further the root *vel* is found with the meaning " to sound,"[69] and to will, to wish " (libido!).

The motive of encoiling is mother symbolism.[70] This is verified by the fact that the trees, for example, bring forth again (like the whale in the legend of Jonah). They do that very generally, thus in the Greek legend the $Μελίαι$ $νύμφαι$* of the ash trees are the mothers of the race of men of the Iron Age. In northern mythology, Askr, the ash tree, is the primitive father. His wife, Embla, is the " Emsige," the active one, and not, as was earlier believed, the aspen. *Askr* probably means, in the first place, the phallic spear of the ash tree. (Compare the Sabine custom of parting the bride's hair with the lance.) The Bundehesh symbolizes the first people, Meschia and Meschiane, as the tree Reivas, one part of which places a branch in a hole of the other part. The material which, according to the northern myth, was animated by the god when he created men [71] is designated as *trê* = wood, tree.[72] I recall also $ὕλη$ = wood, which in Latin is called *materia*. In the wood of the " world-ash," Ygdrasil, a human pair hid themselves at the end of the world, from whom sprang the race of the renewed world.[73] The Noah motive is easily recognized in this conception (the night journey on the sea) ; at the same time, in the symbol of Ygdrasil, a mother idea is again apparent. At the moment of the destruction of the world the " world-ash " becomes the guardian mother, the tree of death and life, one "$ἐγκόλπιον$."† [74] This function of rebirth of the " world-ash " also helps to elucidate the representation met with in the Egyptian Book of the

---

* Melian Virgins.   † Pregnant.

Dead, which is called "the gate of knowledge of the
soul of the East":

"I am the pilot in the holy keel, I am the steersman who allows
no rest in the ship of Râ.[75] I know that tree of emerald green
from whose midst Râ rises to the height of the clouds."[76]

Ship and tree of the dead (death ship and death tree)
are here closely connected. The conception is that Râ,
born from the tree, ascends (Osiris in the Erika). The
representation of the sun-god Mithra is probably explained in the same way. He is represented upon the
Heddernheim relief, with half his body arising from the
top of a tree. (In the same way numerous other monuments show Mithra half embodied in the rock, and illustrate a rock birth, similar to Men.) Frequently there is
a stream near the birthplace of Mithra. This con-
glomeration of symbols is also found in the birth of
Aschanes, the first Saxon king, who grew from the Harz
rocks, which are in the midst of the wood [77] near a fountain.[78] Here we find all the mother symbols united—
earth, wood, water, three forms of tangible matter. We
can wonder no longer that in the Middle Ages the tree
was poetically addressed with the title of honor, "mistress." Likewise it is not astonishing that the Christian
legend transformed the tree of death, the cross, into
the tree of life, so that Christ was often represented on
a living and fruit-bearing tree. This reversion of the
cross symbol to the tree of life, which even in Babylon
was an important and authentic religious symbol, is also
considered entirely probable by Zöckler,[79] an authority

CHRIST ON THE TREE OF LIFE

on the history of the cross. The pre-Christian meaning of the symbol does not contradict this interpretation; on the contrary, its meaning is life. The appearance of the cross in the sun worship (here the cross with equal arms, and the swastika cross, as representative of the sun's rays), as well as in the cult of the goddess of love (Isis with the crux ansata, the rope, the speculum veneris ♀, etc.), in no way contradicts the previous historical meaning. The Christian legend has made abundant use of this symbolism.

The student of mediæval history is familiar with the representation of the cross growing above the grave of Adam. The legend was that Adam was buried on Golgotha. Seth had planted on his grave a branch of the "paradise tree," which became the cross and tree of death of Christ.[80] We all know that through Adam's guilt sin and death came into the world, and Christ through his death has redeemed us from the guilt. To the question in what had Adam's guilt consisted it is said that the unpardonable sin to be expiated by death was that he dared to pick a fruit from the paradise tree.[81] The results of this are described in an Oriental legend. One to whom it was permitted to cast one look into Paradise after the fall saw the tree there and the four streams. But the tree was withered, and in its branches lay an infant. (The mother had become pregnant.[82])

This remarkable legend corresponds to the Talmudic tradition that Adam, before Eve, already possessed a demon wife, by name Lilith, with whom he *quarrelled for mastership*. But Lilith raised herself into the air through the magic of the name of God and hid herself in the sea. Adam forced her back with the help of three angels.[83] Lilith became a nightmare, a Lamia, who threatened those with child and who kidnapped the newborn child. The parallel myth is that of the Lamias, the spectres of the night, who terrified the children. The original legend is that Lamia enticed Zeus, but the jealous Hera, however, caused Lamia to bring only dead children into the world. Since that time the raging Lamia is the persecutor of children, whom she destroys wherever she can. This motive frequently recurs in fairy tales, where the mother often appears directly as a murderess or as a *devourer of men;* [84] a German paradigm is the well-known tale of Hansel and Gretel. Lamia is actually a large, voracious fish, which establishes the connection with the whale-dragon myth so beautifully worked out by Frobenius, in which the sea monster devours the sun-hero for rebirth and where the hero must employ every stratagem to conquer the monster. Here again we meet with the idea of the "terrible mother" in the form of the voracious fish, the mouth of death.[85] In Frobenius there are numerous examples where the monster has devoured not only men but also animals, plants, an entire country, all of which are redeemed by the hero to a glorious rebirth.

The Lamias are typical nightmares, the feminine nature of which is abundantly proven.[86] Their universal peculiarity is that they ride upon their victims. Their counterparts are the spectral horses which bear their riders along in a mad gallop. One recognizes very easily in these symbolic forms the type of anxious dream which, as Riklin shows,[87] has already become important for the interpretation of fairy tales through the investigation of Laistner.[88] The typical riding takes on a special aspect through the results of the analytic investigation of infantile psychology; the two contributions of Freud and myself [89] have emphasized, on one side, the anxiety significance of the horse, on the other side the sexual meaning of the phantasy of riding. When we take these experiences into consideration, we need no longer be surprised that the maternal " world-ash " Ygdrasil is called in German " the frightful horse." Cannegieter [90] says of nightmares:

" Abigunt eas nymphas (matres deas, mairas) hodie rustici osse capitis equini tectis injecto, cujusmodi ossa per has terras in rusticorum villis crebra est animadvertere. Nocte autem ad concubia equitare creduntur et equos fatigare ad longinqua itinera." *

The connection of nightmare and horse seems, at first glance, to be present also etymologically—nightmare and mare. The Indo-Germanic root for märe is *mark*. Märe is the horse, English mare; Old High German *marah* (male horse) and *meriha* (female horse); Old Norse *merr* (*mara* = nightmare); Anglo-Saxon *myre* (*maira*). The French " cauchmar " comes from *calcare* = to tread, to step (of iterative meaning, therefore, " to tread " or press down). It was also said of the cock who

---

* Even to-day the country people drive off these nymphs (mother goddesses, Maira) by throwing a bone of the head of a horse upon the roof—bones of this kind can often be seen throughout the land on the farmhouses of the country people. By night, however, they are believed to ride at the time of the first sleep, and they are believed to tire out their horses by long journeys.

stepped upon the hen. This movement is also typical for
the nightmare; therefore, it is said of King Vanlandi,
" Mara trad han," the Mara trod on him in sleep even to
death.[91] A synonym for nightmare is the "troll" or
"treter"[92] (treader). This movement (*calcare*) is
proven again by the experience of Freud and myself with
children, where a special infantile sexual significance is
attached to stepping or kicking.

The common Aryan root *mar* means "to die"; therefore, *mara* the "dead" or "death." From this results
mors, μόρος = fate (also μοῖρα[93]). As is well known,
the Nornes sitting under the "world-ash" personify fate
like Clotho, Lachesis and Atropos. With the Celts the
conception of the Fates probably passes into that of
matres and *matronæ*, which had a divine significance
among the Germans. A well-known passage in Julius
Cæsar ("De Bello Gallico," i: 50) informs us of this
meaning of the mother:

> "Ut matres familias eorum sortibus et vaticinationibus [94] decla-
> rarent, utrum prœlium committi ex usu esset, nec ne." *

In Slav *mara* means "witch"; poln. *mora* = demon,
nightmare; *mōr* or *mōre* (Swiss-German) means "sow,"
also as an insult. The Bohemian *mura* means "nightmare" and "evening moth, Sphinx." This strange connection is explained through analysis where it often
occurs that animals with movable shells (Venus shell) or
wings are utilized for very transparent reasons as symbols of the female genitals.[95] The Sphingina are the twi-

* That these matrons should declare by lots whether it would be to their
advantage or not to engage in battle.

light moths; they, like the nightmare, come in the darkness. Finally, it is to be observed that the sacred olive
tree of Athens is called "μορία" (that was derived from
μόρος). Halirrhotios wished to cut down the tree, but
killed himself with the axe in the attempt.

The sound resemblance of *mar, mère* with *meer* = sea
and Latin *mare* = sea is remarkable, although etymologically accidental. Might it refer back to " the great primitive idea of the mother " who, in the first place, meant to
us our individual world and afterwards became the symbol of all worlds? Goethe said of the mothers: " They
are encircled by images of all creatures." The Christians, too, could not refrain from reuniting their mother
of God with water. " Ave Maris stella " is the beginning of a hymn to Mary. Then again it is the horses
of Neptune which symbolize the waves of the sea. It is
probably of importance that the infantile word ma-ma
(mother's breast) is repeated in its initial sound in all
possible languages, and that the mothers of two religious
heroes are called Mary and Maya. That the mother is
the horse of the child is to be seen most plainly in the
primitive custom of carrying the child on the back or letting it ride on the hip. Odin hung on the " world-
ash," the mother, his " horse of terror." The Egyptian
sun-god sits on the back of his mother, the heavenly
cow.

We have already seen that, according to Egyptian conceptions, Isis, the mother of god, played an evil trick on
the sun-god with the poisonous snake; also Isis behaved
treacherously toward her son Horus in Plutarch's tradi-

tion. That is, Horus vanquished the evil Typhon, who murdered Osiris treacherously (terrible mother = Typhon). Isis, *however, set him free again.* Horus thereupon rebelled, *laid hands on his mother and tore the regal ornaments from her head,* whereupon Hermes gave her a cow's head. Then Horus conquered Typhon a second time. Typhon, in the Greek legend, is a monstrous dragon. Even without this confirmation it is evident that the battle of Horus is the typical battle of the sun-hero with the whale-dragon. Of the latter we know that it is a symbol of the "dreadful mother," of the voracious jaws of death, where men are dismembered and ground up.[96] Whoever vanquishes this monster has gained a new or eternal youth. For this purpose one must, in spite of all dangers, descend into the belly of the monster [97] (journey to hell) and spend some time there. (Imprisonment by night in the sea.)

The battle with the night serpent signifies, therefore, the conquering of the mother, who is suspected of an infamous crime, that is, the betrayal of the son. A full confirmation of the connection comes to us through the fragment of the Babylonian epic of the creation, discovered by George Smith, mostly from the library of Asurbanipal. The period of the origin of the text was probably in the time of Hammurabi (2,000 B.C.). We learn from this account of creation [98] that the sun-god Ea, the son of the depths of the waters and the god of wisdom,[99] had conquered Apsû. Apsû is the creator of the great gods (he existed in the beginning in a sort of trinity with Tiâmat—the mother of gods and Mumu, his vizier).

Ea conquered the father, but Tiâmat plotted revenge. She prepared herself for battle against the gods.

" Mother Hubur, who created everything,
  Procured invincible weapons, gave birth to giant snakes
  With pointed teeth, relentless in every way;
  Filled their bellies with poison instead of blood,
  Furious gigantic lizards, clothed them with horrors,
  Let them swell with the splendor of horror, formed them rearing,
  Whoever sees them shall die of terror.
  Their bodies shall rear without turning to escape.
  She arrayed the lizards, dragons and Laḥamen,
  Hurricanes, mad dogs, scorpion men,
  Mighty storms, fishmen and rams.
  With relentless weapons, without fear of conflict,
  Powerful are Tiâmat's commands, irresistible are they.

" After Tiâmat had powerfully done her work
  She conceived evil against the gods, her descendants;
  In order to revenge Apsu, Tiâmat did evil.
  When Ea now heard this thing
  He became painfully anxious, sorrowfully he sat himself.
  He went to the father, his creator, Anšar,
  To relate to him all that Tiâmat plotted.
  Tiâmat, our mother, has taken an aversion to us,
  Has prepared a riotous mob, furiously raging."

The gods finally opposed Marduk, the god of spring, the victorious sun, against the fearful host of Tiâmat. Marduk prepared for battle. Of his chief weapon, which he created, it is said:

" He created the evil wind, Imḥullu, the south storm and the
      hurricane,
  The fourth wind, the seventh wind, the whirlwind and the
      harmful wind,
  Then let he loose the winds, which he had created, the seven:
  To cause confusion within Tiâmat, they followed behind him,

Then the lord took up the cyclone, his great weapon;
For his chariot he mounted the stormwind, the incomparable,
    the terrible one."

His chief weapon is the wind and a net, with which he
will entangle Tiâmat.   He approaches Tiâmat and challenges her to a combat.

" Then Tiâmat and Marduk, the wise one of the gods, came to-
        gether,
    Rising for the fight, approaching to the battle:
    Then the lord spread out his net and caught her.
    He let loose the Imḫullu in his train at her face,
    Then Tiâmat now opened her mouth as wide as she could.
    He let the Imḫullu rush in so that her lips could not close;
    With the raging winds he filled her womb.
    Her inward parts were seized and she opened wide her mouth.
    He touched her with the spear, dismembered her body,
    He slashed her inward parts, and cut out her heart,
    Subdued her and put an end to her life.
    He threw down her body and stepped upon it."

After Marduk slew the mother, he devised the creation of the world.

" There the lord rested contemplating her body,
    Then divided he the Colossus, planning wisely.
    He cut it apart like a flat fish, into two parts,[100]
    One half he took and with it he covered the Heavens."

In this manner Marduk created the universe from the
mother. It is clearly evident that the killing of the
mother-dragon here takes place under the idea of a wind
fecundation with negative accompaniments.

The world is created from the mother, that is to say,
from the libido taken away from the mother through sac-

rifice. We shall have to consider this significant formula more closely in the last chapter. The most interesting parallels to this primitive myth are to be found in the literature of the Old Testament, as Gunkel [101] has brilliantly pointed out. It is worth while to trace the psychology of these parallels.

Isaiah li: 9:
(9) " Awake, awake, put on strength, O arm of the Lord; awake as in the ancient days, in the generation of old. Art thou not it that hath cut Rahab, and wounded the dragon?
(10) " Art thou not it which hath dried the sea, the waters of the great deep, that hath made the depths of the sea a way for the ransomed to pass over? "

The name of Rahab is frequently used for Egypt in the Old Testament, also dragon. Isaiah, chapter xxx, verse 7, calls Egypt " the silent Rahab," and means, therefore, something evil and hostile. Rahab is the well-known whore of Jericho, who later, as the wife of Prince Salma, became the ancestress of Christ. Here Rahab appeared as the old dragon, as Tiâmat, against whose evil power Marduk, or Jehovah, marched forth. The expression " the ransomed " refers to the Jews freed from bondage, but it is also mythological, for the hero again frees those previously devoured by the whale. (Frobenius.)

Psalm lxxxix: 10:
" Thou hast broken Rahab in pieces, as one that is slain."

Job xxvi: 12-13:
" He divideth the sea with his power, and by his understanding he smiteth through the proud.

" By his spirit he hath garnished the heavens, his hand hath formed the crooked serpent."

Gunkel places Rahab as identical with Chaos, that is, the same as Tiâmat. Gunkel translates " the breaking to pieces " as " violation." Tiâmat or Rahab as the mother is also the whore. Gilgamesh treats Ischtar in this way when he accuses her of whoredom. This insult towards the mother is very familiar to us from dream analysis. The dragon Rahab appears also as Leviathan, the water monster (maternal sea).

Psalm lxxiv:
(13) " Thou didst divide the sea by thy strength: thou brakest the heads of the dragons in the waters.
(14) " Thou brakest the heads of Leviathan in pieces and gavest him to be meat to the people inhabiting the wilderness.
(15) " Thou didst cleave the fountain and the flood: thou didst dry up mighty rivers."

While only the phallic meaning of the Leviathan was emphasized in the first part of this work, we now discover also the maternal meaning. A further parallel is:

Isaiah xxvii: 1:
" In that day, the Lord with his cruel and great and strong sword shall punish Leviathan, the piercing serpent, even Leviathan that crooked serpent, and he shall slay the dragon that is in the sea."

We come upon a special motive in Job, chap. xli, v. 1:

" Canst thou draw out Leviathan with an hook? or his tongue with a cord which thou lettest down? Canst thou put an hook in his nose? or bore his jaw through with a thorn?"

Numerous parallels to this motive are to be found among exotic myths in Frobenius, where the maternal sea monster was also fished for. The comparison of the mother libido with the elementary powers of the sea and the powerful monsters borne by the earth show how invincibly great is the power of that libido which we designate as maternal.

We have already seen that the incest prohibition prevents the son from reproducing himself through the mother. But this must be done by the god, as is shown with remarkable clearness and candor in the pious Egyptian mythology, which has preserved the most ancient and simple concepts. Thus Chnum, the " moulder," the " potter," the " architect," moulds his egg upon the potter's wheel, for he is " the immortal growth," " the reproduction of himself and his own rebirth, the creator of the egg, which emerged from the primitive waters." In the Book of the Dead it says:

" I am the sublime falcon (the Sun-god), which has come forth from his egg."

Another passage in the Book of the Dead reads:

" I am the creator of Nun, who has taken his place in the underworld. My nest is not seen and my egg is not broken."

A further passage reads:

" that great and noble god in his egg: who is his own originator of that which has arisen from him." [102]

Therefore, the god Nagaga-uer is also called the " great cackler." (Book of the Dead.) " I cackle like

a goose and I whistle like a falcon." The mother is reproached with the incest prohibition as an act of wilful
maliciousness by which she excludes the son from immortality. Therefore, a god must at least rebel, overpower
and chastise the mother. (Compare Adam and Lilith,
above.) The "overpowering" signifies incestuous
rape.[103] Herodotus [104] has preserved for us a valuable
fragment of this religious phantasy.

" And how they celebrate their feast to Isis in the city of
Busiris, I have already previously remarked. After the sacrifice,
all of them, men and women, full ten thousand people, begin to
beat each other. But it would be sin for me to mention for whom
they do beat each other.

" But in Papremis they celebrated the sacrifice with holy actions,
as in the other places. About the time when the sun sets, some
few priests are busy around the image; most of them stand at
the entrance with wooden clubs, and others who would fulfil a
vow, more than a thousand men, also stand in a group with
wooden cudgels opposite them.

" Now on the eve of the festival, they take the image out in
a small and gilded temple into another sacred edifice. Then the
few who remain with the image draw a four-wheeled chariot upon
which the temple stands with the image which it encloses. But
the others who stand in the anterooms are not allowed to enter.
Those under a vow, who stand by the god, beat them off. Now
occurs a furious battle with clubs, in which they bruise each other's
bodies and as I believe, many even die from their wounds: notwithstanding this, the Egyptians consider that none die.

" The natives claim that this festival gathering was introduced
for the following reason: in this sanctuary lived the mother of
Ares.[105] Now Ares was brought up abroad and when he became
a man he came to have *intercourse with his mother*. The servants
of his mother who had seen him did not allow him to enter peace-
fully, but prevented him; at which he fetched people from another city, who mistreated the servants and had entrance to his

mother. Therefore, they asserted that this slaughter was introduced at the feast for Ares."

It is evident that the pious here fight their way to a share
in the mystery of the raping of the mother.[106] This is the
part which belongs to them,[107] while the heroic deed belongs to the god.[108] By Ares is meant the Egyptian Typhon,
as we have good reasons to suppose. *Thus Typhon represents the evil longing for the mother* with which other
myth forms reproach the mother, according to the well-
known example. The death of Balder, quite analogous
to the death of Osiris (attack of sickness of Rê), because
of the wounding by the branch of the mistletoe, seems to
need a similar explanation. It is recounted in the myth
how all creatures were pledged not to hurt Balder, save
only the mistletoe, which was forgotten, presumably because it was too young. This killed Balder. Mistletoe
is a parasite. The female piece of wood in the fire-boring
ritual was obtained [109] from the wood of a parasitical or
creeping plant, the fire mother. The " mare " rests upon
" Marentak," in which Grimm suspects the mistletoe.
The mistletoe was a remedy against barrenness. In Gaul
the Druid alone was allowed to climb the holy oak amid
solemn ceremonies after the completed sacrifice, in order
to cut off the ritual mistletoe.[110] This act is a religiously
limited and organized incest. That which grows on the
tree is the child,[111] which man might have by the mother;
then man himself would be in a renewed and rejuvenated
form; and precisely this is what man cannot have, because
the incest prohibition forbids it. As the Celtic custom
shows, the act is performed by the priest only, with the

observation of certain ceremonies; the hero god and the redeemer of the world, however, do the unpermitted, the superhuman thing, and through it purchase immortality. The dragon, who must be overcome for this purpose, means, as must have been for some time clearly seen, the resistance against the incest. Dragon and serpent, especially with the characteristic accumulation of anxiety attributes, are the symbolic representations of anxiety which correspond to the repressed incest wish. It is, therefore, intelligible, when we come across the tree with the snake again and again (in Paradise the snake even tempts to sin). The snake or dragon possesses in particular the meaning of treasure guardian and defender. The phallic, as well as the feminine, meaning of the dragon [112] indicates that it is again a symbol of the sexual neutral (or bisexual) libido, that is to say, a symbol of the *libido in opposition*. In this significance the black horse, Apaosha, the demon of opposition, appears in the old Persian song, Tishtriya, where it obstructs the sources of the rain lake. The white horse Tishtriya makes two futile attempts to vanquish Apaosha; at the third attempt, with the help of Ahuramazda, he is successful. [113] Whereupon the sluices of heaven open and a fruitful rain pours down upon the earth. [114] In this song one sees very beautifully in the choice of symbol how libido is opposed to libido, will against will, the discordance of primitive man with himself, which he recognizes again in all the adversity and contrasts of external nature.

The symbol of the tree encoiled by the serpent may also be translated as the mother defended from incest by resistance. This symbol is by no means rare upon Mithraic monuments. The rock encircled by a snake is to be comprehended similarly, because Mithra is one born from a rock. The menace of the new-born by the snake (Mithra, Hercules) is made clear through the legend of Lilith and Lamia. Python, the dragon of Leto, and Poine, who devastates the land of Crotopus, are sent by the father of the new-born. This idea indicates the localization, well known in psychoanalysis, of the incest anxiety in the father. The father represents the active repulse of the incest wish of the son. The crime, unconsciously wished for by the son, is imputed to the father under the guise of a pretended murderous purpose, this being the cause of the mortal fear of the son for the father, a frequent neurotic symptom. In conformity with this idea, the monster to be overcome by the young hero is frequently a giant, the guardian of the treasure or the woman. A striking example is the giant Chumbaba in the Gilgamesh epic, who protected the garden of Ishtar; [115] he is overcome by Gilgamesh, whereby Ishtar is won. Thereupon she makes erotic advances towards Gilgamesh.[116] This data should be sufficient to render intelligible the rôle of Horus in Plutarch, especially the violent usage of Isis. Through overpowering the mother the hero becomes equal to the sun; he reproduces himself. He wins the strength of the invincible sun, the power of eternal rejuvenation. We thus understand a series of representations from the Mithraic myth on the Heddernheim relief. There we see, first of all, the birth of Mithra from the top of the tree; the next representa-

tion shows him carrying the conquered bull (comparable
to the monstrous bull overcome by Gilgamesh). This
bull signifies the concentrated significance of the monster,
the father, who as giant and dangerous animal embodies
the incest prohibition, and agrees with the individual
libido of the sun-hero, which he overcomes by self-sacrifice. The third picture represents Mithra, when he
grasps the head ornament of the sun, the nimbus. This
act recalls to us, first of all, the violence of Horus towards
Isis; secondly, the Christian basic thought, *that those who
have overcome attain the crown of eternal life.* On the
fourth picture Sol kneels before Mithra. These last two
representations show plainly that Mithra has taken to
himself the strength of the sun, so that he becomes the
lord of the sun as well. He has conquered " his animal
nature," the bull. The animal knows no incest prohibition; man is, therefore, man because he conquers the
incest wish, that is, the animal nature. Thus Mithra has
sacrificed his animal nature, the incest wish, and with that
has overcome the mother, that is to say, " the terrible
death-bringing mother." A solution is already anticipated in the Gilgamesh epic through the formal renunciation of the horrible Ishtar by the hero. The overcoming
of the mother in the Mithraic sacrifice, which had almost
an ascetic character, took place no longer by the archaic
overpowering, but through the renunciation, the sacrifice
of the wish. The primitive thought of incestuous reproduction through entrance into the mother's womb had
already been displaced, because man was so far advanced
in domestication that he believed that the eternal life of

BULL-SACRIFICE OF MITHRA

the sun is reached, not through the perpetration of incest, but through the sacrifice of the incest wish. This important change expressed in the Mithraic mystery finds its full expression for the first time in the symbol of the crucified God. A bleeding human sacrifice was hung on the tree of life for Adam's sins.[117] The first-born sacrifices its life to the mother when he suffers, hanging on the branch, a disgraceful and painful death, a mode of death which belongs to the most ignominious forms of execution, which Roman antiquity had reserved for only the lowest criminal. Thus the hero dies, as if he had committed the most shameful crime; he does this by returning into the birth-giving branch of the tree of life, at the same time paying for his guilt with the pangs of death. The animal nature is repressed most powerfully in this deed of the highest courage and the greatest renunciation; therefore, a greater salvation is to be expected for humanity, because such a deed alone seems appropriate to expiate Adam's guilt.

As has already been mentioned, the hanging of the sacrifice on the tree is a generally widespread ritual custom, Germanic examples being especially abundant. The ritual consists in the sacrifice being pierced by a spear.[118] Thus it is said of Odin (Edda, Havamal):

> "I know that I hung on the windswept tree
> Nine nights through,
> Wounded by a spear, dedicated to Odin
> I myself to myself."

The hanging of the sacrifice to the cross also occurred in America prior to its discovery. Müller[119] mentions the

Fejervaryian manuscript (a Mexican hieroglyphic kodex),
at the conclusion of which there is a colossal cross, in the
middle of which there hangs a bleeding divinity. Equally
interesting is the cross of Palenque; [120] up above is a
bird, on either side two human figures, who look at the
cross and hold a child against it either for sacrifice or
baptism. The old Mexicans are said to have invoked the
favor of Centeotls, "the daughter of heaven and the
goddess of wheat," every spring by nailing upon the cross
a youth or a maiden and by shooting the sacrifice with
arrows.[121] The name of the Mexican cross signifies
"tree of our life or flesh." [122]

An effigy from the Island of Philae represents Osiris
in the form of a crucified god, wept over by Isis and
Nephthys, the sister consort.[123]

The meaning of the cross is certainly not limited to
the tree of life, as has already been shown. Just as the
tree of life has also a phallic sub-meaning (as libido symbol), so there is a further significance to the cross than
life and immortality.[124] Müller uses it as a sign of rain
and of fertility, because it appears among the Indians
distinctly as a magic charm of fertility. It goes without
saying, therefore, that it plays a rôle in the sun cult. It
is also noteworthy that the sign of the cross is an important sign for the keeping away of all evil, like the ancient
gesture of Manofica. The phallic amulets also serve the
same purpose. Zöckler appears to have overlooked the
fact that the phallic Crux Ansata is the same cross which
has flourished in countless examples in the soil of antiquity. Copies of this Crux Ansata are found in many

places, and almost every collection of antiquities possesses one or more specimens.[125]

Finally, it must be mentioned that the form of the human body is imitated in the cross as of a man with arms outspread. It is remarkable that in early Christian representations Christ is not nailed to the cross, but stands before it with arms outstretched.[126] Maurice [127] gives a striking basis for this interpretation when he says:

" It is a fact not less remarkable than well attested, that the Druids in their groves were accustomed to select the most stately and beautiful tree as an emblem of the deity they adored, and cutting off the side branches, they affixed two of the largest of them to the highest part of the trunk, in such a manner that those branches extended on each side like the arms of a man, and together with the body presented the appearance of a huge cross; and in the bark in several places was also inscribed the letter T (tau)." [128]

" The tree of knowledge " of the Hindoo Dschaina sect assumes human form; it was represented as a mighty, thick trunk in the form of a human head, from the top of which grew out two longer branches hanging down at the sides and one short, vertical, uprising branch crowned by a bud or blossom-like thickening.[129] Robertson in his " Evangelical Myths " mentions that in the Assyrian system there exists the representation of the divinity in the form of a cross, in which the vertical beam corresponds to a human form and the horizontal beam to a pair of conventionalized wings. Old Grecian idols such, for example, as were found in large numbers in Aegina have a similar character, an immoderately long head and arms slightly raised, wing-shaped, and in front distinct breasts.[130]

I must leave it an open question as to whether the symbol of the cross has any relation to the two pieces of wood in the religious fire production, as is frequently claimed. It does appear, however, as if the cross symbol actually still possessed the significance of "union," for this idea belongs to the fertility charm, and especially to the thought of eternal rebirth, which is most intimately bound up with the cross. The thought of "union," expressed by the symbol of the cross, is met with in "Timaios" of Plato, where the world soul is conceived as stretched out between heaven and earth in the form of an X (Chi); hence in the form of a "St. Andrew's cross." When we now learn, furthermore, that the world soul contains in itself *the world as a body,* then this picture inevitably reminds us of the mother.

(*Dialogues of Plato.* Jowett, Vol. II, page 528.)
"And in the center he put the soul, which he diffused through the whole, and also spread over all the body round about, and he made one solitary and only heaven, a circle moving in a circle, having such excellence as to be able to hold converse with itself, and needing no other friendship or acquaintance. Having these purposes in view he created the world to be a blessed god."

This highest degree of inactivity and freedom from desire, symbolized by the *being enclosed within itself,* signifies divine blessedness. The only human prototype of this conception is the child in the mother's womb, or rather more, the adult man in the continuous embrace of the mother, from whom he originates. Corresponding to this mythologic-philosophic conception, the enviable Diogenes inhabited a tub, thus giving mythologic expression to the blessedness and resemblance to the Divine in his freedom from desire. Plato says as follows of the bond of the world soul to the world body:

" Now God did not make the soul after the body, although we have spoken of them in this order; for when he put them together he would never have allowed that the elder should serve the younger, but this is what we say at random, because we ourselves too are very largely affected by chance. Whereas he made the soul in origin and excellence prior to and older than the body, to be the ruler and mistress, of whom the body was to be the subject."

It seems conceivable from other indications that the conception of the soul in general is a derivative of the mother-imago, that is to say, a symbolic designation for the amount of libido remaining in the mother-imago. (Compare the Christian representation of the soul as the bride of Christ.) The further development of the world soul in " Timaios '" takes place in an obscure fashion in mystic numerals. When the mixture was completed the following occurred:

" This entire compound he divided lengthways into two parts, which he joined to one another at the center like the figure of an X."

This passage approaches very closely the division and union of Atman, who, after the division, is compared to a man and a woman who hold each other in an embrace. Another passage is worth mentioning:

" After the entire union of the soul had taken place, according to the master's mind, he formed all that is corporeal within this, and joined it together so as to penetrate it throughout."

Moreover, I refer to my remarks about the maternal meaning of the world soul in Plotinus, in Chapter II.

A similar detachment of the symbol of the cross from a concrete figure we find among the Muskhogean Indians, who stretch above the surface of the water (pond or stream) two ropes crosswise and at the point of intersection throw into the water fruits, oil and precious stones as a sacrifice.[131] Here the divinity is evidently the water, not the cross, which designates the place of sacrifice only, through the point of intersection. The sacrifice at the place of union indicates why this symbol was a primitive charm of fertility,[132] why we meet it so frequently in the prechristian era among the goddesses of love (mother goddesses), especially among the Egyptians in Isis and the sun-god. We have already discussed the continuous union of these two divinities. As the cross (Tau [T], Crux Ansata) always recurs in the hand of Tum, the supreme God, the hegemon of the Ennead, it may not be superfluous to say something more of the destination of Tum. The Tum of On-Heliopolis bears the name " the father of his mother "; what that means needs no explanation; Jusas or Nebit-Hotpet, the goddess joined to him, *was called sometimes the mother, sometimes the daughter, sometimes the wife of the god.* The day of the beginning of autumn is designated in the Heliopolitan inscriptions as the " festival of the goddess Jusasit," as " the arrival of the sister for the purpose of uniting with her father." It is the day in which "the goddess Mehnit completes her work, so that the god Osiris may enter into the left eye." (By which the moon is. meant.[133]) The day is also called the filling up of the sacred eye with its needs. The heavenly cow with the moon eye, the cow-headed Isis, takes to herself in the autumn equinox the seed which procreates Horus. (Moon as keeper of the seed.) The "eye" evidently represents the genitals, as in the myth of Indra, who had to bear spread over his whole body the likeness of Yoni (vulva), on account of a Bathsheba outrage, but was so far pardoned by the gods that the disgraceful likeness of Yoni was changed into eyes.[134] The "pupil" in the eye is a child. The great god becomes a child again; he enters the mother's womb in order to renew himself.[135] In a hymn it is said:

"Thy mother, the heavens, stretches forth her arms to thee."

In another place it is said:

"Thou shinest, oh father of the gods, upon the back of thy mother, daily thy mother takes thee in her arms. When thou illuminatest the dwelling of night, thou unitest with thy mother, the heavens."[136]

The Tum of Pitum-Heliopolis not only bears the Crux Ansata as a symbol, but also has this sign as his most frequent surname, that is, ānχ or ānχi, which means "life" or "the living." He is chiefly honored as the demon serpent, Agatho, of whom it is said, "The holy demon serpent Agatho goes forth from the city Nezi." The snake, on account of casting its skin, is the symbol of renewal, as is the scarabæus, a symbol of the sun, of whom it is said that he, being of masculine sex only, reproduces himself.

The name Chnum (another name for Tum, always meaning "the sun-god") comes from the verb χnum, which means "to bind together, to unite." [137] Chnum appears chiefly as the potter, the moulder of his egg. The cross seems, therefore, to be an extraordinarily condensed symbol; its supreme meaning is that of the tree of life, and, therefore, is a symbol of the mother. The symbolization in a human form is, therefore, intelligible. The phallic forms of the Crux Ansata belong to the abstract meaning of "life" and "fertility," as well as to the meaning of "union," which we can now very properly interpret as *cohabitation with the mother for the purpose of renewal.*[138] It is, therefore, not only a very touching but also a very significant naïve symbolism when Mary, in an Old English lament of the Virgin,[139] accuses the cross of being a false tree, which unjustly and without reason destroyed "the pure fruit of her body, her gentle birdling," with a poisonous draught, the draught of death, which is destined only for the guilty descendants of the sinner Adam. Her son was not a sharer in that guilt. (Compare with this the cunning of Isis with the fatal draught of love.) Mary laments:

"Cross, thou art the evil stepmother of my son, so high hast thou hung him that I cannot even kiss his feet! Cross, thou art my mortal enemy, thou hast slain my little blue bird!"

The holy cross answers:

" Woman, I thank thee for my honor: thy splendid fruit, which now I bear, shines as a red blossom.[140] Not alone to save thee but to save the whole world this precious flower blooms in thee." [141]

Santa Crux says of the relation to each other of the two mothers (Isis in the morning and Isis in the evening) :

" Thou hast been crowned as Queen of Heaven on account of the child, which thou hast borne. But I shall appear as the shining relic to the whole world, at the day of judgment. I shall then raise my lament for thy divine son innocently slain upon me."

Thus the murderous mother of death unites with the mother of life in bringing forth a child. In their lament for the dying God, and as outward token of their union, Mary kisses the cross, and is reconciled to it.[142] The naïve Egyptian antiquity has preserved for us the union of the contrasting tendencies in the mother idea of Isis. Naturally this imago is merely a symbol of the libido of the son for the mother, and describes the conflict between love and incest resistance. The criminal incestuous purpose of the son appears projected as criminal cunning in the mother-imago. The separation of the son from the mother signifies the separation of man from the generic consciousness of animals, from that infantile archaic thought characterized by the absence of individual consciousness.

It was only the power of the incest prohibition which created the self-conscious individual, who formerly had been thoughtlessly one with the tribe, and in this way alone did the idea of individual and final death become possible. Thus through the sin of Adam death came into the world. This, as is evident, is expressed figuratively, that is, in contrast form. The mother's defence against the incest appears to the son as a malicious act, which delivers him over to the fear of death. This conflict faces us in the Gilgamesh epic in its original freshness and passion, where also the incest wish is projected onto the mother.

The neurotic who cannot leave the mother has good reasons; the fear of death holds him there. It seems as if no idea and no word were strong enough to express the meaning of this. Entire religions were constructed in order to give words to the immensity of this conflict. This struggle for expression which continued down through the centuries certainly cannot have its source in the restricted realm of the vulgar conception of incest. Rather one must understand the law which is ultimately expressed as " Incest prohibition " as coercion to domestication, and consider the religious systems as institutions which first receive, then organize and gradually sublimate, the motor forces of the animal nature not immediately available for cultural purposes.

We will now return to the visions of Miss Miller. Those now following need no further detailed discussion. The next vision is the image of a " purple bay." The symbolism of the sea connects smoothly with that which precedes. One might think here in addition of the reminiscences of the Bay of Naples, which we came across in Part I. In the sequence of the whole, however, we must not overlook the significance of the " bay." In

French it is called *une baie,* which probably corresponds to a bay in the English text. It might be worth while here to glance at the etymological side of this idea. Bay is generally used for something which is open, just as the Catalonian word *badia (bai)* comes from *badar,* "to open." In French *bayer* means "to have the mouth open, to gape." Another word for the same is *Meerbusen,* "bay or gulf"; Latin *sinus,* and a third word is golf (gulf), which in French stands in closest relation to *gouffre* = abyss. Golf is derived from " κόλπος," [143] which also means "bosom" and "womb," "mother-womb," also "vagina." It can also mean a fold of a dress or pocket; it may also mean a deep valley between high mountains. These expressions clearly show what primitive ideas lie at their base. They render intelligible Goethe's choice of words at that place where Faust wishes to follow the sun with winged desire in order in the everlasting day "to drink its eternal light":

> "The mountain chain with all its gorges deep,
> Would then no more impede my godlike motion;
> And now before mine eyes expands the ocean,
> With all its bays, in shining sleep!"

Faust's desire, like that of every hero, inclines towards the mysteries of rebirth, of immortality; therefore, his course leads to the sea, and down into the monstrous jaws of death, the horror and narrowness of which at the same time signify the new day.

> "Out on the open ocean speeds my dreaming:
> The glassy flood before my feet is gleaming,
> A new day beckons to a newer shore!

A fiery chariot borne on buoyant pinions,
Sweeps near me now! I soon shall ready be
To pierce the ether's high, unknown dominions,
To reach new spheres of pure activity!
This Godlike rapture, this supreme existence. . . .

.   .   .   .   .   .

"Yes, let me dare those gates to fling asunder,
Which every man would fain go slinking by!
'Tis time, through deeds this word of truth to thunder;
That with the height of God's Man's dignity may vie!
Nor from that gloomy gulf to shrink affrighted,
Where fancy doth herself to self-born pangs compel,—
To struggle toward that pass benighted,
Around whose narrow mouth flame all the fires of Hell:—
To take this step with cheerful resolution,
Though Nothingness should be the certain swift conclusion!"

It sounds like a confirmation, when the succeeding vision of Miss Miller's is *une falaise à pic,* "a steep, precipitous cliff." (Compare *gouffre.*) The entire series of individual visions is completed, as the author observes, by a confusion of sounds, somewhat resembling "wa-ma, wa-ma." This has a very primitive, barbaric sound. Since we learn from the author nothing of the subjective roots of this sound, nothing is left us but the suspicion that this sound might be considered, taken in connection with the whole, as a slight mutilation of the well-known call ma-ma.

CHAPTER VI

THE BATTLE FOR DELIVERANCE FROM THE MOTHER .

THERE now comes a pause in the production of visions by Miss Miller; then the activity of the unconscious is resumed very energetically.

A forest with trees and bushes appears.

After the discussions in the preceding chapter, there is need only of a hint that the symbol of the forest coincides essentially with the meaning of the holy tree. The holy tree is found generally in a sacred forest inclosure or in the garden of Paradise. The sacred grove often takes the place of the taboo tree and assumes all the attributes of the latter. The erotic symbolism of the garden is generally known. The forest, like the tree, has mythologically a maternal significance. In the vision which now follows, the forest furnishes the stage upon which the dramatic representation of the end of Chiwantopel is played. This act, therefore, takes place in or near the mother.

First, I will give the beginning of the drama as it is in the original text, up to the first attempt at sacrifice. At the beginning of the next chapter the reader will find the continuation, the monologue and the sacrificial scene. The drama begins as follows:

" The personage Chiwantopel, came from the south, on horse-back; around him a cloak of vivid colors, red, blue and white. An Indian in a costume of doe skin, covered with beads and ornamented with feathers advances, squats down and prepares to let fly an arrow at Chiwantopel. The latter presents his breast in an attitude of defiance, and the Indian, fascinated by that sight, slinks away and disappears within the forest."

The hero, Chiwantopel, appears on horseback. This fact seems of importance, because as the further course of the drama shows (see Chapter VIII) the horse plays no indifferent rôle, but suffers the same death as the hero, and is even called " faithful brother " by the latter. These allusions point to a remarkable similarity between horse and rider. There seems to exist an intimate con-nection between the two, which guides them to the same destiny. We already have seen that the symbolization of " the libido in resistance " through the " terrible mother " in some places runs parallel with the horse.[1] Strictly speaking, it would be incorrect to say that the horse is, or means, the mother. The mother idea is a libido symbol, and the horse is also a libido symbol, and at some points the two symbols intersect in their significances. The com-mon feature of the two ideas lies in the libido, especially in the libido repressed from incest. The hero and the horse appear to us in this setting like an artistic formation of the idea of humanity with its repressed libido, whereby the horse acquires the significance of the animal uncon-scious, which appears domesticated and subjected to the will of man. Agni upon the ram, Wotan upon Sleipneir, Ahuramazda upon Angromainyu,[2] Jahwe upon the mon-strous seraph, Christ upon the ass,[3] Dionysus upon the ass, Mithra upon the horse, Men upon the human-footed horse, Freir upon the golden-bristled boar, etc., are parallel representations. The chargers of mythology are always invested with great significance; they very often appear anthropomorphized. Thus, Men's horse has human forelegs; Balaam's ass, human speech; the retreating bull, upon whose back Mithra springs in order to strike him down, is, according to a Persian legend, actually the God himself. The mock crucifix of the Palatine represents the crucified with an ass's head, perhaps in reference to the ancient legend that in the temple of Jerusalem the image of an ass was worshipped. As Drosselbart (horse's mane) Wotan is half-human, half-horse.[4] An old German riddle very prettily shows this unity between horse and horseman.[5] "Who are the two, who travel to Thing? Together they have three eyes, ten feet[6] and one tail; and thus they travel over the land." Legends ascribe properties to the horse, which psychologically belong to the unconscious of man; horses are clairvoyant and clairaudient; they show the way when the lost wanderer is helpless; they have mantic powers. In the Iliad the horse prophesies evil. They hear the words which the corpse speaks when it is taken to the grave—words which men cannot hear. Cæsar learned from his human-footed horse (probably taken from the identification of Cæsar with the Phrygian Men) that he was to conquer the world. An ass prophesied to Augustus the victory of Actium. The horse also sees phantoms. All these things correspond to typical manifestations of the unconscious. Therefore, it is perfectly intelligible

that the horse, as the image of the wicked animal component of man, has manifold connections with the devil.
The devil has a horse's foot; in certain circumstances a
horse's form. At crucial moments he suddenly shows a
cloven foot (proverbial) in the same way as in the abduc-
tion of Hadding, Sleipneir suddenly looked out from behind Wotan's mantle.[7] Just as the nightmare rides on
the sleeper, so does the devil, and, therefore, it is said
that those who have nightmares are ridden by the devil.
In Persian lore the devil is the steed of God. The devil,
like all evil things, represents sexuality. Witches have
intercourse with him, in which case he appears in the
form of a goat or horse. The unmistakably phallic
nature of the devil is communicated to the horse as well;
hence this symbol occurs in connections where this is the
only meaning which would furnish an explanation. It is
to be mentioned that Loki generates in the form of a
horse, just as does the devil when in horse's form, as an
old fire god. Thus the lightning was represented theriomorphically as a horse.[8] An uneducated hysteric told me
that as a child she had suffered from extreme fear of
thunder, because every time the lightning flashed she saw
immediately afterwards a huge black horse reaching upwards as far as the sky.[9] It is said in a legend that the
devil, as the divinity of lightning, casts a horse's foot
(lightning) upon the roofs. In accordance with the
primitive meaning of thunder as fertilizer of the earth,
the phallic meaning is given both to lightning and the
horse's foot. In mythology the horse's foot really has
the phallic function as in this dream. An uneducated

patient who originally had been violently forced to coitus by her husband very often dreams (after separation) that a wild horse springs upon her and kicks her in the abdomen with his hind foot. Plutarch has given us the following words of a prayer from the Dionysus orgies:

ἐλθεῖν ἥρως Διόνυσε ᾿Αλιον ἐς ναὸν ἁγνὸν σὺν Χαρίτεσσιν ἐς ναὸν τῷ βοέῳ ποδὶ θύων, ἄξιε ταῦρε, ἄξιε ταῦρε.*¹⁰

Pegasus with his foot strikes out of the earth the spring Hippocrene. Upon a Corinthian statue of Bellerophon, which was also a fountain, the water flowed out from the horse's hoof. Balder's horse gave rise to a spring through his kick. Thus the horse's foot is the dispenser of fruitful moisture.¹¹ A legend of lower Austria, told by Jaehns, informs us that a gigantic man on a white horse is sometimes seen riding over the mountains. This means a speedy rain. In the German legend the goddess of birth, Frau Holle, appears on horseback. Pregnant women near confinement are prone to give oats to a white horse from their aprons and to pray him to give them a speedy delivery. It was originally the custom for the horse to rub against the woman's genitals. The horse (like the ass) had in general the significance of a priapic animal.¹² Horse's tracks are idols dispensing blessing and fertility. Horse's tracks established a claim, and were of significance in determining boundaries, like the priaps of Latin antiquity. Like the phallic Dactyli, a horse opened the mineral riches of the Harz Moun-

---

* Come, O Dionysus, in thy temple of Elis, come with the Graces into thy holy temple: come in sacred frenzy with the bull's foot.

tains with his hoof. The horseshoe, an equivalent for horse's foot,[13] brings luck and has apotropaic meaning. In the Netherlands an entire horse's foot is hung up in the stable to ward against sorcery. The analogous effect of the phallus is well known; hence the phalli at the gates. In particular the horse's leg turned lightning aside, according to the principle " similia similibus."

Horses also symbolize the wind, that is to say, the tertium comparationis is again the libido symbol. The German legend recognizes the wind as the wild huntsman in pursuit of the maiden. Stormy regions frequently derive their names from horses, as the White Horse Mountain of the Lüneburger heath. The centaurs are typical wind gods, and have been represented as such by Böcklin's artistic intuition.[14]

Horses also signify fire and light. The fiery horses of Helios are an example. The horses of Hector are called Xanthos (yellow, bright), Podargos (swift-footed), Lampos (shining) and Aithon (burning). A very pronounced fire symbolism was represented by the mystic Quadriga, mentioned by Dio Chrysostomus. The supreme God always drives his chariot in a circle. Four horses are harnessed to the chariot. The horse driven on the periphery moves very quickly. He has a shining coat, and bears upon it the signs of the planets and the Zodiac.[15] This is a representation of the rotary fire of heaven. The second horse moves more slowly, and is illuminated only on one side. The third moves still more slowly, and the fourth rotates around himself. But once the outer horse set the second horse on fire with his fiery

breath, and the third flooded the fourth with his streaming sweat.   Then the horses dissolve and pass over into
the substance of the strongest and most fiery, which now
becomes the charioteer.   The horses also represent the
four elements.   The catastrophe signifies the conflagration of the world and the deluge, whereupon the division
of the God into many parts ceases, and the divine unity
is restored.[16]   Doubtless the Quadriga may be understood
astronomically as a *symbol of time.*   We already saw in
the first part that the stoic representation of Fate is a
fire symbol.   It is, therefore, a logical continuation of
the thought, when time, closely related to the conception
of destiny, exhibits this same libido symbolism.   Brihâda-
ranyaka-Upanishad, i: 1, says:

" The morning glow verily is the head of the sacrificial horse,
the sun his eye, the wind his breath, the all-spreading fire his
mouth, the year is the belly of the sacrificial horse.   The sky is
his back, the atmosphere the cavern of his body, the earth the vault
of his belly.   The poles are his sides, in between the poles his ribs,
the seasons his limbs, the months and fortnights his joints.   Days
and nights are his feet, stars his bones, clouds his flesh.   The food
he digests is the deserts, the rivers are his veins, the mountains his
liver and lungs, the herbs and trees his hair; the rising sun is his
fore part, the setting sun his after part.   The ocean is his kinsman,
the sea his cradle."

The horse undoubtedly here stands for a time symbol,
and also for the entire world.   We come across in the
Mithraic religion, a strange God of Time, Aion,
called Kronos or Deus Leontocephalus, because his
stereotyped representation is a lion-headed man, who,
standing in a rigid attitude, is encoiled by a snake, whose

head projects forward from behind over the lion's
head. The figure holds in each hand a key, on the chest
rests a thunderbolt, upon his back are the four wings of
the wind; in addition to that, the figure sometimes bears
the Zodiac on his body. Additional attributes are a cock
and implements. In the Carolingian psalter of Utrecht,
which is based upon ancient models, the Sæculum-Aion is
represented as a naked man with a snake in his hand. As
is suggested by the name of the divinity, he is a symbol
of time, most interestingly composed from libido
symbols. The lion, the zodiac sign of the greatest summer heat,[17] is the symbol of the most mighty desire.
("My soul roars with the voice of a hungry lion," says
Mechthild of Magdeburg.) In the Mithra mystery the
serpent is often antagonistic to the lion, corresponding to
that very universal myth of the battle of the sun with the
dragon.

In the Egyptian Book of the Dead, Tum is even designated as a he-cat, because as such he fought the snake,
Apophis. The encoiling also means the engulfing, the
entering into the mother's womb. Thus time is defined
by the rising and setting of the sun, that is to say, through
the death and renewal of the libido. The addition of the
cock again suggests time, and the addition of implements
suggests the creation through time. ("Durée créatrice,"
Bergson.) Oromazdes and Ahriman were produced
through Zrwanakarana, the "infinitely long duration."
Time, this empty and purely formal concept, is expressed
in the mysteries by transformations of the creative power,
the libido. Macrobius says:

"Leonis capite monstratur praesens tempus—quia conditio ejus valida fervensque est." *

Philo of Alexandria has a better understanding:

"Tempus ab hominibus pessimis putatur deus volentibus Ens essentiale abscondere—pravis hominibus tempus putatur causa rerum mundi, sapientibus vero et optimis non tempus sed Deus." † [18]

In Firdusi [19] time is often the symbol of fate, the libido nature of which we have already learned to recognize. The Hindoo text mentioned above includes still more—its symbol of the horse contains the whole world; his kinsman and his cradle is the sea, the mother, similar to the world soul, the maternal significance of which we have seen above. Just as Aion represents the libido in an embrace, that is to say, in the state of death and of rebirth, so here the cradle of the horse is the sea, i. e. the libido is in the mother, dying and rising again, like the symbol of the dying and resurrected Christ, who hangs like ripe fruit upon the tree of life.

We have already seen that the horse is connected through Ygdrasil with the symbolism of the tree. The horse is also a " tree of death "; thus in the Middle Ages the funeral pyre was called St. Michael's horse, and the neo-Persian word for coffin means " wooden horse." [20] The horse has also the rôle of psycho-pompos; he is the steed to conduct the souls to the other world—horse-

---

* The present time is indicated by the head of the lion—because his condition is strong and impetuous.

† Time is thought by the wickedest people to be a divinity who deprives willing people of essential being; by good men it is considered to be the Cause of the things of the world, but to the wisest and best it does not seem time, but God.

women fetch the souls (Valkyries). Neo-Greek songs represent Charon on a horse. These definitions obviously lead to the mother symbolism. The Trojan horse was the only means by which the city could be conquered; because only he who has entered the mother and been reborn is an invincible hero. The Trojan horse is a magic charm, like the " Nodfyr," which also serves to overcome necessity. The formula evidently reads, " In order to overcome the difficulty, thou must commit incest, and once more be born from thy mother." It appears that striking a nail into the sacred tree signifies something very similar. The " Stock im Eisen " in Vienna seems to have been such a palladium.

Still another symbolic form is to be considered. Occasionally the devil rides upon a three-legged horse. The Goddess of Death, Hel, in time of pestilence, also rides upon a three-legged horse.[21] The gigantic ass, which is three-legged, stands in the heavenly rain lake Vourukasha; his urine purifies the water of the lake, and from his roar all useful animals become pregnant and all harmful animals miscarry. The Triad further points to the phallic significance. The contrasting symbolism of Hel is blended into one conception in the ass of Vourukasha. The libido is fructifying as well as destroying.

These definitions, as a whole, plainly reveal the fundamental features. The horse is a libido symbol, partly of phallic, partly of maternal significance, like the tree. It represents the libido in this application, that is, the libido repressed through the incest prohibition.

In the Miller drama an Indian approaches the hero, ready to shoot an arrow at him. Chiwantopel, however, with a proud gesture, exposes his breast to the enemy. This idea reminds the author of the scene between Cassius and Brutus in Shakespeare's " Julius Cæsar." A misunderstanding has arisen between the two friends, when Brutus reproaches Cassius for withholding from him the money for the legions. Cassius, irritable and angry, breaks out into the complaint:

> " Come, Antony, and young Octavius, come,
> Revenge yourselves alone on Cassius,
> For Cassius is a-weary of the world:
> Hated by one he loves: braved by his brother:
> Check'd like a bondman; *all his faults observed:*
> Set in a note-book, learn'd and conn'd by rote,
> To cast into my teeth. O I could weep
> My spirit from mine eyes!—There is my dagger,
> And here my naked breast; within, a heart
> Dearer than Plutus' mine, richer than gold:
> If that thou beest a Roman, take it forth:
> I, that denied thee gold, will give my heart.
> Strike, as thou didst at Cæsar; for I know
> When thou didst hate him worst, thou lov'dst him better
> Than ever thou lov'dst Cassius."

The material here would be incomplete without mentioning the fact that this speech of Cassius shows many analogies to the agonized delirium of Cyrano (compare Part I), only Cassius is far more theatrical and overdrawn. Something childish and hysterical is in his manner. Brutus does not think of killing him, but administers a very chilling rebuke in the following dialogue:

BRUTUS: Sheathe your dagger::
           Be angry when you will, it shall have scope:
           Do what you will, dishonor shall be humor.
           O Cassius, you are yoked with a lamb
           That carries anger as the flint bears fire:
           Who, much enforced, shows a hasty spark,
           And straight is cold again.

CASSIUS: Hath Cassius liv'd
           To be but mirth and laughter to his Brutus
           When grief and blood ill-tempered vexeth him?

BRUTUS: When I spoke that, I was ill-tempered too.

CASSIUS: Do you confess so much? Give me your hand.

BRUTUS: And my heart too.

CASSIUS: O Brutus!

BRUTUS: What's the matter?

CASSIUS: Have not you love enough to bear with me
           When that rash humor *which my mother gave me*
           Makes me forgetful?

BRUTUS: Yes, Cassius, and from henceforth
           When you are over earnest with your Brutus,
           He'll think your mother chides and leave you so.

The analytic interpretation of Cassius's irritability plainly reveals that at these moments he identifies himself with the mother, and his conduct, therefore, is truly feminine, as his speech demonstrates most excellently. For his womanish love-seeking and desperate subjection under the proud masculine will of Brutus calls forth the friendly remark of the latter, that Cassius is yoked with a lamb, that is to say, has something very weak in his character, which is derived from the mother. One recognizes in this without any difficulty the analytic hall-marks of an infantile disposition, which, as always, is characterized by a prevalence of the parent-imago, here the mother-imago. An infantile individual is infantile because he has freed himself insufficiently, or not at all, from the childish environment, that is, from his adaptation to his parents. Therefore, on one side, he reacts falsely towards the world, as a child towards his parents, always demanding love and immediate reward for his feelings; on the other side, on account of the close connection to the parents, he identifies himself with them. The infantile individual behaves like the father and mother. He is not in a condition to live for himself and to find the place to which he belongs. Therefore, Brutus very justly takes it for granted that the " mother chides " in Cassius, not he himself. The psychologically valuable fact which we gather here is the information *that Cassius is infantile and identified* with the mother. The hysterical behavior is due to the circumstance that Cassius is still, in part, a lamb, and *an innocent and entirely harmless child.* He remains, as far as his emotional life is concerned, still far behind himself. This we often see among people who, as masters, apparently govern life and fellow-creatures; they have remained children in regard to the demands of their love nature.

The figures of the Miller dramas, being children of the creator's phantasy, depict, as is natural, those traits of character which belong to the author. The hero, the wish figure, is represented as most distinguished, because the hero always combines in himself all wished-for ideals. Cyrano's attitude is certainly beautiful and impressive; Cassius's behavior has a theatrical effect. Both heroes prepare to die effectively, in which attempt Cyrano succeeds. This attitude betrays a wish for death in the unconscious of our author, the meaning of which we have already discussed at length as the motive for her poem of the moth. The wish of young girls to die is only an indirect expression, which remains a pose, even in case of real death, for death itself can be a pose. Such an outcome merely adds beauty and value to the pose under certain conditions. That the highest summit of life is expressed through the symbolism of death is a well-known fact; for creation beyond one's self means personal death. The coming generation is the end of the preceding one. This symbolism is frequent in erotic speech. The lascivious speech between Lucius and the wanton servant-maid in Apuleius ("Metamorphoses," lib. ii: 32) is one of the clearest examples:

"Proeliare, inquit, et fortiter proeliare: nec enim tibi cedam, nec terga vortam. Cominus in aspectum, si vir es, dirige; et grassare naviter, et occide moriturus. Hodierna pugna non habet missionem.—Simul ambo corruimus inter mutuos amplexus animas anhelantes." *

This symbolism is extremely significant, because it shows how easily a contrasting expression originates and

---

* "Fight," she said, "and fight bravely, for I will not give away an inch nor turn my back. Face to face, come on if you are a man! Strike home, do your worst and die! The battle this day is without quarter . . . till, weary in body and mind, we lie powerless and gasping for breath in each other's arms."

how equally intelligible and characteristic such an expression is. The proud gesture with which the hero offers himself to death may very easily be an indirect expression which challenges the pity or sympathy of the other, and thus is doomed to the calm analytic reduction to which Brutus proceeds. The behavior of Chiwantopel is also suspicious, because the Cassius scene which serves as its model betrays indiscreetly that the whole affair is merely infantile and one which owes its origin to an overactive mother imago. When we compare this piece with the series of mother symbols brought to light in the previous chapter, we must say that the Cassius scene merely confirms once more what we have long supposed, that is to say, that the motor power of these symbolic visions arises from an infantile mother transference, that is to say, from an undetached bond to the mother.

In the drama the libido, in contradistinction to the inactive nature of the previous symbols, assumes a threatening activity, a conflict becoming evident, in which the one part threatens the other with murder. The hero, as the ideal image of the dreamer, is inclined to die; he does not fear death. In accordance with the infantile character of this hero, it would most surely be time for him to take his departure from the stage, or, in childish language, to die. Death is to come to him in the form of an arrow-wound. Considering the fact that heroes themselves are very often great archers or succumb to an arrow-wound (St. Sebastian, as an example), it may not be superfluous to inquire into the meaning of death through an arrow.

We read in the biography of the stigmatized nun Katherine Emmerich [22] the following description of the evidently neurotic sickness of her heart:

" When only in her novitiate, she received as a Christmas present from the holy Christ a very tormenting heart trouble for the whole period of her nun's life. God showed her inwardly the purpose; it was on account of the decline of the spirit of the order, especially for the sins of her fellow-sisters. But what rendered this trouble most painful was the gift which she had possessed from youth, namely, to see before her eyes the inner nature of man as he really was. She felt the heart trouble physically as if her heart was continually pierced by arrows. [23] These arrows—and this represented the still worse mental suffering—she recognized as the thoughts, plots, secret speeches, misunderstandings, scandal and uncharitableness, in which her fellow-sisters, wholly without reason and unscrupulously, were engaged against her and her god-fearing way of life."

It is difficult to be a saint, because even a patient and long-suffering nature will not readily bear such a violation, and defends itself in its own way. The companion of sanctity is temptation, without which no true saint can live. We know from analytic experience that these temptations can pass unconsciously, so that only their equivalents would be produced in consciousness in the form of symptoms. We know that it is proverbial that heart and smart (Herz and Schmerz) rhyme. It is a well-known fact that hysterics put a physical pain in place of a mental pain. The biographer of Emmerich has comprehended that very correctly. Only her interpretation of the pain is, as usual, projected. It is always the others who secretly assert all sorts of evil things about her, and this she pretended gave her the pains. [24] The case, how-

ever, bears a somewhat different aspect. The very difficult renunciation of all life's joys, this death before the
bloom, is generally painful, and especially painful are the
unfulfilled wishes and the attempts of the animal nature to
break through the power of repression. The gossip and
jokes of the sisters very naturally centre around these
most painful things, so that it must appear to the saint
as if her symptoms were caused by this. Naturally, again,
she could not know that gossip tends to assume the rôle
of the unconscious, which, like a clever adversary, always
aims at the actual gaps in our armor.

A passage from Gautama Buddha embodies this idea: [25]

> " A wish earnestly desired
> Produced by will, and nourished
> When gradually it must be thwarted,
> Burrows like an arrow in the flesh."

The wounding and painful arrows do not come from
without through gossip, which only attacks externally,
but they come from ambush, from our own unconscious.
This, rather than anything external, creates the defense-
less suffering. It is our *own repressed and unrecognized
desires which fester like arrows in our flesh.*[26] In another
connection this was clear to the nun, and that most literally. It is a well-known fact, and one which needs no
further proof to those who understand, that these mystic
scenes of union with the Saviour generally are intermingled with an enormous amount of sexual libido.[27] Therefore, it is not astonishing that the scene of the stigmata
is nothing but an incubation through the Saviour, only

slightly changed metaphorically, as compared with the ancient conception of "unio mystica," as cohabitation with the god. Emmerich relates the following of her stigmatization:

"I had a contemplation of the sufferings of Christ, and implored him to let me feel with him his sorrows, and prayed five paternosters to the honor of the five sacred wounds. Lying on my bed with outstretched arms, I entered into a great sweetness and into an endless thirst for the torments of Jesus. Then I saw a light descending upon me: it came obliquely from above. It was a crucified body, living and transparent, with arms extended, but without a cross. The wounds shone brighter than the body; they were five circles of glory, coming forth from the whole glory. I was enraptured and my heart was moved with great pain and yet with sweetness from longing to share in the torments of my Saviour. And my longings for the sorrows of the Redeemer increased more and more on gazing on his wounds, and passed from my breast, through my hands, sides and feet to his holy wounds: then from the hands, then from the sides, then from the feet of the figure threefold shining red beams ending below in an arrow, shot forth to my hands, sides and feet."

The beams, in accordance with the phallic fundamental thought, are threefold, terminating below in an arrow-point.[28] Like Cupid, the sun, too, has its quiver, full of destroying or fertilizing arrows, sun rays,[29] which possess phallic meaning. On this significance evidently rests the Oriental custom of designating brave sons as arrows and javelins of the parents. "To make sharp arrows" is an Arabian expression for "to generate brave sons." The Psalms declare (cxxvii:4):

"Like as the arrows in the hands of the giant; even so are the young children."

(Compare with this the remarks previously made about " boys.") Because of this significance of the arrow it is intelligible why the Scythian king Ariantes, when he wished to prepare a census, demanded an arrow-head from each man. A similar meaning attaches equally to the lance. Men are descended from the lance, because the ash is the mother of lances. Therefore, the men of the Iron Age are derived from her. The marriage custom to which Ovid alludes (" Comat virgineas hasta recurva comas "—*Fastorum,* lib. ii: 560) has already been mentioned. Kaineus issued a command that his lance be honored. Pindar relates in the legend of this Kaineus:

" He descended into the depths, splitting the earth with a straight foot." [30] .

He is said to have originally been a maiden named Kainis, who, because of her complaisance, was transformed into an invulnerable man by Poseidon. Ovid pictures the battle of the Lapithæ with the invulnerable Kaineus; how at last they covered him completely with trees, because they could not otherwise touch him. Ovid says at this place:

" Exitus in dubio est: alii sub inania corpus
　　Tartara detrusum silvarum mole ferebant,
　　Abnuit Ampycides: medioque ex aggere fulvis
　　Vidit avem pennis liquidas exire sub auras." *

* The result is doubtful: the body borne down by the weight of the forest is carried into empty Tartaros: Ampycides denies this: from out of the midst of the mass, he sees a bird with tawny feathers issue into the liquid air.

Roscher considers this bird to be the golden plover (Charadrius pluvialis), which borrows its name from the fact that it lives in the χαράδρα, a crevice in the earth. By his song he proclaims the approaching rain. Kaineus was changed into this bird.

We see again in this little myth the typical constituents of the libido myth: original bisexuality, immortality (invulnerability) through entrance into the mother (splitting the mother with the foot, and to become covered up) and resurrection as a bird of the soul and a bringer of fertility (ascending sun). When this type of hero causes his·lance to be worshipped, it probably means that his lance is a valid and equivalent expression of himself.

From our present standpoint, we understand in a new sense that passage in Job, which I mentioned in Chapter IV of the first part of this book:

" He has set me up for his mark.

" His archers compass me round about, he cleaveth my reins asunder, and doth not spare:—he poureth out my gall upon the ground.

" He breaketh me with breach upon breach: he runneth upon me like a giant."—*Job* xvi: 12-13-14.

Now we understand this symbolism as an expression for·the soul torment caused by the onslaught of the unconscious desires. The libido festers in his flesh, a cruel god has taken possession of him and pierced him with his painful libidian projectiles, with thoughts, which overwhelmingly pass through him. (As a dementia præcox patient once said to me during his recovery: " To-day a

thought suddenly thrust itself through me.") This same
idea is found again in Nietzsche in Zarathustra:

The Magician

Stretched out, shivering
Like one half dead whose feet are warmed,
Shaken alas! by unknown fevers,
Trembling from the icy pointed arrows of frost,
Hunted by Thee, O Thought!
Unutterable! Veiled! Horrible One!
Thou huntsman behind the clouds!
Struck to the ground by thee,
Thou mocking eye that gazeth at me from the dark!
————— Thus do I lie
Bending, writhing, tortured
With all eternal tortures,
Smitten
By thee, cruelest huntsman,
Thou unfamiliar God.

Smite deeper!
Smite once more:
Pierce through and rend my heart!
What meaneth this torturing
With blunt-toothed arrows?
Why gazeth thou again,
Never weary of human pain,
With malicious, God-lightning eyes,
Thou wilt not kill,
But torture, torture?

No long-drawn-out explanation is necessary to enable
us to recognize in this comparison the old, universal idea
of the martyred sacrifice of God, which we have met previously in the Mexican sacrifice of the cross and in the
sacrifice of Odin.[31] This same conception faces us in

the oft-repeated martyrdom of St. Sebastian, where, in
the delicate-glowing flesh of the young god, all the pain
of renunciation which has been felt by the artist has been
portrayed. An artist always embodies in his artistic work
a portion of the mysteries of his time. In a heightened
degree the same is true of the principal Christian symbol,
the crucified one pierced by the lance, the conception of
the man of the Christian era tormented by his wishes,
crucified and dying in Christ.

This is not torment which comes from without, which
befalls mankind; but that he himself is the hunter, mur-
derer, sacrificer and sacrificial knife is shown us in another
of Nietzsche's poems, wherein the apparent dualism is
transformed into the soul conflict through the use of the
same symbolism:

> " Oh, Zarathustra,
> Most cruel Nimrod!
> Whilom hunter of God
> The snare of all virtue,
> An arrow of evil!
> Now
> Hunted by thyself
> Thine own prey
> Pierced through thyself,
> Now
> Alone with thee
> Twofold in thine own knowledge
> Mid a hundred mirrors
> False to thyself,
> Mid a hundred memories
> Uncertain
> Ailing with each wound
> Shivering with each frost

Caught in thine own snares,
Self knower!
Self hangman!

" Why didst thou strangle thyself
With the noose of thy wisdom?
Why hast thou enticed thyself
Into the Paradise of the old serpent?
Why hast thou crept
Into thyself, thyself? . . ."

The deadly arrows do not strike the hero from without, but it is he himself who, in disharmony with himself, hunts, fights and tortures himself. Within himself will has turned against will, libido against libido—therefore, the poet says, " Pierced through thyself," that is to say, wounded by his own arrow. Because we have discerned that the arrow is a libido symbol, the idea of " penetrating or piercing through " consequently becomes clear to us. It is a phallic act of union with one's self, a sort of self-fertilization (introversion) ; also a self-violation, a self-murder; therefore, Zarathustra may call himself his own hangman, like Odin, who sacrifices himself to Odin.

The wounding by one's own arrow means, first of all, *the state of introversion.* What this signifies we already know—the libido sinks into its " own depths " (a well-known comparison of Nietzsche's) and finds there below, in the shadows of the unconscious, the substitute for the upper world, which it has abandoned: *the world of memories* (" 'mid a hundred memories "), the strongest and most influential of which are the early infantile memory pictures. It is the world of the child, this paradise-like

state of earliest childhood, from which we are separated
by a hard law.   In this subterranean kingdom slumber
sweet feelings of home and the endless hopes of all that
is to be.   As Heinrich in the " Sunken Bell," by Gerhart
Hauptmann, says, in speaking of his miraculous work:

> " There is a song lost and forgotten,
>   A song of home, a love song of childhood,
>   Brought up from the depths of the fairy well,
>   Known to all, but yet unheard."

However, as Mephistopheles says, " The danger is
great."   These depths are enticing; they are the mother
and—death.   When the libido leaves the bright upper
world, whether from the decision of the individual or
from decreasing life force, then it sinks back into its own
depths, into the source from which it has gushed forth,
and turns back to that point of cleavage, the umbilicus,
through which it once entered into this body.   This point
of cleavage is called the mother, because from her comes
the source of the libido.   Therefore, when some great
work is to be accomplished, before which weak man re-
coils, doubtful of his strength, his libido returns to that
source—and this is the dangerous moment, in which the
decision takes place between annihilation and new life.
If the libido remains arrested in the wonder kingdom of
the inner world,[32] then the man has become for the world
above a phantom, then he is practically dead or des-
perately ill.[33]   But if the libido succeeds in tearing itself
loose and pushing up into the world above, then a miracle
appears.   This journey to the underworld has been a

fountain of youth, and new fertility springs from his apparent death. This train of thought is very beautifully gathered into a Hindoo myth: Once upon a time, Vishnu sank into an ecstasy (introversion) and during this state of sleep bore Brahma, who, enthroned upon the lotus flower, arose from the navel of Vishnu, bringing with him the Vedas, which he diligently read. (Birth of creative thought from introversion.) But through Vishnu's ecstasy a devouring flood came upon the world. (Devouring through introversion, symbolizing the danger of entering into the mother of death.) A demon taking advantage of the danger, stole the Vedas from Brahma and hid them in the depths. (Devouring of the libido.) Brahma roused Vishnu, and the latter, transforming himself into a fish, plunged into the flood, fought with the demon (battle with the dragon), conquered him and recaptured the Vedas. (Treasure obtained with difficulty.)

Self-concentration and the strength derived therefrom correspond to this primitive train of thought. It also explains numerous sacrificial and magic rites which we have already fully discussed. Thus the impregnable Troy falls because the besiegers creep into the belly of a wooden horse; for he alone is a hero who is reborn from the mother, like the sun. But the danger of this venture is shown by the history of Philoctetes, who was the only one in the Trojan expedition who knew the hidden sanctuary of Chryse, where the Argonauts had sacrificed already, and where the Greeks planned to sacrifice in order to assure a safe ending to their undertaking. Chryse was a nymph upon the island of Chryse; according to the account of the scholiasts in Sophocles's "Philoctetes," this nymph loved Philoctetes, and cursed him because he spurned her love.   This characteristic projection, which is also met with in the Gilgamesh epic, should be referred back, as suggested, to the repressed incest wish of the son, who is represented through the projection as if the mother had the evil wish, for the refusal of which the son was given over to death.   In reality, however, the son becomes mortal by separating himself from the mother. His fear of death, therefore, corresponds to the repressed wish to turn back to the mother, and causes him to believe that the mother threatens or pursues him.   The teleological significance of this *fear of persecution* is evident; *it is to keep son and mother apart.*

The curse of Chryse is realized in so far that Philoctetes, according to one version, when approaching his altar, injured himself in his foot with one of his own deadly poisonous arrows, or, according to another version [34] (this is better and far more abundantly proven), *was bitten in his foot by a poisonous serpent.*[35]   From then on he is ailing.[36]

This very typical wound, which also destroyed Rê, is described in the following manner in an Egyptian hymn:

> " The ancient of the Gods moved his mouth,
>   He cast his saliva upon the earth,
>   And what he spat, fell upon the ground.
>   With her hands Isis kneaded that and the soil
>   Which was about it, together:
>   From that she created a venerable worm,
>   And made him like a spear.

She did not twist him living around her face,
But threw him coiled upon the path,
Upon which the great God wandered at ease
Through all his lands.

" The venerable God stepped forth radiantly,
The gods who served Pharaoh accompanied him,
And he proceeded as every day.
Then the venerable worm stung him. . . .
The divine God opened his mouth
And the voice of his majesty echoed even to the sky.
And the gods exclaimed: Behold!
Thereupon he could not answer,
His jaws chattered,
All his limbs trembled
And the poison gripped his flesh,
As the Nile seizes upon the land."

In this hymn Egypt has again preserved for us a primitive conception of the serpent's sting. The aging of the autumn sun as an image of human senility is symbolically traced back to the mother through the poisoning by the serpent. The mother is reproached, because her malice causes the death of the sun-god. The serpent, the primitive symbol of fear,[37] illustrates the repressed tendency to turn back to the mother, because the only possibility of security from death is possessed by the mother, as the source of life.

Accordingly, only the mother can cure him, sick unto death, and, therefore, the hymn goes on to depict how the gods were assembled to take counsel:

" And Isis came with her wisdom:
Her mouth is full of the breath of life,
Her words banish sorrow,
And her speech animates those who no longer breathe.

She said: 'What is that; what is that, divine father?
Behold, a worm has brought you sorrow——'

" 'Tell me thy name, divine father,
Because the man remains alive, who is called by his name.' "

Whereupon Ré replied:

" ' I am he, who created heaven and earth, and piled up the hills,
And created all beings thereon.
I am he, who made the water and caused the great flood,
Who produced the bull of his mother,
Who is the procreator,' etc.

" The poison did not depart, it went further,
The great God was not cured.
Then said Isis to Rê:
' Thine is not the name thou hast told me.
Tell me true that the poison may leave thee,
For he whose name is spoken will live.' "

Finally Ré decides to speak his true name. He is approximately healed (imperfect composition of Osiris); but he has lost his power, and finally he retreats to the heavenly cow.

The poisonous worm is, if one may speak in this way, a " negative " phallus, a deadly, not an animating, form of libido; therefore, a wish for death, instead of a wish for life. The " true name " is soul and magic power; hence a symbol of libido. What Isis demands is the retransference of the libido to the mother goddess. This request is fulfilled literally, for the aged god turns back to the divine cow, the symbol of the mother.[38] This symbolism is clear from our previous explanations. The onward urging, living libido which rules the consciousness of the son, demands separation from the mother. The longing of the child for the mother is a hindrance on the path to this, taking the form of a psychologic resistance, which is expressed empirically in the neurosis by all manners of fears, that is to say, the fear of life. The more a person withdraws from adaptation to reality, and falls into slothful inactivity, the greater becomes his anxiety (cum grano salis), which everywhere besets him at each point as a hindrance upon his path. The fear springs from the mother, that is to say, from the longing to go back to the mother, which is opposed to the adaptation to reality. This is the way in which the mother has become apparently the malicious pursuer. Naturally, it is not the actual mother, although the actual mother, with the abnormal tenderness with which she sometimes pursues her child, even into adult years, may gravely injure it through a willful prolonging of the infantile state in the child. It is rather the mother-imago, which becomes the Lamia. The mother-imago, however, possesses its power solely and exclusively from the son's tendency not only to look and to work forwards, but also to glance backwards to the pampering sweetness of childhood, to that glorious state of irresponsibility and security with which the protecting mother-care once surrounded him.[39]

The retrospective longing acts like a paralyzing poison upon the energy and enterprise; so that it may well be compared to a poisonous serpent which lies across our path. Apparently, it is a hostile demon which robs us of energy, but, in reality, it is the individual unconscious, the retrogressive tendency of which begins to overcome the conscious forward striving. The cause of this can be, for example, the natural aging which weakens the energy, or it may be great external difficulties, which cause man to break down and become a child again, or it may be, and this is probably the most frequent cause, the woman who enslaves the man, so that he can no longer free himself, and becomes a child again.⁴⁰ It may be of significance also that Isis, as sister-wife of the sun-god, creates the poisonous animal from the spittle of the god, which is perhaps a substitute for sperma, and, therefore, is a symbol of libido. She creates the animal from the libido of the god; that means she receives his power, making him weak and dependent, so that by this means she assumes the dominating rôle of the mother. (Mother transference to the wife.) This part is preserved in the legend of Samson, in the rôle of Delilah, who cut off Samson's hair, the sun's rays, thus robbing him of his strength.⁴¹ Any weakening of the adult man strengthens the wishes of the unconscious; therefore, the decrease of strength appears directly as the backward striving towards the mother.

There is still to be considered one more source of the reanimation of the mother-imago. We have already met it in the discussion of the mother scene in " Faust," that is to say, *the willed introversion of a creative mind,* which, retreating before its own problem and inwardly collecting its forces, dips at least for a moment into the source of life, in order there to wrest a little more strength from the mother for the completion of its work. It is a mother-child play with one's self, in which lies much weak self-admiration and self-adulation ("Among a hundred mirrors"—Nietzsche); *a Narcissus state,* a strange spectacle, perhaps, for profane eyes. The separation from the mother-imago, the birth out of one's self, reconciles all conflicts through the sufferings. This is probably meant by Nietzsche's verse:

> "Why hast thou enticed thyself
> Into the Paradise of the old serpent?
> Why hast thou crept
> Into thyself, thyself? . . .

> "A sick man now
> Sick of a serpent's poison,[42]
> A captive now
> Whom the hardest destiny befell
> In thine own pit;
> Bowed down as thou workest
> Encaved within thyself,
> Burrowing into thyself,
> Helpless,
> Stiff,
> A corpse.
> Overwhelmed with a hundred burdens,
> Overburdened by thyself.
> A wise man,
> A self-knower,
> The wise Zarathustra;
> Thou soughtest the heaviest burden
> And foundest thou thyself. . . ."

The symbolism of this speech is of the greatest richness. He is buried in the depths of *self, as if in the earth;* really a dead man who has turned back to mother earth;[43] a Kaineus "piled with a hundred burdens" and pressed down to death; the one who groaning bears the heavy burden of his own libido, of that libido which draws him back to the mother. Who does not think of the Taurophoria of Mithra, who took his bull (according to the Egyptian hymn, " the bull of his mother "), that is, his love for his mother, the heaviest burden upon his back, and with that entered upon the painful course of the so-called Transitus! [44] This path of passion led to the *cave,* in which the bull was sacrificed. Christ, too, had to bear the cross,[45] the symbol of his love for the mother, and he carried it to the place of sacrifice where the lamb was slain in the form of the God, the infantile man, a " self-executioner," and then to burial in the subterranean sepulchre.[46]

That which in Nietzsche appears as a poetical figure of speech is really a primitive myth. It is as if the poet still possessed a dim idea or capacity to feel and reactivate those imperishable phantoms of long-past worlds of thought in the words of our present-day speech and in the images which crowd themselves into his phantasy. Hauptmann also says: " Poetic rendering is that which allows the echo of the primitive word to resound through the form." [47]

The sacrifice, with its mysterious and manifold meaning, which is rather hinted at than expressed, passes unrecognized in the unconscious of our author. The arrow is not shot, the hero Chiwantopel is not yet fatally poisoned and ready for death through self-sacrifice. We now can say, according to the preceding material, this sacrifice means renouncing the mother, that is to say, *re-*

nunciation of all bonds and limitations which the soul has taken with it from the period of childhood into the adult life. From various hints of Miss Miller's it appears that at the time of these phantasies she was still living in the circle of the family, evidently at an age which was in urgent need of independence. That is to say, man does not live very long in the infantile environment or in the bosom of his family without real danger to his mental health. Life calls him forth to independence, and he who gives no heed to this hard call because of childish indolence and fear is threatened by a neurosis, and once the neurosis has broken out it becomes more and more a valid reason to escape the battle with life and to remain for all time in the morally poisoned infantile atmosphere.

The phantasy of the arrow-wound belongs in this struggle for personal independence. The thought of this resolution has not yet penetrated the dreamer. On the contrary, she rather repudiates it. After all the preceding, it is evident that the symbolism of the arrow-wound through direct translation must be taken as a coitus symbol. The " Occide moriturus " attains by this means the sexual significance belonging to it. Chiwantopel naturally represents the dreamer. But nothing is attained and nothing is understood through one's reduction to the coarse sexual, because it is a commonplace that the unconscious shelters coitus wishes, the discovery of which signifies nothing further. *The coitus wish under this aspect is really a symbol for the individual demonstration of the libido separated from the parents, of the conquest of an independent life.* This step towards a new life means, at the same time, the death of the past life.[48] Therefore, Chiwantopel is the infantile hero [49] (the son, the child, the lamb, the fish) who is still enchained by the fetters of childhood and who has to die as a symbol of the incestuous libido, and with that sever the retrogressive bond. For the entire libido is demanded for the battle of life, and there can be no remaining behind. The dreamer cannot yet come to this decision, which will tear aside all the sentimental connections with father and mother, and yet it must be made in order to follow the call of the individual destiny.

CHAPTER VII

THE DUAL MOTHER RÔLE

After the disappearance of the assailant, Chiwantopel begins the following monologue:

"From the extreme ends of these continents, from the farthest lowlands, after having forsaken the palace of my father, I have been wandering aimlessly during a hundred moons, always pursued by my mad desire to find 'her who will understand.' With jewels I have tempted many fair ones, with kisses I have tried to snatch the secret of their hearts, with acts of bravery I have conquered their admiration. (He reviews the women he has known.) Chita, the princess of my race . . . she is a little fool, vain as a peacock, having nought in her head but jewels and perfume. Ta-nan, the young peasant, . . . bah, a mere sow, no more than a breast and a stomach, caring only for pleasure. And then Ki-ma, the priestess, a true parrot, repeating hollow phrases learnt from the priests; all for show, without real education or sincerity, suspicious poseur and hypocrite! . . . Alas! Not one who understands me, not one who resembles me, not one who has a soul sister to mine. There is not one among them all who has known my soul, not one who could read my thought; far from it; not one capable of seeking with me the luminous summits, or of spelling with me the superhuman word, love."

Here Chiwantopel himself says that his journeying and wandering is a quest for that other, and for the meaning of life which lies in union with her. In the first part of this work we merely hinted gently at this possibility. The fact that the seeker is masculine and the sought-for of feminine sex is not so astonishing, because the chief object of the unconscious transference is the mother, as has probably been seen from that which we have already learned. The daughter takes a male attitude towards the mother. The genesis of this adjustment can only be suspected in our case, because objective proof is lacking. Therefore, let us rather be satisfied with inferences. " She who will understand " means the mother, in the infantile language. At the same time, it also means the life companion. As is well known, the sex contrast concerns the libido but little. The sex of the object plays a surprisingly slight rôle in the estimation of the unconscious. The object itself, taken as an objective reality, is but of slight significance. (But it is of greatest importance whether the libido is transferred or introverted.) The original concrete meaning of *erfassen,* "to seize," *begreifen,* " to touch," etc., allows us to recognize clearly the under side of the wish—to find a congenial person. But the " upper " intellectual half is also contained in it, and is to be taken into account at the same time. One might be inclined to assume this tendency if it were not that our culture abused the same, for the misunderstood woman has become almost proverbial, which can only be the result of a wholly distorted valuation. On the one side, our culture undervalues most extraordinarily the importance of sexuality; on the other side, sexuality breaks out as a direct result of the repression burdening it at every place where it does not belong, and makes use of such an indirect manner of expression that one may expect to meet it suddenly almost anywhere. Thus the

idea of the intimate comprehension of a human soul,
which is in reality something very beautiful and pure, is
soiled and disagreeably distorted through the entrance
of the indirect sexual meaning.[1] The secondary meaning
or, better expressed, the misuse, which repressed and
denied sexuality forces upon the highest soul functions,
makes it possible, for example, for certain of our opponents to scent in psychoanalysis prurient erotic confes-
sionals. These are subjective wish-fulfilment deliria
which need no contra arguments. This misuse makes the
wish to be " understood " highly suspicious, if the natural
demands of life have not been fulfilled. Nature has *first
claim* on man; only long afterwards does the luxury of
intellect come. The mediæval ideal of life for the sake
of death needs gradually to be replaced by a natural conception of life, in which the normal demands of men are
thoroughly kept in mind, so that the desires of the animal
sphere may no longer be compelled to drag down into
their service the high gifts of the intellectual sphere in
order to find an outlet. We are inclined, therefore, to
consider the dreamer's wish for understanding, first of
all, as a repressed striving towards the natural destiny.
This meaning coincides absolutely with psychoanalytic
experience, that there are countless neurotic people who
apparently are prevented from experiencing life because
they have an unconscious and often also a conscious re-
pugnance to the sexual fate, under which they imagine
all kinds of ugly things. There is only too great an inclination to yield to this pressure of the unconscious sexuality and to experience the dreaded (unconsciously hoped

for) disagreeable sexual experience, so as to acquire by that means a legitimately founded horror which retains them more surely in the infantile situation. This is the reason why so many people fall into that very state towards which they have the greatest abhorrence.

That we were correct in our assumption that, in Miss Miller, it is a question of the battle for independence is shown by her statement that the hero's departure from his father's house reminds her of the fate of the young Buddha, who likewise renounced all luxury to which he was born in order to go out into the world to live out his destiny to its completion. Buddha gave the same heroic example as did Christ, who separated from his mother, and even spoke bitter words (Matthew, chap. x, v. 34):

" Think not that I am come to send peace on earth: I came not to send peace, but a sword.

(35) "For I am come to set a man at variance against his father, and the daughter against her mother, and the daughter-in-law against her mother-in-law.

(36) "And a man's foes shall be they of his own household.

(37) "He that loveth father or mother more than me is not worthy of me."

Or Luke, chap. xii, v. 51:

" Suppose ye that I am come to give peace on earth? I tell you, Nay: but rather division.

(52) "For from henceforth there shall be five in one house divided, three against two, and two against three.

(53) "The father shall be divided against the son, and the son against the father; the mother against the daughter, and the daughter against the mother; the mother-in-law against the

daughter-in-law, and the daughter-in-law against her mother-in-law."

Horus snatched from his mother her head adornment, the power. Just as Adam struggled with Lilith, so he struggles for power. Nietzsche, in " Human, All Too Human," expressed the same in very beautiful words:

" One may suppose that a mind, in which the ' type of free mind ' is to ripen and sweeten at maturity, has had its decisive crisis in a great detachment, so that before this time it was just so much the more a fettered spirit and appeared chained forever to its corner and its pillar.[2] What binds it most firmly? What cords are almost untearable? Among human beings of a high and exquisite type, it would be duties: that reverence, which is suitable for youth, that modesty and tenderness for all the old honored and valued things, that thankfulness for the earth from which they grew, for the hand which guided them, for the shrine where they learnt to pray:—their loftiest moments themselves come to bind them the firmest, to obligate them the most permanently. The great detachment comes suddenly for people so bound.

" ' Better to die than to live here,'—thus rings the imperative voice of seduction: and this here, this ' at home ' is all, that it (the soul) has loved until now! A sudden terror and suspicion against that which it has loved, a lightning flash of scorn towards that which is called ' duty,' a rebellious, arbitrary, volcanic, impelling desire for travelling, for strange countries, estrangements, coolness, frigidity, disillusionments, a hatred of love, perhaps a sacrilegious touch and glance backwards[3] there where just now it adored and loved, perhaps a blush of shame over what it has just done, and at the same time an exultation over having done it, an intoxicating internal joyous thrill, in which a victory reveals itself —a victory? Over what? Over whom? An enigmatic, doubtful, questioning victory, but the first triumph. Of such woe and pain is formed the history of the great detachment. It is like a disease which can destroy men,—this first eruption of strength and will towards self-assertion."[4]

The danger lies, as is brilliantly expressed by Nietzsche, in isolation in one's self:

" Solitude surrounds and embraces him ever more threatening, ever more constricting, ever more heart-strangling, the terrible Goddess and Mater sæva cupidinum."

The libido taken away from the mother, who is abandoned only reluctantly, becomes threatening as a serpent, the symbol of death, for the relation to the mother must cease, *must die, which itself almost causes man's death.* In " Mater sæva cupidinum " the idea attains rare, almost conscious, perfection.

I do not presume to try to paint in better words than has Nietzsche the psychology of the wrench from childhood.

Miss Miller furnishes us with a further reference to a material which has influenced her creation in a more general manner; this is the great Indian epic of Longfellow, " The Song of Hiawatha."

If my readers have had patience to read thus far, and to reflect upon what they have read, they frequently must have wondered at the number of times I introduce for comparison such apparently foreign material and how often I widen the base upon which Miss Miller's creations rest. Doubts must often have arisen whether it is justifiable to enter into important discussions concerning the psychologic foundations of myths, religions and culture in general on the basis of such scanty suggestions. It might be said that behind the Miller phantasies such a

thing is scarcely to be found. I need hardly emphasize
the fact that I, too, have sometimes been in doubt. I
had never read "Hiawatha" until, in the course of my
work, I came to this part. "Hiawatha," a poetical compilation of Indian myths, gives me, however, a justification for all preceding reflections, because this epic contains an unusual number of mythologic problems. This
fact is probably of great importance for the wealth of
suggestions in the Miller phantasies. We are, therefore,
compelled to obtain an insight into this epic.

Nawadaha sings the songs of the epic of the hero
Hiawatha, the friend of man:

> " There he sang of Hiawatha,
> Sang the songs of Hiawatha,
> Sang his wondrous birth and being,
> How he prayed and how he fasted,
> How he lived and toiled and suffered,
> That the tribes of men might prosper,
> That he might advance his people."

The teleological meaning of the hero, as that symbolic
figure which unites in itself libido in the form of admiration and adoration, in order to lead to higher sublima-
tions by way of the symbolic bridges of the myths, is
anticipated here. Thus we become quickly acquainted
with Hiawatha as a savior, and are prepared to hear all
that which must be said of a savior, of his marvellous
birth, of his early great deeds, and his sacrifice for his
fellow-men.

The first song begins with a fragment of evangelism:
Gitche Manito, the " master of life," tired of the quarrels

of his human children, calls his people together and makes
known to them the joyous message:

> " I will send a prophet to you,
> A Deliverer of the nations,
> Who shall guide you and shall teach you,
> Who shall toil and suffer with you.
> If you listen to his counsels,
> You will multiply and prosper.
> If his warnings pass unheeded,
> You will fade away and perish! "

Gitche Manito, the Mighty, " the creator of the nations," is represented as he stood erect " on the great Red
Pipestone quarry."

> " From his footprints flowed a river,
> Leaped into the light of morning,
> O'er the precipice plunging downward
> Gleamed like Ishkoodah, the comet."

The water flowing from his footsteps sufficiently
proves the phallic nature of this creator. I refer to the
earlier utterances concerning the phallic and fertilizing
nature of the horse's foot and the horse's steps, and especially do I recall Hippocrene and the foot of Pegasus.[5]
We meet with the same idea in Psalm lxv, vv. 9 to 11:

" Thou visitest the earth, and waterest it; thou makest it very
plenteous.

" The river of God is full of water; thou preparest their corn,
for so thou providest for the earth.

" Thou waterest her furrows: thou sendest rain into the little
valleys thereof; thou makest it soft with the drops of rain, and
blessest the increase of it.

" Thou crownest the year with thy goodness; and thy paths
drop fatness."

Wherever the fertilizing God steps, there is fruitfulness. We already have spoken of the symbolic meaning of treading in discussing the nightmares. Kaineus passes into the depths, "splitting the earth with a foot outstretched." Amphiaraus, another chthonic hero, sinks into the earth, which Zeus has opened for him by a stroke of lightning. (Compare with that the above-mentioned vision of a hysterical patient, who saw a black horse after a flash of lightning: identity of horse's footstep and flash of lightning.) By means of a flash of lightning heroes were made immortal.[6] Faust attained the mothers when he stamped his foot.

"Stamp and descend, stamping thou'lt rise again."

The heroes in the sun-devouring myths often stamp at or struggle in the jaws of the monster. Thus Tor stamped through the ship's bottom in battle with the monster, and *went as far as the bottom of the sea.* (Kaineus.) (Concerning "kicking" as an infantile phantasy, see above.) The regression of the libido to the presexual stage makes this preparatory action of treading either a substitution for the coitus phantasy or for the phantasy of re-entrance into the mother's womb. The comparison of water flowing from the footsteps with a comet is a light symbolism for the fructifying moisture (sperma). According to an observation by Humboldt (Kosmos), certain South American Indian tribes call the meteors "urine of the stars." Mention is also made of how Gitche Manito makes fire. He blows upon a forest, so that the trees, rubbing upon each other, burst into flame. This demon is, therefore, an excellent libido symbol; he also produced fire.

After this prologue in the second song, the hero's previous history is related. The great warrior, Mudjekeewis (Hiawatha's father), has cunningly overcome the great bear, " the terror of the nations," and stolen from him the magic " belt of wampum," a girdle of shells. Here we meet the motive of the " treasure attained with difficulty," which the hero rescues from the monster. Who the bear is, is shown by the poet's comparisons. Mudjekeewis strikes the bear on his head after he has robbed him of the treasure.

> " With the heavy blow bewildered
>   Rose the great Bear of the mountains,
>   But his knees beneath him trembled,
>   And he whimpered *like a woman*."

Mudjekeewis said derisively to him:

> " Else you would not cry, and whimper,
>   Like a *miserable woman!*
>
>   .   .   .   .   .
>
>   But you, Bear! sit here and whimper,
>   And disgrace your tribe by crying,
>   Like a wretched Shaugodaya,
>   Like a *cowardly old woman!* "

These three comparisons with a woman are to be found near each other on the same page. Mudjekeewis has, like a true hero, once more torn life from the jaws of death, from the all-devouring " terrible mother." This deed, which, as we have seen, is also represented as a journey to hell, " night journey through the sea," the conquering of the monster from within, signifies at the same time entrance into the mother's womb, a rebirth, the results of which are perceptible also for Mudjekeewis. As in the Zosimos vision, here too the entering one becomes the breath of the wind or spirit.   Mudjekeewis becomes the west wind, the fertilizing breath, the father of winds.[7] His sons become the other winds.   An intermezzo tells of them and of their love stories, of which I will mention only the courtship of Wabuns, the East Wind, because here the erotic wooing of the wind is pictured in an especially beautiful manner.   Every morning he sees a beautiful girl in a meadow, whom he eagerly courts:

> " Every morning, gazing earthward,
>   Still the first thing he beheld there
>   Was her blue eyes looking at him,
>   Two blue lakes among the rushes."

The comparison with water is not a matter of secondary importance, because " from wind and water " shall man be born anew.

> " And he wooed her with caresses,
>   Wooed her with his smile of sunshine,
>   With his flattering words he wooed her,
>   With his sighing and his singing,
>   Gentlest whispers in the branches,
>   Softest music, sweetest odors," etc.

In these onomatopoetic verses the wind's caressing courtship is excellently expressed.[8]

The third song presents the previous history of Hiawatha's mother. His grandmother, when a maiden, lived in the moon. There she once swung upon a liana, but a jealous lover cut off the liana, and Nokomis, Hiawatha's grandmother, fell to earth. The people, who saw her fall downwards, thought that she was a *shooting star*. This marvellous descent of Nokomis is more plainly illustrated by a later passage of this same song; there little Hiawatha asks the grandmother what is the moon. Nokomis teaches him about it as follows: The moon is the body of a *grandmother*, whom a warlike grandson has cast up there in wrath. Hence the moon is the *grandmother*. In ancient beliefs, the moon is also the gathering place of departed souls,[9] the guardian of seeds; therefore, once more a place of the origin of life of predominantly feminine significance. The remarkable thing is that Nokomis, falling upon the earth, gave birth to a daughter, Wenonah, subsequently the mother of Hiawatha. The throwing upwards of the mother, and her falling down and bringing forth, seems to contain something typical in itself. Thus a story of the seventeenth century relates that a mad bull threw a pregnant woman as high as a house, and tore open her womb, and the child fell without harm upon the earth. On account of his wonderful birth, this child was considered a hero or doer of miracles, but he died at an early age. The belief is widespread among lower savages that the sun is feminine and the moon masculine. Among the Namaqua, a Hottentot tribe, the opinion is prevalent that the sun consists of transparent bacon.

"The people, who journey on boats, draw it down by magic every evening, cut off a suitable piece and then give it *a kick so that it flies up again into the sky.*"—*Waitz:* "Anthropologie," II, 342.

The infantile nourishment comes from the mother. In the Gnostic phantasies we come across a legend of the origin of man which possibly belongs here: the female archons bound to the vault of Heaven are unable, on account of its quick rotation, to keep their young within them, but let them fall upon the earth, from which men arise. Possibly there is here a connection with barbaric midwifery, the letting fall of the parturient. The assault upon the mother is already introduced with the adventure of Mudjekeewis, and is continued in the violent handling of the " grandmother," Nokomis, who, as a result of the cutting of the liana and the fall downwards, seems in some way to have become pregnant. The " cutting of the branch," the plucking, we have already recognized as mother incest. (See above.) That well-known verse, " Saxonland, where beautiful maidens grow upon trees," and phrases like " picking cherries in a neighbor's garden," allude to a similar idea. The fall downwards of Nokomis deserves to be compared to a poetical figure in Heine.

> " A star, a star is falling
>   Out of the glittering sky!
> The star of Love! I watch it
>   Sink in the depths and die.
>
> " The leaves and buds are falling
>   From many an apple-tree;

> I watch the mirthful breezes
> Embrace them wantonly . . ."

Wenonah later was courted by the caressing West Wind, and becomes pregnant. Wenonah, as a young moon-goddess, has the beauty of the moonlight. Nokomis warns her of the dangerous courtship of Mudjekeewis, the West Wind. But Wenonah allows herself to become infatuated, and conceives from the breath of the wind, from the πνεῦμα, a son, our hero.

> " And the West-Wind came at evening,
>
> .   .   .   .   .   .
>
> Found the beautiful Wenonah,
> Lying there amid the lilies,
> Wooed her with his words of sweetness,
> Wooed her with his soft caresses,
> Till she bore a son in sorrow,
> Bore a son of love and sorrow."

Fertilization through the breath of the spirit is already a well-known precedent for us. The star or comet plainly belongs to the birth scene as a libido symbol; Nokomis, too, comes to earth as a shooting star. Mörike's sweet poetic phantasy has devised a similar divine origin.

> " And she who bore me in her womb,
>   And gave me food and clothing.
> She was a maid—a wild, brown maid,
>   Who looked on men with loathing.

> " She fleered at them and laughed out loud,
>   And bade no suitor tarry;
> ' I'd rather be the Wind's own bride
>   Than have a man and marry.'

" Then came the Wind and held her fast
His captive, love-enchanted;
And lo, by him a merry child
Within her womb was planted."

Buddha's marvellous birth story, retold by Sir Edwin Arnold, also shows traces of this.[10]

" Maya, the Queen . . .
Dreamed a strange dream, dreamed that a star from heaven—
Splendid, six-rayed, in color rosy-pearl,
Whereof the token was an Elephant
Six-tusked and white as milk of Kamadhuk—
Shot through the void; and shining into her,
Entered her womb upon the right." [11]

During Maya's conception a wind blows over the land:

" A wind blew
With unknown freshness over lands and seas."

After the birth the four genii of the East, West, South and North come to render service as bearers of the palanquin. (The coming of the wise men at Christ's birth.) We also find here a distinct reference to the " four winds." For the completion of the symbolism there is to be found in the Buddha myth, as well as in the birth legend of Christ, besides the impregnation by star and wind, also the fertilization by an animal, here an elephant, which with its phallic trunk fulfilled in Maya the Christian method of fructification through the ear or the head. It is well known that, in addition to the dove, the unicorn is also a procreative symbol of the Logos.

Here arises the question why the birth of a hero always

had to take place under such strange symbolic circumstances? It might also be imagined that a hero arose
from ordinary surroundings and gradually grew out of
his inferior environment, perhaps with a thousand troubles and dangers. (And, indeed, this motive is by no
means strange in the hero myth.) It might be said that
superstition demands strange conditions of birth and generation; but why does it demand them?

The answer to this question is: that the birth of the
hero, as a rule, is not that of an ordinary mortal, but is
a rebirth from the mother-spouse; hence it occurs under
mysterious ceremonies. Therefore, in the very beginning, lies the motive of the two mothers of the hero. As
Rank [12] has shown us through many examples, the hero
is often obliged to experience exposure, and upbringing
by foster parents, and in this manner he acquires the two
mothers. A striking example is the relation of Hercules
to Hera. In the Hiawatha epic Wenonah dies after the
birth and Nokomis takes her place. Maya dies after the
birth [13] and Buddha is given a stepmother. The stepmother is sometimes an animal (the she-wolf of Romulus
and Remus, etc.). The twofold mother may be replaced
by the motive of twofold birth, which has attained a
lofty significance in the Christian mythology; namely,
through baptism, which, as we have seen, represents rebirth. Thus man is born not merely in a commonplace
manner, but also born again in a mysterious manner, by
means of which he becomes a participator of the kingdom
of God, of immortality. Any one may become a hero
in this way who is generated anew through his own

mother, because only through her does he share in immortality. Therefore, it happened that the death of Christ on the cross, which creates universal salvation, was understood as "baptism"; that is to say, as rebirth through the second mother, the mysterious tree of death. Christ says:

"But I have a baptism to be baptized with: and how am I straitened till it be accomplished!"—*Luke* xii: 50.

He interprets his death agony symbolically as birth agony.

The motive of the two mothers suggests the thought of self-rejuvenation, and evidently expresses the fulfilment of the wish that it *might be possible for the mother to bear me again;* at the same time, applied to the heroes, it means one is a hero who is borne again by her who has previously been his mother; that is to say, *a hero is he who may again produce himself through his mother.*

The countless suggestions in the history of the procreation of the heroes indicate the latter formulations. Hiawatha's father first overpowered the mother under the symbol of the bear; then himself becoming a god, he procreates the hero. What Hiawatha had to do as hero, Nokomis hinted to him in the legend of the origin of the moon; he is forcibly to throw his mother upwards (or throw downwards?); then she would become pregnant by this act of violence and could bring forth a daughter. This rejuvenated mother would be allotted, according to the Egyptian rite, as a daughter-wife to the sun-god, the father of his mother, for self-reproduction. What action

Hiawatha takes in this regard we shall see presently. We have already studied the behavior of the pre-Asiatic gods related to Christ. Concerning the pre-existence of Christ, the Gospel of St. John is full of this thought. Thus the speech of John the Baptist:

" This is he of whom I said, After me cometh a man which is preferred before me; for he was before me."—*John* i: 30.

Also the beginning of the gospel is full of deep mythologic significance:

" In the beginning was the Word, and the Word was with God, and the Word was God.   The same was in the beginning with God.
(3) " All things were made by him, and without him was not anything made that was made.
(4) " In him was life, and the *life* was the *light of men.*
(5) " And the light shineth in darkness; and the darkness comprehendeth it not.
(6) " There was a man sent from God whose name was John.
(7) " The same came for a witness, to bear witness of the Light.
(8) " He was not that Light, but was sent to bear witness of that Light.
(9) " That was the true Light, which lighteth every man that cometh into the world."

This is the proclamation of the reappearing light, the reborn sun, which formerly was, and which will be again. In the baptistry at Pisa, Christ is represented bringing the tree of life to man; his head is surrounded by a sun halo.   Over this relief stand the words INTROITUS SOLIS.

Because the one born was his own procreator, the history of his procreation is strangely concealed under symbolic events, which are meant to conceal and deny it; hence the extraordinary assertion of the virgin conception. This is meant to hide the incestuous impregnation. But do not let us forget that this naïve assertion plays an unusually important part in the ingenious symbolic bridge, which is to guide the libido out from the incestuous bond to higher and more useful applications, which indicate a new kind of immortality; that is to say, immortal work.

The environment of Hiawatha's youth is of importance :

> " By the shores of Gitche Gumee,
> By the shining Big-Sea-Water,
> Stood the wigwam of Nokomis,
> Daughter of the Moon, Nokomis.
> Dark behind it rose the forest,
> Rose the black and gloomy pine-trees,
> Rose the firs with cones upon them.
> Bright before it beat the water,
> Beat the clear and sunny water,
> Beat the shining Big-Sea-Water."

In this environment Nokomis brought him up. Here she taught him the first words, and told him the first fairy tales, and the sounds of the water and the wood were intermingled, so that the child learned not only to understand man's speech, but also that of Nature :

> " At the door on summer evenings
> Sat the little Hiawatha;
> Heard the whispering of the pine-trees,
> Heard the lapping of the water,
> Sounds of music, words of wonder:
> ' Minne-wawa!' [14] said the pine-trees,
> ' Mudway-aushka!' [15] said the water."

Hiawatha hears human speech in the sounds of Nature; thus he understands Nature's speech. The wind says, " Wawa." The cry of the wild goose is " Wawa." Wah-wah-taysee means the small glowworm which enchants him. Thus the poet paints most beautifully the gradual gathering of external nature into the compass of the subjective,[16] and the intimate connection of the primary object to which the first lisping words were applied, and from which the first sounds were derived, with the secondary object, the wider nature which usurps imperceptibly the mother's place, and takes possession of those sounds heard first from the mother, and also of those feelings which we all discover later in ourselves in all the warm love of Mother Nature. The later blending, whether pantheistic-philosophic or æsthetic, of the sentimental, cultured man with nature is, looked at retrospectively, a reblending with the mother, who was our primary object, and with whom we truly were once wholly one.[17] Therefore, it is not astonishing when we again see emerging in the poetical speech of a modern philosopher, Karl Joël, the old pictures which symbolize the unity with the mother, illustrated by the confluence of subject and object. In his recent book, " Seele und Welt " (1912), Joël writes as follows, in the chapter called " Primal Experience "[18]:

" I lay on the seashore, the shining waters glittering in my dreamy eyes; at a great distance fluttered the soft breeze; throbbing, shimmering, stirring, lulling to sleep comes the wave beat to the shore—or to the ear? I know not. Distance and nearness become blurred into one; without and within glide into each

other. Nearer and nearer, *dearer and more homelike sounds the
beating of the waves;* now, like a thundering pulse in my head it
strikes, and now it beats over my soul, devours it, embraces it,
while it itself at the same time floats out like the blue waste of
waters. Yes, without and within are one. Glistening and foam-
ing, flowing and fanning and roaring, the entire symphony of the
stimuli experienced sounds in one tone, all thought becomes one
thought, which becomes one with feeling; the world exhales in
the soul and the soul dissolves in the world. Our small life is
encircled by a great sleep—*the sleep of our cradle, the sleep of our
grave, the sleep of our home, from which we go forth in the morning, to which we again return in the evening;* our life but the
short journey, the interval between the emergence from the original oneness and the sinking back into it! Blue shimmers the
infinite sea, wherein dreams the jelly fish of the primitive life,
toward which without ceasing our thoughts hark back dimly
through eons of existence. For every happening entails a change
and a guarantee of the unity of life. At that moment when they
are no longer blended together, in that instant man lifts his *head,
blind and dripping, from the depths* of the stream of experience,
from the oneness with the experience; at that moment of parting
when the unity of life in startled surprise detaches the Change
and holds it away from itself as something alien, at this moment
of alienation the aspects of the experience have been substantial-
ized into subject and object, and in that moment consciousness is
born."

Joël paints here, in unmistakable symbolism, the confluence of subject and object as the reunion of mother
and child. The symbols agree with those of mythology,
even in their details. The encircling and devouring motive is distinctly suggested. The sea, devouring the sun
and giving birth to it anew, is already an old acquaintance. The moment of the rise of consciousness, the separation of subject and object is a birth; truly philosophical

thought hangs with lame wings upon the few great primitive pictures of human speech, above the simple, all-surpassing greatness of which no thought can rise. The idea of the jelly fish is not " accidental." Once when I was explaining to a patient the maternal significance of water at this contact with the mother complex, she experienced a very unpleasant feeling. " It makes me squirm," she said, " as if I touched a jelly fish." Here, too, the same idea! The blessed state of sleep before birth and after death is, as Joël observed, something like old shadowy memories of that unsuspecting, thoughtless state of early childhood, where as yet no opposition disturbed the peaceful flow of dawning life, to which the inner longing always draws us back again and again, and from which the active life must free itself anew with struggle and death, so that it may not be doomed to destruction. Long before Joël, an Indian chieftain had said the same thing in similar words to one of the restless wise men :

" Ah, my brother, you will never learn to know the happiness of thinking nothing and doing nothing: this is next to sleep; this is the most delightful thing there is. Thus we were before birth, thus we shall be after death." [19]

We shall see in Hiawatha's later fate how important his early impressions are in his choice of a wife. Hiawatha's first deed was to kill a roebuck with his arrow:

" Dead he lay there in the forest,
   By the ford across the river."

This is typical of Hiawatha's deeds. Whatever he kills, for the most part, lies *next to or in the water,* some-

times half in the water and half on the land.[20] It seems
that this must well be so. The later adventures will
teach us why this must be so. The buck was no ordinary
animal, but a magic one; that is to say, one with an additional unconscious significance. Hiawatha made for himself gloves and moccasins from its hide; the gloves imparted such strength to his arms that he could crumble
rocks to dust, and the moccasins had the virtue of the
seven-league boots. By enwrapping himself in the buck's
skin he really became a giant. This motive, together with
the death of the animal at the ford,[21] in the water, reveals the fact that the parents are concerned, whose
gigantic proportions as compared with the child are of
great significance in the unconscious. The "toys of
giants" is a wish inversion of the infantile phantasy.
The dream of an eleven-year-old girl expresses this:

" I am as high as a church steeple; then a policeman comes. I
tell him, ' If you say anything, I will cut off your head. ' "

The "policeman," as the analysis brought out, referred to the father, whose gigantic size was over-com-
pensated by the church steeple. In Mexican human sacrifices, the gods were represented by criminals, who were
slaughtered, and flayed, and the Corybantes then clothed
themselves in the bloody skins, in order to illustrate the
resurrection of the gods.[22] (The snake's casting of his
skin as a symbol of rejuvenation.)

Hiawatha has, therefore, conquered his parents, primarily the mother, although in the form of a male animal (compare the bear of Mudjekeewis) ; and from that

comes his giant's strength. He has taken on the parent's skin and now has himself become a great man. Now he started forth to his first great battle to fight with the father Mudjekeewis, in order to avenge his dead mother Wenonah. Naturally, under this figure of speech hides the thought that he slays the father, in order to take possession of the mother. Compare the battle of Gilgamesh with the giant Chumbaba and the ensuing conquest of Ishtar. The father, in the psychologic sense, merely represents the personification of the incest prohibition; that is to say, resistance, which defends the mother. Instead of the father, it may be a fearful animal (the great bear, the snake, the dragon, etc.) which must be fought and overcome. The hero is a hero because he sees in every difficulty of life resistance to the forbidden treasure, and fights that resistance with the complete yearning which strives towards the treasure, attainable with difficulty, or unattainable, the yearning which paralyzes and kills the ordinary man.

Hiawatha's father is Mudjekeewis, the west wind; the battle, therefore, takes place in the west. Thence came life (impregnation of Wenonah); thence also came death (death of Wenonah). Hiawatha, therefore, fights the typical battle of the hero for rebirth in the western sea, the battle with the devouring terrible mother, this time in the form of the father. Mudjekeewis, who himself had acquired a divine nature, through his conquest of the bear, now is overpowered by his son:

" Back retreated Mudjekeewis,
    Rushing westward o'er the mountains,

Stumbling westward down the mountains,
Three whole days retreated fighting,
Still pursued by Hiawatha
To the doorways of the West-Wind,
To the portals of the Sunset,
To the earth's remotest border,
Where into the empty spaces
Sinks the sun, as a flamingo
Drops into her nest at nightfall."

The "three days" are a stereotyped form representing the stay in the sea prison of night. (Twenty-first until twenty-fourth of December.) Christ, too, remained three days in the underworld. "The treasure, difficult to attain," is captured by the hero during this struggle in the west. In this case the father must make a great concession to the son; he gives him divine nature,[23] that very wind nature, the immortality of which alone protected Mudjekeewis from death. He says to his son:

" I will share my kingdom with you,
Ruler shall you be henceforward,
Of the Northwest-Wind, Keewaydin,
Of the home-wind, the Keewaydin."

That Hiawatha now becomes ruler of the home-wind has its close parallel in the Gilgamesh epic, where Gilgamesh finally receives the magic herb from the wise old Utnapishtim, who dwells in the West, which brings him safe once more over the sea to his home; but this, when he is home again, is retaken from him by a serpent.

When one has slain the father, one can obtain possession of his wife, and when one has conquered the mother, one can free one's self.

On the return journey Hiawatha stops at the clever arrow-maker's, who possesses a lovely daughter:

> " And he named her from the river,
> From the water-fall he named her,
> Minnehaha, Laughing Water."

When Hiawatha, in his earliest childhood dreaming, felt the sounds of water and wind press upon his ears, he recognized in these sounds of nature the speech of his mother. The murmuring pine trees on the shore of the great sea, said " Minnewawa." And above the murmuring of the winds and the splashing of the water he found his earliest childhood dreams once again in a woman, " Minnehaha," the laughing water. And the hero, before all others, finds in woman the mother, in order to become a child again, and, finally, to solve the riddle of immortality.

The fact that Minnehaha's father is a skilful arrow-maker betrays him as the father of the hero (and the woman he had with him as the mother). The father of the hero is very often a skilful carpenter, or other artisan. According to an Arabian legend, Tare,[24] Abraham's father, was a skilful master workman, who could carve arrows from any wood; that is to say, in the Arabian form of speech, he was a procreator of splendid sons.[25] Moreover, he was a maker of images of gods. Tvashtar, Agni's father, is the maker of the world, a smith and carpenter, the discoverer of fire-boring. Joseph, the father of Jesus, was also a carpenter; likewise Kinyras, Adonis's father, who is said to have invented the hammer, the lever, roofing and mining. Hephæstus, the father of Hermes, is an artistic master workman and sculptor. In fairy tales, the father of the hero is very modestly the traditional wood-cutter. These conceptions were also alive in the cult of Osiris. There the divine image was carved out of a tree trunk and then placed within the hollow of the tree. (Frazer: "Golden Bough," Part IV.) In Rigveda, the world was also hewn out of a tree by the world-sculptor. The idea that the hero is his own procreator [26] leads to the fact that he is invested with paternal attributes, and reversedly the heroic attributes are given to the father. In Mânî there exists a beautiful union of the motives. He accomplishes his great labors as a religious founder, hides himself for years in a cave, he dies, is skinned, stuffed and hung up (hero). Besides he is an artist, and has a crippled foot. A similar union of motives is found in Wieland, the smith.

Hiawatha kept silent about what he saw at the old arrow-maker's on his return to Nokomis, and he did nothing further to win Minnehaha. But now something happened, which, if it were not in an Indian epic, would rather be sought in the history of a neurosis. Hiawatha introverted his libido; that is to say, he fell into an extreme resistance against the "real sexual demand" (Freud); he built a hut for himself in the wood, in order to fast there and to experience dreams and visions. For the first three days he wandered, as once in his earliest youth, through a forest and looked at all the animals and plants:

" ' Master of life! ' he cried, desponding,
  ' Must our lives depend on these things? ' "

The question whether our lives must depend upon
" these things " is very strange. It sounds as if life were
derived from these things; that is to say, from nature
in general. Nature seems suddenly to have assumed a
very strange significance. This phenomenon can be explained only through the fact that a great amount of
libido was stored up and now is given to nature. As is
well known, men of even dull and prosy minds, in the
springtime of love, suddenly become aware of nature,
and even make poems about it. But we know that libido,
prevented from an actual way of transference, always re-
verts to an earlier way of transference. Minnehaha, the
laughing water, is so clearly an allusion to the mother
that the secret yearning of the hero for the mother is
powerfully touched. Therefore, without having undertaken anything, he goes home to Nokomis; but there again
he is driven away, because Minnehaha already stands in
his path.

He turns, therefore, even further away, into that early
youthful period, the tones of which recall Minnehaha
most forcibly to his thoughts, where he learnt to hear
the mother-sounds in the sounds of nature. In this very
strange revival of the impressions of nature we recognize
a regression to those earliest and strongest nature impressions which stand next to the subsequently extinguished, even stronger, impressions which the child received from the mother. The glamour of this feeling for
her is transferred to other objects of the childish environ-

ment (father's house, playthings, etc.), from which later those magic blissful feelings proceed, which seem to be peculiar to the earliest childish memories. When, therefore, Hiawatha hides himself in the lap of nature, it is really the mother's womb, and it is to be expected that he will emerge again new-born in some form.

Before turning to this new creation arising from introversion, there is still a further significance of the preceding question to be considered: whether life is dependent upon " these things " ? Life may depend upon these things in the degree that they serve *for nourishment.* We must infer in this case that suddenly the question of nutrition came very near the hero's heart. (This possibility will be thoroughly proven in what follows.) The question of nutrition, indeed, enters seriously into consideration. First, because regression to the mother necessarily revives that special path of transference; namely, that of nutrition through the mother. As soon as the libido regresses to the presexual stage, there we may expect to see the function of nutrition and its symbols put in place of the sexual function. Thence is derived an essential root of the displacement from below upwards (Freud), because, in the presexual stage, the principal value belongs not to the genitals, but to the mouth. Secondly, because the hero fasted, his hunger becomes predominant. Fasting, as is well known, is employed to silence sexuality; also, it expresses symbolically the resistance against sexuality, translated into the language of the presexual stage. On the fourth day of his fast the hero ceased to address himself to nature;

he lay exhausted, with half-closed eyes, upon his couch, sunk deep in dreams, the picture of extreme introversion.

We have already seen that, in such circumstances, an infantile internal equivalent for reality appears, in the place of external life and reality. This is also the case with Hiawatha:

> " And he saw a youth approaching,
>   Dressed in garments green and yellow,
>   Coming through the purple twilight,
>   Through the splendor of the sunset;
>   Plumes of green bent o'er his forehead,
>   And his hair was soft and golden."

This remarkable apparition reveals himself in the following manner to Hiawatha:

> " From the Master of Life descending,
>   I, the friend of man, Mondamin,
>   Come to warn you and instruct you,
>   How by struggle and by labor
>   You shall gain what you have prayed for.
>   Rise up from your bed of branches;
>   Rise, O youth, and wrestle with me!"

Mondamin is the maize: a god, who is eaten, arising from Hiawatha's introversion. His hunger, taken in a double sense, his longing for the nourishing mother, gives birth from his soul to another hero, the edible maize, the son of the earth mother. Therefore, he again arises at sunset, symbolizing the entrance into the mother, and in the western sunset glow he begins again the mystic struggle with the self-created god, the god who has originated entirely from the longing for the nourishing mother.

The struggle is again the struggle for liberation from this destructive and yet productive longing. Mondamin is, therefore, equivalent to the mother, and the struggle with him means the overpowering and impregnation of the mother. This interpretation is entirely proven by a myth of the Cherokees, " who invoke it (the maize) under the name of ' The Old Woman,' in allusion to a myth that it sprang from the blood of an old woman killed by her disobedient sons ' " : [27]

> " Faint with famine, Hiawatha
> Started from his bed of branches,
> From the twilight of his wigwam
> Forth into the flush of sunset
> Came, and wrestled with Mondamin;
> At his touch he felt new courage
> Throbbing in his brain and bosom,
> Felt new life and hope and vigor
> Run through every nerve and fibre."

The battle at sunset with the god of the maize gives Hiawatha new strength; and thus it must be, because the fight for the individual depths, against the paralyzing longing for the mother, gives creative strength to men. Here, indeed, is the source of all creation, but it demands heroic courage to fight against these forces and to wrest from them the " treasure difficult to attain." He who succeeds in this has, in truth, attained the best. Hiawatha wrestles with himself for his creation.[28] The struggle lasts again the charmed three days. The fourth day, just as Mondamin prophesied, Hiawatha conquers him, and Mondamin sinks to the ground in death. As Mondamin

previously desired, Hiawatha digs his grave in mother
earth, and soon afterwards from this grave the young
and fresh maize grows for the nourishment of mankind.

Concerning the thought of this fragment, we have
therein a beautiful parallel to the mystery of Mithra,
where first the battle of the hero with his bull occurs.
Afterwards Mithra carries in " transitus " the bull into
the cave, where he kills him. From this death all fertility grows, all that is edible.[29] The cave corresponds
to the grave. The same idea is represented in the Christian mysteries, although generally in more beautiful
human forms. The soul struggle of Christ in Geth-
semane, where he struggles with himself in order to complete his work, then the " transitus," the carrying of the
cross,[30] where he takes upon himself the symbol of the
destructive mother, and therewith takes himself to the
sacrificial grave, from which, after three days, he tri-
umphantly arises; all these ideas express the same fundamental thoughts. Also, the symbol of eating is not lacking in the Christian mystery. Christ is a god who is eaten
in the Lord's Supper. His death transforms him into
bread and wine, which we partake of in grateful memory
of his great deed.[31] The relation of Agni to the Soma-
drink and that of Dionysus to wine [32] must not be omitted
here. An evident parallel is Samson's rending of the
lion, and the subsequent inhabitation of the dead lion by
honey bees, which gives rise to the well-known German
riddle:

" Speise ging von dem Fresser und Süssigkeit von dem Starken
(Food went from the glutton and sweet from the strong)." [33]

THE DUAL MOTHER RÔLE

In the Eleusinian mysteries these thoughts seem to have played a rôle. Besides Demeter and Persephone, Iakchos is a chief god of the Eleusinian cult; he was the " puer æternus," the eternal boy, of whom Ovid says the following:

> " Tu puer æternus, tu formosissimus alto
> Conspiceris cœlo tibi, cum sine cornibus astas,
> Virgineum caput est," etc.*

In the great Eleusinian festival procession the image of Iakchos was carried. It is not easy to say which god is Iakchos, possibly a boy, or a new-born son, similar to the Etrurian Tages, who bears the surname " the freshly ploughed boy," because, according to the myth, he arose from the furrow of the field behind the peasant, who was ploughing. This idea shows unmistakably the Mondamin motive. The plough is of well-known phallic meaning; the furrow of the field is personified by the Hindoos as woman. The psychology of this idea is that of a coitus, referred back to the presexual stage (stage of nutrition). The son is the edible fruit of the field. Iakchos passes, in part, as son of Demeter or of Persephone, also appropriately as consort of Demeter. (Hero as procreator of himself.) He is also called τῆς Δήμητρος δαίμων (Δαίμων equals libido, also Mother libido.) He was identified with Dionysus, especially with the Thracian Dionysus-Zagreus, of whom a typical fate of rebirth was related. Hera had goaded the Titans against Zagreus,

---

* Thou boy eternal, thou most beautiful one seen in the heavens, without horns standing, with thy virgin head, etc.

who, assuming many forms, sought to escape them, until they finally took him when he had taken on the form of a bull. In this form he was killed (Mithra sacrifice) and dismembered, and the pieces were thrown into a cauldron; but Zeus killed the Titans by lightning, and swallowed the still-throbbing heart of Zagreus. Through this act he gave him existence once more, and Zagreus as Iakchos again came forth.

Iakchos carries the torch, the phallic symbol of procreation, as Plato testifies. In the festival procession, the sheaf of corn, the cradle of Iakchos, was carried. (λῖκνον, mystica vannus Iacchi.) The Orphic legend[34] relates that Iakchos was brought up by Persephone, when, after three years' slumber in the λῖκνον,* he awoke. This statement distinctly suggests the Mondamin motive. The 20th of Boedromion (the month Boedromion lasts from about the 5th of September to the 5th of October) is called Iakchos, in honor of the hero. On the evening of this day the great torchlight procession took place on the seashore, in which the quest and lament of Demeter was represented. The rôle of Demeter, who, seeking her daughter, wanders over the whole earth without food or drink, has been taken over by Hiawatha in the Indian epic. He turns to all created things without obtaining an answer. As Demeter first learns of her daughter from the subterranean Hecate, so does Hiawatha first find the one sought for, Mondamin,[35] in the deepest introversion (descent to the mother). Hiawatha produces from himself, Mondamin, as a mother produces the son. The

* A winnowing fan used as cradle.

longing for the mother also includes the producing mother (first devouring, then birth-giving). Concerning the real contents of the mysteries, we learn through the testimony of Bishop Asterius, about 390 A.D., the following:

" Is not there (in Eleusis) the gloomiest descent, and the most solemn communion of the hierophant and the priestess; between him and her alone? Are the torches not extinguished, and does not the vast multitude regard as their salvation that which takes place between the two in the darkness? " [36]

That points undoubtedly to a ritual marriage, which was celebrated subterraneously in mother earth. The Priestess of Demeter seems to be the representative of the earth goddess, perhaps the furrow of the field.[37] The descent into the earth is also the symbol of the mother's womb, and was a widespread conception under the form of cave worship. Plutarch relates of the Magi that they sacrificed to Ahriman, εἰς τόπον ἀνήλιον.* Lukian lets the magician Mithrobarzanes εἰς χωρίον ἔρημον καὶ ὑλῶδες καὶ ἀνήλιον,† descend into the bowels of the earth. According to the testimony of Moses of the Koran, the sister Fire and the brother Spring were worshipped in Armenia in a cave. Julian gave an account from the Attis legend of a κατάβασις εἰς ἄντρον,‡ from whence Cybele brings up her son lover, that is to say, gives birth to him.[38] The cave of Christ's birth, in Bethlehem ('House of Bread'), is said to have been an Attis spelæum.

* In a sunless place.
† Descend into a sunless desert place.
‡ Descent into a cave.

A further Eleusinian symbolism is found in the festival of Hierosgamos, in the form of the *mystic chests,* which, according to the testimony of Clemens of Alexandria, may have contained pastry, salt and fruits. The synthema (confession) of the mystic transmitted by Clemens is suggestive in still other directions:

" I have fasted, I have drunk of the barleydrink, I have taken from the chest and after I have labored, I have placed it back in the basket, and from the basket into the chest."

The question as to what lay in the chest is explained in detail by Dieterich.[39] The labor he considers a phallic activity, which the mystic has to perform. In fact, representations of the mystic basket are given, wherein lies a phallus surrounded by fruits.[40] Upon the so-called Lovatelli tomb vase, the sculptures of which are understood to be Eleusinian ceremonies, it is shown how a mystic caressed the serpent entwining Demeter. The caressing of the fear animal indicates a religious conquering of incest.[41] According to the testimony of Clemens of Alexandria, a serpent was in the chest. The serpent in this connection is naturally of phallic nature, the phallus which is forbidden in relation to the mother. Rohde mentions that in the Arrhetophories, pastry, in the form of phalli and serpents, were thrown into the cave near the Thesmophorion. This custom was a petition for the bestowal of children and harvest.[42] The snake also plays a large part in initiations under the remarkable title ὁ διὰ κόλπου θεός. * Clemens observes that the symbol

* He who achieved divinity through the womb.

of the Sabazios mysteries is ὁ διὰ κόλπων θεός, δράκων δὲ ἐστι καὶ οὗτος διελκόμενος τοῦ κόλπου τῶν τελουμέ-νων.*

Through Arnobius we learn:

"Aureus coluber in sinum demittitur consecratis et eximitur rursus ab inferioribus partibus atque imis." †

In the Orphic Hymn 52, Bacchus is invoked by ὑποκόλπιε,‡ which indicates that the god enters into man as if through the female genitals.[43] According to the testimony of Hippolytus, the hierophant in the mystery exclaimed ἱερὸν ἔτεκε πότνια κοῦρον, Βριμὼ βριμόν (the revered one has brought forth a holy boy, Brimos from Brimo). This Christmas gospel, "Unto us a son is born," is illustrated especially through the tradition[44] that the Athenians "secretly show to the partakers in the Epoptia, the great and wonderful and most perfect Epoptic mystery, *a mown stalk of wheat.*"[45]

The parallel for the motive of death and resurrection is the motive of losing and finding. The motive appears in religious rites in exactly the same connection, namely, in spring festivities similar to the Hierosgamos, where the image of the god was hidden and found again. It is an uncanonical tradition that Moses left his father's house when twelve years old to teach mankind. In a similar manner Christ is lost by his parents, and they find him again as a teacher of wisdom, just as in the Mo-

* He who achieved divinity through the womb; he is a serpent, and he was drawn through the womb of those who were being initiated.

† The golden serpent is crowded into the breast of the initiates and is then drawn out through the lowest parts.

‡ O Fœtus, he who is in the vagina or womb.

hammedan legend Moses and Joshua lose the fish, and
in his place Chidher, the teacher of wisdom, appears
(like the boy Jesus in the temple); so does the corn god,
lost and believed to be dead, suddenly arise again from
his mother into renewed youth. (That Christ was laid
in the manger is suggestive of fodder. Robertson, therefore, places the manger as parallel to the liknon.)

We understand from these accounts why the Eleusinian mysteries were for the mystic so rich in comfort for
the hope of a better world. A beautiful Eleusinian epitaph shows this:

" Truly, a beautiful secret is proclaimed by the blessed Gods!
    Mortality is not a curse, but death a blessing! "

The hymn to Demeter [46] in the mysteries also says the
same:

" Blessed is he, the earth-born man, who hath seen this!
    Who hath not shared in these divine ceremonies,
    He hath an unequal fate in the obscure darkness of death."

Immortality is inherent in the Eleusinian symbol; in a
church song of the nineteenth century by Samuel Preis-
werk we discover it again:

" The world is yours, Lord Jesus,
    The world, on which we stand,
    Because it is thy world
    It cannot perish.
    Only the wheat, before it comes
    Up to the light in its fertility,
    Must die in the bosom of the earth
    First freed from its own nature.

" Thou goest, O Lord, our chief,
 To heaven through thy sorrows,
 And guide him who believes
 In thee on the same path.
 Then take us all equally
 To share in thy sorrows and kingdoms,
 Guide us through thy gate of death,
 Bring thy world into the light."

Firmicus relates concerning the Attis mysteries:

" Nocte quadam simulacrum in lectica supinum ponitur et per numeros digestis fletibus plangitur; deinde cum se ficta lamentatione satiaverint, lumen infertur: tunc a sacerdote omnium qui flebant fauces unguentur, quibus perunctis sacerdos hoc lento murmure susurrat: 'Θαρρεῖτε μύσται τοῦ θεοῦ σεσωσμένου· ἔσται γὰρ ἡμῖν ἐκ πόνου σωτηρία.' " *

Such parallels show how little human personality and how much divine, that is to say, universally human, is found in the Christ mystery. No man is or, indeed, ever was, a hero, for the hero is a god, and, therefore, impersonal and generally applicable to all. Christ is a " spirit," as is shown in the very early Christian interpretation. In different places of the earth, and in the most varied forms and in the coloring of various periods, the Savior-hero appears as a fruit of the entrance of the libido into the personal maternal depths. The Bacchian consecrations represented upon the Farnese relief contain

* On a certain night an image is placed lying down in a litter; there is weeping and lamentations among the people, with beatings of bodies and tears. After a time, when they have become exhausted from the lamentations, a light appears; then the priest anoints the throats of all those who were weeping, and softly whispers, " Take courage, O initiates of the Redeemed Divinity; you shall achieve salvation through your grief."

a scene where a mystic wrapped in a mantle, drawn over his head, was led to Silen, who holds the "λῖχνον" (chalice), covered with a cloth. The covering of the head signifies death. The mystic dies, figuratively, like the seed corn, grows again and comes to the corn har‑ vest. Proclus relates that the mystics were buried up to their necks. The Christian church as a place of religious ceremony is really nothing but the grave of a hero (cata‑ combs). The believer descends into the grave, in order to rise from the dead with the hero. That the meaning underlying the church is that of the mother's womb can scarcely be doubted. The symbols of Mass are so dis‑ tinct that the mythology of the sacred act peeps out everywhere. It is the magic charm of rebirth. The ven‑ eration of the Holy Sepulchre is most plain in this re‑ spect. A striking example is the Holy Sepulchre of St. Stefano in Bologna. The church itself, a very old polyg‑ onal building, consists of the remains of a temple to Isis. The interior contains an artificial spelæum, a so-called Holy Sepulchre, into which one creeps through a very little door. After a long sojourn, the believer reappears reborn from this mother's womb. An Etruscan ossuarium in the archæological museum in Florence is at the same time a statue of Matuta, the goddess of death; the clay figure of the goddess is hollowed within as a receptacle for the ashes. The representations indicate that Matuta is the mother. Her chair is adorned with sphinxes, as a fitting symbol for the mother of death.

Only a few of the further deeds of Hiawatha can in‑ terest us here. Among these is the battle with Mishe‑

THE SO-CALLED HOLY SEPULCHRE OF S. STEFANO AT BOLOGNA

Nahma, the fish-king, in the eighth song. This deserves to be mentioned as a typical battle of the sun-hero. Mishe-Nahma is a fish monster, who dwells at the bottom of the waters. Challenged by Hiawatha to battle, he devours the hero, together with his boat:

> " In his wrath he darted upward,
> Flashing leaped into the sunshine,
> Opened his great jaws, and swallowed
> Both canoe and Hiawatha.

> " Down into that darksome cavern
> Plunged the headlong Hiawatha,
> As a log on some black river
> Shoots and plunges down the rapids,
> Found himself in utter darkness,
> Groped about in helpless wonder,
> Till he felt a great heart beating,
> Throbbing in that utter darkness.
> And he smote it in his anger,
> With his fist, the heart of Nahma,
> Felt the mighty king of fishes
> Shudder through each nerve and fibre.

> .   .   .   .

> Crosswise then did Hiawatha
> Drag his birch-canoe for safety,
> Lest from out the jaws of Nahma,
> In the turmoil and confusion,
> Forth he might be hurled, and perish."

It is the typical myth of the work of the hero, distributed over the entire world. He takes to a boat, fights with the sea monster, is devoured, he defends himself against being bitten or crushed [47] (resistance or stamping motive); having arrived in the interior of the " whale dragon," he seeks the vital organ, which he cuts off

or in some way destroys. Often the death of the
monster occurs as the result of a fire which the hero
secretly makes within him; he mysteriously creates in the
womb of death life, the rising sun. Thus dies the fish,
which drifts ashore, where, with the assistance of
" birds," the hero again attains the light of day.[48]   The
bird in this sense probably means the reascent of the sun,
the longing of the libido, the rebirth of the phœnix.
(The longing is very frequently represented by the symbol of hovering.)   The sun symbol of the bird rising from
the water is (etymologically) contained in the singing
swan.   "Swan" is derived from the root *sven*, like
sun and tone. (See the preceding.)   This act signifies
rebirth, and the bringing forth of life from the mother,[49]
and by this means the ultimate destruction of death,
which, according to a Negro myth, has come into the
world, through the mistake of an old woman, who, at
the time of the general casting of skins (for men renewed their youth through casting their skin like
snakes), drew on, through absent-mindedness, her old
skin instead of a new one, and as a result died.   But the
effect of such an act could not be of any duration.   Again
and again troubles of the hero are renewed, always under
the symbol of deliverance from the mother.   Just as Hera
(as the pursuing mother) is the real source of the great
deeds of Hercules, so does Nokomis allow Hiawatha no
rest, and raises up new difficulties in his path, in form of
desperate adventures in which the hero may perhaps conquer, but also, perhaps, may perish.   The libido of mankind is always in advance of his consciousness; unless his

MATUTA, AN ETRUSCAN PIETÀ

libido calls him forth to new dangers he sinks into slothful inactivity or, on the other hand, childish longing for
the mother overcomes him at the summit of his existence,
and he allows himself to become pitifully weak, instead
of striving with desperate courage towards the highest.
The mother becomes the demon, who summons the hero
to adventure, and who also places in his path the poisonous serpent, which will strike him. Thus Nokomis, in the
ninth song, calls Hiawatha, points with her hand to the
west, where the sun sets in purple splendor, and says to
him:

> " Yonder dwells the great Pearl-Feather,
> Megissogwon, the Magician,
> Manito of Wealth and Wampum,
> Guarded by his fiery serpents,
> Guarded by the black pitch-water.
> You can see his fiery serpents,
> The Kenabeek, the great serpents,
> Coiling, playing in the water."

This danger lurking in the west is known to mean
death, which no one, even the mightiest, escapes. This
magician, as we learn, also killed the father of Nokomis.
Now she sends her son forth to avenge the father
(Horus). Through the symbols attributed to the magician it may easily be recognized what he symbolizes.
Snake and water belong to the mother, the snake as a
symbol of the repressed longing for the mother, or, in
other words, as a symbol of resistance, encircles protectingly and defensively the maternal rock, inhabits the cave,
winds itself upwards around the mother tree and guards

the precious hoard, the "mysterious" treasure. The black Stygian water is, like the black, muddy spring of Dhulqarnein, the place where the sun dies and enters into rebirth, the maternal sea of death and night. On his journey thither Hiawatha takes with him the magic oil of Mishe-Nahma, which helps his boat through the waters of death. (Also a sort of charm for immortality, like the dragon's blood for Siegfried, etc.)

First, Hiawatha slays the great serpent. Of the "night journey in the sea" over the Stygian waters it is written:

> "All night long he sailed upon it,
> Sailed upon that sluggish water,
> Covered with its mould of ages,
> Black with rotting water-rushes,
> Rank with flags, and leaves of lilies,
> Stagnant, lifeless, dreary, dismal,
> Lighted by the shimmering moonlight
> And by will-o'-the-wisps illumined,
> Fires by ghosts of dead men kindled,
> In their weary night encampments."

The description plainly shows the character of a water of death. The contents of the water point to an already mentioned motive, that of encoiling and devouring. It is said in the "Key to Dreams of Jagaddeva":[50]

"Whoever in dreams surrounds his body with bast, creepers or ropes, with snake-skins, threads, or tissues, dies."

I refer to the preceding arguments in regard to this. Having come into the west land, the hero challenges the magician to battle. A terrible struggle begins. Hiawatha is powerless, because Megissogwon is invulnerable. At evening Hiawatha retires wounded, despairing for a while, in order to rest:

> " Paused to rest beneath a pine-tree,
>   From whose branches trailed the mosses,
>   And whose trunk was coated over
>   With the Dead-man's Moccasin-leather,
>   With the fungus white and yellow."

This protecting tree is described as coated over with the moccasin leather of the dead, the fungus. This investing of the tree with anthromorphic attributes is also an important rite wherever tree worship prevails, as, for example, in India, where each village has its sacred tree, which is clothed and in general treated as a human being. The trees are anointed with fragrant waters, sprinkled with powder, adorned with garlands and draperies. Just as among men, the piercing of the *ears was performed as an apotropaic charm against death, so does it occur with the holy tree.* Of all the trees of India there is none more sacred to the Hindoos than the Aswatha (Ficus religiosa). It is known to them as Vriksha Raja (king of trees), Brahma, Vishnu and Mahesvar live in it, and the worship of it is the worship of the triad. Almost every Indian village has an Aswatha,[51] etc. This " village linden tree," well known to us, is here clearly characterized as the mother symbol; it contains the three gods.

Hence, when Hiawatha retires to rest under the pine-tree,[52] it is a dangerous step, because he resigns himself to the mother, whose garment is the garment of death (the devouring mother). As in the whale-dragon, the

hero also in this situation needs a " helpful bird "; that
is to say, the helpful animals, which represent the benevolent parents:

> " Suddenly from the boughs above him
> Sang the Mama, the woodpecker;
> ' Aim your arrows, Hiawatha,
> At the head of Megissogwon,
> Strike the tuft of hair upon it,
> At their roots the long black tresses;
> There alone can he be wounded.' "

Now, amusing to relate, Mama hurried to his help.
It is a peculiar fact that the woodpecker was also the
" Mama " of Romulus and Remus, who put nourishment
into the mouths of the twins with his beak.[53]   (Compare
with that the rôle of the vulture in Leonardo's dream.
The vulture is sacred to Mars, like the woodpecker.)
With the maternal significance of the woodpecker, the
ancient Italian folk-superstition agrees: that from the
tree upon which this bird nested any nail which has been
driven in will soon drop out again.[54]   The woodpecker
owes its special significance to the circumstance that he
hammers holes into trees.   (" To drive nails in," as
above!)   It is, therefore, understandable that he was
made much of in the Roman legend as an old king of
the country, a possessor or ruler of the holy tree, the
primitive image of the Paterfamilias.   An old fable relates how Circe, the spouse of King Picus, transformed
him into the Picus Martius, the woodpecker.   The sorcer-
ess is the " new-creating mother," who has " magic influence " upon the sun-husband.   She kills him, trans-

forms him into the soul-bird, the unfulfilled wish. Picus was also understood as the wood demon and incubus, as well as the soothsayer, all of which fully indicate the mother libido.[55] Picus was often placed on a par with Picumnus by the ancients. Picumnus is the inseparable companion of Pilumnus, and both are actually called *infantium dii,* " the gods of little children." Especially it was said of Pilumnus that he defended new-born children against the destroying attacks of the wood demon, Silvanus. (Good and bad mother, the motive of the two mothers.)

The benevolent bird, a wish thought of deliverance which arises from introversion,[56] advises the hero to shoot the magician under the hair, which is the only vulnerable spot. This spot is the " phallic " point,[57] if one may venture to say so; it is at *the top of the head,* at the *place where the mystic birth from the head takes place,* which even today appears in children's sexual theories. Into that Hiawatha shoots (one may say, very naturally) three arrows [58] (the well-known phallic symbol), and thus kills Megissogwon. Thereupon he steals the magic wampum armor, which renders him invulnerable (means of immortality). He significantly leaves the dead lying in the water—because the magician is the fearful mother:

> " On the shore he left the body,
> Half on land and half in water,
> In the sand his feet were buried,
> And his face was in the water."

Thus the situation is the same as with the fish king, because the monster is the personification of the water

of death, which in its turn represents the devouring
mother. This great deed of Hiawatha's, where he has
vanquished the mother as the death-bringing demon,[59]
is followed by his marriage with Minnehaha.

A little fable which the poet has inserted in the later
song is noteworthy. An old man is transformed into a
youth, by *crawling through a hollow oak tree.*

In the fourteenth song is a description of how Hiawatha discovers writing. I limit myself to the description of two hieroglyphic tokens:

> "Gitche Manito the Mighty,
>   He, the Master of Life, was painted
>   As an egg, with points projecting
>   To the four winds of the heavens.
>   Everywhere is the Great Spirit,
>   Was the meaning of this symbol."

The world lies in the egg, which encompasses it at
every point; it is the cosmic woman with child, the symbol of which Plato as well as the Vedas has made use of.
This mother is like the air, which is everywhere. But air
is spirit; the mother of the world is a spirit:

> "Mitche Manito the Mighty,
>   He the dreadful Spirit of Evil,
>   As a serpent was depicted,
>   As Kenabeek, the great serpent."

But the spirit of evil is fear, is the forbidden desire,
the adversary who opposes not only each individual heroic
deed, but life in its struggle for eternal duration as well,
and who introduces into our body the poison of weak-

ness and age through the treacherous bite of the serpent. It is all that is retrogressive, and as the model of our first world is our mother, all retrogressive tendencies are towards the mother, and, therefore, are disguised under the incest image.

In both these ideas the poet has represented in mythologic symbols the libido arising from the mother and the libido striving backward towards the mother.

There is a description in the fifteenth song how Chibiabos, Hiawatha's best friend, the amiable player and singer, the embodiment of the joy of life, was enticed by the evil spirits into ambush, fell through the ice and was drowned. Hiawatha mourns for him so long that he succeeds, with the aid of the magician, in calling him back again. But the revivified friend is only a spirit, and he becomes master of the land of spirits. (Osiris, lord of the underworld; the two Dioscuri.) Battles again follow, and then comes the loss of a second friend, Kwasind, the embodiment of physical strength.

In the twentieth song occur famine and the death of Minnehaha, foretold by two taciturn guests from the land of death; and in the twenty-second song Hiawatha prepares for a final journey to the west land:

> " I am going, O Nokomis,
>   On a long and distant journey,
>   To the portals of the Sunset,
>   To the regions of the home-wind,
>   Of the Northwest-Wind Keewaydin.

> " One long track and trail of splendor,
>   Down whose stream, as down a river,

Westward, westward, Hiawatha
Sailed into the fiery sunset,
Sailed into the purple vapors,
Sailed into the dusk of evening.

" Thus departed Hiawatha,
Hiawatha the Beloved,
In the glory of the sunset,
In the purple mists of evening,
To the regions of the home-wind,
Of the Northwest-Wind, Keewaydin,
To the Islands of the Blessed,
To the kingdom of Ponemah,
To the land of the Hereafter! "

The sun, victoriously arising, tears itself away from the embrace and clasp, from the enveloping womb of the sea, and sinks again into the maternal sea, into night, the all-enveloping and the all-reproducing, leaving behind it the heights of midday and all its glorious works. This image was the first, and was profoundly entitled to become the symbolic carrier of human destiny; in the morning of life man painfully tears himself loose from the mother, from the domestic hearth, to rise through battle to his heights. Not seeing his worst enemy in front of him, but bearing him within himself as a deadly longing for the depths within, for drowning in his own source, for becoming absorbed into the mother, his life is a constant struggle with death, a violent and transitory delivery from the always lurking night. This death is no external enemy, but a deep personal longing for quiet and for the profound peace of non-existence, for a dreamless sleep in the ebb and flow of the sea of life. Even in his highest endeavor for harmony and equilibrium, for philosophic depths and artistic enthusiasm, he seeks death, immobility, satiety and rest. If, like Peirithoos, he tarries too long in this place of rest and peace, he is overcome by torpidity, and the poison of the serpent paralyzes him for all time. If he is to live he must fight and sacrifice his longing for the past, in order to rise to his own heights. And having reached the noonday heights, he must also *sacrifice the love for his own achievement,* for he may not loiter. The sun also sacrifices its greatest strength in order to hasten onwards to the fruits of autumn, which are the seeds of immortality; fulfilled in children, in works, in posthumous fame, in a new order of things, all of which in their turn begin and complete the sun's course over again.

The " Song of Hiawatha " contains, as these extracts show, a material which is very well adapted to bring into play the abundance of ancient symbolic possibilities, latent in the human mind, and to stimulate it to the creation of mythologic figures. But the products always contain the same old problems of humanity, which rise again and again in new symbolic disguise from the shadowy world of the unconscious. Thus Miss Miller is reminded through the longing of Chiwantopel, of another mythic cycle which appeared in the form of Wagner's " Siegfried." Especially is this shown in the passage in Chiwantopel's monologue, where he exclaims, " There is not one who understands me, not one who resembles me, not one who has a soul sister to mine." Miss Miller observes that the sentiment of this passage has the greatest analogy with the feelings which Siegfried experienced for Brunhilde.

This analogy causes us to cast a glance at the song of Siegfried, especially at the relation of Siegfried and Brunhilde. It is a well-recognized fact that Brunhilde, the Valkyr, gives protection to the birth (incestuous) of Siegfried, but while Sieglinde is the human mother, Brunhilde has the rôle of " spiritual mother " (mother-imago); however, unlike Hera towards Hercules, she is not a pursuer, but benevolent. This sin, in which she is an accomplice, by means of the help she renders, is the reason for her banishment by Wotan. The strange birth of Siegfried from the sister-wife distinguishes him as Horus, as the *reborn son,* a reincarnation of the retreating Osiris—Wotan. The birth of the young son, of the hero, results, indeed, from mankind, who, however, are merely the human bearers of the cosmic symbolism. Thus the birth is protected by the spirit mother (Hera, Lilith) : she sends Sieglinde with the child in her womb (Mary's flight) on the " night journey on the sea " to the east:

> " Onward, hasten;
> Turn to the East.
>
> .   .   .   .
>
> O woman, thou cherishest
> The sublimest hero of the world
> In thy sheltering womb."

The motive of dismemberment is found again in the broken sword of Siegmund, which was kept for Siegfried. From the dismemberment life is pieced together again. (The Medea wonder.) Just as a smith forges the pieces together, so is the dismembered dead again put together. (This comparison is also found in

" Timaios " of Plato: the parts of the world joined together with pegs.)   In the Rigveda, 10, 72, the creator of the world, Brahmanaspati, is a smith.

> " Brahmanaspati, as a blacksmith,
>   Welded the world together."

The sword has the significance of the phallic sun power; therefore, a sword proceeds from the mouth of the apocalyptic Christ; that is to say, the procreative fire, the word, or the procreative Logos.   In Rigveda, Brahmanaspati is also a prayer-word, which possessed an ancient creative significance: [60]

> " And this prayer of the singers, expanding from itself,
>   Became a cow, which was already there before the world,
>   Dwelling together in the womb of this god,
>   Foster-children of the same keeper are the gods."
>   —*Rigveda* x: 31.

The Logos became a cow; that is to say, the mother, who is pregnant with the gods.   (In Christian uncanonical phantasies, where the Holy Ghost has feminine significance, we have the well-known motive of the two mothers, the earthly mother, Mary, and the spiritual mother, the Holy Ghost.)   The transformation of the Logos into the mother is not remarkable in itself, because the origin of the phenomenon fire-speech seems to be the mother-libido, according to the discussion in the earlier chapter.   The *spiritual is the mother-libido*.   The significance of the sword, in the Sanskrit conception, têjas, is probably partly determined by its sharpness, as is shown above, in its connection with the libido conception.

The motive of pursuit (the pursuing Sieglinde, analogous to Leto) is not here bound up with the spiritual mother, but with Wotan, therefore corresponding to the Linos legend, where the father of the wife is also the pursuer. Wotan is also the father of Brunhilde. Brunhilde stands in a peculiar relation to Wotan. Brunhilde says to Wotan:

> " Thou speakest to the will of Wotan
> By telling me what thou wishest:
> Who . . . am I
> Were I not thy will? "

> *Wotan:*
> I take counsel only with myself,
> When I speak with thee . . .

Brunhilde is also somewhat the " angel of the face," that creative will or word,[61] emanating from God, also the Logos, which became the child-bearing woman. God created the world through his word; that is to say, his mother, the woman who is to bring him forth again. (He lays his own egg.)   This peculiar conception, it seems to me, can be explained by assuming that the libido overflowing into speech (thought) has preserved its sexual character to an extraordinary degree as a result of the inherent inertia.   In this way the " word " had to execute and fulfil all that was denied to the sexual wish; namely, the return into the mother, in order to attain eternal duration.   The " word " fulfils this wish by itself becoming the daughter, the wife, the mother of the God, who brings him forth anew.[62]

Wagner has this idea vaguely in his mind in Wotan's lament over Brunhilde:

> " None as she knew my inmost thought;
> None knew the source of my will
> As she;
> She herself was
> The creating womb of my wish;
> And so now she has broken
> The blessed union! "

Brunhilde's sin is the favoring of Siegmund, but, behind this, lies incest: this is projected into the brother-sister relation of Siegmund and Sieglinde; in reality, and archaically expressed, Wotan, the father, has entered into his self-created daughter, in order to rejuvenate himself. But this fact must, of course, be veiled. Wotan is rightly indignant with Brunhilde, for she has taken the Isis rôle and through the birth of the son has deprived the old man of his power. The first attack of the death serpent in the form of the son, Siegmund, Wotan has repelled; he has broken Siegmund's sword, but Siegmund rises again in a grandson. This inevitable fate is always helped by the woman; hence the wrath of Wotan.

At Siegfried's birth Sieglinde dies, as is proper. The foster-mother [63] is apparently not a woman, but a chthonic god, a crippled dwarf, who belongs to that tribe which renounces love.[64] The Egyptian god of the underworld, the crippled shadow of Osiris (who celebrated a melancholy resurrection in the sexless semi-ape Harpocrates), is the tutor of Horus, who has to avenge the death of his father.

Meanwhile Brunhilde sleeps the enchanted sleep, like a Hierosgamos, upon a mountain, where Wotan has put her to sleep [65] with the magic thorn (Edda), surrounded by the flames of Wotan's fire (equal to libido [66]), which wards off every one. But Mime becomes Siegfried's enemy and wills his death through Fafner. Here Mime's dynamic nature is revealed; he is a masculine representation of the terrible mother, also a foster-mother of demoniac nature, who places the poisonous worm (Typhon) in her son's (Horus's) path. Siegfried's longing for the mother drives him away from Mime, and his travels begin with the mother of death, and lead through vanquishing the " terrible mother " [67] to the woman:

> *Siegfried:*
> Off with the imp!
> I ne'er would see him more!
> Might I but know what my mother was like
> That will my thought never tell me!
> Her eyes' tender light
> Surely did shine
> Like the soft eyes of the doe!

Siegfried decides to separate from the demon which was the mother in the past, and he gropes forward with the longing directed towards the mother. Nature acquires a hidden maternal significance for him (" doe "); in the tones of nature he discovers a suggestion of the maternal voice and the maternal language:

> *Siegfried:*
> Thou gracious birdling,
> Strange art thou to me!

Dost thou in the wood here dwell?
Ah, would that I could take thy meaning!
Thy song something would say—
Perchance—of my loving mother!

This psychology we have already encountered in Hiawatha. By means of his dialogue with the bird (bird, like wind and arrow, represents the wish, the winged longing) Siegfried entices Fafner from the cave. His desires turn back to the mother, and the chthonic demon, the cave-dwelling terror of the woods, appears. Fafner is the protector of the treasure; in his cave lies the hoard, the source of life and power. The mother possesses the libido of the son, and jealously does she guard it. Translated into psychological language, this means the positive transference succeeds only through the release of the libido from the mother-imago, the incestuous object in general. Only in this manner is it possible to gain one's libido, the incomparable treasure, and this requires a mighty struggle, the whole battle of adaptation.[68] The Siegfried legend has abundantly described the outcome of this battle with Fafner. According to the Edda, Siegfried eats Fafner's heart, the seat of life. He wins the magic cap, through whose power Alberich had changed himself into a serpent. This refers to the motive of casting the skin, rejuvenation. By means of the magic cap one can vanish and assume different shapes. The vanishing probably refers to dying and to the invisible presence; that is, existence in the mother's womb. A luck-bringing cap, amniotic covering, the new-born child occasionally wears over his head (the caul). Moreover,

Siegfried drinks the dragon's blood, which makes it possible for him to understand the language of birds, and consequently he enters into a peculiar relation with Nature, a dominating position, the result of his knowledge, and finally wins the treasure.

Hort is a mediæval and Old High German word with the meaning of "collected and guarded treasure"; Gothic, *huzd;* Old Scandinavian, *hodd;* Germanic *hozda,* from pre-Germanic *kuzdhó*—for *kudtho* —"the concealed." Kluge [69] adds to this the Greek κεύθω, ἔκυθον = "to hide, to conceal." Also *hut* (*hut,* to guard; English, hide), Germanic root *hud,* from Indo-Germanic *kuth* (questionable), to Greek κεύθω and κύσθος, "cavity," feminine genitals. Prellwitz,[70] too, traces Gothic *huzd,* Anglo-Saxon *hyde,* English hide and hoard, to Greek κεύθω. Whitley Stokes traces English hide, Anglo-Saxon *hydan,* New High German *Hütte,* Latin *cûdo* = helmet; Sanskrit *kuhara* (cave?) to primitive Celtic *koudo* = concealment; Latin, *occultatio.*

The assumption of Kluge is also supported in other directions; namely, from the point of view of the primitive idea:

"There exists in Athens [71] a sacred place (a Temenos) of Ge, with the surname Olympia. Here the ground is torn open for about a yard in width; and they say, after the flood at the time of Deucalion, that the water receded here; and every year they throw into the fissure wheatmeal, kneaded with honey."

We have observed previously that among the Arrhetophorian, pastry in the form of snakes and phalli, was thrown into a crevice in the earth. This was mentioned in connection with the ceremonies of fertilizing the earth. We have touched slightly already upon the sacrifice in the earth crevice among the Watschandies. The flood of death has passed characteristically into the crevice of the earth; that is, back into the mother again; because from the mother the universal great death has come in the first place. The flood is simply the counterpart of the vivifying and all-producing water: Ὠκεανοῦ, ὅσ περ γένεσις πάντεσσι τέτυκται.* One sacrifices the honey cake to the mother, so that she may spare one from death. Thus every year in Rome a gold sacrifice was thrown into the lacus Curtius, into the former fissure in the earth, which could only be closed through the sacrificial death of Curtius. He was the typical hero, who has journeyed into the underworld, in order to conquer the danger threatening the Roman state from the opening of the abyss. (Kaineus, Amphiaraos.) In the Amphiaraion of Oropos those healed through the temple incubation threw their gifts of gold into the sacred well, of which Pausanias says:

"If any one is healed of a sickness through a saying of the oracle, then it is customary to throw a silver or gold coin into the well; because here Amphiaraos has ascended as a god."

It is probable that this oropic well is also the place of his " Katabasis " (descent into the lower world). There were many entrances into Hades in antiquity. Thus near Eleusis there was an abyss, through which Aidoneus passed up and down, when he kidnapped Cora. (Dragon

* Ocean, who arose to be the producer of all.

and maiden: the libido overcome by resistance, life replaced by death.) There were crevices in the rocks,
through which souls could ascend to the upper world. Behind the temple of Chthonia in Hermione lay a sacred
district of Pluto, with a ravine through which Hercules
had brought up Cerberus; in addition, there was an
" Acherusian " lake.[72] This ravine was, therefore, the
entrance to the place where death was conquered. The
lake also belongs here as a further mother symbol, for
symbols appear massed together, as they are surrogates,
and, therefore, do not afford the same satisfaction of desire as accorded by reality, so that the unsatisfied remnant of the libido must seek still further symbolic outlets.
The ravine in the Areopagus in Athens was considered
the seat of inhabitants of the lower world. An old
Grecian custom [73] suggests a similar idea. Girls were
sent into a cavern, where a poisonous snake dwelt, as a
test of virginity. If they were bitten by the snake, it was
a token that they were no longer chaste. We find this
same motive again in the Roman legend of St. Silvester,
at the end of the fifth century: [74]

" Erat draco immanissimus in monte Tarpeio, in quo est Capitolium collocatum. Ad hunc draconem per CCCLXV gradus,
quasi ad infernum, magi cum virginibus sacrilegis descendebant
semel in mense cum sacrificiis et lustris, ex quibus esca poterat
tanto draconi inferri. Hic draco subito ex improviso ascendebat
et licet non ingrederetur vicinos tamen aeres flatu suo vitiabat.
Ex quo mortalitas hominum et maxima luctus de morte veniebat
infantum. (Lilith motive.) Sanctus itaque Silvester cum haberet
cum paganis pro defensione veritatis conflictum, ad hoc venit ut
dicerent ei pagani: ' Silvester descende ad draconem et fac eum

in nomine Dei tui vel uno anno ab interfectione generis humani cessare." *

St. Peter appeared to Silvester in a dream and advised him to close his door to the underworld with chains, according to the model in Revelation, chap. xx:

(1) "And I saw an angel come down from heaven, having the key of the bottomless pit, and a great chain in his hand.

(2) "And he laid hold on the dragon, that old serpent, which is the Devil and Satan, and bound him a thousand years.

(3) "And cast him into the bottomless pit, and shut him up, and set a seal upon him."

The anonymous author of a writing, " De Promissionibus," [75] of the beginning of the fifth century, mentions a very similar legend:

"Apud urbem Romam specus quidam fuit in quo draco miræ magnitudinis mechanica arte formatus, gladium ore gestans,[76] oculis rutilantibus gemmis [77] metuendus ac terribilis apparebat. Hinc annuæ devotæ virgines floribus exornatæ, eo modo in sacrificio dabantur, quatenus inscias munera deferentes gradum scalæ, quo certe ille arte diaboli draco pendebat, contingentes impetus venientis gladii perimeret, ut sanguinem funderet innocentem. Et hunc quidam monachus, bene ob meritum cognitus Stiliconi tunc patricio, eo modo subvertit; baculo, manu, singulos gradus palpandos inspiciens, statim ut illum tangens fraudem

* There was a huge dragon on Mount Tarpeius, where the Capitolium stands. Once a month, with sacrilegious maidens, the priests descended 365 steps into the hell of this dragon, carrying expiatory offerings of food for the dragon. Then the dragon suddenly and unexpectedly arose, and, though he did not come out, he poisoned the air with his breath. Thence came the mortality of man and the deepest sorrow for the death of the children. When, for the defence of truth, St. Silvester had had a conflict with the heathen, it came to this that the heathen said: " Silvester, go down to the dragon, and in the name of thy God make him desist from the killing of mankind."

diabolicam repperit, eo transgresso descendens, draconem scidit, misitque in partes: ostendens et hic deos non esse qui manu fiunt." *

The *hero battling with the dragon has much in common with the dragon,* and also he takes over his qualities; for example, invulnerability. As the footnotes show, the similarity is carried still further (sparkling eyes, sword in his mouth). Translated psychologically, the dragon is merely the son's repressed longing, striving towards the mother; therefore, the son is the dragon, as even Christ is identified with the serpent, which, once upon a time, similia similibus, had controlled the snake plague in the Wilderness. John iii: 14. *As a serpent he is to be crucified; that is to say, as one striving backwards towards the mother, he must die hanging or suspended on the mother tree.* Christ and the dragon of the Antichrist are in the closest contact in the history of their appearance and their cosmic meaning. (Compare Bousset, the Antichrist.) The legend of the dragon concealed

* Near the city of Rome there was a certain cavern in which appeared a dragon of remarkable size, mechanically produced, brandishing a sword in his mouth, his eyes glittering like gems, fearful and terrible. Hither came virgins every year, devoted to this service, adorned with flowers, who were given to him in sacrifice. Bringing these gifts, they unknowingly descended the steps to a point where, with diabolical cunning, the dragon was suspended, striking those who came a blow with the sword, so that the innocent blood was shed. Now, there was a certain monk who, on account of his good deeds, was well known to Stilico, the patrician; he killed this dragon as follows: He examined each separate step carefully, both with a rod and his own hand, until, discovering the false step, he exposed the diabolical fraud. Then, jumping over this step, he went down and killed the dragon, cutting him to pieces, demonstrating that one who could be destroyed by human hand could not be a divinity.

in the Antichrist myth belongs to the life of the hero, and, therefore, is immortal. In none of the newer forms of myth are the pairs of opposites so perceptibly near as in that of Christ and Antichrist. (I refer to the remarkable psychologic description of this problem in Mereschkowski's romance, "Leonardo da Vinci.") That the dragon is only an artifice is a useful and delightfully rationalistic conceit, which is most significant for that period. In this way the dismal gods were effectually vulgarized. The schizophrenic insane readily make use of this mechanism, in order to depreciate efficient personalities. One often hears the stereotyped lament, "It is all a play, artificial, made up," etc. A dream of a "schizophrenic" is most significant; he is sitting in a dark room, which has only a single small window, through which he can see the sky. The sun and moon appear, but they are only made artificially from oil paper. (Denial of the deleterious incest influence.)

The descent of the three hundred and sixty-five steps refers to the sun's course, to the cavern of death and rebirth. That this cavern actually stands in a relation to the subterranean mother of death can be shown by a note in Malalas, the historian of Antioch,[78] who relates that Diocletian consecrated there a crypt to Hecate, to which one descends by three hundred and sixty-five steps. Cave mysteries seem to have been celebrated for Hecate in Samothrace as well. The serpent also played a great part as a regular symbolic attribute in the service of Hecate. The mysteries of Hecate flourished in Rome towards the end of the fourth century, so that the two foregoing

legends might indeed relate to her cult. Hecate [79] is a
real spectral goddess of night and phantoms, a Mar; she
is represented as riding, and in Hesiod occurs as the
patron of riders. She sends the horrible nocturnal fear
phantom, the Empusa, of whom Aristophanes says that
she appears inclosed in a *bladder swollen with blood*.
According to Libanius, the mother of Aischines is also
called Empusa, for the reason that ἐκ σκοτεινῶν τόπων
τοῖς παισὶν καὶ ταῖς γυναιξίν ὡρμᾶτο."*

Empusa, like Hecate, has *peculiar* feet; one foot is
made of brass, the other of ass' dung. Hecate has snake-
like feet, which, as in the triple form ascribed to Hecate,
points to her phallic libido nature. [80] In Tralles, Hecate
appears next to Priapus; there is also a Hecate Aphro-
disias. Her symbols are the key, [81] the whip, [82] the snake, [83]
the dagger [84] and the torch. [85] As mother of death, dogs
accompany her, the significance of which we have previously discussed at length. As guardian of the door of
Hades and as Goddess of dogs, she is of threefold form,
and really identified with Cerberus. Thus Hercules, in
bringing up Cerberus, brings the conquered mother of
death into the upper world. As spirit mother (moon!),
she sends madness, lunacy. (This mythical observation
states that " the mother " sends madness; by far the majority of the cases of insanity consist, in fact, in the domination of the individual by the material of the incest
phantasy.) In the mysteries of Cerberus, a rod,
called λευκόφυλλος,† was broken off. This rod protected

---

* Out of dark places she rushes on children and women.
† White-leaved.

the purity of virgins, and caused any one who touched the plant to become insane. We recognize in this the motive of the sacred tree, which, as mother, must not be touched, an act which only an insane person would commit. Hecate, as nightmare, appears in the form of Empusa, in a vampire rôle, or as Lamia, as devourer of men; perhaps, also, in that more beautiful guise, "The Bride of Corinth." She is the mother of all charms and witches, the patron of Medea, because the power of the "terrible mother" is magical and irresistible (working upward from the unconscious). In Greek syncretism, she plays a very significant rôle. She is confused with Artemis, who also has the surname ἑκάτη,* "the one striking at a distance" or "striking according to her will," in which we recognize again her superior power. Artemis is the huntress, with hounds, and so Hecate, through confusion with her, becomes κυνηγετική, the wild nocturnal huntress. (God, as huntsman, see above.) She has her name in common with Apollo, ἕκατος ἑκάεργος.† From the standpoint of the libido theory, this connection is easily understandable, because Apollo merely symbolizes the more positive side of the same amount of libido. The confusion of Hecate with Brimo as subterranean mother is understandable; also with Persephone and Rhea, the primitive all-mother. Intelligible through the maternal significance is the confusion with Ilithyia, the midwife. Hecate is also the direct goddess of births, κουροτρόφος,‡ the multiplier of cat-

---

* Far-shooting Hecate.   † Far-shooting, the far-darting.
‡ Goddess of birth.

tle, and goddess of marriage. Hecate, orphically, occupies the centre of the world as Aphrodite and Gaia, even as the world soul in general. On a carved gem [86] she is represented carrying the cross on her head. The beam on which the criminal was scourged is called ἑκάτη.* To her, as to the Roman Trivia, the triple roads, or *Scheideweg,* "forked road," or crossways were dedicated. And where roads branch off or unite sacrifices of dogs were brought her; there the bodies of the executed were thrown; the sacrifice occurs at the *point of crossing.* Etymologically, *scheide,* "sheath"; for example, swordsheath, sheath for water-shed and sheath for vagina, is identical with *scheiden,* "to split," or "to separate." The meaning of a sacrifice at this place would, therefore, be as follows: to offer something to the mother at the place of junction or at the fissure. (Compare the sacrifice to the chthonic gods in the abyss.) The Temenos of Ge, the abyss and the well, are easily understood as the gates of life and death,[87] " past which every one gladly creeps " (Faust), and sacrifices there his obolus or his πελανοί,† instead of his body, just as Hercules soothes Cerberus with the honey cakes. (Compare with this the mythical significance of the dog!) Thus the crevice at Delphi, with the spring, Castalia, was the seat of the chthonic dragon, Python, who was conquered by the sun-hero, Apollo. (Python, incited by Hera, pursued Leta, pregnant with Apollo; but she, on the floating island of Delos [nocturnal journey on the sea], gave birth to her child, who later slew the Python; that is to say, conquered in

---

* Hecate.　　　　　　　　† Sacrificial cakes offered to the gods.

it the spirit mother.) In Hierapolis (Edessa) the temple
was erected above the crevice through which the flood
had poured out, and in Jerusalem the foundation stone
of the temple covered the great abyss,[88] just as Christian
churches are frequently built over caves, grottoes, wells,
etc. In the Mithra grotto,[89] and all the other sacred
caves up to the Christian catacombs, which owe their
significance not to the legendary persecutions but to the
worship of the dead,[90] we come across the same fundamental motive. The burial of the dead in a holy place
(in the " garden of the dead," in cloisters, crypts, etc.)
is restitution to the mother, with the certain hope of resurrection by which such burial is rightfully rewarded.
The animal of death which dwells in the cave had to be
soothed in early times through human sacrifices; later
with natural gifts.[91] Therefore, the Attic custom gives
to the dead the μελιτοῦττα, to pacify the dog of hell,
the three-headed monster at the gate of the underworld.
A more recent elaboration of the natural gifts seems to be
the obolus for Charon, who is, therefore, designated by
Rohde as the second Cerberus, corresponding to the
Egyptian dog-faced god Anubis.[92] Dog and serpent of
the underworld (Dragon) are likewise identical. In
the tragedies, the Erinnyes are serpents as well as dogs;
the serpents Tychon and Echidna are parents of the serpents—Hydra, the dragon of the Hesperides, and Gorgo;
and of the dogs, Cerberus, Orthrus, Scylla.[93] Serpents
and dogs are also protectors of the treasure. The
chthonic god was probably always a serpent dwelling in a
cave, and was fed with πελανοί.* In the Asclepiadean of

* Ritual sacrificial food offered to the gods.

the later period, the sacred serpents were scarcely visible, meaning that they probably existed only figuratively.[94] Nothing was left but the hole in which the snake was said‹ to dwell.   There the πελανοί* were placed; later the obolus was thrown in.   The sacred cavern in the temple of Kos consisted of a rectangular pit, upon which was laid a stone lid, with a square hole; this arrangement serves the purpose of a treasure house.   The snake hole had become a slit for money, a " sacrificial box," and the cave had become a " treasure."   That this development, which Herzog traces, agrees excellently with the actual condition is shown by a discovery in the temple of Asclepius and Hygieia in Ptolemais:

" An encoiled granite snake, with arched neck, was found.   In the middle of the coil is seen a narrow slit, polished by usage, just large enough to allow a coin of four centimeters diameter at most to fall through.   At the side are holes for handles to lift the heavy pieces, the under half of which is used as a cover."—*Herzog, Ibid.*, p. 212.

The serpent, as protector of the hoard, now lies on the treasure house.   The fear of the maternal womb of death has become the guardian of the treasure of life. That the snake in this connection is really a symbol of death, that is to say, of the dead libido, results from the fact that the souls of the dead, like the chthonic gods, appear as *serpents,* as dwellers in the kingdom of the mother of death.[95]   This development of symbol allows us to recognize easily the transition of the originally very primitive significance of the crevice in the earth as mother to the

* Ritual sacrificial food offered to the gods.

meaning of treasure house, and can, therefore, support the etymology of *Hort*, " hoard, treasure," as suggested by Kluge. κεύθω, belonging to κεῦθος, means the innermost womb of the earth (Hades); κύσθος, that Kluge adds, is of similar meaning, cavity or womb. Prellwitz does not mention this connection. Fick,[96] however, compares New High German *hort*, Gothic *huzd*, to Armenian *kust*, " abdomen "; Church Slavonian *čista*, Vedic *kostha* = abdomen, from the Indo-Germanic root *koustho -s* = viscera, lower abdomen, room, store-room. Prellwitz compares κύσθος κύστις = urinary bladder, bag, purse; Sanskrit *kustha-s* = cavity of the loins; then κύτος = cavity, vault; κύτις = little chest, from κνέω = I am pregnant. Here, from κύτος = cave, κύαρ = hole, κύαθος = cup, κύλα = depression under the eye, κῦμα = swelling, wave, billow, κῦρος = power, force, κύριος = lord, Old Iranian *caur*, *cur* = hero; Sanskrit *çura -s* = strong, hero. The fundamental Indo-Germanic roots [97] are *kevo* = to swell, to be strong. From that the above-mentioned κνέω, κύαρ, κῦρος and Latin *cavus* = hollow, vaulted, cavity, hole; *cavea* = cavity, enclosure, cage, scene and assembly; *caulæ* = cavity, opening, enclosure, stall [98]; *kuéyô* = swell; participle, *kueyonts* = swelling; *en-kueyonts* = pregnant. ἐγκυέων = Latin *inciens* = pregnant; compare Sanskrit *vi-çváyan* = swelling; *kûro -s (kevaro -s)*, strong, powerful hero.

The treasure which the hero fetches from the dark cavern is swelling life; it is himself, the hero, new-born from the anxiety of pregnancy and the birth throes.

Thus the Hindoo fire-bringer is called Matariçvan, meaning the one swelling in the mother. The *hero striving
towards the mother is the dragon, and when he separates
from the mother he becomes the conqueror of the
dragon.*[99] This train of thought, which we have already
hinted at previously in Christ and Antichrist, may be
traced even into the details of Christian phantasy. There
is a series of mediæval pictures [100] in which the communion cup contains a dragon, a snake or some sort of
small animal.[101]

The cup is the receptacle, the maternal womb, of the
god resurrected in the wine; the cup is the cavern where
the serpent dwells, the god who sheds his skin, in the
state of metamorphosis; for Christ is also the serpent.
These symbolisms are used in an obscure connection in
I Corinthians, verse 10: Paul writes of the Jews who
" were all baptized unto Moses in the cloud and in the
sea " (also reborn) and " did all drink the same spiritual
drink; for they drank of that spiritual rock that followed
them, and that rock was Christ." They drank from the
mother (the generative rock, birth from the rock) the
milk of rejuvenation, the mead of immortality, and this
Rock was Christ, here identified with the mother, because
he is the symbolic representative of the mother libido.
When we drink from the cup, then we drink from the
mother's breast immortality and everlasting salvation.
Paul wrote of the Jews that they ate and then rose up
to dance and to indulge in fornication, and then twenty-
three thousand of them were swept off by the plague of
serpents. The remedy for the survivors, however, was

the sight of a serpent hanging on a pole. From it was derived the cure.

"The cup of blessing which we bless, is it not the communion of the blood of Christ? The bread which we break, is it not the communion of the body of Christ? For we being many are one bread, and one body; for we are all partakers of one bread."— *I Corinthians* x: 16, 17.

Bread and wine are the body and the blood of Christ; the food of the immortals who are brothers with Christ, ἀδελφοί, those who come from the same womb. We who are reborn again from the mother are all heroes together with Christ, and enjoy immortal food. As with the Jews, so too with the Christians, there is imminent danger of unworthy partaking, for this mystery, which is very closely related psychologically with the subterranean Hierosgamos of Eleusis, involves a mysterious union of. man in a spiritual sense,[102] which was constantly misunderstood by the profane and was retranslated into his language, where mystery is equivalent to orgy and secrecy to vice.[103] A very interesting blasphemer and sectarian of the beginning of the nineteenth century named Unternährer has made the following comment on the last supper:

"The communion of the devil is in this brothel. All they sacrifice here, they sacrifice to the devil and not to God. There they have the devil's cup and the devil's dish; *there they have sucked the head of the snake*,[104] there they have fed upon the iniquitous bread and drunken the wine of wickedness." [105]

Unternährer is an adherent or a forerunner of the "theory of living one's own nature." He dreams of himself as a sort of priapic divinity; he says of himself:

" Black-haired, very charming and handsome in countenance, and every one enjoys listening to thee on account of the amiable speeches which come from thy mouth; therefore the maids love thee."

He preaches " the cult of nakedness."

" Ye fools and blind men, behold God has created man in his image, as male and female, and has blessed them and said, ' Be fruitful and multiply and fill the earth, and make it subject to thee.' Therefore, he has given the greatest honor to these poor members and has placed them naked in the garden," etc.

" Now are the fig leaves and the covering removed, because thou hast turned to the Lord, for the Lord is the Spirit, and where the spirit of the Lord is, there is freedom,[106] there the clearness of the Lord is mirrored with uncovered countenance. This is precious before God, and this is the glory of the Lord, and the adornment of our God, when you stand in the image and honor of your God, as God created you, naked and not ashamed.

· " Who can ever praise sufficiently in the sons and daughters of the living God those parts of the body which are destined to procreate?

" In the lap of the daughters of Jerusalem is the gate of the Lord, and the Just will go into the temple there, to the altar.[107] And in the lap of the sons of the living God is the water-pipe of the upper part, which is a tube, like a rod, to measure the temple and altar. And under the water-tube the sacred stones are placed, as a sign and testimony of the Lord, who has taken to himself the seed of Abraham.

" Out of the seeds in the chamber of the mother, God creates a man with his hands, as an image of himself. Then the mother house and the mother chamber is opened in the daughters of the Living God, and God himself brings forth a child through them. Thus God creates children from the stones, for the seed comes from the stones." [108]

History teaches in manifold examples how the religious mysteries are liable to change suddenly into sexual orgies

because they have originated from an overvaluation of the
orgy.   It is characteristic that this priapic divinity [109] returns again to the old symbol of the snake, which in the
mystery enters into the faithful, fertilizing and spiritual-
izing them, although it originally possessed a phallic significance.   In the mysteries of the Ophites, the festival
was really celebrated with serpents, in which the animals
were even kissed.   (Compare the caressing of the snake
of Demeter in the Eleusinian mysteries.)   In the sexual
orgies of the modern Christian sects the phallic kiss plays
a very important rôle.   Unternährer was an uncultivated,
crazy peasant, and it is unlikely that the Ophitic religious
ceremonies were known to him.

The phallic significance is expressed negatively or mysteriously through the serpent, which always points to a
secret related thought.   This related thought connects
with the mother; thus, in a dream a patient found the
following imagery: " A serpent shot out from a moist
cave and bit the dreamer in the region of the genitals."
This dream took place at the instant when the patient
was convinced of the truth of the analysis, and began
to free himself from the bond of his mother complex.
The meaning is: I am convinced that I am inspired and
poisoned by the mother.   The contrary manner of expression is characteristic of the dream.   At the moment
when he felt the impulse to go forwards he perceived the
attachment to the mother.   Another patient had the following dream during a relapse, in which the libido was
again wholly introverted for a time: " She was entirely
filled within by a great snake; only one end of the tail

peeped out from her arm. She wanted to seize it, but it
escaped her." A patient with a very strong introversion
(catatonic state) complained to me that a snake was
stuck in her throat.[110] This symbolism is also used by
Nietzsche in the "vision" of the shepherd and the
snake :[111]

"And verily, what I saw was like nothing I ever saw before.
I saw a young shepherd, writhing, choking, twitching with a con-
vulsed face, from whose mouth hung a black, heavy serpent.

"Did I ever see so much disgust and pallid fear upon a countenance?[112] Might he have been sleeping, and the snake crept
into his mouth—there it bit him fast?

"My hand tore at the serpent and tore—in vain!—I failed to
tear the serpent out of his mouth. Then there cried out of me:
'Bite! Bite! Its head off! Bite!' I exclaimed; all my horror,
my hate, my disgust, my compassion, all the good and bad cried
out from me in one voice.

"Ye intrepid ones around me! solve for me the riddle which I
saw, make clear to me the vision of the lonesomest one.

"For it was a vision and a prophecy; what did then I behold
in parable? And who is it who is still to come?

"Who is the shepherd into whose mouth crept the snake? Who
is the man into whose throat all the heaviness and the blackest
would creep?[113]

"But the shepherd bit, as my cry had told him; he bit with a
huge bite! Far away did he spit the head of the serpent—and
sprang up.

"No longer shepherd, no longer man, a transfigured being, an
illuminated being, who laughed! Never yet on earth did a man
laugh as he laughed!

"O my brethren, I heard a laugh which was no human
laughter—and now a thirst consumeth me, a longing that is never
allayed.

"My longing for this laugh eats into me. Oh, how can I
suffer still to live! And how now can I bear to die!"[114]

The snake represents the introverting libido. Through introversion one is fertilized, inspired, regenerated and reborn from the God. In Hindoo philosophy this idea of creative, intellectual activity has even cosmogenic significance. The unknown original creator of all things is, according to Rigveda 10, 121, Prajâpati, the "Lord of Creation." In the various Brahmas, his cosmogenic activity was depicted in the following manner

"Prajâpati desired: 'I will procreate myself, I will be manifold.' He performed Tapas; after he had performed Tapas he created these worlds."

The strange conception of Tapas is to be translated, according to Deussen,[115] as "he heated himself with his own heat,[116] with the sense of 'he brooded, he hatched.'" Here the hatcher and the hatched are not two, but one and the same identical being. As Hiranyagarbha, Prajâpati is the egg produced from himself, the world-egg, from which he hatches himself. He creeps into himself, he becomes his own uterus, becomes pregnant with himself, in order to give birth to the world of multiplicity. Thus Prajâpati through the way of introversion changed into something new, the multiplicity of the world. It is of especial interest to note how the most remote things come into contact. Deussen observes:

"In the degree that the conception of Tapas (heat) becomes in hot India the symbol of exertion and distress, the 'tapo atapyata' began to assume the meaning of self-castigation and became related to the idea that creation is an act of *self-renunciation* on the part of the Creator."

Self-incubation and self-castigation and introversion are very closely connected ideas.¹¹⁷ The Zosimos vision mentioned above betrays the same train of thought, where it is said of the place of transformation: ὁ τόπος τῆς ἀσκήσεως.* We have already observed that the place of transformation is really the uterus. Absorption in one's self (introversion) is an entrance into one's own uterus, and also at the same time asceticism. In the philosophy of the Brahmans the world arose from this activity; among the post-Christian Gnostics it produced the revival and spiritual rebirth of the individual, who was born into a new spiritual world. The Hindoo philosophy is considerably more daring and logical, and assumes that creation results from introversion in general, as in the wonderful hymn of Rigveda, 10, 29, it is said:

> " What was hidden in the shell,
> Was born through the power of fiery torments.
> ·From this first arose love,
> As the germ of knowledge,
> The wise found the roots of existence in non-existence,
> By investigating the heart's impulses." ¹¹⁸

This philosophical view interprets the world as an emanation of the libido, and this must be widely accepted from the theoretic as well as the psychologic standpoint, for the function of reality is an instinctive function, having the character of biological adaptation. When the insane Schreber brought about the end of the world through his libido-introversion, he expressed an entirely rational psychologic view, just as Schopenhauer wished to abolish

* The place of discipline.

through negation (holiness, asceticism) the error of the primal will, through which the world was created. Does not Goethe say:

> " You follow a false trail;
> Do not think that we are not serious;
> Is not the kernel of nature
> In the hearts of men? "

The hero, who is to accomplish the rejuvenation of the world and the conquest of death, is the libido, which, brooding upon itself in introversion, coiling as a snake around its own egg, apparently threatens life with a poisonous bite, in order to lead it to death, and from that darkness, conquering itself, gives birth to itself again. Nietzsche knows this conception: [119]

> " How long have you sat already upon your misfortune.
> Give heed! lest you hatch an egg,
> A basilisk egg
> Of your long travail."

The hero is himself a serpent, himself a sacrificer and a sacrificed. The hero himself is of *serpent nature;* therefore, Christ compares himself with the serpent; therefore, the redeeming principle of the world of that Gnostic sect which styled itself the Ophite was the serpent. The serpent is the Agatho and Kako demon. It is, indeed, intelligible, when, in the Germanic saga, they say that the heroes had serpents' eyes.[120] I recall the parallel previously drawn between the eyes of the Son of man and those of the Tarpeian dragon. In the already mentioned mediæval pictures, the dragon, instead of the

Lord, appeared in the cup; the dragon who with changeful, serpent glances [121] guarded the divine mystery of renewed rebirth in the maternal womb. In Nietzsche the old, apparently long extinct idea is again revived: [122]

> " Ailing with tenderness, just as the thawing wind,
> Zarathustra sits waiting, waiting on his hill,
> Sweetened and cooked in his own juice,
> Beneath his summits,
> Beneath his ice he sits,
> Weary and happy,
> A Creator on his seventh day.
> Silence!
> It is my truth!
> From hesitating eyes—
> From velvety shadows
> Her glance meets mine,
> Lovely, mischievous, the glance of a girl.
> She divines the reason of my happiness,
> She divines me—ha! what is she plotting?
> A purple dragon lurks
> In the abyss of her maiden glance.[123]
> Woe to thee, Zarathustra,
> Thou seemest like some one
> Who has swallowed gold,
> Thy belly will be slit open." [124]

In this poem nearly all the symbolism is collected which we have elaborated previously from other connections. Distinct traces of the primitive identity of serpent and hero are still extant in the myth of Cecrops. Cecrops is himself half-snake, half-man. Originally, he probably was the Athenian snake of the citadel itself. As a buried god, he is like Erechtheus, a chthonic snake god. Above his subterranean dwelling rises the Parthenon, the temple of the virgin goddess (compare the analogous idea of the Christian church). The casting of the skin of the god, which we have already mentioned in passing, stands in the closest relation to the nature of the hero. We have spoken already of the Mexican god who casts his skin. It is also told of Mani, the founder of the Manichaean sect, that he was killed, skinned, stuffed and hung up.[125] That is the death of Christ, merely in another mythological form.[126]

Marsyas, who seems to be a substitute for Attis, the son-lover of Cybele, was also skinned.[127] Whenever a Scythian king died, slaves and horses were slaughtered, skinned and stuffed, and then set up again.[128] In Phrygia, the representatives of ·the father-god were killed and skinned. The same was done in Athens with an ox, who was skinned and stuffed and again hitched to the plough.

In this manner the revival of the fertility of the earth was celebrated.[129]

This readily explains the fragment from the Sabazios mysteries, transmitted to us by Firmicus:[130] Ταῦρος δρά-κοντος καὶ πατὴρ ταύρου δράκων*.

The active fructifying (upward striving) form of the libido is changed into the negative force striving downwards towards death. The hero as zodion of spring (ram, bull) conquers the depths of winter; and beyond the summer solstice is attacked by the unconscious longing for death, and is bitten by the snake. However, he himself is the snake. But he is at war with himself, and, therefore, the descent and the end appear to him as the

* The bull, father of the serpent, and the serpent, father of the bull.

malicious inventions of the mother of death, who in this way wishes to draw him to herself. The mysteries, however, consolingly promise that there is no contradiction [131] or disharmony when life is changed into death: ταῦρος δράκοντος καὶ πατήρ ταύρου δράκων.

Nietzsche, too, gives expression to this mystery: [132]

> " *Here do I sit now,*
> That is, I'm swallowed down
> By this the smallest oasis—
> —It opened up just yawning,
> Its loveliest maw agape.
> Hail! hail! to that whalefish,
> When he for his guests' welfare
> Provided thus!
>
> .   .   .   . .   .
>
> Hail to his belly
> If he had also
> Such a lovely oasis belly—
> The desert grows, woe to him
> Who hides the desert!
> Stone grinds on stone, the desert
> Gulps and strangles.
> The monstrous death gazes, glowing brown,
> And chews—his life is his chewing . . .
> Forget not, O man, burnt out by lust,
> Thou art the stone, the desert,
> Thou art death! "

The serpent symbolism of the Last Supper is explained by the identification of the hero with the serpent: The god is buried in the mother: as fruit of the field, as food coming from the mother and at the same time as drink of immortality he is received by the mystic, or as a serpent he unites with the mystic. All these symbols represent the liberation of the libido from the incestuous fixation through which new life is attained. The liberation is accomplished under symbols, which represent the activity of the incest wish.

It might be justifiable at this place to cast a glance upon psychoanalysis as a method of treatment. In practical analysis it is important, first of all, to discover the libido lost from the control of consciousness. (It often happens to the libido as with the fish of Moses in the Mohammedan legend; it sometimes " takes its course in a marvellous manner into the sea.") Freud says in his important article, " Zur Dynamik der Übertragung " : [133]

" The libido has retreated into regression and again revives the infantile images."

This means, mythologically, that the sun is devoured by the serpent of the night, the treasure is concealed and guarded by the dragon: substitution of a present mode of adaptation by an infantile mode, which is represented by the corresponding neurotic symptoms. Freud continues:

" Thither the analytic treatment follows it and endeavors to seek out the libido again, to render it accessible to consciousness, and finally to make it serviceable to reality. Whenever the analytic investigation touches upon the libido, withdrawn into its hiding-place, a struggle must break out; all the forces, which have caused the regression of the libido, will rise up as resistance against the work, in order to preserve this new condition."

Mythologically this means: the hero seeks the lost sun, the fire, the virgin sacrifice, or the treasure, and fights the typical fight with the dragon, with the libido in resistance. As these parallels show, psychoanalysis mobiles a part of the life processes, the fundamental importance of which properly illustrates the significance of this process.

After Siegfried has slain the dragon, he meets the father, Wotan, plagued by gloomy cares, for the primitive mother, Erda, has placed in his path the snake, in order to enfeeble his sun. He says to Erda:

> *Wanderer:*
>   All-wise one,
>   Care's piercing sting by thee was planted
>   In Wotan's dauntless heart
>   With fear of shameful ruin and downfall.
>   Filled was his spirit by tidings
>   Thou didst foretell.
>   Art thou the world's wisest of women?
>   Tell to me now
>   How a god may conquer his care.
>
> *Erda:*
>   Thou art not
>   What thou hast said.

It is the same primitive motive which we meet in Wagner: the mother has robbed her son, the sun-god, of the joy of life, through a poisonous thorn, and deprives him of his power, which is connected with the name. Isis demands the name of the god; Erda says, " Thou art not what thou hast said." But the " Wanderer " has found the way to conquer the fatal charm of the mother, the fear of death:

> " The eternals' downfall
>   No more dismays me,
>   Since their doom I willed.

" I leave to thee, loveliest Wälsung,
   Gladly my heritage now.
To the ever-young
   In gladness yieldeth the god ! "

These wise words contain, in fact, the saving thought. It is not the mother who has placed the poisonous worm in our path, but our libido itself wills to complete the course of the sun to mount from morn to noon, and, passing beyond noon, to hasten towards evening, not at war with itself, but willing the descent and the end.[134]

Nietzsche's Zarathustra teaches:

" I praise thee, my death, the free death, which comes to me because I want it.

" And when shall I want it?

" He who has a goal and an heir wants death at the proper time for his goal and his heir.

" And this is the great noonday, when man in the middle of his course stands between man and superman, and celebrates his path towards evening as his highest hope: because it is the path to a new morning.

" He who is setting will bless his own going down because it is a transition : and the sun of his knowledge will be at high noon."

Siegfried conquers the father Wotan and takes possession of Brunhilde. The first object that he sees is her horse; then he believes that he beholds a mail-clad man. He cuts to pieces the protecting coat of mail of the sleeper. (Overpowering.) When he sees it is a woman, terror seizes him:

" My heart doth falter and faint;
   On whom shall I call
That he may help me?

Mother! Mother!
Remember me!

" Can this be fearing?
Oh, mother! Mother!
Thy dauntless child!
A woman lieth asleep:—
And she now has taught him to fear!

" Awaken! Awaken!
Holiest maid!
Then life from the sweetness of lips
Will I win me—
E'en tho' I die in a kiss."

In the duet which follows the mother is invoked:

" O mother, hail!
Who gave thee thy birth! "

The confession of Brunhilde is especially characteristic:

" O knewest thou—joy of the world,
How I have ever loved thee!
Thou wert my gladness,
My care wert thou!
Thy life I sheltered;
Or ere it was thine,
Or ere thou wert born,
My shield was thy guard." [115]

The pre-existence of the hero and the pre-existence of
Brunhilde as his wife-mother are clearly indicated from
this passage.

Siegfried says in confirmation:

" Then death took not my mother?
Bound in sleep did she lie? "

The mother-imago, which is the symbol of the dying and resurrected libido, is explained by Brunhilde to the hero, as his own will:

> " Thyself am I
> If blest I be in thy love."

The great mystery of the Logos entering into the mother for rebirth is proclaimed with the following words by Brunhilde:

> " O Siegfried, Siegfried,
> Conquering light!
> I loved thee ever,
> For I divined
> The thought that Wotan had hidden—
> The thought that I dared
> Not to whisper— [136]
> That all unclearly
> Glowed in my bosom
> Suffered and strove;
> For which I flouted
> Him, who conceived it: [136]
> For which in penance
> Prisoned I lay,
> While thinking it not
> And feeling only,
> For, in my thought,
> Oh, should you guess it?
> Was only my love for thee."

The erotic similes which now follow distinctly reveal the motive of rebirth:

> *Siegfried:*
> A glorious flood
> Before me rolls.

> With all my senses
> I only see
> Its buoyant, gladdening billows.
> Though in the deep
> I find not my face,
> Burning, I long
> For the water's balm;
> And now as I am,
> Spring in the stream.[137]
> O might its billows
> Engulf me in bliss."

The motive of plunging into the maternal water of re-birth (baptism) is here fully developed. An allusion to the "terrible mother" imago, the mother of heroes, who teaches them fear, is to be found in Brunhilde's words (the horse-woman, who guides the dead to the other side):

> "Fearest thou, Siegfried?
> Fearest thou not
> The wild, furious woman?"

The orgiastic "Occide moriturus" resounds in Brunhilde's words:

> "Laughing let us be lost—
> Laughing go down to death!"

And in the words

> "Light-giving love,
> Laughing death!"

is to be found the same significant contrast.

The further destinies of Siegfried are those of the Invictus: the spear of the gloomy, one-eyed Hagen strikes Siegfried's vulnerable spot. The old sun, who has become the god of death, the one-eyed Wotan, smites his off-spring, and once again ascends in eternal rejuvenation. The course of the invincible sun has supplied the mystery of human life with beautiful and imperishable symbols; it became a comforting fulfilment of all the yearning for immortality, of all desire of mortals for eternal life.

Man leaves the mother, the source of libido, and is driven by the eternal thirst to find her again, and to drink renewal from her; thus he completes his cycle, and returns again into the mother's womb. Every obstacle which obstructs his life's path, and threatens his ascent, wears the shadowy features of the "terrible mother," who paralyzes his energy with the consuming poison of the stealthy, retrospective longing. In each conquest he wins again the smiling love and life-giving mother—images which belong to the intuitive depths of human feeling, the features of which have become mutilated and irrecognizable through the progressive development of the surface of the human mind. The stern necessity of adaptation works ceaselessly to obliterate the last traces of these primitive landmarks of the period of the origin of the human mind, and to replace them along lines which are to denote more and more clearly the nature of real objects.

CHAPTER VIII

THE SACRIFICE

AFTER this long digression, let us return to Miss Miller's vision. We can now answer the question as to the significance of Siegfried's longing for Brunhilde. It is the striving of the libido away *from the mother towards the mother*. This paradoxical sentence may be translated as follows: as long as the libido is satisfied merely with phantasies, it moves in itself, in its own depths, in the mother.[1] When the longing of our author rises in order to escape the magic circle of the incestuous and, therefore, pernicious, object, and it does not succeed in finding reality, then the object is and remains irrevocably the mother. Only the overcoming of the obstacles of reality brings the deliverance from the mother, who is the continuous and inexhaustible source of life for the creator, but death for the cowardly, timid and sluggish.

Whoever is acquainted with psychoanalysis knows how often neurotics cry out against their parents. To be sure, such complaints and reproaches are often justified on account of the common human imperfections, but still more often they are reproaches which should really be directed towards themselves. Reproach and hatred are always futile attempts to free one's self apparently from the parents, but in reality from one's own hindering longing for the parents. Our author proclaims through the mouth of her infantile hero Chiwantopel a series of insults against her own family. We can assume that she must renounce all these tendencies, because they contain an unrecognized wish. This hero, of many words, who performs few deeds and indulges in futile yearnings, is the libido which has not fulfilled its destiny, but which turns round and round in the kingdom of the mother, and, in spite of all its longing, accomplishes nothing. Only he can break this magic circle who possesses the courage of the will to live and the heroism to carry it through. Could this yearning hero-youth, Chiwantopel, but put an end to his existence, he would probably rise again in the form of a brave man seeking real life. This necessity imposes itself upon the dreamer as a wise counsel and hint of the unconscious in the following monologue of Chiwantopel. He cries sadly:

" In all the world, there is not a single one! I have sought among a hundred tribes. I have watched a hundred moons, since I began. Can it be that there is not a solitary being who will ever know my soul? Yes, by the sovereign God, yes! But ten thousand moons will wax and wane before that pure soul is born. And it is from another world that her parents will come to this one. She will have pale skin and pale locks. She will know sorrow before her mother bears her. Suffering will accompany her; she will seek also, and she will find, no one who understands her. Temptation will often assail her soul—but she will not yield. In her dreams, I will come to her, and she will understand. *I have kept my body inviolate.* I have come ten thousand moons before her epoch, and she will come ten thousand moons too late. But she will understand! There is only once in all the ten thousand moons that a soul like hers is born."

Thereupon a green serpent darts from the bushes, glides towards him and stings him on the arm, then attacks the horse, which succumbs first. Then Chiwantopel says to his horse:

" ' Adieu, faithful brother! Enter into rest! I have loved you, and you have served me well. Adieu. Soon I will rejoin you! ' Then to the snake: ' Thanks, little sister, you have *put an end to my wanderings.*' "

Then he cried with grief and spoke his prayer:

" ' Sovereign God, take me soon! I have tried to know thee, and to keep thy law! O, do not suffer my body to fall into corruption and decay, and to furnish the vultures with food! ' A smoking crater is perceived at a distance, the rumbling of an earthquake is heard, followed by a trembling of the ground."

Chiwantopel cries in the delirium of suffering, while the earth covers his body:

" I have kept my body inviolate. Ah! She understands. Ja-ni-wa-ma, Ja-ni-wa-ma, thou who comprehendeth me."

Chiwantopel's prophecy is a repetition of Longfellow's " Hiawatha," where the poet could not escape sentimentality, and at the close of the career of the hero, Hiawatha, he brings in the Savior of the white people, in the guise of the arriving illustrious representatives of the Christian religion and morals. (One thinks of the work of redemption of the Spaniards in Mexico and Peru!) With this prophecy of Chiwantopel, the personality of the author is again placed in the closest relation to the hero, and, indeed, as the real object of Chiwantopel's longing.

Most certainly the hero would have married her, had she lived at his time; but, unfortunately, she comes too late. The connection proves our previous assertion that the libido moves round in a circle. The author loves herself; that is to say, she, as the hero, is sought by one who comes too late. This motive of coming too late is characteristic of the infantile love: the father and the mother cannot be overtaken. The separation of the two personalities by ten thousand moons is a wish fulfilment; with that the incest relation is annulled in an effectual manner. This white heroine will seek without being understood. (She is not understood, because she cannot understand herself rightly.) And she will not find. But in dreams, at least, they will find each other, " and she will understand." The next sentence of the text reads:

" I have kept my body inviolate."

This proud sentence, which naturally only a woman can express, because man is not accustomed to boast in that direction, again confirms the fact that all enterprises have remained but dreams, that the body has remained " inviolate." When the hero visits the heroine in a dream, it is clear what is meant. This assertion of the hero's, that he has remained inviolate, refers back to the unsuccessful attempt upon his life in the previous chapter (huntsman with the arrow), and clearly explains to us what was really meant by this assault; that is to say, the refusal of the coitus phantasy. Here the wish of the unconscious obtrudes itself again, after the hero had repressed it the first time, and thereupon he painfully and hysterically utters this monologue. " Temptation will often assail her soul—but it will not yield." This very bold assertion reduces—noblesse oblige—the unconscious to an enormous infantile megalomania, which is always the case when the libido is compelled, through similar circumstances, to regressions. " Only once in all the ten thousand moons is a soul born like mine!" Here the unconscious ego expands to an enormous degree, evidently in order to cover with its boastfulness a large part of the neglected duty of life. But punishment follows at its heels. Whoever prides himself too much on having sustained no wound in the battle of life lays himself open to the suspicion that his fighting has been with words only, whilst actually he has remained far away from the firing-line. This spirit is just the reverse of the pride of those savage women, who point with satisfaction to the countless scars which were given them by their men in the sexual fight for supremacy. In accordance with this, and in logical continuation of the same, all that follows is expressed in figurative speech. The orgiastic " Occide moriturus " in its admixture with the reckless laughter of the Dionysian frenzy confronts us here in sorry disguise with a sentimental stage trickery worthy of our posthumous edition of " Christian morals." In place of the positive phallus, the negative appears, and leads the hero's horse (his libido animalis), not to satisfaction, but into eternal peace—also the fate of the hero. This end means that the mother, represented as the jaws of death, devours the libido of the daughter. Therefore, instead of life and procreative growth, only phantastic self-oblivion results.

This weak and inglorious end has no elevating or illuminating meaning so long as we consider it merely as the solution of an individual erotic conflict. The fact that the symbols under which the solution takes place have actually a significant aspect, reveals to us that behind the individual mask, behind the veil of " individuation," a primitive idea stands, the severe and serious features of which take from us the courage to consider the sexual meaning of the Miller symbolism as all-sufficient.

It is not to be forgotten that the *sexual phantasies of the neurotic and the exquisite sexual language of dreams* are regressive phenomena. The sexuality of the unconscious is not what it seems to be; *it is merely a symbol;* it is a thought bright as day, clear as sunlight, a decision, a step forward to every goal of life—but expressed in the unreal sexual language of the unconscious, and in the thought form of an earlier stage; a resurrection, so to speak, of earlier modes of adaptation. When, therefore, the unconscious pushes into the foreground the coitus wish, negatively expressed, it means somewhat as follows: under similar circumstances primitive man acted in such and such a manner. The mode of adaptation which to-day is unconscious for us is carried on by the savage Negro of the present day, whose undertakings beyond those of nutrition appertain to sexuality, characterized by violence and cruelty. Therefore, in view of the archaic mode of expression of the Miller phantasy, we are justified in assuming the correctness of our interpretation for the lowest and nearest plane only. A deeper stratum of meaning underlies the earlier assertion that the figure of

Chiwantopel has the character of Cassius, who has a lamb as a companion. Therefore, Chiwantopel is the portion of the dreamer's libido bound up with the mother (and, therefore, masculine); hence he is her infantile personality, the childishness of character, which as yet is unable to understand that one must leave father and mother, when the time is come, in order to serve the destiny of the entire personality. This is outlined in Nietzsche's words:

" Free dost thou call thyself? Thy dominant thought would I hear and not that thou hast thrown off a yoke. Art thou one who had the right to throw off a yoke? There are many who throw away their last value when they throw away their servitude."

Therefore, when Chiwantopel dies, it means that herein is a fulfilment of a wish, that this infantile hero, who cannot leave the mother's care, may die. And if with that the bond between mother and daughter is severed, a great step forward is gained both for inner and outer freedom. But man wishes to remain a child too long; he would fain stop the turning of the wheel, which, rolling, bears along with it the years; man wishes to keep his childhood and eternal youth, rather than to die and suffer corruption in the grave. (" O, do not suffer my body to fall into decay and corruption.") Nothing brings the relentless flight of time and the cruel perishability of all blossoms more painfully to our consciousness than an inactive and empty life. *Idle dreaming is the mother of the fear of death,* the sentimental deploring of what has been and the vain turning back of the clock. Although man can forget in the long- (perhaps too long) guarded feelings of youth, in the dreamy state of stubbornly held remembrances, that the wheel rolls onward, nevertheless mercilessly does the gray hair, the relaxation of the skin and the wrinkles in the face tell us, that whether or not we expose the body to the destroying powers of the whole struggle of life, the poison of the stealthily creeping serpent of time consumes our bodies, which, alas! we so dearly love. Nor does it help if we cry out with the melancholy hero Chiwantopel, " I have kept my body inviolate "; flight from life does not free us from the law of age and death. The neurotic who seeks to get rid of the necessities of life wins nothing and lays upon himself the frightful burden of a premature age and death, which must appear especially cruel on account of the total emptiness and meaninglessness of his life. If the libido is not permitted to follow the progressive life, which is willing to accept all dangers and all losses, then it follows the other road, sinking into its own depths, working down into the old foreboding regarding the immortality of all life, to the longing for rebirth.

Hölderlin exemplifies this path in his poetry and his life. I leave the poet to speak in his song:

To the Rose.

" In the Mother-womb eternal,
　　Sweetest queen of every lea,
　Still the living and supernal
　　Nature carries thee and me.

" Little rose, the storm's fierce power
　　Strips our leaves and alters us;
　Yet the deathless germ will tower
　　To new blooms, miraculous."

The following comments may be made upon the parable of this poem: The rose is the symbol of the beloved woman ("Haidenröslein," heather rose of Goethe). The rose blooms in the " rose-garden " of the maiden; therefore, it is also a direct symbol of the libido. When the poet dreams that he is with the rose in the mother-womb of nature, then, psychologically, the fact is that his libido is with the mother. Here is an eternal germination and renewal. We have come across this motive already in the Hierosgamos hymn (Iliad XIV): The nuptials in the blessed West; that is to say, the union in and with the mother. Plutarch shows us this motive in naïve form in his tradition of the Osiris myth; Osiris and Isis copulating in the mother's womb. This is also perceived by Hölderlin as the enviable prerogative of the gods—to enjoy everlasting infancy. Thus, in Hyperion, he says:

" Fateless, like the sleeping nursling,
Breathe the Heavenly ones;
Chastely guarded in modest buds,
Their spirits blossom eternally,
And their quiet eyes
Gaze out in placid
Eternal serenity."

This quotation shows the meaning of heavenly bliss. Hölderlin never was able to forget this first and greatest happiness, the dreamy picture of which estranged him from real life. Moreover, in this poem, the ancient *motive of the twins* in the mother's womb is intimated. (Isis and Osiris in the mother's womb.) The motive is archaic. There is a legend in Frobenius of how the great serpent (appearing from the little serpent in the hollow tree, through the so-called stretching out of the serpent) has finally devoured all men (devouring mother—death), and only a pregnant woman remains alive; she digs a ditch, covers it with a stone (grave—mother's womb), and, living there, she gives birth to twins, the subsequent dragon-killers (the hero in double form, man and phallus, man and woman, man with his libido, the dying and rising sun).

This existence together in the mother is to be found also very beautifully expressed in an African myth (Frobenius):

" In the beginning, Obatala, the heaven, and Odudua, the earth, his wife, lay pressed firmly together in a calabas."

The guarding " in a modest bud " is an idea which has appeared already in Plutarch, where it is said that the sun was born in the morning from a flower bud. Brahma, too, comes from the bud, which also gave birth in Assam to the first human pair.

Humanity.
(An unfinished poem.)

" Scarcely sprouted from the waters, O Earth,
    Are thy old mountain tops and diffuse odors,
    While the first green islands, full of young woods, breathe delight
    Through the May air over the Ocean.

" And joyfully the eye of the Sun-god looked down
    Upon the firstlings of the trees and flowers;
    Laughing children of his youth, born from thee;
    When on the fairest of the islands . . .

Once lay thy most beautiful child under the grapes;
Lay after a mild night; in the dawn,
In the daybreak a child born to thee, O Earth!
And the boy looks up familiarly
To his Father, Helios,
And, tasting the sweet grapes,
He picked the sacred vine for his nurse,
And soon he is grown; the beasts
Fear him, for he is different from them:
This man; he is not like thee, the father,
For the lofty soul of the father,
Is in him boldly united with thy pleasures,
And thy sadness, O Earth,
He may resemble the eternal Nature,
The mother of Gods, the terrible Mother.

" Ah! therefore, O Earth,
His presumption drives him away from thy breast,
And thy gifts are vain, the tender ones;
Ever and ever too high does the proud heart beat.

" Out from the sweet meadow of his shores
Man must go into the flowerless waters,
And tho his groves shine with golden fruit,
Like the starry night, yet he digs,
He digs caves in the mountains, and seeks in the mines,
Far from the sacred rays of his father,
Faithless also to the Sun-god,
Who does not love weaklings, and mocks at cares.

" Ah! freer do the birds of the wood breathe:
Although the breast of man heaves wilder and more proudly,
His pride becomes fear, and the tender flowers
Of his peace do not bloom for long."

This poem betrays to us the beginning of the discord
between the poet and nature; he begins to be estranged
from reality, the natural actual existence.   It is a re-

markable idea how the little child chooses "the vine for his nurse." This Dionysian allusion is very old. In the significant blessing of Jacob it is said of Judah (Genesis, chap. xlix, verse 11):

"Binding his foal unto the vine, and his ass's colt unto the choice vine."

A Gnostic gem has been preserved upon which there is a representation of an ass suckling her foal, above which is the symbol of Cancer, and the circumscription D.N.I.H.Y.X.P.S.: Dominus Noster Jesus Christus, with the supplement Dei filius. As Justinus Martyr indignantly observes, the connections of the Christian legend with that of Dionysus are unmistakable. (Compare, for example, the miracle of the wine.) In the last-named legend the ass plays an important rôle. Generally speaking, the ass has an entirely different meaning in the Mediterranean countries than with us—an economic one. Therefore, it is a benediction when Jacob says (Genesis, chap. xlix, verse 14):

"Issachar is a strong ass couching down between two burdens."

The above-mentioned thought is altogether Oriental. Just as in Egypt the new-born sun is a bull-calf, in the rest of the Orient it can easily be an ass's foal, to whom the vine is the nurse. Hence the picture in the blessing of Jacob, where it is said of Judah:

"His eyes are ruddy with wine and his teeth white with milk."

The mock crucifix of the Palatine, with an ass's head, evidently alludes to a very significant background.

To Nature.

" While about thy veil I lingered, playing,
    And, like any bud, upon thee hung,[2]
Still I felt thy heart in every straying
    Sound about my heart that shook and clung.
While I groped with faith and painful yearning,
    To your picture, glowing and unfurled,
Still I found a place for all my burning
    Tears, and for my love I found a world!

" To the Sun my heart, before all others,
    Turned and felt its potent magicry;
And it called the stars its little brothers,[3]
    And it called the Spring, God's melody;
And each breeze in groves or woodlands fruity
    Held thy spirit—and that same sweet joy
Moved the well-springs of my heart with beauty—
    Those were golden days without alloy.

" Where the Spring is cool in every valley,[4]
    And the youngest bush and twig is green,
And about the rocks the grasses rally,
    And the branches show the sky between,
There I lay, imbibing every flower
    In a rapt, intoxicated glee,
And, surrounded by a golden shower,
    From their heights the clouds sank down to me.[5]

" Often, as a weary, wandering river
    Longs to join the ocean's placid mirth,
I have wept and lost myself forever
    In the fulness of thy love, O Earth!
Then—with all the ardor of my being—
    Forth I rushed from Time's slow apathy,
Like a pilgrim home from travel, fleeing
    To the arms of rapt Eternity.

" *Blessed be childhood's golden dreams, their power*
    Hid from me Life's dismal poverty:

All the heart's rich germs ye brought to flower;
Things I could not reach, ye gave to me! °
In thy beauty and thy light, O Nature,
    Free from care and from compulsion free,
Fruitful Love attained a kingly stature,
    Rich as harvests reaped in Arcady.

" That which brought me up, is dead and riven,
    Dead the youthful world which was my shield;
And this breast, which used to harbor heaven,
    Dead and dry as any stubble-field.
Still my Springlike sorrows sing and cover
    With their friendly comfort every smart—
But the morning of my life is over
    And the Spring has faded from my heart. . . .

" Shadows are the things that once we cherished;
    Love itself must fade and cannot bide;
Since the golden dreams of youth have perished,
    Even friendly Nature's self has died.
Heart, poor heart, those days could never show it—
    How far-off thy home, and where it lies . . .
Now, alas, thou nevermore wilt know it
    If a dream of it does not suffice."

Palinodia.

" What gathers about me, Earth, in your dusky, friendly green?
    What are you blowing towards me, Winds, what do you bring
        again?
    There is a rustling in all the tree-tops. . . .

    .   .   .   .   .

" Why do you wake my soul?
    Why do ye stir in me the past, ye Kind ones?
    Oh, spare me, and let them rest; oh, do not mock
    Those ashes of my joy. . . .

" O change your changeless gods—
    And grow in your youth over the old ones.

And if you would be akin to the mortals
The young girls will blossom for you.
And the young heroes will shine;
And, sweeter than ever,
Morning will play upon the cheeks of the happy ones;
And, ravishing-sweet, you will hear
The songs of those who are without care. . . .

" Ah, once the living waves of song
  Surged out of every bush to me;
  And still the heavenly ones glanced down upon me,
  Their eyes shining with joy."

.   .   .

The separation from the blessedness of childhood,
from youth even, has taken the golden glamour from
nature, and the future is hopeless emptiness. But what
robs nature of its glamour, and life of its joy, is the
poison of the retrospective longing, which harks back, in
order to sink into its own depths:

Empedocles.

" Thou seekest life—and a godly fire springs to thee,
  Gushing and gleaming, from the deeps of the earth;
  And, with shuddering longing,
  Throws thee down into the flames of Aetna.

" So, through a queen's wanton whim,
  Pearls are dissolved in wine—restrain her not!
  Didst thou not throw thy riches, Poet,
  Into the bright and bubbling cup!

" Still thou art holy to me, as the Power of Earth
  Which took thee away, lovely assassin! . . .
  And I would have followed the hero to the depths,
  Had Love not held me."

This poem betrays the secret longing for the maternal depths.[7]

He would like to be sacrificed in the chalice, dissolved in wine like pearls (the " crater " of rebirth), yet love holds him within the light of day. The libido still has an object, for the sake of which life is worth living. But were this object abandoned, then the libido would sink into the realm of the subterranean, the mother, who brings forth again:

Obituary.
(Unfinished poem.)

" Daily I go a different path.
  Sometimes into the green wood, sometimes to the bath in the
     spring;
  Or to the rocks where the roses bloom.
  From the top of the hill I look over the land,
  Yet nowhere, thou lovely one, nowhere in the light do I find
     thee;
  And in the breezes my words die away,
  The sacred words which once we had.

" Aye, thou art far away, O holy countenance!
  And the melody of thy life is kept from me,
  No longer overheard. And, ah, where are
  Thy magic songs which once soothed my heart
  With the peace of Heaven?
  How long it is, how long!
  The youth is aged; the very earth itself, which once smiled on me,
  Has grown different.

" Oh, farewell! The soul of every day departs, and, departing,
     turns to thee—
  And over thee there weeps
  The eye that, becoming brighter,
  Looks down,
  There where thou tarriest."

This distinctly suggests a renunciation, an envy of one's own youth, that time of freedom which one would like to retain through a deep-rooted dislike to all duty and endeavor which is denied an immediate pleasure reward. Painstaking work for a long time and for a remote object is not in the nature of child or primitive man. It is difficult to say if this can really be called laziness, but it seems to have not a little in common with it, in so far as the psychic life on a primitive stage, be it of an infantile or archaic type, possesses an extreme inertia and irresponsibility in production and non-production.

The last stanza portends evil, a gazing towards the other land, the distant coast of sunrise or sunset; love no longer holds the poet, the bonds with the world are torn and he calls loudly for assistance to the mother:

Achilles.

" Lordly son of the Gods! Because you lost your loved one,
  You went to the rocky coast and cried aloud to the flood,
  Till the depths of the holy abyss heard and echoed your grief,
  From the far reaches of your heart. Down, deep down, far
    from the clamor of ships,
  Deep under the waves, in a peaceful cave,
  Dwelt the beautiful Thetis, she who protected you, the Goddess
    of the Sea,
  Mother of the youth was she; the powerful Goddess,
  She who once had lovingly nursed him,
  On the rocky shore of his island; she who had made him a hero
  With the might of her strengthening bath and the powerful song
    of the waves.
  And the mother, mourning, hearkened to the cry of her child,
  And rose, like a cloud, from the bed of the sea,
  Soothing with tender embraces the pains of her darling;
  And he listened, while she, caressing, promised to soften his grief.

"Son of the Gods! Oh, were I like you, then could I confidently
Call on the Heavenly Ones to hearken to my secret grief.
But never shall I see this—I shall bear the disgrace
As if I never belonged to her, even though she thinks of me with
     tears.
Beneficent Ones! And yet Ye hear the lightest prayers of men.
Ah, how rapt and fervently I worshipped you, holy Light,
Since I have lived, the Earth and its fountains and woodlands,
Father Ether—and my heart has felt you about me, so ardent
     and pure—
Oh, soften my sorrows, ye Kind Ones,
That my soul may not be silenced, may not be struck dumb too
     early;
That I may live and thank Ye, O Heavenly Powers,
With joyful songs through all the hurrying days.
Thank ye for gifts of the past, for the joys of vanished Youth—
And then, pray, take me, the lonely one,
Graciously, unto yourselves."

These poems describe more plainly than could be depicted with meagre words the persistent arrest and the constantly growing estrangement from life, the gradual deep immersion into the maternal abyss of the individual being. The apocalyptic song of Patmos is strangely related to these songs of retrogressive longing. It enters as a dismal guest surrounded by the mist of the depths, the gathering clouds of insanity, bred through the mother. In it the primitive thoughts of the myth, the suggestion clad in symbols, of the sun-like death and resurrection of life, again burst forth. Similar things are to be found in abundance among sick people of this sort.

I reproduce some significant fragments from Patmos:

          " Near is the God
          And hard to comprehend,

> But where Danger threatens
> The Rescuer appears."

These words mean that the libido has now sunk to the lowest depths, where " the danger is great." (Faust, Part II, Mother scene.) There " the God is near "; there man may find the inner sun, his own nature, sun-like and self-renewing, hidden in the mother-womb like the sun in the nighttime:

> ". . . In Chasms
> And in darkness dwell
> The eagles; and fresh and fearlessly
> The Sons of the Alps pass swiftly over the abyss
> Upon lightly swinging bridges."

With these words the dark phantastic poem passes on. The eagle, the bird of the sun, dwells in darkness—the libido has hidden itself, but high above it the inhabitants of the mountains pass, probably the gods (" Ye are walking above in the light "), symbols of the sun wandering across the sky, like the eagle flying over the depths:

> ". . . Above and around are reared
> The summits of Time,
> And the loved ones, though near,
> Live on deeply separated mountains.
> So give us waters of innocence,
> And give us wings of true understanding,
> With which to pass across and to return again."

The first is a gloomy picture of the mountains and of time—although caused by the sun wandering over the mountains, the following picture a nearness, and at the same time separation, of the lovers, and seems to hint at life in the underworld,[8] where he is united with all that once was dear to him, and yet cannot enjoy the happiness of reunion, because it is all shadows and unreal and devoid of life. Here the one who descends drinks the waters of innocence, the waters of childhood, the drink of rejuvenation,[9] so wings may grow, and, winged, he may soar up again into life, like the winged sun, which arises like a swan from the water (" Wings, to pass across and to return again ") :

> " . . . So I spoke, and lo, a genie
> Carried me off, swifter than I had imagined,
> And farther than ever I had thought
> From my own house!
> It grew dark
> As I went in the twilight.
> The shadowy wood,
> And the yearning brooks of my home-land
> Grew vague behind me—
> And I knew the country no longer."

After the dark and obscure words of the introduction, wherein the poet expresses the prophecy of what is to come, the sun journey begins (" night journey in the sea ") towards the east, towards the ascent, towards the mystery of eternity and rebirth, of which Nietzsche also dreams, and which he expressed in significant words:

" Oh, how could I not be ardent for eternity, and for the nuptial ring of rings—the ring of the return! Never yet have I found the woman from whom I wish children, unless she would be this woman whom I love; for I love thee, O eternity."

Hölderlin expresses this same longing in a beautiful symbol, the individual traits of which are already familiar to us:

> ". . . But soon in a fresh radiance
> Mysteriously
> Blossoming in golden smoke,
> With the rapidly growing steps of the sun,
> Making a thousand summits fragrant,
> Asia arose!
> And, dazzled,
> I sought one whom I knew;
> For unfamiliar to me were the broad roads,
> Where from Tmolus
> Comes the gilded Pactol,
> And Taurus stands and Messagis—
> And the gardens are full of flowers.
> But high up in the light
> The silvery snow gleams, a silent fire;
> And, as a symbol of eternal life,
> On the impassable walls,
> Grows the ancient ivy.[10]
> And carried by columns of living cedars and laurels
> Are the solemn, divinely built palaces."

The symbol is apocalyptic, the maternal city in the land of eternal youth, surrounded by the verdure and flowers of imperishable spring.[11] The poet identifies himself here with John, who lived on Patmos, who was once associated with "the sun of the Highest," and saw him face to face:

> "There at the Mystery of the Vine they met,
> There at the hour of the Holy Feast they gathered,   .
> And—feeling the approach of Death in his great, quiet soul,

The Lord, pouring out his last love, spoke,
And then he died.
Much could be said of it—
How his triumphant glance,
The happiest of all,
Was seen by his companions, even at the last.

.   .   .   .

Therefore he sent the Spirit unto them,
And the house trembled, solemnly;
And, with distant thunder,
The storm of God rolled over the cowering heads
Where, deep in thought,
The heroes of death were assembled. . . .
Now, when he, in parting,
Appeared once more before them,
Then the kingly day, the day of the sun, was put out,
And the gleaming sceptre, formed of his rays,
Was broken—and suffered like a god itself.
Yet it shall return and glow again
When the right time comes."

The fundamental pictures are the sacrificial death and the resurrection of Christ, like the self-sacrifice of the sun, which voluntarily breaks its sceptre, the fructifying rays, in the certain hope of resurrection. The following comments are to be noted in regard to "the sceptre of rays": Spielrein's patient says, "God pierces through the earth with his rays." The earth, in the patient's mind, has the meaning of woman. She also comprehends the sunbeam in mythologic fashion as something solid: "Jesus Christ has shown me his love, by striking against the window with a sunbeam." Among other insane patients I have come across the same idea of the solid substance of the sunbeam. Here there is also a hint of the phallic nature of the instrument which is associated with the hero. Thor's hammer, which, cleaving the earth, penetrates deeply into it, may be compared to the foot of Kaineus. The hammer is retained in the interior of the earth, like the treasure, and, in the course of time, it gradually comes again to the surface ("the treasure blooms"), meaning that it was born again from the earth. (Compare what has been said concerning the etymology of "swelling.") On many monuments Mithra holds a peculiar object in his hands, which Cumont compares to a half-filled tube. Dieterich proves from his papyrus text that the object is the shoulder of the bull, the bear constellation. The shoulder has an indirect phallic meaning, for it is the part which is wanting in Pelops. Pelops was slaughtered by his father, Tantalus, dismembered, and boiled in a kettle, to make a meal for the gods. Demeter had unsuspectingly eaten the shoulder from this feast, when Zeus discovered the outrage. He had the pieces thrown back into the kettle, and, with the help of the life-dispensing Clotho, Pelops was regenerated, and the shoulder which was missing was replaced by an ivory one. This substitution is a close parallel to the substitution of the missing phallus of Osiris. Mithra is represented in a special ceremony, holding the bull's shoulder over Sol, his son and vice-regent. This scene may be compared to a sort of dedication, or accolade (something like the ceremony of confirmation). The blow of the hammer as a generating, fructifying, inspiring function is retained as a folk-custom and expressed by striking with the twig of life, which has the significance

of a charm of fertility. In the neuroses, the sexual meaning of castigation plays an important part, for among
many children castigation may elicit a sexual orgasm.
The ritual act of striking has the same significance of
generating (fructifying), and is, indeed, merely a variant
of the original phallic ceremonial. Of similar character
to the bull's shoulder is the cloven hoof of the devil, to
which a sexual meaning also appertains. The ass's jawbone wielded by Samson has the same worth. In the
Polynesian Maui myth the jawbone, the weapon of the
hero, is derived from the man-eating woman, Muri-
ranga-whenua, whose body swells up enormously from
lusting for human flesh (Frobenius). Hercules' club is
made from the wood of the maternal olive tree. Faust's
key also " knows the mothers." The libido springs from
the mother, and with this weapon alone can man overcome death.

It corresponds to the phallic nature of the ass's jawbone, that at the place where Samson threw it God caused
a spring to gush forth [12] (springs from the horse's tread,
footsteps, horse's hoof). To this relation of meanings
belongs the magic wand, the sceptre in general.
Σκῆπτρον belongs to σκᾶπος, σκηπάνων, σκήπων =
staff; σκηπτός = storm-wind; Latin *scapus* = shaft,
stock, scapula, shoulder; Old High German *Scaft* =
spear, lance.[13] We meet once more in this compilation
those connections which are already well known to us:
Sun-phallus as tube of the winds, lance and shoulder-
blade.

The passage from Asia through Patmos to the Chris-

tian mysteries in the poem of Hölderlin is apparently a
superficial connection, but in reality a very ingenious train
of thought; namely, the entrance into death and the land
beyond as a self-sacrifice of the hero, for the attainment
of immortality.   At this time, when the sun has set, when
love is apparently dead, man awaits in mysterious joy
the renewal of all life:

> ". . . And Joy it was
> From now on
> To live in the loving night and see
> The eyes of innocence hold the unchanging
> Depths of all wisdom."

Wisdom dwells in the depths, the wisdom of the mother:
being one with it, insight is obtained into the meaning
of deeper things, into all the deposits of primitive times,
the strata of which have been preserved in the soul.
Hölderlin, in his diseased ecstasy, feels once more the
greatness of the things seen, but he does not care to bring
up to the light of day that which he had found in the
depths—in this he differs from Faust.

> " And it is not an evil, if a few
> Are lost and never found, and if the speech
> Conceals the living sound;
> Because each godly work resembles ours;
> And yet the Highest does not plan it all—
> The great pit bears two irons,
> And the glowing lava of Aetna. . . .
> Would I had the power
> To build an image and see the Spirit—
> See it as it was!"

He allows only one hope to glimmer through, formed in scanty words:

> " He wakes the dead;
> They who are not enchained and bound,
> They who are not unwrought.
> . . . And if the Heavenly Ones
> Now, as I believe, love me—
> . . . Silent is his sign [14]
> In the dusky sky. And one stands under it
> His whole life long—for Christ still lives."

But, as once Gilgamesh, bringing back the magic herb from the west land, was robbed of his treasure by the demon serpent, so does Hölderlin's poem die away in a painful lament, which betrays to us that no victorious resurrection will follow his descent to the shadows:

> ". . . Ignominiously
> A power tears our heart away,
> For sacrifices the heavenly ones demand."

This recognition, that man must sacrifice the retrogressive longing (the incestuous libido) before the " heavenly ones " tear away the sacrifice, and at the same time the entire libido, came too late to the poet. Therefore, I take it to be a wise counsel which the unconscious gives our author, to sacrifice the infantile hero. This sacrifice is best accomplished, as is shown by the most obvious meaning, through a complete devotion to life, in which all the libido unconsciously bound up in familial bonds, must be brought outside into human contact. For it is necessary for the well-being of the adult individual, who in his childhood was merely an atom revolving in a rotary system, to become himself the centre of a new system. That such a step implies the solution or, at least, the energetic treatment of the individual sexual problem is obvious, for unless this is done the unemployed libido will inexorably remain fixed in the incestuous bond, and will prevent individual freedom in essential matters. Let us keep in mind that Christ's teaching separates man from his family without consideration, and in the talk with Nicodemus we saw the specific endeavor of Christ to procure activation of the incest libido. Both tendencies serve the same goal—the liberation of man; the Jew from his extraordinary fixation to the family, which does not imply higher development, but greater weakness and more uncontrolled incestuous feeling, produced the compensation of the compulsory ceremonial of the cult and the religious fear of the incomprehensible Jehovah. When man, terrified by no laws and no furious fanatics or prophets, allows his incestuous libido full play, and does not liberate it for higher purposes, then he is under the influence of unconscious compulsion. For compulsion is the unconscious wish. (Freud.) He is under the dominance of the libido εἱμαρμένη* and his destiny does not lie in his own hands; his adventures, Τύχαι καὶ Μοῖραι,† fall from the stars. His unconscious incestuous libido, which thus is applied in its most primitive form, fixes the man, as regards his love type, in a corresponding primitive stage, the stage of ungovernableness and surrender to the emotions. Such was the psychologic situation of

* Fate.   † Chances and fates.

the passing antiquity, and the Redeemer and Physician of that time was he who endeavored to educate man to the sublimation of the incestuous libido.[15]   The destruction of slavery was the necessary condition of that sublimation, for antiquity had not yet recognized the duty of work and work as a duty, as a social need of fundamental importance. Slave labor was compulsory work, the counterpart of the equally disastrous compulsion of the libido of the privileged.   It was only the obligation of the individual to work which made possible in the long run that regular " drainage " of the unconscious, which was inundated by the continual regression of the libido.   Indolence is the beginning of all vice, because in a condition of slothful dreaming the libido has abundant opportunity for sinking into itself, in order to create compulsory obligations by means of regressively re-animated incestuous bonds.   The best liberation is through *regular work*.[16]   Work, however, is salvation only when it is a free act, and has in itself nothing of infantile compulsion.   In this respect, religious ceremony appears in a high degree as organized inactivity, and at the same time as the forerunner of modern work.

Miss Miller's vision treats the problem of the sacrifice of the infantile longing, in the first place, as an individual problem, but if we cast a glance at the form of this presentation, then we will become aware that here it must concern something, which is also a problem of humanity in general.   For the symbols employed, the serpent which killed the horse [17] and the hero voluntarily sacrificing himself, are primitive figures of phantasies and religious myths streaming up from the unconscious.

In so far as the world and all within it is, above all, a thought, which is credited with transcendental "substance" through the empirical need of the same, there results from the sacrifice of the regressive libido the creation of the world; and, psychologically speaking, the world in general. For him who looks backward the world, and even the infinite starry sky, is the mother [18] who bends over and encloses him on all sides, and from the renunciation of this idea and from the longing for this idea arises the image of the world. From this most simple fundamental thought, which perhaps appears strange to us only because it is conceived according to the *principle of desire and not the principle of reality*,[19] results the significance of the cosmic sacrifice. A good example of this is the slaying of the Babylonian primitive mother Tiâmat, the dragon, whose body is destined to form the heaven and the earth. We come upon this thought in its most complete form in Hindoo philosophy of the most ancient date; namely, in songs of Rigveda. In Rigveda 10: 81, 4, the song inquires:

" What was the tree, what wood in sooth produced it, from which
    they fashioned out the earth and heaven?
Ye thoughtful men inquire within your spirit, whereon he stood
    when he established all things."

Viçvakarman, the All-Creator, who created the world from the unknown tree, did so as follows:

" He who, sacrificing, entered into all these beings
    As a wise sacrificer, our Father, who,
    Striving for blessings through prayer,
    Hiding his origin,
    Entered this lowly world,
    What and who has served him
    As a resting-place and a support? " [20]

Rigveda 10: 90, gives answer to these questions.
Purusha is the primal being who

". . . covered earth on every side and
    Spread ten fingers' breadth beyond."

One sees that Purusha is a sort of Platonic world soul,
who surrounds the world from without. Of Purusha it
is said:

" Being born he overtopped the earth
    Before, behind, and in all places."

The mother symbolism is plain, it seems to me, in the
idea of Purusha. He represents the mother-imago and
the libido of the child clinging to her. From this assumption all that follows is very easily explained:

" As sacrificial animal on the bed of straw
    Was dedicated the Purusha,
    Who was born on the straw,
    Whom the Gods, the Blest, and the Wise,
    Meeting there, sacrificed."

This verse is very remarkable; if one wishes to stretch
this mythology out on the procrustean bed of logic, sore
violence would have to be committed. It is an incredibly

phantastic conception that, beside the gods, ordinary
" wise men " unite in sacrificing the primitive being, aside
from the circumstance that, beside the primitive being,
nothing had existed in the beginning (that is to say, before
the sacrifice), as we shall soon see. If the great mystery
of the mother sacrifice is meant thereby, then all becomes
clear:

> " From that great general sacrifice
> The dripping fat was gathered up.
> He formed the creatures of the air,
> And animals both wild and tame.
> From that great general sacrifice
> Richas and Sama-hymns were born;
> Therefrom the metres were produced,
> The Yajus had its birth from it.
>
> " The moon was gendered from his mind
> And from his eye the Sun had birth;
> Indra and Agni from his mouth
> Were born, and Vâyu from his breath.
>
> " Forth from his navel came midair;
> The sky was fashioned from his head;
> Earth from his feet, and from his ears
> The regions. Thus they formed the worlds."

It is evident that by this is meant not a physical, but a
psychological cosmogony. The world arises when man
discovers it. He discovers it when he sacrifices the
mother; that is to say, when he has freed himself from
the midst of his unconscious lying in the mother. That
which impels him forward to this discovery may be interpreted psychologically as the so-called " Incest bar-

rier " of Freud. The incest prohibition places an end to the childish longing for the food-giving mother, and compels the libido, gradually becoming sexual, into the path of the biological aim. The libido forced away from the mother by the incest prohibition seeks for the sexual object in the place of the forbidden mother. In this wider psychologic sense, which expresses itself in the allegoric language of the "incest prohibition," "mother," etc., must be understood Freud's paradoxical sentence, " Originally we have known only sexual objects." [21] This sentence must be understood psychologically throughout, in the sense of a world image created from within outwards, which has, in the first place, nothing to do with the so-called " objective " idea of the world. This is to be understood as a new edition of the subjective idea of the world corrected by reality. Biology, as a science of objective experience, would have to reject unconditionally Freud's proposition, for, as we have made clear above, the function of reality can only be partly sexual; in another equally important part it is self-preservation. The matter appears different for that thought which accompanies the biological function as an epiphenomenon. As far as our knowledge reaches, the individual act of thought is dependent wholly or in greatest part on the existence of a highly differentiated brain, whereas the function of reality (adaptation to reality) is something which occurs in all living nature as wholly independent from the act of thought. This important proposition of Freud's applies only to the act of thought, for thinking, as we may recognize from manifold traces, arose dynami-

cally from the libido, which was split off from the original
object at the "incest barrier" and became actual when
the first budding sexual emotions began to flow in the
current of the libido which goes to the mother. Through
the incest barrier the sexual libido is forced away from the
identification with the parents, and introverted for lack
of adequate activity. It is the sexual libido which forces
the growing individual slowly away from his family. If
this necessity did not exist, then the family would always
remain clustered together in a solid group. Hence the
neurotic always renounces a complete erotic experience,[22]
in order that he may remain a child. Phantasies seem to
arise from the introversion of the sexual libido. Since the
first childish phantasies most certainly do not attain the
quality of a conscious plan, and as phantasies likewise (even
among adults) are almost always the direct derivates of
the unconscious, it is, therefore, highly probable that the
first phantastic manifestations arise from an act of regression. As we illustrated earlier, the regression goes
back to the presexual stage, as many traces show. Here
the sexual libido obtains again, so to speak, that universal
capacity of application, or capacity for displacement,
which it actually possessed at that stage when the sexual
application was not yet discovered. Naturally, no adequate object is found in the presexual stage for the regressive sexual libido, but only surrogates, which always leave
a wish; namely, the wish to have the surrogate as similar
as possible to the sexual goal. This wish is secret, however, for it is really an incest wish. The unsatisfied unconscious wish creates innumerable secondary objects,

symbols for the primitive object, the mother (as the Rigveda says, the creator of the world, "hiding his origin," enters into things). From this the thought or the phantasies proceed, as a desexualized manifestation of *an originally sexual libido.*

From the standpoint of the libido, the term "incest barrier" corresponds to one aspect, but the matter, however, may be considered from another point of view.

The time of undeveloped sexuality, about the third and the fourth year, is, at the same time, considered externally, the period when the child finds himself confronted with increased demands from the world of reality. He can walk, speak and independently attend to a number of other things. He sees himself in a relation to a world of unlimited possibilities, but in which he dares to do little or nothing, because he is as yet too much of a baby and cannot get on without his mother. At this time mother should be exchanged for the world. Against this the past rises as the greatest resistance; this is always so whenever man would undertake a new adaptation. In spite of all evidence and against all conscious resolutions, the unconscious (the past) always enforces its standpoint as resistance. In this difficult position, precisely at this period of developing sexuality, we see the dawning of the mind. The problem of the child at this period is the discovery of the world and of the great trans-subjective reality. For that he must lose the mother; every step out into the world means a step away from the mother. Naturally, all that which is retrogressive in men rebels against this step, and energetic attempts are

made against this adaptation in the first place. Therefore, this period of life is also that in which the first
clearly developed neuroses arise. The tendency of this
age is one directly opposed to that of dementia præcox.
The child seeks to win the world and to leave the mother
(this is a necessary result). The dementia præcox patient, however, seeks to leave the world and to regain the
subjectivity of childhood. We have seen that in dementia præcox the recent adaptation to reality is replaced
by an archaic mode of adaptation; that is to say, the
recent idea of the world is rejected in favor of an archaic
idea of the world. When the child renounces his task of
adaptation to reality, or has considerable difficulties in
this direction, then we may expect that the recent adaptation will again be replaced by archaic modes of adaptation. It would, therefore, be conceivable that through
regression in children archaic products would naturally
be unearthed; that is to say, old ways of functioning of
the thought system, which is inborn with the brain differentiation, would be awakened.

According to my available but as yet unpublished material, a remarkably archaic and at the same time generally applicable character seems to appertain to infantile
phantasy, quite comparable with the products of dementia præcox. It does not seem improbable that through
regression at this age those same associations of elements
and analogies are reawakened which formerly constituted
the archaic idea of the world. When we now attempt to
investigate the nature of these elements, a glance at the
psychology of myths is sufficient to show us that the

archaic idea was chiefly sexual anthropomorphism. It appears that these things in the unconscious childish phantasy play an extraordinary rôle, as we can recognize from examples taken at random. Just as the sexualism of neuroses is not to be taken literally but as regressive phantasy and symbolic compensation for a recent unachieved adaptation, so is the sexualism of the early infantile phantasy, especially the incest problem, a regressive product of the revival of the archaic modes of function, outweighing actuality. On this account I have expressed myself very vaguely in this work, I am sure, in regard to the incest problem. This is done in order not to be responsible for the idea that I understand by it a gross sexual inclination towards the parents. The true facts of the case are much more complicated, as my investigations point out. Originally incest probably never possessed particularly great significance as such, because cohabitation with an old woman for all possible motives could hardly be preferred to mating with a young woman. It seems that the mother has acquired incestuous significance only psychologically. Thus, for example, the incestuous unions of antiquity were not a result of a love inclination, but of a special superstition, which is most intimately bound up with the mythical ideas here treated. A Pharaoh of the second dynasty is said to have married his sister, his daughter and his granddaughter; the Ptolemies were accustomed also to marriage with sisters; Kambyses married his sister; Artaxerxes married his two daughters; Qobad I (sixth century A. D.) married his daughter. The Satrap Sysimithres married his mother. These incestuous unions are explained by the circumstance that in the Zend Avesta the marriage of relatives was directly commanded; [23] it emphasized the resemblance of rulers to the divinity, and, therefore, was more of an artificial than a natural arrangement, because it originated more from a theoretical than from a biological inclination. (A practical impetus towards that lay often in the peculiar laws of inheritance left over from the *Mutter recht,* " maternal right " [matriarchal], period.) The confusion which certainly frequently involved the barbarians of antiquity in regard to the choice of their sexual objects cannot very well be measured by the standard of present-day love psychology. In any case, the incest of the semi-animal past is in no way proportionate to the enormous significance of the incest phantasy among civilized people. This disproportion enforces the assumption that the incest prohibition which we meet even amongst relatively lower races concerns rather the mythical ideas than the biological damage; therefore, the ethnical prohibition almost always concerns the mother and seldom the father. Incest prohibition can be understood, therefore, as a result of regression, and as the result of a libidinous anxiety, which regressively attacks the mother. Naturally, it is difficult or impossible to say from whence this anxiety may have come. I merely venture to suggest that it may have been a question of a primitive separation of the pairs of opposites which are hidden in the will of life: the will for life and for death. It remains obscure what adaptation the primitive man tried to evade through introversion and regression to the parents; but, according to the analogy of the soul life in general, it may be assumed that the libido, which disturbed the initial equilibrium of becoming and of ceasing to be, had been stored up in the attempt to make an especially difficult adaptation, and from which it recedes even today.

After this long digression, let us turn back to the song of the Rigveda. Thinking and a conception of the world arose from a shrinking back from stern reality, and it is only after man has regressively assured himself again of the protective parental power [24] that he enters life wrapped in a dream of childhood shrouded in magic superstititions; that is to say, " thinking," [25] for he, timidly sacrificing his best and assuring himself of the favor of the invisible powers, step by step develops to greater power, in the degree that he frees himself from his retrogressive longing and the original lack of harmony in his being.

Rigveda 10, 90, concludes with the exceedingly significant verse, which is of greatest importance for the Christian mysteries as well:

" Gods, sacrificing, rendered homage to the sacrifice: these were
    the earliest holy ordinances,
The mighty ones attained the height of heaven, there where the
    Sâdhyas, goddesses of old, are dwelling."

Through the sacrifice a fulness of power was attained, which extends up to the power of the " parents." Thus the sacrifice has also the meaning of a psychologic maturation process.

In the same manner that the world originated through sacrifice, through the renunciation of the retrospective mother libido, thus, according to the teachings of the Upanishads, is produced the new condition of man, which may be termed the immortal. This new condition is again attained through a sacrifice; namely, through the sacrificial horse which is given a cosmic significance in the teaching of the Upanishads. What the sacrificial horse means is told by Brihadâranyaka-Upanishad 1 : 1 :

" Om!

" 1. The dawn is truly the head of the sacrificial horse, the sun his eye, the wind his breath, his mouth the all-spreading fire, the year is the body of the sacrificial horse. The sky is his back, the atmosphere his body cavity, the earth the vault of his belly, the poles are his sides, the space between the poles his ribs, the seasons his limbs, the months and half-months his joints, day and night his feet, the stars his bones, the clouds his flesh, the food, which he digests, are the deserts; the rivers, his veins; liver and lungs, the mountains; the herbs and trees, his hair; the rising sun is his fore-part, the setting sun his hind-part. When he shows his teeth, that is lightning; when he trembles, that is thunder; when he urinates, that is rain; his voice is speech.

" 2. The day, in truth, has originated for the horse as the sacrificial dish, which stands before him; his cradle is in the world-sea towards the East; the night has originated for him as the sacrificial dish, which stands behind him; its cradle is in the world-sea of the evening; these two dishes originated in order to surround the horse. As a charger he generated the gods, as champion he produced the Gandharvas, as a racer the demons, as horse man-kind. The Ocean is his relative, the ocean his cradle."

As Deussen remarks, the sacrificial horse has the significance of a *renunciation of the universe.* When the horse is sacrificed, then the world is sacrificed and de-

stroyed, as it were—a train of thought which Schopenhauer also had in mind, and which appears as a product of
a diseased mind in Schreber.[26] The horse in the above
text stands between two sacrificial vessels, from one of
which it comes and to the other of which it goes, just as
the sun passes from morning to evening. The horse,
therefore, signifies the libido, which has passed into the
world. We previously saw that the "mother libido"
must be sacrificed in order to produce the world; here the
world is destroyed by the repeated sacrifice of the same
libido, which once belonged to the mother. The horse
can, therefore, be substituted as a symbol for this libido,
because, as we saw, it had manifold connections with
the mother.[27] The sacrifice of the horse can only
produce another state of introversion, which is similar to that before the creation of the world. The
position of the horse between the two vessels, which represent the producing and the devouring mother, hint at
the idea of life enclosed in the ovum; therefore, the vessels are destined to "surround" the horse. That this
is actually so the Brihadâranyaka-Upanishad 3 : 3 proves:

"1. From where have the descendants of Parikshit come, that
I ask thee, Yâjñavalkya! From where came the descendants of
Parikshit?

"2. Yâjñavalkya spake: 'He has told thee, they have come
from where all come, who offer up the sacrificial horse. That is
to say, this world extends so far as two and thirty days of the
chariot of the Gods (the sun) reach. This (world) surrounds
the earth twice around. This earth surrounds the ocean twice
around. There is, as broad as the edge of a razor or as the wing
of a fly, a space between (the two shells of the egg of the world).

These were brought by Indra as a falcon to the wind: and the
wind took them up into itself and carried them where were the
offerers of the sacrificial horse.   Somewhat like this he spoke
(Gandharva to thee) and praised the wind.'

" Therefore is the wind the special (vyashti) and the wind the
universal (samashti).   He, who knows this, defends himself from
dying again."

As this text tells us, the offerers of the sacrificial horse
come in that *narrowest fissure* between the shells of the
egg of the world, at that place, where the shells *unite and
where they are divided.*   The fissure *(vagina)* in the maternal world soul is designated by Plato in " Timaeus " by
X, the symbol of the cross.   Indra, who as a falcon has
stolen the soma (the treasure attainable with difficulty),
brings, as Psychopompos, the souls to the wind, to the
generating pneuma, which carries them forward to the
fissure or vagina, to the point of union, to the entrance
into the maternal egg.   This train of thought of the
Hindoo philosophy briefly and concisely summarizes the
sense of innumerable myths; at the same time it is a
striking example of the fact that philosophy is internally
nothing else but a refined and sublimated mythology.   It
is brought to this refined state by the influence of the cor-
rector of reality.[28]   We have emphasized the fact that
in the Miller drama the horse is the first to die, as the
animal brother of the hero.   (Corresponding to the early
death of the half-animal Eabani, the brother friend of
Gilgamesh.)   This sacrificial death recalls the whole
category of mythological animal sacrifices.   Volumes
could be filled with parallels, but we must limit ourselves
here to suggestions.   The sacrificial animal, where it has

lost the primitive meaning of the simple sacrificial gift, and has taken a higher religious significance, stands in a close relation to both the hero and the divinity. The animal represents the god himself; [29] thus the bull [30] represents Zagreus, Dionysus and Mithra; the lamb represents Christ, [31] etc. As we are aware, the animal symbols represent the animal libido. The sacrifice of the animal means, therefore, the sacrifice of the animal nature. This is most clearly expressed in the religious legend of Attis. Attis is the son lover of the divine mother, Agdistis Cybele. Agdistis was characteristically androgynous, [32] as symbol of the mother-libido, like the tree; really a clear indication that the mother-imago has in addition to the significance of the likeness of the real mother the meaning of the mother of humanity, the libido in general. Driven mad by the insanity-breeding mother enamored of him, he emasculates himself, and that under a pine tree. (The pine tree plays an important rôle in his service. Every year a pine tree was wreathed about and upon it an image of Attis was hung, and then it was cut down, which represents the castration.) The blood, which spurted to the earth, was transformed into budding violets. Cybele now took this pine tree, bore it into her cavern and there wept over it. (Pietà.) The chthonic mother takes her son with her into the cavern—namely, into the womb— according to another version. Attis was transformed into the pine tree. The tree here has an essentially phallic meaning; on the contrary, the attaching of the image of Attis to the tree refers also to the maternal meaning. ("To be attached to the mother.") In Ovid ("Metamorphoses," Book X) the pine tree is spoken of as follows:

> " Grata deum matri, siquidem Cybeleius Attis
> Exuit hac hominem, truncoque induruit illo." *

The transformation into the pine tree is evidently a burial in the mother, just as Osiris was overgrown by the heather. Upon the Attis bas-relief of Coblenz Attis appears *growing out of a tree,* which is interpreted by Mannhardt as the " life-principle " of vegetation inherent in the tree. It is probably a tree birth, just as with Mithra. (Relief of Heddernheim.) As Firmicus observes, in the Isis and Osiris cult and also in the cult of the virgin Persephone, tree and image had played a rôle.[33] Dionysus had the surname Dendrites, and in Boeotia he is said to have been called ἔνδενδρος, meaning " in a tree." (At the birth of Dionysus, Megaira planted the pine tree on the Kithairon.) The Pentheus myth bound up with the Dionysus legend furnishes the remarkable and supplementary counterpart to the death of Attis, and the subsequent lamentation. Pentheus,[34] curious to espy the orgies of the Maenades, *climbed upon a pine tree,* but he was observed by his mother; the Maenades cut down the tree, and Pentheus, taken for an animal, was torn by them in frenzy,[35] his own mother being the first to rush upon him. In this myth the phallic meaning of the tree (cutting down, castration) and its maternal significance (mounting and the

---

* Beloved of the mother of the gods, inasmuch as the Cybeline Attis sheds his human shape in this way and stiffens into this tree trunk.

sacrificial death of the son) is present; at the same time the supplementary counterpart to the Pietà is apparent, the "terrible mother." The feast of Attis was celebrated as a lamentation and then as a joy in the spring. (Good Friday and Easter.) The priests of Attis-Cybele worship were often eunuchs, and were called Galloi.[36] The archigallus was called Atys (Attis).[37] Instead of the animal castration, the priests merely scratched their arms until they bled. (Arm in place of phallus, "the twisting of arms.") A similar symbolism of the sacrificial impulse is met in the Mithraic religion, where essential parts of the mysteries consist in the catching and the subduing of the bull.

A parallel figure to Mithra is the primitive man Gayomard. He was created together with his bull, and the two lived for six thousand years in a blissful state. But when the world came into the cycle of the seventh sign of the Zodiac (Libra) the evil principle entered. Libra is astrologically the so-called positive domicile of Venus; the evil principle, therefore, came under the dominion of the goddess of love (destruction of the sun-hero through the mother-wife—snake, whore, etc). As a result, after thirty years, Gayomard and his bull died. (The trials of Zartusht lasted also thirty years; compare the span of Christ's life.) Fifty-five species of grain came from the dead bull, twelve kinds of salubrious plants, etc. The sperma of the bull entered into the moon for purification, but the sperma of Gayomard entered into the sun. This circumstance possibly suggests a rather feminine meaning of bull. Gosh or Drvâçpa is the soul of the bull, and was worshipped as a female divinity.   She would not, at first, from diffidence, become the goddess of the herds, until the coming of Zarathustra was announced to her as consolation.   This has its parallel in the Hindoo Purâna, where the coming of Krishna was promised the earth.   (A complete analogy to Christ.[38]) She, too, travels in her chariot, like Ardvîçûra, the goddess of love.   The soul of the bull is, therefore, decidedly feminine.   This myth of Gayomard repeats only in an altered form the primitive conception of the closed ring of a male-female divinity, self-begetting and forth-bringing.

Like the sacrificial bull, the fire, the sacrifice of which we have already discussed in Chapter III, has a feminine nature among the Chinese, according to the commentaries [39] of the philosopher Tschwang-Tse:

"The spirit of the hearth is called Ki. He is clad in bright red, which resembles fire, and appears as a lovely, attractive maiden."

In the " Book of Rites " it is said:

"Wood is burned in the flames for the spirit of Au. This sacrifice to Au is a sacrifice to old departed women."

These spirits of the hearth and fire are the souls of departed cooks and, therefore, are called " old women." The kitchen god develops from this pre-Buddhistic tradition and becomes later (male sex) the ruler of the family and the *mediator between family and god*. Thus the old feminine fire spirit becomes a species of Logos. (Compare with this the remarks in Chapter III.)

From the bull's sperma the progenitors of the cattle came, as well as two hundred and seventy-two species of useful animals. According to Mînôkhired, Gayomard had destroyed the Dév Azûr, who was considered the demon of evil appetites.[40] In spite of the efforts of Zara-thustra, this demon remained longest on the earth. He was destroyed at last at the resurrection, like Satan in the Apocalypse of John. In another version it is said that Angromainyus and the serpent were left until the last, so as to be destroyed by Ahuramazda himself. Accord-ing to a surmise by Kern, Zarathustra may mean " golden-star " and be identical with Mithra. Mithra's name is connected with neo-Persian *Mihr,* which means " sun and love."

In Zagreus we see that the bull is also identical with the god; hence the bull sacrifice is a god sacrifice, but on a primitive stage. The animal symbol is, so to speak, only a part of the hero; he sacrifices only his animal; therefore, symbolically, renounces only his animal nature. The internal participation in the sacrifice [41] is expressed excellently in the anguished ecstatic countenance of the bull-slaying Mithra. He does it willingly and unwill-ingly [42] hence the somewhat hysterical expression which has some similarity to the well-known mawkish counte-nance of the Crucified of Guido Reni. Benndorf says: [43]

" The features, which, especially in the upper portion, bear an absolutely ideal character, have an extremely morbid expression."

Cumont [44] himself says of the facial expression of the Tauroctonos:

" The countenance, which may be seen in the best reproductions, is that of a young man of an almost feminine beauty; the head has a quantity of curly hair, which, rising up from the forehead, surrounds him as with a halo; the head is slightly tilted backwards, so that the glance is directed towards the heavens, and the contraction of the brows and the lips give a strange expression of sorrow to the face." [45]

The Ostian head of Mithra Tauroctonos, illustrated in Cumont, has, indeed, an expression which we recognize in our patients as one of sentimental resignation. *Sentimentality is repressed brutality.* Hence the exceedingly sentimental pose, which had its counterpart in the symbolism of the shepherd and the lamb of contemporaneous Christianity, with the addition of infantilism. [46]

Meanwhile, it is only his animal nature which the god sacrifices; that is to say, his sexuality, [47] always in close analogy to the course of the sun. We have learned in the course of this investigation that the part of the libido which erects religious structures is in the last analysis fixed in the mother, and really represents that tie through which we are permanently connected with our origin. Briefly, we may designate this amount of libido as " Mother Libido." As we have seen, this libido conceals itself in countless and very heterogeneous symbols, also in animal images, no matter whether of masculine or feminine nature—differences of sex are at bottom of a secondary value and psychologically do not play the part which might be expected from a superficial observation.

The annual sacrifice of the maiden to the dragon probably represented the most ideal symbolic situation. In order to pacify the anger of the "terrible mother" the most beautiful woman was sacrificed as symbol of man's libido. Less vivid examples are the sacrifice of the first-born and various valuable domestic animals. A second ideal case is the self-castration in the service of the mother (Dea Syria, etc.), a less obvious form of which is circumcision. By that at least only a portion is sacrificed.[48] With these sacrifices, the object of which in ideal cases is to symbolize the libido drawing away from the mother, life is symbolically renounced in order to regain it. By the sacrifice man ransoms himself from the fear of death and reconciles the destroying mother. In those later religions, where the hero, who in olden times overcomes all evil and death through his labors, has become the divine chief figure, he becomes the priestly sacrificer and the regenerator of life. But as the hero is an imaginary figure and his sacrifice is a transcendental mystery, the significance of which far exceeds the value of an ordinary sacrificial gift, this deepening of the sacrificial symbolism regressively resumes the idea of the human sacrifice. This is partly due to the preponderance of phantastic additions, which always take their subject-matter from greater depths, and partly due to the higher religious occupation of the libido, which demanded a more complete and equivalent expression. Thus the relation between Mithra and his bull is very close. It is the hero himself in the Christian mysteries who sacrifices himself voluntarily. The hero, as we have sufficiently shown, is the infantile personality longing for the mother, who as Mithra sacrifices the wish (the libido), and as Christ

gives himself to death both willingly and unwillingly.
Upon the monuments of the Mithraic religion we often
meet a strange symbol: a crater (mixing bowl) encóiled
by a serpent, sometimes with a lion, who as antagonist
opposes the serpent.[49]   It appears as if the two were
fighting for the crater.   The crater symbolizes, as we
have seen, the mother, the serpent the resistance defend-
ing her, and the lion the greatest strength and strongest
will.[50]   The struggle is for the mother.   The serpent takes
part almost regularly in the Mithraic sacrifice of the
bull, moving towards the blood flowing from the wound.
It seems to follow from that that the life of the bull
(blood) is sacrificed to the serpent.   Previously we have
pointed out the mutual relationship between serpent and
bull, and found there that the bull symbolizes the living
hero, the shining sun, but that the serpent symbolizes the
dead, buried or chthonic hero, the invisible sun.   As the
hero is in the mother in the state of death, the serpent
is also, as the symbol of the fear of death, the sign of
the devouring mother.   The sacrifice of the bull to the
serpent, therefore, signifies a willing renunciation of life,
in order to win it from death.   Therefore, after the sacrifice of the bull, wonderful fertility results.   The antagonism between serpent and lion over the crater is to
be interpreted as a battle over the fruitful mother's
womb, somewhat comparable to the more simple symbolism of the Tishtriya song, where the demon Apaosha,
the black horse, has possession of the rain lake, and the
white horse, Tishtriya, must banish him from it.   Death
from time to time lays its destroying hand upon life and

fertility and the libido disappears, by entering into the mother, from whose womb it will be born renewed. It, therefore, seems very probable that the significance of the Mithraic bull sacrifice is also that of the sacrifice of the mother who sends the fear of death. As the contrary of the Occide moriturus is also intended here, so is the act of sacrifice an impregnating of the mother; the chthonic snake demon drinks the blood; that is to say, the libido (sperma) of the hero committing incest. Life is thus immortalized for the hero because, like the sun, he generates himself anew. After all the preceding materials, it can no longer be difficult to recognize in the Christian mysteries the human sacrifice, or the sacrifice of the son to the mother.[51] Just as Attis emasculates himself on account of the mother, so does Christ himself hang upon the tree of life,[52] the wood of martyrdom, the ἑκάτη,* the chthonic mother, and by that redeems creation from death. By entering again into the mother's womb (Matuta, Pietà of Michelangelo) he redeems in death the sin in life of the primitive man, Adam, in order symbolically through his deed [53] to procure for the innermost and most hidden meaning of the religious libido its highest satisfaction and most pronounced expression. The martyrdom of Christ has in Augustine as well actually the meaning of a Hierosgamos with the mother (corresponding to the Adonis festival, where Venus and Adonis were laid upon the nuptial couch) :

" Procedit Christus quasi sponsus de thalamo suo, præsagio nuptiarum exiit ad campum sæculi; pervenit usque ad crucis

* Hecate.

torum (torus has the meaning of bed, pillow, concubine, bier) et
ibi firmavit ascendendo conjugium: ubi cum sentiret anhelantem
in suspiriis creaturam commercio pietatis se pro conjuge dedit ad
pœnam et copulavit sibi perpetuo iure matronam."

This passage is perfectly clear. A similar death over-
takes the Syrian Melcarth, who, riding upon a sea horse,
was annually burned. Among the Greeks he is called
Melicertes, and was represented riding upon a dolphin.
The dolphin is also the steed of Arion. We have learned
to recognize previously the maternal significance of
dolphin, so that in the death of Melcarth we can once
more recognize the negatively expressed Hierosgamos
with the mother. (Compare Frazer " Golden Bough,"
IV, p. 87.) This figurative expression is of the greatest
teleological significance. Through its symbol it leads
that libido which inclines backward into the original,
primitive and impulsive upwards to the spiritual by investing it with a mysterious but fruitful function. It is
superfluous to speak of the effect of this symbol upon
the unconscious of Occidental humanity. A glance over
history shows what creative forces were released in this
symbol.[54]

The comparison of the Mithraic and the Christian
sacrifice plainly shows wherein lies the superiority of the
Christian symbol; it is the frank admission that not only
are the lower wishes to be sacrificed, but the whole personality. The Christian symbol demands complete devotion; it compels a veritable self-sacrifice to a higher
purpose, while the Sacrificium Mithriacum, remaining
fixed on a primitive symbolic stage, is contented with an

animal sacrifice. The religious effect of these symbols must be considered as an orientation of the unconscious by means of imitation.

In Miss Miller's phantasy there is internal compulsion, in that she passes from the horse sacrifice to the self-sacrifice of the hero. Whereas the first symbolizes renunciation of the sexual wishes, the second has the deeper and ethically more valuable meaning of the sacrifice of the infantile personality. The object of psychoanalysis has frequently been wrongly understood to mean the renunciation or the gratification of the ordinary sexual wish, while, in reality, the problem is the sublimation of the infantile personality, or, expressed mythologically, a sacrifice and rebirth of the infantile hero.[55] In the Christian mysteries, however, the resurrected one becomes a supermundane spirit, and the invisible kingdom of God, with its mysterious gifts, are obtained by his believers through the sacrifice of himself on the mother. In psychoanalysis the infantile personality is deprived of its libido fixations in a rational manner; the libido which is thus set free serves for the building up of a personality matured and adapted to reality, who does willingly and without complaint everything required by necessity. (It is, so to speak, the chief endeavor of the infantile personality to struggle against all necessities and to create coercions for itself where none exist in reality.)

The serpent as an instrument of sacrifice has already been abundantly illustrated. (Legend of St. Silvester, trial of the virgins, wounding of Rê and Philoctetes, symbolism of the lance and arrow.) It is the destroying

knife; but, according to the principle of the "Occide
moriturus" also the phallus, the sacrificial act represents
a coitus act as well.[56]   The religious significance of the
serpent as a cave-dwelling, chthonic animal points to a
further thought; namely, to the creeping into the
mother's womb in the form of a serpent.[57]   As the horse
is the brother, so the serpent is the sister of Chiwantopel.
This close relation refers to a fellowship of these animals
and their characters with the hero.   We know of the
horse that, as a rule, he is not an animal of fear, although,
mythologically, he has at times this meaning.   He signifies much more the living, positive part of the libido,
the striving towards continual renewal, whereas the serpent, as a rule, represents the fear, the fear of death,[58]
and is thought of as the antithesis to the phallus.   This
antithesis between horse and serpent, mythologically between bull and serpent, represents an opposition of the
libido within itself, a striving forwards and a striving
backwards at one and the same time.[59]   It is not only
as if the libido might be an irresistible striving forward,
an endless life and will for construction, such as Schopenhauer has formulated in his world will, death and every
end being some malignancy or fatality coming from without, but the libido, corresponding to the sun, also wills
the destruction of its creation.   In the first half of life
its will is for growth, in the second half of life it hints,
softly at first, and then audibly, at its will for death.
And just as in youth the impulse to unlimited growth often
lies under the enveloping covering of a resistance against
life, so also does the will of the old to die frequently lie

under the covering of a stubborn resistance against the end.

This apparent contrast in the nature of the libido is strikingly illustrated by a Priapic statuette in the antique collection at Verona.[60] Priapus smilingly points with his finger to a snake biting off his " membrum." He carries

PRIAPUS AND SERPENT

a basket on his arm, filled with oblong objects, probably phalli, evidently prepared as substitutes.

A similar motive is found in the " Deluge " of Rubens (in the Munich Art Gallery), where a serpent emasculates a man. This motive explains the meaning of the " Deluge "; the maternal sea is also the devouring mother.[61] The phantasy of the world conflagration, of the cataclysmic end of the world in general, is nothing but a mythological projection of a personal individual will for death; therefore, Rubens could represent the essence of the " Deluge " phantasy in the emasculation by the serpent; for the serpent is our own repressed will for the end, for which we find an explanation only with the greatest difficulty.

Concerning the symbolism of the serpent in general, its significance is very dependent upon the time of life and circumstances. The repressed sexuality of youth is symbolized by the serpent, because the arrival of sexuality puts an end to childhood. To age, on the contrary, the serpent signifies the repressed thought of death. With our author it is the insufficiently expressed sexuality which as serpent assumes the rôle of sacrificer and delivers the hero over to death and rebirth.

As in the beginning of our investigation the hero's name forced us to speak of the symbolism of Popocatepetl as belonging to the creating part of the human body, so at the end does the Miller drama again give us an opportunity of seeing how the volcano assists in the death of the hero and causes him to disappear by means of an earthquake into the depths of the earth. As the volcano gave birth and name to the hero, so at the end of the day it devours him again.[62] We learn from the last words of the hero that *his longed-for beloved,* she who alone understands him, is called Ja-ni-wa-ma. We find in this name those lisped syllables familiar to us from the early childhood of the hero, Hiawatha, Wawa, wama, mama. The only one who really understands us is the mother. For *verstehen,* "to understand" (Old High German *firstân),* is probably derived from a primitive Germanic prefix *fri,* identical with περὶ, meaning "roundabout." The Old High German *antfristôn,* "to interpret," is considered as identical with *firstân.* From that results a fundamental significance of the verb *verstehen*, "to understand," as "standing round about something." [63] *Comprehendere* and κατασυλλαμβάνειν express a similar idea as the German *erfassen*, "to grasp, to comprehend." The thing common to these expressions is the surrounding, the enfolding. And there is no doubt that there is nothing in the world which so completely enfolds us as the mother. When the neurotic complains that the world has no understanding, he says indirectly that he misses the mother. Paul Verlaine has expressed this thought most beautifully in his poem, " Mon Rêve Familier ":

My Familiar Dream.

"Often I have that strange and poignant dream
  Of some unknown who meets my flame with flame—
  Who, with each time, is never quite the same,
Yet never wholly different does she seem.
She understands me! Every fitful gleam
  Troubling my heart, she reads aright somehow:
  Even the sweat upon my pallid brow
She soothes with tears, a cool and freshening stream.

"If she is dark or fair? I do not know—
  Her name? Only that it is sweet and low,
  Like those of loved ones who have long since died.
Her look is like a statue's, kind and clear;
  And her calm voice, distant and dignified,
Like those hushed voices that I loved to hear."

NOTES

PART I

INTRODUCTION

[1] He is said to have killed himself when he heard that she whom he so passionately adored was his mother.

[2] "Wish Fulfilment and Symbolism in Fairy Tales." Tr. by W. A. White, M.D.

[3] "Dream and Myth." Deuticke, Wien 1909.

[4] "The Myth of the Birth of the Hero."

[5] "Die Symbolik in den Legenden, Märchen, Gebräuchen und Träumen." *Psychiatrisch.-Neurologische Wochenschrift*, X. Jahrgang.

[6] "On the Nightmare." *Amer. Journ. of Insanity*, 1910.

[7] *Jahrbuch*, 1910, Pt. II.

[8] "Die Frömmigkeit des Grafen Ludwig von Zinzendorf. Ein psychoanalytischer Beitrag zur Kenntnis der religiösen Sublimationprozesse und zur Erklärung des Pietismus." Deuticke, Wien 1910. We have a suggestive hint in Freud's work, "Eine Kindheitserinnerung des Leonardo da Vinci." Deuticke, Wien 1910.

[9] Compare Rank in *Jahrbuch*, Pt. II, p. 465.

CHAPTER I

[1] Compare Liepmann, "Über Ideenflucht," Halle 1904; also Jung, "Diagnost. Assoc. Stud.," p. 103: "Denken als Unterordnung unter eine herrschende Vorstellung"; compare Ebbinghaus, "Kultur der Gegenwart," p. 221. Külpe ("Gr. d. Psychologie," p. 464) expresses himself in a similar manner: "In thinking it is a question of an anticipatory apperception which sometimes governs a greater, sometimes a smaller circle of individual reproductions, and is differentiated from accidental motives of reproduction only by the consequence with which all things outside this circle are held back or repressed."

[2] In his "Psychologia empirica meth. scientif. pertract.," etc., 1732, p. 23, Christian Wolff says simply and precisely: "Cogitatio est actus animae quo sibi rerumque aliarum extra se conscia est."

[3] The moment of adaptation is emphasized especially by William James in his definition of reasoning: "Let us make this ability to deal with novel data the technical differentia of reasoning. This will sufficiently mark it out from common associative thinking, and will immediately enable us to say just what peculiarity it contains."

[4] "Thoughts are shadows of our experiences, always darker, emptier,

485

simpler than these," says Nietzsche. Lotze ("Logik," p. 552) expresses himself in regard to this as follows: "Thought, left to the logical laws of its movement, encounters once more at the end of its regularly traversed course the things suppressed or hidden."

[5] Compare the remarks of Baldwin following in text. The eccentric philosopher Johann Georg Hamann (1730-88) even places intelligence and speech as identical (see Hamann's writings, pub. by Roth, Berlin 1821). With Nietzsche intelligence fares even worse as "speech metaphysics" (Sprachmetaphysik). Friedrich Mauthner goes the furthest in this conception ("Sprache und Psychologie," 1901). For him there exists absolutely no thought without speech, and speaking is thinking. His idea of the "fetish of the word" governing in science is worthy of notice.

[6] Compare Kleinpaul: "Das Leben der Sprache," 3 Bände. Leipzig 1893.

[7] "Jardin d'Épicure," p. 80.

[8] It is difficult to calculate how great is the seductive influence of the primitive word-meaning upon a thought. "Anything which has even been in consciousness remains as an affective moment in the unconscious," says Hermann Paul ("Prinzipien der Sprachgeschichte," 4th ed., 1909, p. 25). The old word-meanings have an after-effect, chiefly imperceptible, "within the dark chamber of the unconscious in the Soul" (Paul). J. G. Hamann, mentioned above, expresses himself unequivocally: "Metaphysics reduces all catchwords and all figures of speech of our empirical knowledge to empty hieroglyphics and types of ideal relations." It is said that Kant learned some things from Hamann.

[9] "Grundriss der Psychologie," p. 365.

[10] "Lehrbuch der Psychologie," X, 26.

[11] James Mark Baldwin: "Thought and Things, or Genetic Logic."

[12] In this connection I must refer to an experiment which Eberschweiler (*Allgemeine Zeitschrift für Psychiatrie,* 1908) has made at my request, which discloses the remarkable fact that in an association experiment the intrapsychic association is influenced by phonetic considerations ("Untersuchungen über den Einfluss der sprachlichen Komponente auf die Assoziation," *Allgemeine Zeitschrift für Psychiatrie,* 1908).

[13] So at least this form of thought appears to Consciousness. Freud says in this connection ("The Interpretation of Dreams," tr. by Brill, p. 418): "It is demonstrably incorrect to state that we abandon ourselves to an aimless course of ideas when we relinquish our reflections, and allow the unwilled ideas to emerge. It can be shown that we are able to reject only those end-presentations known to us, and that immediately upon the cessation of these unknown or, as we inaccurately say, unconscious end-presentations come into play which now determine the course of the unwilled ideas—a thought without end-presentation cannot be produced through any influence we can exert on our own psychic life."

[14] "Grundriss der Psychologie," p. 464.

[15] Behind this assertion stand, first of all, experiences taken from the field of the normal. The undirected thinking is very far removed from "meditation," and especially so as far as readiness of speech is concerned. In psychological experiments I have frequently found that the

subjects of the investigation—I speak only of cultivated and intelligent people, whom I have allowed to indulge in reveries, apparently unintentionally and without previous instruction—have exhibited affect-expressions which can be registered experimentally. But the basic thought of these, even with the best of intentions, they could express only incompletely or even not at all. One meets with an abundance of similar experiences in association experiments and psychoanalysis—indeed, there is hardly an unconscious complex which has not at some time existed as a phantasy in consciousness.

However, more instructive are the experiences from the domain of psychopathology. But those arising in the field of the hysterias and neuroses, which are characterized by an overwhelming transference tendency, are rarer than the experiences in the territory of the introversion type of neuroses and psychoses, which constitute by far the greater number of the mental derangements, at least the collected Schizophrenic group of Bleuler. As has already been indicated by the term "introversion," which I briefly introduced in my study, "Konflikte der kindlichen Seele," pp. 6 and 10, these neuroses lead to an overpowering autoerotism (Freud). And here we meet with this unutterable purely phantastic thinking, which moves in inexpressible symbols and feelings. One gets a slight impression of this when one seeks to examine the paltry and confused expressions of these people. As I have frequently observed, it costs these patients endless trouble and effort to put their phantasies into common human speech. A highly intelligent patient, who interpreted such a phantasy piece by piece, often said to me, " I know absolutely with what it is concerned, I see and feel everything, but it is quite impossible for me to find the words to express it." The poetic and religious introversion gives rise to similar experiences; for example, Paul, in the Epistle to the Romans viii:26—"For we know not what we should pray for as we ought: but the Spirit itself maketh intercession with groanings which cannot be uttered.'

[16] Similarly, James remarks, "The great difference, in fact, between that simple kind of rational thinking which consists in the concrete objects of past experience merely suggesting each other, and reason distinctively so called, is this, that whilst the empirical thinking is only reproductive, reasoning is productive."

[17] Compare the impressive description of Petrarch's ascent of Mt. Ventoux, by Jacob Burckhardt ("Die Kultur der Renaissance in Italien," 1869, p. 235):

"One now awaits a description of the view, but in vain, not because the poet is indifferent to it, but, on the contrary, because the impression affects him all too strongly. His entire past life, with all its follies, passes before him; he recalls that it is ten years ago to-day that he, as a young man, left Bologna, and he turns a yearning glance toward Italy. He opens a book—' Confessions of St. Augustine,' his companion at that time—and his eye falls upon this passage in the tenth chapter: ' and the people went there and admired the high mountains, the wide wastes of the sea and the mighty downward rushing streams, and the ocean and the courses of the stars, and forgot themselves.' His brother, to whom he reads these words, cannot comprehend why, at this point, he closes the book and is silent."

[18] Wundt gives a striking description of the scholastic method in his "Philosophische Studien," XIII, p. 345. The method consists "first in this, that one realizes the chief aim of scientific investigation is the

discovery of a comprehensive scheme, firmly established, and capable of being applied in a uniform manner to the most varied problems; secondly, in that one lays an excessive value upon certain general ideas, and, consequently, upon the word-symbols designating these ideas, wherefore an analysis of word-meanings comes, in extreme cases, to be an empty subtlety and splitting of hairs, instead of an investigation of the real facts from which the ideas are abstracted."

[19] The concluding passage in "Traumdeutung" was of prophetic significance, and has been brilliantly established since then through investigations of the psychoses. "In the psychoses these modes of operation of the psychic mechanism, normally suppressed in the waking state, again become operative, and then disclose their inability to satisfy our needs in the outer world." The importance of this position is emphasized by the views of Pierre Janet, developed independently of Freud, and which deserve to be mentioned here, because they add confirmation from an entirely different side, namely, the biological. Janet makes the distinction in this function of a firmly organized "inferior" and "superior" part, conceived of as in a state of continuous transformation.
"It is really on this superior part of the functions, on their adaptation to present circumstances, that the neuroses depend. The neuroses are the disturbances or the checks in the evolution of the functions—the illnesses depending upon the morbid functioning of the organism. These are characterized by an alteration in the superior part of the functions, in their evolution and in their adaptation to the present moment—to the present state of the exterior world and of the individual, and also by the absence or deterioration of the old parts of these same functions.
"In the place of these superior operations there are developed physical, mental, and, above all, emotional disturbances. This is only the tendency to replace the superior operations by an exaggeration of certain inferior operations, and especially by gross visceral disturbances" ("Les Névroses," p. 383).
The old parts are, indeed, the inferior parts of the functions, and these replace, in a purposeless fashion, the abortive attempts at adaptation. Briefly speaking, the archaic replaces the recent function which has failed. Similar views concerning the nature of neurotic symptoms are expressed by Claparède as well ("Quelques mots sur la définition de l'Hystérie," *Arch. de Psychol.*, I, VII, p. 169).
He understands the hysterogenic mechanism as a "Tendance à la réversion"—as a sort of atavistic manner of reaction.

[20] I am indebted to Dr. Abraham for the following interesting communication: "A little girl of three and a half years had been presented with a little brother, who became the object of the well-known childish jealousy. Once she said to her mother, 'You are two mammas; you are my mamma, and your breast is little brother's mamma.' She had just been looking on with great interest at the process of nursing." It is very characteristic of the archaic thinking of the child for the breast to be designated as "mamma."

[21] Compare especially Freud's thorough investigation of the child in his "Analyse der Phobie eines fünfjährigen Knaben," 1912 *Jahrbuch,* Pt. I. Also my study, "Konflikte der kindlichen Seele," 1912 *Jahrbuch,* Pt. II, p. 33.

[22] "Human, All Too Human," Vol. II, p. 27 and on.

[23] "Sammlung kleiner Schriften zur Neurosenlehre," Pt. II, p. 205.

[24] "Der Künstler, Ansätze zu einer Sexualpsychologie," 1907, p. 36.

[25] Compare also Rank's later book, "The Myth of the Birth of the Hero."

[26] "Wish Fulfilment and Symbolism in Fairy Tales," 1908.

[27] "Dreams and Myths."

[28] Compare with this "Konflikte der kindlichen Seele," p. 6, foot.

[29] Compare Abraham, "Dreams and Myths." New York 1913. The wish for the future is represented as already fulfilled in the past. Later, the childish phantasy is again taken up regressively in order to compensate for the disillusionment of actual life.

[30] Rank: "The Myth of the Birth of the Hero."

[31] Naturally, it could not be said that because this was an institution in antiquity, the same would recur in our phantasy, but rather that in antiquity it was possible for the phantasy so generally present to become an institution. This may be concluded from the peculiar activity of the mind of antiquity.

[32] The Dioscuri married the Leucippides by theft, an act which, according to the ideas of higher antiquity, belonged to the necessary customs of marriage (Preller: "Griechische Mythologie," 1854, Pt. II, p. 68).

[33] See S. Creuzer: "Symbolik und Mythologie," 1811, Pt. III, p. 245.

[34] Compare also the sodomitic phantasies in the "Metamorphoses" of Apuleius. In Herculaneum, for example, corresponding sculptures have been found.

[35] Ferrero: "Les lois psychologiques du symbolisme."

[36] With the exception of the fact that the thoughts enter consciousness already in a high state of complexity, as Wundt says.

[37] Schelling: "Philosophie der Mythologie," Werke, Pt. II, considers the "preconscious" as the creative source, also H. Fichte ("Psychologie," I, p. 508) considers the preconscious region as the place of origin of the real content of dreams.

[38] Compare, in this connection, Flournoy: "Des Indes à la planète Mars." Also Jung: "Zur Psychologie und Pathologie sogenannter okkulter Phänomene," and "Über die Psychologie der Dementia praecox." Excellent examples are to be found in Schreber: "Denkwürdigkeiten eines Nervenkranken." Mutze, Leipzig.

[39] "Jardin d'Épicure."

[40] The figure of Judas acquires a great psychological significance as the priestly sacrificer of the Lamb of God, who, by this act, sacrifices himself at the same time. (Self-destruction.) Compare Pt. II of this work.

[41] Compare with this the statements of Drews ("The Christ Myth"), which are so violently combated by the blindness of our time. Clearsighted theologians, like Kalthoff ("Entstehung des Christentums," 1904), present as impersonal a judgment as Drews. Kalthoff says, "The sources from which we derive our information concerning the origin of Christianity are such that in the present state of historical research no historian would undertake the task of writing the biography of an

historical Jesus." Ibid., p. 10: "To see behind these stories the life of a real historical personage, would not occur to any man, if it were not for the influence of 'rationalistic theology." Ibid., p. 9: "The divine in Christ, always considered an inner attribute and one with the human, leads in a straight line backward from the scholarly man of God, through the Epistles and Gospels of the New Testament, to the Apocalypse of Daniel, in which the theological imprint of the figure of Christ has arisen. At every single point of this line Christ shows superhuman traits; nowhere is He that which critical theology wished to make Him, simply a natural man, an historic individual."

[42] Compare J. Burckhardt's letter to Albert Brenner (pub. by Hans Brenner in the Basle *Jahrbuch,* 1901): "I have absolutely nothing stored away for the special interpretation of Faust. You are well provided with commentaries of all sorts. Hark! let us at once take the whole foolish pack back to the reading-room from whence they have come. What you are destined to find in Faust, that you will find by intuition. Faust is nothing else than pure and legitimate myth, a great primitive conception, so to speak, in which everyone can divine in his own way his own nature and destiny. Allow me to make a comparison: What would the ancient Greeks have said had a commentator interposed himself between them and the Oedipus legend? There was a chord of the Oedipus legend in every Greek which longed to be touched directly and respond in its own way. And thus it is with the German nation and Faust."

[43] I will not conceal the fact that for a time I was in doubt whether I dare venture to reveal through analysis the intimate personality which the author, with a certain unselfish scientific interest, has exposed to public view. Yet it seemed to me that the writer would possess an understanding deeper than any objections of my critics. There is always some risk when one exposes one's self to the world. The absence of any personal relation with Miss Miller permits me free speech, and also exempts me from those considerations due woman which are prejudicial to conclusions. The person of the author is on that account just as shadowy to me as are her phantasies; and, like Odysseus, I have tried to let this phantom drink only enough blood to enable it to speak, and in so doing betray some of the secrets of the inner life.

I have not undertaken this analysis, for which the author owes me but little thanks, for the pleasure of revealing private and intimate matters, with the accompanying embarrassment of publicity, but because I wished to show the secret of the individual as one common to all.

CHAPTER II

[1] A very beautiful example of this is found in C. A. Bernoulli: "Franz Overbeck und Friedrich Nietzsche. Eine Freundschaft," 1908 (Pt. I, p. 72). This author depicts Nietzsche's behavior in Basle society: "Once at a dinner he said to the young lady at his side, 'I dreamed a short time ago that the skin of my hand, which lay before me on the table, suddenly became like glass, shiny and transparent, through which I saw distinctly the bones and the tissues and the play of the muscles. All at once I saw a toad sitting on my hand and at the same time I felt an irresistible compulsion to swallow the beast. I overcame my terrible aversion and gulped it down.' The young lady laughed. 'And do you laugh at that?' Nietzsche asked, his deep eyes fixed on his companion,

half questioning, half sorrowful. The young lady knew intuitively that she did not wholly understand that an oracle had spoken to her in the form of an allegory and that Nietzsche had revealed to her a glimpse into the dark abyss of his inner self." On page 166 Bernoulli continues as follows: "One can perhaps see, behind that harmless pleasure of faultless exactness in dress, a dread of contamination arising from some mysterious and tormenting disgust."

Nietzsche went to Basle when he was very young; he was then just at the age when other young people are contemplating marriage. Seated next to a young woman, he tells her that something terrible and disgusting is taking place in his transparent hand, something which he must take completely into his body. We know what illness caused the premature ending of Nietzsche's life. It was precisely this which he would tell the young lady, and her laughter was indeed discordant.

[2] A whole series of psychoanalytic experiences could easily be produced here to illustrate this statement.

[3] Ferenczi: " IntroJektion und Übertragung," *Jahrbuch,* Pt. I (1912).

CHAPTER III

[1] The choice of words and comparisons is always significant. A psychology of travels and the unconscious forces co-operating with them is yet to be written.

[2] This mental disturbance had until recently the very unfortunate designation, Dementia Praecox, given by Kraepelin. It is extremely unfortunate that this malady should have been discovered by the psychiatrists, for its apparently bad prognosis is due to this circumstance. Dementia praecox is synonymous with therapeutic hopelessness. How would hysteria appear if judged from the standpoint of psychiatry! The psychiatrist naturally sees in the institutions only the worst cases of dementia praecox, and as a consequence of his therapeutic helplessness he must be a pessimist. How deplorable would tuberculosis appear if the physician of an asylum for the incurable described the nosology of this disease! Just as little as the chronic cases of hysteria, which gradually degenerate in insane asylums, are characteristic of real hysteria, just so little are the cases of dementia praecox in asylums characteristic of those early forms so frequent in general practice, and which Janet has described under the name of Psychasthenia. These cases fall under Bleuler's description of Schizophrenia, a name which connotes a psychological fact, and might easily be compared with similar facts in hysteria. The term which I use in my private work for these conditions is Introversion Neurosis, by which, in my opinion, the most important characteristic of the condition is given, namely, the predominance of introversion over transference, which latter is the characteristic feature of hysteria.

In my " Psychology of Dementia Praecox " I have not made any study of the relationship of the Psychasthenia of Janet. Subsequent experience with Dementia Praecox, and particularly the study of Psychasthenia in Paris, have demonstrated to me the essential relationship of Janet's group with the Introversion Neuroses (the Schizophrenia of Bleuler).

[3] Compare the similar views in my article, " Über die Psychologie der Dementia praecox," Halle 1907; and "Inhalt der Psychose," Deuticke, Wien 1908. Also Abraham: " Die psychosexuellen Differenzen der

Hysterie und der Dementia praecox," *Zentralblatt für Nervenheilkunde und Psychiatrie,* 1908. This author, in support of Freud, defines the chief characteristic of dementia praecox as Autoerotism, which as I have asserted is only one of the results of Introversion.

[4] Freud, to whom I am indebted for an essential part of this view, also speaks of "Heilungsversuch," the attempt toward cure, the search for health.

[5] Miss Miller's publication gives no hint of any knowledge of psychoanalysis.

[6] Here I purposely give preference to the term "Imago" rather than to the expression "Complex," in order, by the choice of terminology, to invest this psychological condition, which I include under "Imago," with living independence in the psychical hierarchy, that is to say, with that autonomy which, from a large experience, I have claimed as the essential peculiarity of the emotional complex. (Compare "The Psychology of Dementia Praecox.") My critics, Isserlin especially, have seen in this view a return to medieval psychology, and they have, therefore, rejected it utterly. This "return" took place on my part consciously and intentionally because the phantastic, projected psychology of ancient and modern superstition, especially demonology, furnishes exhaustive evidence for this point of view. Particularly interesting insight and confirmation is given us by the insane Schreber in an autobiography ("Denkwürdigkeiten eines Nervenkranken," Mutze, Leipzig), where he has given complete expression to the doctrine of autonomy. "Imago" has a significance similar on the one hand to the psychologically conceived creation in Spitteler's novel "Imago," and upon the other hand to the ancient religious conception of "imagines et lares."

[7] Compare my article, "Die Bedeutung des Vaters für das Schicksal des Einzelnen."

[8] As is well known, Anaxagoras developed the conception that the living primal power (Urpotenz) of $\nu o\tilde{\nu}\varsigma$ (mind) imparts movement, as if by a blast of wind, to the dead primal power (Urpotenz) of matter. There is naturally no mention of sound. This $\nu o\tilde{\nu}\varsigma$, which is very similar to the later conception of Philo, the $\lambda\acute{o}\gamma o\varsigma$ $\sigma\pi\epsilon\rho\mu\alpha\tau\iota\kappa\acute{o}\varsigma$ of the Gnostics and the Pauline $\pi\nu\epsilon\tilde{\nu}\mu\alpha$ (spirit) as well as to the $\pi\nu\epsilon\tilde{\nu}\mu\alpha$ of the contemporary Christian theologians, has rather the old mythological significance of the fructifying breath of the winds, which impregnated the mares of Lusitania, and the Egyptian vultures. The animation of Adam and the impregnation of the Mother of God by the $\pi\nu\epsilon\tilde{\nu}\mu\alpha$ are produced in a similar manner. The infantile incest phantasy of one of my patients reads: "the father covered her face with his hands and blew into her open mouth."

[9] Haydn's "Creation" might be meant.

[10] See Job xvi: 1-11.

[11] I recall the case of a young insane girl who continually imagined that her innocence was suspected, from which thought she would not allow herself to be dissuaded. Gradually there developed out of her defensive attitude a correspondingly energetic positive erotomania.

[12] Compare the preceding footnote with the text of Miss Miller's.

[13] The case is published in "Zur Psychologie und Pathologie sogenannter okkulter Phänomene." Mutze, Leipzig 1902.

[14] Compare Freud's "Analyse der Phobie eines fünfjährigen Knaben," *Jahrbuch*, Vol. I, 1st half; also Jung: "Konflikte der kindlichen Seele," *Jahrbuch*, II, Vol. I.

[15] Others do not make use of this step, but are directly carried away by Eros.

[16] "La sagesse et la destinée."

[17] This time I shall hardly be spared the reproach of mysticism. But perhaps the facts should be further considered; doubtless the unconscious contains material which does not rise to the threshold of consciousness. The analysis dissolves these combinations into their historical determinants, for it is one of the essential tasks of analysis to render impotent by dissolution the content of the complexes competing with the proper conduct of life. Psychoanalysis works backwards like the science of history. Just as the largest part of the past is so far removed that it is not reached by history, so too the greater part of the unconscious determinants is unreachable. History, however, knows nothing of two kinds of things, that which is hidden in the past and that which is hidden in the future. Both perhaps might be attained with a certain probability; the first as a postulate, the second as an historical prognosis. In so far as to-morrow is already contained in to-day, and all the threads of the future are in place, so a more profound knowledge of the past might render possible a more or less far-reaching and certain knowledge of the future. Let us transfer this reasoning, as Kant has already done, to psychology. Then necessarily we must come to the same result. Just as traces of memory long since fallen below the threshold of consciousness are accessible in the unconscious, so too there are certain very fine subliminal combinations of the future, which are of the greatest significance for future happenings in so far as the future is conditioned by our own psychology. But just so little as the science of history concerns itself with the combinations for the future, which is the function of politics, so little, also, are the psychological combinations for the future the object of analysis; they would be much more the object of an infinitely refined psychological synthesis, which attempts to follow the natural current of the libido. This we cannot do, but possibly this might happen in the unconscious, and it appears as if from time to time, in certain cases, significant fragments of this process come to light, at least in dreams. From this comes the prophetic significance of the dream long claimed by superstition.
The aversion of the scientific man of to-day to this type of thinking, hardly to be called phantastic, is merely an overcompensation to the very ancient and all too great inclination of mankind to believe in prophesies and superstitions.

[18] Dreams seem to remain spontaneously in the memory just so long as they give a correct résumé of the psychologic situation of the individual.

[19] How paltry are the intrinsic ensemble and the detail of the erotic experience, is shown by this frequently varied love song which I quote in its epirotic form:

EPIROTIC LOVE SONG
(*Zeitschrift des Vereines für Volkskunde*, XII, p. 159.)

O Maiden, when we kissed, then it was night; who saw us?
A night Star saw us, and the moon,
And it leaned downward to the sea, and gave it the tidings,

Then the Sea told the rudder, the rudder told the sailor,
The sailor put it into song, then the neighbor heard it,
Then the priest heard it and told my mother,
From her the father heard it, he got in a burning anger,
They quarrelled with me and commanded me and they have forbidden me
Ever to go to the door, ever to go to the window.
And yet I will go to the window as if to my flowers,
And never will I rest till my beloved is mine.

[20] Job xli:13 (Leviathan).

"21. His breath kindleth coals, and a flame goeth out of his mouth.

"22. In his neck remaineth strength, and sorrow is turned into joy before him.

"24. His heart is as firm as a stone; yea, as hard as a piece of the nether millstone.

"25. When he raiseth up himself, the mighty are afraid: by reason of breakings they purify themselves.

"33. Upon earth there is not his like who is made without fear.

"34. He beholdeth all high things: he is a king over all the children of pride."

Chapter xlii.

"1. Then Job answered the Lord, and said,

"2. I know that thou canst do everything, and that no thought can be withholden from thee."

[21] The theriomorphic attributes are lacking in the Christian religion except as remnants, such as the Dove, the Fish and the Lamb. The latter is also represented as a Ram in the drawings in the Catacombs. Here belong the animals associated with the Evangelists which particularly need historical explanation. The Eagle and the Lion were definite degrees of initiation in the Mithraic mysteries. The worshippers of Dionysus called themselves βόες because the god was represented as a bull; likewise the ἄρκτοι of Artemis, conceived of as a she-bear. The Angel might correspond to the ἡλιόδρομοι of the Mithras mysteries. It is indeed an exquisite invention of the Christian phantasy that the animal coupled with St. Anthony is the pig, for the good saint was one of those who were subjected to the devil's most evil temptations.

[22] Compare Pfister's notable article: "Die Frömmigkeit des Grafen Ludwig von Zinzendorf." Wien 1910.

[23] The Book of Job, originating at a later period under non-Jewish influences, is a striking presentation of individual projection psychology.

[24] "If we say we have no sin, we deceive ourselves, and the truth is not in us" (I John i:8).

[25] "Surely he has borne our griefs and carried our sorrows" (Isaiah liii:4).

[26] "Bear ye one another's burdens" (Galatians vi:2).

[27] God is Love, corresponding to the platonic "Eros" which unites humanity with the transcendental.

[28] Compare Reitzenstein ("Die hellenistischen Mysterienreligionen," Leipzig and Berlin 1910, p. 20): "Among the various forms with which a primitive people have represented the highest religious consecration, union with God, belongs necessarily that of the sexual union, in which man attributes to his semen the innermost nature and power of God.

That which was in the first instance wholly a sensual act becomes in the most widely separated places, independently, a sacred act, in which the god is represented by a human deputy or his symbol the Phallus."

[29] Take as an example among many others the striking psychologic description of the fate of Alypius, in the " Confessions " of St. Augustine (Bk. VI, Ch. 7): " Only the moral iniquity of Carthage, expressed in the absolute wildness of its worthless spectacles, had drawn him down into the whirlpool of this misery. [Augustine, at that time a teacher of Logic, through his wisdom had converted Alypius.] He rose up after those words from the depths of the mire, into which he had willingly let himself be submerged, and which had blinded him with fatal pleasure. He stripped the filth from off his soul with courageous abstemiousness. All the snares of the Hippodrome no longer perplexed him. Thereupon Alypius went to Rome in order to study law; there he became a backslider. He was transported to an unbelievable degree by an unfortunate passion for gladiatorial shows. Although in the beginning he abominated and cursed these shows, one evening some of his friends and fellow-students, whom he met after they had dined, in spite of his passionate refusals and the exertion of all the power of his resistance, dragged him with friendly violence to the Amphitheatre on the occasion of a cruel and murderous exhibition. At the time he said to them, ' If you drag my body to that place and hold it there, can you turn my mind and my eyes to that spectacle? ' In spite of his supplications they dragged him with them, eager to know if he would be able to resist the spectacle. When they arrived they sat down where place was still left, and all glowed with inhuman delight. He closed his eyes and forbade his soul to expose itself to such danger. O, if he had also stopped up his ears! When some one fell in combat and all the people set up a mighty shout, he stifled his curiosity and prepared proudly to scorn the sight, confident that he could view the spectacle if he so desired. And his soul was overcome with terrible wounds, like the wounds of the body which he desired to see, and souls more miserable than the one whose fall had caused the outcry, which pressing through his ears, had opened his eyes, so that his weakness had been bared. Through this he could be struck and thrown down, for he had the feeling of confidence more than strength, and he was the weaker because he trusted himself to this and not to Thee. When he saw the blood, then at the same time he drew in the desire for blood, and no longer turned away but directed his looks thither. The fury took possession of him and yet he did not know it; he took delight in the wicked combat and was intoxicated by the bloody pleasure. Now he was no longer the same as when he had come, and he was the true accomplice of those who first had dragged him there. What more is there to say? He saw, he cried out, he was inflamed, and he carried away with him the insane longing, which enticed him again to return, not only in the company of those who first had dragged him with them, but going ahead of all and leading others."

[30] Compare the prayer of the so-called Mithraic Liturgy (pub. by Dieterich). There, characteristic places are to be found, such for instance as: τῆς ἀνθρωπίνης μου ψυχικῆς δυνάμεως ἣν ἐγὼ πάλιν μεταπαραλήμψομαι μετὰ τὴν ἐνεστῶσαν καὶ κατεπείγουσάν με πικρὰν ἀνάγκην ἀχρεοκόπητον (The human soul force which I, weighed down by guilt, would again attain, because of the present bitter need oppressing me). ἐπικαλοῦμαι ἕνεκα τῆς

κατεπειγούσης καὶ πικρᾶς ἀπαραιτήτου ἀνάγκης (On account of the oppressing bitter and inexorable need).

From the speech of the High Priest (Apuleius: "Metamorphoses," lib. XI, 248) a similar train of thought may be gathered. The young philosopher Lucius was changed into an ass, that continuously rutting animal which Isis hated. Later he was released from the enchantment and initiated into the mysteries of Isis. When he was freed from the spell the priest speaks as follows: "Lubrico virentis aetatulae, ad serviles delapsus voluptates, curiositatis improsperae sinistrum praemium reportasti.—Nam in eos, quorum sibi vitas servitium Deae nostrae majestas vindicavit, non habet locum casus infestus—in tutelam jam receptus es Fortunae, sed videntis" (But falling into the slavery of pleasure, in the wantonness of buxom youth, you have reaped the inauspicious reward of your ill-fated curiosity—for direful calamity has no power over those whose lives the majesty of our Goddess has claimed for her own service.—You are now received under the guardianship of fortune, but of a fortune who can see). In the prayer to the Queen of Heaven, Isis, Lucius says: "Qua fatorum etiam inextricabiliter contorta retractas licia et Fortunae tempestates mitigas, et stellarum noxios meatus cohibes" (By which thou dost unravel the inextricably entangled threads of the fates, and dost assuage the tempests of fortune and restrain the malignant influences of the stars).—Generally it was the purpose of the rite to destroy the "evil compulsion of the star" by magic power.

The power of fate makes itself felt unpleasantly only when everything goes against our will; that is to say when we no longer find ourselves in harmony with ourselves. As I endeavored to show in my article, "Die Bedeutung des Vaters," etc., the most dangerous power of fate lies in the infantile libido fixation, localized in the unconscious. The power of fate reveals itself at closer range as a compulsion of the libido; wherefore Maeterlinck justly says that a Socrates could not possibly be a tragic hero of the type of Hamlet. In accordance with this conception the ancients had already placed εἱμαρμένη (destiny) in relation to "Primal Light," or "Primal Fire." In the Stoic conception of the primal cause, the warmth spread everywhere, which has created everything and which is therefore Destiny. (Compare Cumont: "Mysterien des Mithra," p. 83.) This warmth is, as will later be shown, a symbol of the libido. Another conception of the Ananke (necessity) is, according to the Book of Zoroaster, περὶ φύσεως (concerning nature), that the air as wind had once a connection with fertility. I am indebted to Rev. Dr. Keller of Zurich for calling my attention to Bergson's conception of the "durée créatrice."

[31] Schiller says in "Wallenstein": "In your breast lie the constellations of your fate." "Our fates are the result of our personality," says Emerson in his "Essays." Compare with this my remarks in "Die Bedeutung des Vaters."

[32] The ascent to the "Idea" is described with unusual beauty in Augustine (Bk. X, Ch. 8). The beginning of Ch. 8 reads: "I will raise myself over this force of my nature, step by step ascending to Him who has made me. I will come to the fields and the spacious palaces of my memory."

[33] The followers of Mithra also called themselves Brothers. In philosophical speech Mithra was Logos emanating from God. (Cumont: "Myst. des Mithra," p. 102.)

Besides the followers of Mithra there existed many Brotherhoods which were called Thiasai and probably were the organizations from which the Church developed later. (A. Kalthoff: "Die Entstehung des Christentums.")

[34] Augustine, who stood in close relation to that period of transition not only in point of time but also intellectually, writes in his "Confessions" (Bk. VI, Ch. 16):
"Nor did I, unhappy, consider from what source it sprung, that even on these things, foul as they were, I with pleasure discoursed with my carnal pleasures. And yet these friends I loved for themselves only, and friends; nor could I, even according to the notions I then had of happiness, be happy without friends, amid what abundance soever of I felt that I was beloved of them for myself only. O, crooked paths! Woe to the audacious soul, which hoped, by forsaking Thee, to gain some better thing! Turned it hath, and turned again, upon back, sides, and belly, yet all was painful, and Thou alone rest!" (Trans. by Pusey.)
It is not only an unpsychologic but also an unscientific method of procedure to characterize offhand such effects of religion as suggestion. Such things are to be taken seriously as the expression of the deepest psychologic need.

[35] Both religions teach a pronounced ascetic morality, but at the same time a morality of action. The last is true also of Mithracism. Cumont says that Mithracism owed its success to the value of its morale: "This stimulated to action in an extraordinary degree" ("Myst. des Mithra"). The followers of Mithra formed a "sacred legion" for battle against evil, and among them were virgins (nuns) and continents (ascetics). Whether these brotherhoods had another meaning—that is, an economic-communistic one—is something I will not discuss now. Here only the religious-psychologic aspects interest us. Both religions have in common the idea of the divine sacrifice. Just as Christ sacrificed himself as the Lamb of God, so did Mithra sacrifice his Bull. This sacrifice in both religions is the heart of the Mysteries. The sacrificial death of Christ means the salvation of the world; from the sacrifice of the bull of Mithra the entire creation springs.

[36] This analytic perception of the roots of the Mystery Religions is necessarily one-sided, just as is the analysis of the basis of the religious poem. In order to understand the actual causes of the repression in Miss Miller one must delve into the moral history of the present; just as one is obliged to seek in the ancient moral and economic history the actual causes of repression which have given rise to the Mystery cults. This investigation has been brilliantly carried out by Kalthoff. (See his book, "Die Entstehung des Christentums," Leipzig 1904.) I also refer especially to Pohlmann's "Geschichte des antiken Kommunismus und Sozialismus"; also to Bücher: "Die Aufstände der unfreien Arbeiter 143 bis 129 v. Chr.," 1874.
The other cause of the enormous introversion of the libido in antiquity is probably to be found in the fact that an unbelievably large part of the people suffered in the wretched state of slavery. It is inevitable that finally those who bask in good fortune would be infected in the mysterious manner of the unconscious, by the deep sorrow and still deeper misery of their brothers, through which some were driven into orgiastic furies. Others, however, the better ones, sank into that strange world-weariness and satiety of the intellectuals of that time. Thus from two sources the great introversion was made possible.

[37] Compare Freud: "The Interpretation of the Dream."

[38] Compare Freud: "Sublimation," in "Three Contributions to the Sexual Theory."

[39] In a manner which is closely related to my thought, Kalthoff ("Entstehung des Christentums") understands the secularizing of the religious interest as a new incarnation of the λόγος (word). He says: "The profound grasp of the soul of nature evidenced in modern painting and poetry, the living intuitive feeling which even science in its most austere works can no longer do without, enables us easily to understand how the Logos of Greek philosophy which assigned its place in the world to the old Christ type, clothed in its world-to-come significance celebrated a new incarnation."

[40] It seems, on account of the isolation of the cult, that this fact was the cause of its ruin as well, because the eyes of that time were blinded to the beauty of nature. Augustine (Bk. X, Ch. 6) very justly remarks: "But they [men] were themselves undone through love for her [creation]."

[41] Augustine (ibid.): "But what do I love when I love Thee, Oh God? Not the bodily form, nor the earthly sweetness, nor the splendor of the light, so dear to these eyes; nor the sweet melodies of the richly varied songs; not the flowers and the sweet scented ointments and spices of lovely fragrance; not manna and honey; not the limbs of the body whose embraces are pleasant to the flesh. I do not love these when I love my God, and yet the light, the voice, the fragrance, the food, the embrace of my inner man; when these shine into my soul, which no space contains, which no time takes away, where there is a fragrance which the wind does not blow away, where there is a taste which no gluttony diminishes and where harmony abides which no satiety can remove—that is what I love, when I love my God." (Perhaps a model for Zarathustra: "Die sieben Siegel," Nietzsche's works, VI, p. 33 ff.)

[42] Cumont: "Die Mysterien des Mithra. Ein Beitrag zur Religionsgeschichte der römischen Kaiserzeit." Übersetzt von Gehrich, Leipzig 1903, p. 109.

[43] 41st Letter to Lucilius.

[44] Ibid.

CHAPTER IV

[1] Complexes are apt to be of the greatest stability, although their outward forms of manifestation change kaleidoscopically. A large number of experimental studies have entirely convinced me of this fact.

[2] Julian the Apostate made the last, unsuccessful attempt to cause the triumph of Mithracism over Christianity.

[3] This solution of the libido problem was brought about in a similar manner by the flight from the world during the first Christian century. (The cities of the Anchorites in the deserts of the Orient.) People mortified themselves in order to become spiritual and thus escape the extreme brutality of the decadent Roman civilization. Asceticism is forced sublimation, and is always to be found where the animal impulses are still so strong that they must be violently exterminated. The masked self-murder of the ascetic needs no further biologic proof.

Chamberlain ("Foundations of the Nineteenth Century") sees in the problem a biologic suicide because of the enormous amount of illegitimacy among Mediterranean peoples at that time. I believe that illegitimacy tends rather to mediocrity and to living for pleasure. It appears after all that there were, at that time, fine and noble people who, disgusted with the frightful chaos of that period which was merely an expression of the disruption of the individual, put an end to their lives, and thus caused the death of the old civilization with its endless wickedness.

[4] Δίκη (Justice), daughter of Zeus and Themis, who, after the Golden Age, forsook the degenerate earth.

[5] Thanks to this eclogue, Virgil later attained the honor of being a semi-Christian poet. To this he owes his position as guide to Dante.

[6] Both are represented not only as Christian, but also as Pagan. Essener and Therapeuten were quasi orders of the Anchorites living in the desert. Probably, as, for instance, may be learned from Apuleius ("Metamorphoses," lib. XI), there existed small settlements of mystics or consecrated ones around the sacred shrines of Isis and Mithra. Sexual abstinence and celibacy were also known.

[7] "Below the hills, a marshy plain
Infects what I so long have been retrieving:
This stagnant pool likewise to drain
Were now my latest and my best achieving.
To many millions following let me furnish soil."

The analogy of this expression with the quotation above is striking.

[8] Compare Breuer and Freud: "Studien über Hysterie"; also Bleuler: "Die Psychoanalyse Freuds," *Jahrbuch*, 1910, Vol. II, 2nd half.

[9] Faust (in suicide monologue):

"Out on the open ocean speeds my dreaming!
The glassy flood before my feet is gleaming!
A new day beckons to a newer shore!

A fiery chariot, borne on buoyant pinions,
Sweeps near me now; I soon shall ready be
To pierce the ether's high, unknown dominions,
To reach new spheres of pure activity!
This godlike rapture, this supreme existence
Do I, but now a worm, deserve to track?
Yes, resolute to reach some brighter distance;
On Earth's fair sun I turn my back!

·   ·   ·   ·   ·

Ah, that no wing can lift me from the soil,
Upon its tract to follow, follow soaring!
Then would I see eternal Evening gild
The silent world beneath me glowing.

·   ·   ·   ·   ·

And now before mine eyes expands the ocean,
With all its bays in shining sleep!

·   ·   ·   ·   ·

The newborn impulse fires my mind,
I hasten on, his beams eternal drinking."

We see it is the same longing and the same sun.

[10] Compare Jung: "Diagnost. Assoc. Stud."; also "The Psychology of Dementia Praecox," Chs. II and III.

[11] According to the Christian conception *God is Love.*

[12] Apuleius ("Met.," lib. XI, 257): "At manu dextera gerebam flammis adultam facem: et caput decora corona cinxerat palmae candidae foliis in modum radiorum prosistentibus. Sic ad instar solis exornato et in vicem simulacri constituto" (Then in my right hand I carried a burning torch; while a graceful chaplet encircled my head, the shining leaves of the palm tree projecting from it like rays of light. Thus arrayed like the sun, and placed so as to resemble a statue).

[13] The parallel in the Christian mysteries is the crowning with the crown of thorns, the exhibition and mocking of the Savior.

[14] In the same way the Sassanian Kings called themselves "Brothers of the Sun and of the Moon." In Egypt the soul of every ruler was a reduplication of the Sun Horus, an incarnation of the sun.

[15] "The rising at day out of the Underworld." Erman: "Aegypten," p. 409.

[16] Compare the coronation above. Feather, a symbol of power. Feather crown, a crown of rays, halo. Crowning, as such, is an identification with the sun. For example, the spiked crown upon the Roman coins made its appearance at the time when the Cæsars were identified with *Sol invictus* ("Solis invicti comes"). The halo is the same, that is to say, an image of the sun, just as is the tonsure. The priests of Isis had smooth-shaven heads like stars. (See Apuleius, "Metamorphoses.")

[17] Compare with this my statements in "Über die Bedeutung des Vaters für das Schicksal des Einzelnen." Deuticke, Wien.

[18] In the text of the so-called Mithra Liturgy are these lines: "Ἐγώ εἰμι σύμπλανος ὑμῖν ἀστὴρ καὶ ἐκ τοῦ βάθους ἀναλάμπων—ταῦτά σου εἰπόντος εὐθέως ὁ δίσκος ἀπλωθήσεται" (I am a star wandering about with you and flaming up from the depths. When thou hast said this, immediately the disc of the sun will unfold). The mystic through his prayers implored the divine power to cause the disc of the sun to expand. In the same way Rostand's "Chantecler" causes the sun to rise by his crowing.

"For verily I say unto you, If ye have faith as a grain of mustard seed, ye shall say unto this mountain, Remove hence to yonder place; and it shall remove; and nothing shall be impossible unto you" (Matthew xvii:20).

[19] Compare especially the words of the Gospel of John: "I and my Father are one" (John x:30). "He that hath seen me hath seen the Father" (John xiv:9). "Believe me that I am in the Father, and the Father in me" (John xiv:11). "I came forth from the Father, and am come into the world; again, I leave the world, and go to the Father" (John xvi:28). "I ascend unto my Father, and your Father; and to my God, and your God" (John xx:17).

[20] See the footnote on p. 137 of text.

[21] Two-bodied: an obscure epithet, if one does not admit that the dual life of the redeemed, taught in the mysteries of that time, was attributed to God, that is to say, to the libido. Compare the Pauline conception of the σῶμα σαρκικόν and πνευματικόν (carnal and spiritual body). In the Mithraic worship, Mithra seems to be the divine spirit, while Helios

is the material god; to a certain extent the visible lieutenant of the divinity. Concerning the confusion between Christ and Sol, see below.

[22] Compare Freud: "Three Contributions to the Sexual Theory."

[23] Renan ("Dialogues et fragments philosophiques," p. 168) says: "Before religion had reached the stage of proclaiming that God must be put into the absolute and ideal, that is to say, beyond this world, one worship alone was reasonable and scientific: that was the worship of the sun."

[24] Buber: "Ekstat. Konfess.," p. 51 and on.

[25] "Liebesgesänge an Gott," cited by Buber: "Ekstat. Konfess.," p. 40. An allied symbolism is found in Carlyle: "The great fact of existence is great to him. Fly as he will, he can not get out of the awful presence of this reality. His mind is so made; he is great by that first of all. Fearful and wonderful, real is life, real is death, is this universe to him. Though all men should forget its truth, and walk in a vain show, he can not. At all moments the Flame-image glares in upon him" ("Heroes and Hero-Worship").

One can select from literature at random. For example, S. Friedländer (Berlin-Halensee) says in *Jugend*, 1910, No. 35, p. 823: "Her longing demands from the beloved only the purest. Like the sun, it burns to ashes with the flame of excessive life, which refuses to be light," and so on.

[26] Buber: Ibid., p. 45.

[27] I emphasize this passage because its idea contains the psychological root of the "Wandering of the soul in Heaven," the conception of which is very ancient. It is a conception of the wandering sun which from its rising to its setting wanders over the world. The wandering gods are representations of the sun, that is, symbols of the libido. This comparison is indelibly impressed in the human phantasy as is shown by the poem of Wesendonck:

GRIEF.

The sun, every evening weeping,
Reddens its beautiful eyes for you;
When early death seizes you,
Bathing in the mirror of the sea.

Still in its old splendor
The glory rises from the dark world;
You awaken anew in the morning
Like a proud conqueror.

Ah, why then should I lament,
When my heart, so heavy, sees you?
Must the sun itself despair?
Must the sun set?

And does death alone bear life?
Do griefs alone give joys?
O, how grateful I am that
Such pains have given me nature!

Another parallel is in the poem of Ricarda Huch:

As the earth, separating from the sun,
Withdraws in quick flight into the stormy night,

Starring the naked body with cold snow,
Deafened, it takes away the summer joy.
And sinking deeper in the shadows of winter,
Suddenly draws close to that which it flees,
Sees itself warmly embraced with rosy light
Leaning against the lost consort.
Thus I went, suffering the punishment of exile,
Away from your countenance, into the ancient place.
Unprotected, turning to the desolate north,
Always retreating deeper into the sleep of death;
And then would I awake on your heart,
Blinded by the splendor of the dawn.

[28] The whistling and snapping is a tasteless, archaic relic, an allurement for the theriomorphic divinity, probably also an infantile reminiscence (quieting the child by whistling and snapping). Of similar significance is the roaring at the divinity. ("Mithr. Lit.," p. 13): "You are to look at him and give forth a long roar, as with a horn, using all your breath, pressing your sides, and kiss the amulet . . . etc." "My soul roars with the voice of a hungry lion," says Mechthild von Magdeburg. "As the hart panteth after the water brooks, so panteth my soul after God."—Psalms xlii: 2. The ceremonial custom, as so often happens, has dwindled into a figure of speech. Dementia praecox, however, revivifies the old custom, as in the "Roaring miracle" of Schreber. See the latter's "Denkwürdigkeiten eines Nervenkranken," by which he demands that God, i.e. the Father, so inadequately oriented with humanity, take notice of his existence.

The infantile reminiscence is clear, that is, the childish cry to attract the attention of the parent to himself; the whistling and smacking for the allurement of the theriomorphic attribute, the "helpful animal." (See Rank: "The Myth of the Birth of the Hero.")

[29] The water-god Sobk, appearing as a crocodile, was identified with Rê.

[30] Erman: "Aegypten," p. 354.

[31] Erman: Ibid., p. 355.

[32] Compare above ἀστέρας πενταδακτυλιαίους ("five-fingered stars").

[33] The bull Apis is a manifestation of Ptah. The bull is a well-known symbol of the sun.

[34] Amon.

[35] Sobk of Faijum.

[36] The God of Dedu in the Delta, who was worshipped as a piece of wood. (Phallic.)

[37] This reformation, which was inaugurated with much fanaticism, soon broke down.

[38] Apuleius, "Met.," lib. XI, p. 239.

[39] It is noteworthy that the humanists too (I am thinking of an expression of the learned Mutianus Rufus) soon perceived that antiquity had but two gods, that is, a masculine god and a feminine god.

[40] Not only was the light- or fire-substance ascribed to the divinity but also to the soul; as for example in the system of Mâni, as well as

among the Greeks, where it was characterized as a fiery breath of air. The Holy Ghost of the New Testament appears in the form of flames around the heads of the Apostles, because the πνεῦμα was understood to mean "fiery" (Dieterich: Ibid., p. 116). Very similar is the Iranian conception of Hvarenô, by which is meant the "Grace of Heaven" through which a monarch rules. By "Grace" is understood a sort of fire or shining glory, something very substantial (Cumont: Ibid., p. 70). We come across conceptions allied in character in Kerner's "Seherin von Prevorst," and in the case published by me, "Psychologie und Pathologie sogenannter occulter Phänomene." Here not only the souls consist of a spiritual light-substance, but the entire world is constructed according to the white-black system of the Manichæans—and this by a fifteen-year-old girl! The intellectual over-accomplishment which I observed earlier in this creation, is now revealed as a consequence of energetic introversion, which again roots up deep historical strata of the soul and in which I perceive a regression to the memories of humanity condensed in the unconscious.

[41] I add to this a quotation from Firmicus Maternus (Mathes. I, 5, 9, cit. by Cumont: "Textes et Monuments," I, p. 40): "Cui (animo) descensus per orbem solis tribuitur" (To this spirit the descent through the orb of the sun is attributed).

[42] St. Hieronymus remarks, concerning Mithra who was born in a miraculous manner from a rock, that this birth was the result of "solo aestu libidinis" (merely through the heat of the libido) (Cumont: "Textes et Monuments," I, p. 163).

[43] Mead: "A Mithraic Ritual." London 1907, p. 22.

[44] I am indebted to my friend and co-worker, Dr. Riklin, for the knowledge of the following case which presents an interesting symbolism. It concerns a paranoic who passed over into a manifest megalomaniac in the following way: She suddenly saw a *strong light,* a *wind blew* upon her, she felt as if "her heart turned over," and from that moment she knew that God had visited her and was in her.
I wish to refer here to the interesting correlation of mythological and pathological forms disclosed in the analytical investigation of Dr. S. Spielrein, and expressly emphasize that she has discovered the symbolisms presented by her in the *Jahrbuch,* through independent experimental work, in no way connected with my work.

[45] According to the Chaldean teaching the sun occupies the middle place in the choir of the seven planets.

[46] The Great Bear consists of seven stars.

[47] Mithra is frequently represented with a knife in one hand and a torch in the other. The knife as an instrument of sacrifice plays an important rôle in his myth.

[48] Ibid.

[49] Compare with this the scarlet mantle of Helios in the Mithra liturgy. It was a part of the rites of the various cults to be dressed in the bloody skins of the sacrificial animals, as in the Lupercalia, Dionysia and Saturnalia, the last of which has bequeathed to us the Carnival, the typical figure of which, in Rome, was the priapic Pulcinella.

⁵⁰ Compare the linen-clad retinue of Helios. Also the bull-headed gods wear white περιζώματα (aprons).

⁵¹ The title of Mithra in Vendidad XIX, 28; cit. by Cumont: " Textes et Monuments," p. 37.

⁵² The development of the sun symbol in Faust does not go as far as an anthropomorphic vision. It stops in the suicide scene at the chariot of Helios ("A fiery chariot borne on buoyant pinions sweeps near me now "). The fiery chariot comes to receive the dying or departing hero, as in the ascension of Elijah or of Mithra. (Similarly Francis of Assisi.) In his flight Faust passes over the sea, just as does Mithra. The ancient Christian pictorial representations of the ascension of Elijah are partly founded upon the corresponding Mithraic representations. The horses of the sun-chariot rushing upwards to Heaven leave the solid earth behind, and pursue their course over a water god, Oceanus, lying at their feet. (Cumont: " Textes et Monuments." Bruxelles 1899, I, p. 178.)

⁵³ Compare my article, " Psych. und Path. sog. occ. Phän."

⁵⁴ Quoted from Pitra: " Analecta sacra," cit. by Cumont: " Textes et Monuments," p. 355.

⁵⁵ Cited from Usener: " Weihnachtsfest," p. 5.

⁵⁶ The passage from Malachi is found in chap. iv, 2: " But unto you that fear my name shall the Sun of Righteousness arise with healing in His wings " (feathers). This figure of speech recalls the Egyptian sun symbol.

⁵⁷ Cumont: " Textes et Monuments," t. I, p. 355. περὶ ἀστρονόμων.

⁵⁸ The pictures in the Catacombs contain much symbolism of the sun. The Swastika cross, for example—a well-known image of the sun, wheel of the sun, or sun's feet—is found upon the garment of Fossor Diogenes in the cemetery of Peter and Marcellinus. The symbols of the rising sun, the bull and the ram, are found in the Orpheus fresco of the cemetery of the holy Domitilla. Similarly the ram and the peacock (which, like the phœnix, is the symbol of the sun) is found upon an epitaph of the Callistus Catacomb.

⁵⁹ Compare the countless examples in Görres: " Die christliche Mystik."

⁶⁰ Compare Leblant: " Sarcophages de la Gaule," 1880. In the " Homilies " of Clement of Rome (" Hom.," II, 23, cit. by Cumont) it is said: Τῷ κυρίῳ γεγονάσιν δώδεκα ἀπόστολοι τῶν τοῦ ἡλίου δώδεκα μηνῶν φέροντες τὸν ἀριθμόν (The twelve apostles of the Lord, having the number of the twelve months of the sun). As is apparent, this idea is concerned with the course of the sun through the Zodiac. Without wishing to enter upon an interpretation of the Zodiac, I mention that, according to the ancient view (probably Chaldean), the course of the sun was represented by a snake which carried the signs of the Zodiac on its back (similarly to the Leontocephalic God of the Mithra mysteries). This view is proven by a passage from a Vatican Codex edited by Cumont in another connection (190, saec. XIII, p. 229, p. 85): ''τότε ὁ πάνσοφος δημιουργὸς ἄκρῳ νεύματι ἐκίνησε τὸν μέγαν δράκοντα σὺν τῷ κεκοσμημένῳ στεφάνῳ, λέγω δὴ τὰ ιβ' ζῴδια, βαστάζοντα ἐπὶ τοῦ νώτου αὐτοῦ" (The all-wise maker of the world set in motion the great dragon with the adorned crown, with a command

at the end. I speak now of the twelve images borne on the back of this).

This inner connection of the ζῴδια (small images) with the zodiacal snake is worthy of notice and gives food for thought. The Manichæan system attributes to Christ the symbol of the snake, and indeed of the snake on the tree of Paradise. For this the quotation from John gives far-reaching justification (John iii: 14): "And as Moses lifted up the serpent in the wilderness, even so must the son of man be lifted up." An old theologian, Hauff ("Biblische Real- und Verbalkonkordanz," 1834), makes this careful observation concerning this quotation: "Christ considered the Old Testament story an unintentional symbol of the idea of the atonement." The almost bodily connection of the followers with Christ is well known. (Romans xii: 4): "For as we have many members in one body, and all members have not the same office, so we being many are one body in Christ, and every one members one of another." If confirmation is needed that the zodiacal signs are symbols of the libido, then the sentence in John i: 29, "Behold the Lamb of God, which taketh away the sin of the world," assumes a significant meaning.

[61] According to an eleventh-century manuscript in Munich; Albrecht Wirth: "Aus orientalischen Chroniken," p. 151. Frankfurt 1894.

[62] Abeghian: "Der armenische Volksglaube," p. 41, 1899.

[63] Compare Aigremont: "Fuss- und Schuhsymbolik," Leipzig 1909.

[64] Attis was later assimilated with Mithra. Like Mithra he was represented with the Phrygian cap (Cumont: "Myst. des Mith.," p. 65). According to the testimony of Hieronymus, the manger (Geburtshöhle) at Bethlehem was originally a sanctuary (Spelaeum) of Attis (Usener: "Weihnachtsfest," p. 283).

[65] Cumont ("Die Mysterien des Mithra," p. 4) says of Christianity and Mithracism: "Both opponents perceived with astonishment how similar they were in many respects, without being able to account for the causes of this similarity."

[66] Our present-day moral views come into conflict with this wish in so far as it concerns the erotic fate. The erotic adventures necessary for so many people are often all too easily given up because of moral opposition, and one willingly allows himself to be discouraged because of the social advantages of being moral.

[67] The poetical works of Lord Byron.

[68] Edmond Rostand: "Cyrano de Bergerac," Paris 1898.

[69] The projection into the "cosmic" is the primitive privilege of the libido, for it enters into our perception naturally through all the avenues of the senses, apparently from without, and in the form of pain and pleasure connected with the objects. This we attribute to the object without further thought, and we are inclined, in spite of our philosophic considerations, to seek the causes in the object, which often has very little concern with it. (Compare this with the Freudian conception of Transference, especially Firenczi's remarks in his paper, "Introjektion und Übertragung," *Jahrbuch*, Vol. I, p. 422.) Beautiful examples of direct libido projection are found in erotic songs:

> "Down on the strand, down on the shore,
> A maiden washed the kerchief of her lover;
> And a soft west wind came blowing over the shore,

> Lifted her skirt a little with its breeze
> And let a little of her ankles be seen,
> And the seashore became as bright as all the world."
> > (Neo-Grecian Folksong from Sanders: "Das Volks-
> > leben der Neugriechen," 1844, p. 81, cit. *Zeit-
> > schrift des Vereines für Volkskunde*, Jahrgang XII,
> > 1902, p. 166.)

> "In the farm of Gymir I saw
> A lovely maiden coming toward me;
> From the brilliance of her arm glowed
> The sky and all the everlasting sea."
> > (From the Edda, tr. (into Ger.) by H. Gering, p.
> > 53; *Zeitschrift für Volkskunde*, Jahrgang XII, 1902,
> > p. 167.)

Here, too, belong all the miraculous stories of cosmic events, phenomena occurring at the birth and death of heroes. (The Star of Bethlehem; earthquakes, the rending asunder of the temple hangings, etc., at the death of Christ.) The omnipotence of God is the manifest omnipotence of the libido, the only actual doer of wonders which we know. The symptom described by Freud, as the "omnipotence of thought" in Compulsion Neuroses arises from the "sexualizing" of the intellect. The historical parallel for this is the magical omnipotence of the mystic, attained by introversion. The "omnipotence of thought" corresponds to the identification with God of the paranoic, arrived at similarly through introversion.

[70] Comparable to the mythological heroes who after their greatest deeds fall into spiritual confusion.

[71] Here I must refer you to the blasphemous piety of Zinzendorf, which has been made accessible to us by the noteworthy investigation of Pfister.

[72] Anah is really the beloved of Japhet, the son of Noah. She leaves him because of the angel.

[73] The one invoked is really a star. Compare Miss Miller's poem.

[74] Really an attribute of the wandering sun.

[75] Compare Miss Miller's poem.

> "My poor life is gone,
>
> ———————— then having gained
> One raptured glance, I'll die content,
> For I the source of beauty, warmth and life
> Have in his perfect splendor once beheld."

[76] The light-substance of God.

[77] The light-substance of the individual soul.

[78] The bringing together of the two light-substances shows their common origin; they are the symbols of the libido. Here they are figures of speech. In earlier times they were doctrines. According to Mechthild von Magdeburg the soul is made out of love ("Das fliessende Licht der Gottheit," herausgegeben von Escherich, Berlin 1909).

[79] Compare what is said above about the snake symbol of the libido.

The idea that the climax means at the same time the end, even death, forces itself here.

[80] Compare the previously mentioned pictures of Stuck: Vice, Sin and Lust, where the woman's naked body is encircled by the snake. Fundamentally it is a symbol of the most extreme fear of death. The death of Cleopatra may be mentioned here.

[81] Encircling by the serpent.

PART II

CHAPTER I

[1] This is the way it appears to us from the psychological standpoint. See below.

[2] Samson as Sun-god. See Steinthal: "Die Sage von Simson," *Zeitschrift für Völkerpsychologie*, Vol. II.

[3] I am indebted for the knowledge of this fragment to Dr. Van Ophuijsen of The Hague.

[4] Rudra, properly father of the Maruts (winds), a wind or sun god, appears here as the sole creator God, as shown in the course of the text. The rôle of creator and fructifier easily belongs to him as wind god. I refer to the observations in Part I concerning Anaxagoras and to what follows.

[5] This and the following passages from the Upanishads are quoted from: "The Upanishads," translated by R. G. S. Mead and J. C. Chattopâdhyâya. London 1896.

[6] In a similar manner, the Persian sun-god Mithra is endowed with an immense number of eyes.

[7] Whoever has in himself, God, the sun, is immortal, like the sun. Compare Pt. I, Ch. 5.

[8] He was given that name because he had introduced the phallic cult into Greece. In gratitude to him for having buried the mother of the serpents, the young serpents cleaned his ears, so that he became clairaudient and understood the language of birds and beasts.

[9] Compare the vase picture of Thebes, where the Cabiri are represented in noble and in caricatured form (in Roscher: "Lexicon," s. Megaloi Theoi).

[10] The justification for calling the Dactyli thumbs is given in a note in Pliny: 37, 170, according to which there were in Crete precious stones of iron color and thumblike shape which were called Idaean Dactyli.

[11] Therefore, the dactylic metre or verse.

[12] See Roscher: "Lexicon of Greek and Roman Mythology," s. Dactyli.

[13] According to Jensen: "Kosmologie," p. 292, Oannes-Ea is the educator of men.

[14] Inman: "Ancient Pagan and Modern Christian Symbolism."

[15] Varro identifies the μεγάλοι θεοί with the Penates. The Cabiri might be simulacra duo virilia Castoris et Pollucis in the harbor of Samothrace.

[16] In Brasiae on the Laconian coast and in Pephnos some statues only a foot high with caps on their heads were found.

[17] That the monks have again invented cowls seems of no slight importance.

[18] *Zentralblatt für Psychoanalyse,* II, p. 187.

[19] The typical motive of the youthful teacher of wisdom has also been introduced into the Christ myth in the scene of the twelve-year-old Jesus in the temple.

[20] Next to this, there is a female figure designated as KPATEIA, which means " one who brings forth " (Orphic).

[21] Roscher: "Lexicon," s. v. Megaloi Theoi.

[22] Roscher: "Lexicon," s. v. Phales.

[23] Compare Freud's evidence, *Zentralblatt für Psychoanalyse,* I, p. 188. I must remark at this place that etymologically penis and penates are not grouped together. On the contrary, πέος, πόσϑη, Sanskrit *pása-ḥ,* Latin *penis,* were given with the Middle High German *visel* (penis) and Old High German *fasel* the significance of fœtus, *proles.* (Walde: "Latin Etymologie," s. Penis.)

[24] Stekel in his "Traumsymbolik" has traced out this sort of representation of the genitals, as has Spielrein also in a case of dementia praecox. 1912 *Jahrbuch,* Vol. III, p. 369.

[25] The figure of Κράτεια, the one who "brings forth," placed beside it is surprising in that the libido occupied in creating religion has apparently developed out of the primitive relation to the mother.

[26] In Freud's paper ("Psychoanalytische Bemerkungen über einen Fall von Paranoia usw.," 1912 *Jahrbuch,* Vol. III, p. 68), which appeared simultaneously with the first part of my book, he makes an observation absolutely parallel to the meaning of my remarks concerning the " libido theory " resulting from the phantasies of the insane Schreber: Schreber's divine rays composed by condensation of sun's rays, nerve fibres and sperma are really nothing else but the libido fixations projected outside and objectively represented, and lend to his delusion a striking agreement with our theory. That the world must come to an end because the ego of the patient attracts all the rays to himself; that later during the process of reconstruction he must be very anxious lest God sever the connection of the rays with him: these and certain other peculiarities of Schreber's delusion sound very like the foregoing endopsychic perceptions, on the assumption of which I have based the interpretation of paranoia.

[27] "Tuscalanarum quaestionum," lib. IV.

[28] "Pro Quint.," 14.

[29] Walde: "Latin Etymological Dictionary," 1910. See libet. *Liberi* (children) is grouped together with *libet* by Nazari ("Riv. di Fil.," XXXVI, 573). Could this be proven, then Liber, the Italian god of procreation, undoubtedly connected with *liberi,* would also be grouped with *libet.* Libitina is the goddess of the dead, who would have nothing in common with Lubentina and Lubentia (attribute of Venus), which belongs to *libet;* the name is as yet unexplained. (Compare the later comments in this work.) *Libare =* to pour (to sacrifice?) and is supposed to have nothing to do with *liber.* The etymology of *libido* shows not only the central setting of the idea, but also the connection with

the German *Liebe* (love). We are obliged to say under these circumstances that not only the idea, but also the word *libido* is well chosen for the subject under discussion.

[30] A corrected view on the conservation of energy in the light of the theory of cognition might offer the comment that this picture is the projection of an endopsychic perception of the equivalent transformations of the libido.

CHAPTER II

[1] Freud: "Three Contributions to the Sexual Theory,' p. 29. Translation by Brill. "In a non-sexual 'impulse' originating from impulses of motor sources we can distinguish a contribution from a stimulus-receiving organ, such as the skin, mucous membrane, and sensory organs. This we shall here designate as an erogenous zone; it is that organ the stimulus of which bestows on the impulse the sexual character."

[2] Freud: Ibid., p. 14. "One definite kind of contiguity, consisting of mutual approximation of the mucous membranes of the lips in the form of a kiss, has among the most civilized nations received a sexual value, though the parts of the body concerned do not belong to the sexual apparatus but form the entrance to the digestive tract."

[3] See Freud: Ibid.

[4] An old view which Möbius endeavored to bring again to its own. Among the newcomers it is Fouillée, Wundt, Beneke, Spencer, Ribot and others, who grant the psychologic primate to the impulse system.

[5] Freud: Ibid., p. 25. "I must repeat that these psychoneuroses, as far as my experience goes, are based on sexual motive powers. I do not mean that the energy of the sexual impulse contributes to the forces supporting the morbid manifestations (symptoms), but I wish distinctly to maintain that this supplies the only constant and the most important source of energy in the neurosis, so that the sexual life of such persons manifests itself either exclusively, preponderately, or partially in these symptoms."

[6] That scholasticism is still firmly rooted in mankind is only too easily proven, and an illustration of this is the fact that not the least of the reproaches directed against Freud, is that he has changed certain of his earlier conceptions. Woe to those who compel mankind to learn anew! "Les savants ne sont pas curieux."

[7] *Jahrbuch,* Vol. III, p. 65.

[8] Schreber's case is not a pure paranoia in the modern sense.

[9] Also in "Der Inhalt der Psychose," 1908.

[10] Compare Jung: "The Psychology of Dementia Praecox," p. 114.

[11] For example, in a frigid woman who as a result of a specific sexual repression does not succeed in bringing the libido sexualis to the husband, the parent imago is present and she produces symptoms which belong to that environment.

[12] Similar transgression of the sexual sphere might also occur in hysterical psychoses; that indeed is included with the definition of the psychosis and means nothing but a general disturbance of adaptation.

[13] "Die psychosexuellen Differenzen der Hysterie und der Dementia praecox," *Zentralblatt für Nervenheilkunde und Psychiatrie,* 1908.

[14] "Introjektion und Übertragung," *Jahrbuch,* Vol. I, p. 422.

[15] See Avenarius: "Menschliche Weltbegriffe," p. 25.

[16] "Welt als Wille und Vorstellung," Vol. I, p. 54.

[17] "Theogonie."

[18] Compare Roscher: "Lexicon," p. 2248.

[19] Drews: "Plotinus," Jena 1907, p. 127.

[20] Ibid., p. 132.

[21] Ibid., p. 135.

[22] Plotinus: "Enneades," II, 5, 3.

[23] Plotinus: "Enneades," IV, 8, 3.

[24] "Enneades," III, 5, 9.

[25] Ibid., p. 141.

[26] Naturally this does not mean that the function of reality owes its existence to the differentiation in procreative instincts exclusively. I am aware of the undetermined great part played by the function of nutrition.

[27] Malthusianism is the artificial setting forth of the natural tendency.

[28] For instance, in the form of procreation as in general of the will.

[29] Freud in his work on paranoia has allowed himself to be carried over the boundaries of his original conception of libido by the facts of this illness. He there uses libido even for the function of reality, which cannot be reconciled with the standpoint of the "Three Contributions."

[30] Bleuler arrives at this conclusion from the ground of other considerations, which I cannot always accept. See Bleuler, "Dementia Praecox," in Aschaffenburg's "Handbuch der Psychiatrie."

[31] See Jung: "Kritik über E. Bleuler: Zur Theorie des schizophrenen Negativismus." *Jahrbuch,* Vol. III, p. 469.

[32] Spielrein: "Über den psychologischen Inhalt eines Falles von Schizophrenie." *Jahrbuch,* Vol. III, p. 329.

[33] His researches are in my possession and their publication is in preparation.

[34] Honegger made use of this example in his lecture at the private psychoanalytic congress in Nürnberg, 1910.

[35] Spielrein: Ibid., pp. 338, 353, 387. For soma as the "effusion of the seed," see what follows.

[36] Compare Berthelot: "Les Alchémistes Grecs," and Spielrein: Ibid., p. 353.

[37] I cannot refrain from observing that this vision reveals the original meaning of alchemy. A primitive magic power for generation, that is to say, a means by which children could be produced without the mother.

[38] Spielrein: Ibid., pp. 338, 345.

[39] I must mention here those Indians who create the first people from the union of a sword hilt and a shuttle.

[40] Ibid., p. 399.

CHAPTER III

[1] Naturally a precursor of onanism.

[2] This true catatonic pendulum movement of the head, I saw arise in the case of a catatonic patient, from the coitus movements gradually shifted upwards. This Freud has described long ago as a shifting from below to above.

[3] She put the small fragments which fell out into her mouth and ate them.

[4] "Dreams and Myths." Vienna 1909. Translated by Wm. A. White, M.D.

[5] A. Kuhn: "Mythologische Studien," Vol. I: "Die Herabkunft des Feuers und des Göttertrankes." Gütersloh 1886. A very readable résumé of the contents is to be found in Steinthal: "Die ursprüngliche Form der Sage von Prometheus," Zeitschrift für Völkerpsychologie und Sprachwissenschaft, Vol. II, 1862; also in Abraham: Ibid.

[6] Also mathnâmi and mâthayati. The root manth or math has a special significance.

[7] Zeitschrift für vergleichende Sprachforschung, Vol. II, p. 395, and Vol. IV, p. 124.

[8] Bapp in Roscher's "Lexicon," Sp. 3034.

[9] Bhrgu = φλεγυ, a recognized connection of sound. See Roscher: Sp. 3034, 54.

[10] For the eagle as a fire token among the Indians, see Roscher: Sp. 3034, 60.

[11] The stem manth according to Kuhn becomes in German mangeln, rollen (referring to washing). Manthara is the butter paddle. When the gods generated the amrta (drink of immortality) by twirling the ocean around, they used the mountain Mandara as the paddle (see Kuhn: Ibid., p. 17). Steinthal calls attention to the Latin expression in poetical speech: mentula = male member, in which ment (manth) was used. I add here also, mentula is to be taken as diminutive for menta or mentha (μίνϑα), Minze. In antiquity the Minze was called "Crown of Aphrodite" (Dioscorides, II, 154). Apuleius called it "mentha venerea"; it was an aphrodisiac. (The opposite meaning is found in Hippocrates: Si quis eam saepe comedat, ejus genitale semen ita colliquescit, ut effluat, et arrigere prohibet et corpus imbecillum reddit, and according to Dioscorides, Minze is a means of preventing conception. (See Aigremont: "Volkserotik und Pflanzenwelt," Vol. I, p. 127). But the ancients also said of Menta: "Menta autem appellata, quod suo odore mentem feriat—mentae ipsius odor animum excitat." This leads us to the root ment—in Latin mens; English, mind—with which the parallel development to pramantha, Προμηϑεύς, would be completed. Still to be added is that an especially strong chin is called mento (mentum). A special development of the chin is given, as we know, to the priapic

figure of Pulcinello, also the pointed beard (and ears) of the satyrs and the other priapic demon, just as in general all the protruding parts of the body can be given a masculine significance and all the receding parts or depressions a feminine significance. This applies also to all other animate or inanimate objects. See Maeder: *Psycho.-Neurol. Wochenschr.*, X. Jahrgang. However, this whole connection is more than a little uncertain.

[12] Abraham observes that in Hebrew the significance of the words for man and woman is related to this symbolism.

[13] "What is called the gulya (pudendum) means the yoni (the birthplace) of the God; the fire, which was born there, is called 'beneficent'" ("Kâtyâyanas Karmapradîpa," I, 7; translated by Kuhn: "Herabkunft des Feuers," p. 67). The etymologic connection between *bohren—geboren* is possible. The Germanic *bŏrôn* (to bore) is primarily related to the Latin *forare* and the Greek φαράω = to plow. Possibly it is an Indo-Germanic root *bher* with the meaning to bear; Sanscrit *bhar-;* Greek φερ-; Latin *fer-;* from this Old High German *beran,* English to bear, Latin *fero* and *fertilis, fordus* (pregnant); Greek φορός. Walde ("Latin Etym.," s. Ferio) traces *forare* to the root *bher-*. Compare with this the phallic symbolism of the plough, which we meet later on.

[14] Weber: "Indische Studien," I, 197; quoted by Kuhn: Ibid., p. 71.

[15] "Rigveda," III, 29—1 to 3.

[16] Or mankind in general. Viçpatni is the feminine wood, viçpati, an attribute of Agni, the masculine. In the instruments of fire lies the origin of the human race, from the same perverse logic as in the beforementioned shuttle and sword-hilt. Coitus as the means of origin of the human race must be denied, from the motive, to be more fully discussed later, of a primitive resistance against sexuality.

[17] Wood as the symbol of the mother is well known from the dream investigation of the present time. See Freud: "Dream Interpretation." Stekel ("Sprache des Traumes," p. 128) explains it as the symbol of the woman. Wood is also a German vulgar term for the breast. ("Wood before the house.") The Christian wood symbolism needs a chapter by itself. The son of Ilâ: Ilâ is the daughter of Manus, the one and only, who with the help of his fish has overcome the deluge, and then with his daughter again procreated the human race.

[18] See Hirt: "Etymologie der neuhochdeutschen Sprache," p. 348.

[19] The capitular of Charlemagne of 942 forbade "those sacrilegious fires which are called Niedfyr." See Grimm: "Mythologie," 4th edition, p. 502. Here there are to be found descriptions of similar fire ceremonies.

[20] Kuhn: Ibid., p. 43.

[21] Preuss: "Globus," LXXXVI, 1905, S. 358.

[22] Compare with this Friedrich Schultze: "Psychologie der Naturvölker," p. 161.

[23] This primitive play leads to the phallic symbolism of the plough. Ἀροῦν means to plough and possesses in addition the poetic meaning of impregnate. The Latin *arare* means merely to plough, but the phrase "fundum alienum arare" means "to pluck cherries in a neighbor's

garden." A striking representation of the phallic plough is found on a vase in the archeological museum in Florence. It portrays a row of six naked ithyphallic men who carry a plough represented phallically (Dieterich: "Mutter Erde," p. 107). The "carrus navalis" of our spring festival (carnival) was at times during the Middle Ages a plough (Hahn: "Demeter und Baubo," quoted by Dieterich: Ibid., p. 109). Dr. Abegg of Zurich called my attention to the clever work of R. Meringer ("Wörter und Sachen. Indogermanische Forschungen," 16, 179/84, 1904). We are made acquainted there with a very far-reaching amalgamation of the libido symbols with the external materials and external activities, which support our previous considerations to an extraordinary degree. Meringer's assumption proceeds from the two Indo-Germanic roots, uen and ueneti. Indo-Germanic *uen Holz, ai. ist. van, vana. Agni is garbhas vanām, "fruit of the womb of the woods."

Indo-Germanic *ueneti signifies "he ploughs": by that is meant the penetration of the ground by means of a sharpened piece of wood and the throwing up of the earth resulting from it. This verb itself is not verified because this very primitive working of the ground was given up at an early time. When a better treatment of the fields was learned, the primitive designation for the ploughed field was given to the pasture, therefore Gothic vinja, νομή, Old Icelandic vin, pasture, meadow. Perhaps also the Icelandic Vanen, as Gods of agriculture, came from that.

From ackern (to plough) sprang coïre (the connection might have been the other way); also Indo-Germanic *uenos (enjoyment of love), Latin venus. Compare with this the root uen = wood. Coïre = passionately to strive; compare Old High German vinnan, to rave or to storm; also the Gothic vēns; ἐλπίς = hope; Old High German wân = expectation, hope; Sanscrit van, to desire or need; further, Wonne (delight, ecstasy); Old Icelandic vinr (beloved, friend). From the meaning ackern (to plough) arises wohnen (to live). This transition has been completed only in the German. From wohnen→gewöhnen, gewohnt sein (to be accustomed), Old Icelandic vanr = gewohnt (to be accustomed); from ackern further→sich mühen, plagen (to take much trouble, wearing work), Old Icelandic vinna, to work: Old High German winnan (to toil hard, to overwork); Gothic vinnan, πάσχειν; vunns, πάθημα. From ackern comes, on the other hand, gewinnen erlangen (to win, to attain), Old High German giwinnan, but also verletzen (to injure): Gothic vunds (wund), wound. Wund in the beginning, the most primal sense, was therefore the ground torn up by the wooden implement. From verletzen (to injure) come schlagen (to strike), besiegen (to conquer): Old High German winna (strife); Old Saxon winnan (to battle).

[24] The old custom of making the "bridal bed" upon the field, which was for the purpose of rendering the field fertile, contains the primitive thought in the most elementary form; by that the analogy was expressed in the clearest manner: Just as I impregnate the woman, so do I impregnate the earth. The symbol leads the sexual libido over to the cultivation of the earth and to its fruitfulness. Compare with that Mannhardt: "Wald- und Feldkulte," where there are abundant illustrations.

[25] Spielrein's patient (Jahrbuch, III, p. 371) associates fire and generation in an unmistakable manner. She says as follows concerning it: "One needs iron for the purpose of piercing the earth and for the purpose of creating fire." This is to be found in the Mithra liturgy as well. In the invocation to the fire god, it is said: ὁ συνδήσας πνεύματι

τὰ πύρινα κλεῖθρα τοῦ οὐρανοῦ (Thou who hast closed up the fiery locks of heaven, with the breath of the spirit,—open to me). "With iron one can create cold people from the stone." The boring into the earth has for her the meaning of fructification or birth. She says: "With the glowing iron one can pierce through mountains. The iron becomes glowing when one pushes it into a stone."

Compare with this the etymology of *bohren* and *gebären* (see above). In the "Bluebird" of Maeterlinck the two children who seek the bluebird in the land of the unborn children, find a boy who bores into his nose. It is said of him: he will discover a new fire, so as to warm the earth again, when it will have grown cold.

[26] Compare with this the interesting proofs in Bücher: "Arbeit und Rhythmus," Leipzig 1899.

[27] Amusement is undoubtedly coupled with many rites, but by no means with all. There are some very unpleasant things.

[28] The Upanishads belong to the Brâhmana, to the theology of the Vedic writings, and comprise the theosophical-speculative part of the Vedic teachings. The Vedic writings and collections are in part of very uncertain age and may reach back to a very distant past because for a long period they were handed down only orally.

[29] The primal and omniscient being, the idea of whom, translated into psychology, is comprehended in the conception of libido.

[30] Âtman is also considered as originally a bisexual being—corresponding to the libido theory. The world sprang from desire. Compare *Brihadâranyaka-Upanishad*, I, 4, 1 (Deussen):

"(1) In the beginning this world was Âtman alone—he looked around: Then he saw nothing but himself.
"(2) Then he was frightened; therefore, one is afraid, when one is alone. Then he thought: Wherefore should I be afraid, since there is nothing beside myself?
"(3) But also he had no joy, therefore one has no joy when one is alone. Then he longed for a companion."

After this there follows the description of his division quoted above. Plato's conception of the world-soul approaches very near to the Hindoo idea. "The soul in no wise needed eyes, because near it there was nothing visible. Nothing was separate from it, nothing approached it, because outside of it there was nothing" ("Timaios").

[31] Compare with this Freud's "Three Contributions to the Sexual Theory."

[32] What seems an apparently close parallel to the position of the hand in the Upanishad text I observed in a little child. The child held one hand before his mouth and rubbed it with the other, a movement which may be compared to that of the violinist. It was an early infantile habit which persisted for a long time afterwards.

[33] Compare Freud: "Bemerkungen über einen Fall von Zwangs-neurose." 1912 *Jahrbuch*, Vol. I, p. 357.

[34] As shown above, in the child the libido progresses from the mouth zone into the sexual zone.

[35] Compare what has been said above about Dactyli. Abundant examples are found in Aigremont: "Fuss- und Schuhsymbolik."

[36] When, in the enormously increased sexual resistance of the present day, women emphasize the secondary signs of sex and their erotic charm by specially designed clothing, that is a phenomenon which belongs in the same general scheme for the heightening of allurement.

[37] It is well known that the orifice of the ear has also a sexual value. In a hymn to the Virgin it is called "quae per aurem concepisti." Rabelais' Gargantua was born through his mother's ear. Bastian ("Beiträge z. vergl. Psychologie," p. 238) mentions the following passage from an old work, "There is not to be found in this entire kingdom, even among the very smallest girls, a maiden, because even in her tender youth she puts a special medicine into her genitals, also in the orifice of her ears; she stretches these and holds them open continuously."—Also the Mongolian Buddha was born from the ear of his mother.

[38] The driving motive for the breaking up of the ring might be sought, as I have already intimated in passing, in the fact that the secondary sexual activity (the transformed coitus) never is or would be adapted to bring about that natural satiety, as is the activity in its real place. With this first step towards transformation, the first step towards the characteristic dissatisfaction was also taken, which later drove man from discovery to discovery without allowing him ever to attain satiety. Thus it looks from the biological standpoint, which however is not the only one possible.

[39] Translated by Mead and Chattopâdhyâya. Sec. 1, Pt. II.

[40] In a song of the Rigveda it is said that the hymns and sacrificial speeches, as well as all creation in general, have proceeded from the "entirely fire consumed" Purusha (primitive man-creator of the world).

[41] Compare Brugsch: "Religion und Myth. d. alt. Aegypter," p. 255 f., and the Egyptian dictionary.

[42] The German word "Schwan" belongs here, therefore it sings when dying. It is the sun. The metaphor in Heine supplements this very beautifully.

> "Es singt der Schwan im Weiher
> Und rudert auf und ab,
> Und immer leiser singend,
> Taucht er ins Flutengrab."

Hauptmann's "Sunken Bell" is a sun myth in which bell = sun = life = libido.

[43] Loosely connected with ag-ilis. See Max Müller: "Vorl. über den Ursprung und die Entwicklung der Religion," p. 237.

[44] An Eranian name of fire is *Nairyôçagha* = masculine word. The Hindoo *Narâçamsa* means wish of men (Spiegel: "Erân. Altertumskunde," II, 49). Fire has the significance of Logos (compare Ch. 7, "Siegfried"). Of *Agni* (fire), Max Müller, in his introduction to "The Science of Comparative Religions," says: "It was a conception familiar to India to consider the fire upon the altar as being at the same time subject and object. The fire burned the sacrifice and was thereby similar to the priest, the fire carried the sacrifice to the gods, and was thereby an intercessor between men and the gods: fire itself, however, repre-

sented also something divine, a god, and when honor was to be shown to this god, then fire was as much the subject as the object of the sacrifice. Hence the first conception, that Agni sacrificed itself, i.e. that it produced for itself its own sacrifice, and next that it brings itself to the sacrifice." The contact of this line of thought with the Christian symbol is plainly apparent. Krishna utters the same thought in the "Bhagavad-Gîtâ," b. IV (translated by Arnold, London 1910):

> "All's then God!
> The sacrifice is Brahm, the ghee and grain
> Are Brahm, the fire is Brahm, the flesh it eats
> Is Brahm, and unto Brahm attaineth he
> Who, in such office, meditates on Brahm."

The wise Diotima sees behind this symbol of fire (in Plato's symposium, c. 23). She teaches Socrates that Eros is "the intermediate being between mortals and immortals, a great Demon, dear Socrates; for everything demoniac is just the intermediate link between God and man." Eros has the task "of being interpreter and messenger from men to the gods, and from the gods to men, from the former for their prayers and sacrifices, from the latter for their commands and for their compensations for the sacrifices, and thus filling up the gap between both, so that through his mediation the whole is bound together with itself." Eros is a son of Penia (poverty, need) generated by Poros intoxicated with nectar. The meaning of Poros is dark; πόρος means way and hole, opening. Zielinski: "Arch. f. Rel. Wissensch.," IX, 43 ff., places him with Phoroneus, identical with the fire-bringer, who is held in doubt; others identify him with primal chaos, whereas others read arbitrarily Κόρος and Μόρος. Under these circumstances, the question arises whether there may not be sought behind it a relatively simple sexual symbolism. Eros would be then simply the son of Need and of the female genitals, for this door is the beginning and birthplace of fire. Diotima gives an excellent description of Eros: "He is manly, daring, persevering, a strong hunter (archer, compare below) and an incessant intriguer, who is constantly striving after wisdom,—a powerful sorcerer, poison mixer and sophist; and he is respected neither as an immortal nor as a mortal, but on the same day he first blooms and blossoms, when he has attained the fulness of the striving, then dies in it but always awakens again to life because of the nature of his father (rebirth!); attainment, however, always tears him down again." For this characterization, compare Chs. V, VI and VII of this work.

[45] Compare Riklin: "Wish Fulfilment and Symbolism in Fairy Tales," translated by Wm. White, M.D., where a child is produced by the parents placing a little turnip in the oven. The motive of the furnace where the child is hatched is also found again in the type of the whale-dragon myth. It is there a regularly recurring motive because the belly of the dragon is very hot, so that as the result of the heat the hero loses his hair—that is to say, he loses the characteristic covering of hair of the adult and becomes a child. (Naturally the hair is related to the sun's rays, which are extinguished in the setting of the sun.) Abundant examples of this motive are in Frobenius: "Das Zeitalter des Sonnengottes," Vol. I. Berlin 1904.

[46] This aspect of Agni is similar to Dionysus, who bears a remarkable parallel to both the Christian and the Hindoo mythology.

[47] "Now everything in the world which is damp, he created from sperma, but this is the soma." *Brihadâraṇyaka-Upaniṣhad*, 1-4.

[48] The question is whether this significance was a secondary development. Kuhn seems to assume this. He says ("Herabkunft des Feuers," p. 18): "However, together with the meaning of the root *manth* already evolved, there has also developed in the Vedas the conception of 'tearing off' due naturally to the mode of procedure."

[49] Examples in Frobenius: "Das Zeitalter des Sonnengottes."

[50] See in this connection Stekel: "Die sexuelle Wurzel der Kleptomanie," *Zeitschrift für Sexualwissenschaft*, 1908.

[51] Even in the Roman Catholic church at various places the custom prevailed for the priest to produce once a year the ceremonial fire.

[52] I must remark that the designation of onanism as a "great discovery" is not merely a play with words on my part. I owe it to two young patients who pretended that they were in possession of a terrible secret; that they had discovered something horrible, which no one had ever known before, because had it been known great misery would have overtaken mankind. Their discovery was onanism.

[53] One must in fairness, however, consider that the demands of life, rendered still more severe by our moral code, are so heavy that it simply is impossible for many people to attain that goal which can be begrudged to no one, namely the possibility of love. Under the cruel compulsion of domestication, what is left but onanism, for those people possessed of an active sexuality? It is well known that the most useful and best men owe their ability to a powerful libido. This energetic libido longs for something more than merely a Christian love for the neighbor.

[54] I am fully conscious that onanism is only an intermediate phenomenon. There always remains the problem of the original division of the libido.

[55] In connection with my terminology mentioned in the previous chapter, I give the name of autoerotic to this stage following the incestuous love. Here I emphasize the erotic as a regressive phenomenon; the libido blocked by the incest barrier regressively takes possession of an older way of functioning anterior to the incestuous object of love. This may be comprehended by Bleuler's terminology, Autismus, that is, the function of pure self-preservation, which is especially distinguished by the function of nutrition. However, the terminology "autismus" cannot very well be longer applied to the presexual material, because it is already used in reference to the mental state of dementia praecox where it has to include autoerotism plus introverted desexualized libido. Autismus designates first of all a pathological phenomenon of regressive character, the presexual material, however, of a normal functioning, the chrysalis stage.

CHAPTER IV

[1] Therefore that beautiful name of the sun-hero Gilgamesh: Wehfrohmensch (pain-joy human being). See Jensen: "Gilgamesh Epic."

[2] Compare here the interesting researches of H. Silberer. 1912 *Jahrbuch*, Vol. I, p. 513.

[3] See Bleuler: *Psychiatr.-neurol. Wochenschrift,* XII. Jahrgang, Nr. 18 to 21.

[4] Compare with this my explanations in *Jahrbuch,* Vol. III, p. 469.

[5] Compare the exhortation by Krishna to the irresolute Arjuna in Bhagavad-Gîtâ: "But thou, be free of the pairs of opposites!" Bk. II, "The Song Celestial," Edwin Arnold.

[6] "Pensées," LIV.

[7] See the following chapter.

[8] Compare John Müller: "Über die phantastischen Gesichtserscheinungen," Coblenz 1826; and Jung: "Occult Phenomena," in Collected Papers on Analytic Psychology.

[9] Also the related doctrine of the Upanishad.

[10] Bertschinger: "Illustrierte Halluzinationen," *Jahrbuch,* Vol. III, p. 69.

[11] How very important is the coronation and sun identification, is shown not alone from countless old customs, but also from the corresponding ancient metaphors in the religious speech: the Wisdom of Solomon v:17: "Therefore, they will receive a beautiful crown from the hand of the Lord." I Peter v:4: "Feed the flock of God . . . and when the chief shepherd shall appear ye shall receive a crown of glory that fadeth not away."
In a church hymn of Allendorf it is said of the soul: "The soul is liberated from all care and pain and in dying it has come to the *crown of joy;* she stands as bride and queen in the *glitter of eternal splendor,* at the side of the great king," etc. In a hymn by Laurentius Laurentii it is said (also of the soul): "The crown is entrusted to the brides because they conquer." In a song by Sacer we find the passage: "Adorn my coffin with garlands just as a conqueror is adorned,—from those springs of heaven, my soul has attained the eternally green crown: the true glory of victory, coming from the son of God who has so cared for me." A quotation from the above-mentioned song of Allendorf is added here, in which we have another complete expression of the primitive psychology of the sun identification of men, which we met in the Egyptian song of triumph of the ascending soul.
(Concerning the soul, continuation of the above passage:) "It [the soul] sees a clear countenance [sun]: his [the sun's] joyful loving nature now restores it through and through: it is a *light in his light.*—Now the *child can see the father:* He feels the gentle emotion of love. Now he can understand the word of Jesus. He himself, the father, has loved you. An unfathomable sea of benefits, an abyss of eternal waves of blessing is disclosed to the enlightened spirit: he beholds the countenance of God, and knows what signifies *the inheritor of God in light and the co-heir of Christ.*—The feeble body rests on the earth: it sleeps until Jesus awakens it. *Then will the dust become the sun,* which now is covered by the dark cavern: Then shall we come together with all the pious, who knows how soon, and will be for eternity with the Lord." I have emphasized the significant passages by italics: they speak for themselves, so that I need add nothing.

[12] In order to avoid misunderstanding I must add that this was absolutely unknown to the patient.

[13] The analysis of an eleven-year-old girl also confirms this. I gave a report of this in the I Congrès International de Pédologie, 1911, in Brussels.

[14] The identity of the divine hero with the mystic is not to be doubted. In a prayer written on papyrus to Hermes, it is said: σὺ γὰρ ἐγὼ καὶ ἐγὼ σύ· τὸ αὸν ὄνομα ἐμὸν καὶ τὸ ἐμὸν σόν· ἐγὼ γὰρ εἰμι τὸ εἰθολόν σου (For thou art I and I am thou, thy name is mine, and mine is thine; for I am thy image). (Kenyon: Greek Papyrus, in the British Museum, 1893, p. 116, Pap. CXXII, 2. Cited by Dieterich: "Mithrasliturgie," p. 79.) The hero as image of the libido is strikingly illustrated in the head of Dionysus at Leiden (Roscher, I, Sp. 1128), where the hair rises like flame over the head. He is—like a flame: "Thy savior will be a flame." Firmicus Maternus ("De Errore Prof. Relig.," 104, p. 28) acquaints us with the fact that the god was saluted as bridegroom, and "young light." He transmits the corrupt Greek sentence, δε νυνφε χαιρε νυνφε νεον φως, with which he contrasts the Christian conception: "Nullum apud te lumen est nec est aliquis qui sponsus mereatur audire: unum lumen est, unus est sponsus. Nominum horum gratiam Christus accepit." Today Christ is still our hero and the bridegroom of the soul. These attributes will be confirmed in regard to Miss Miller's hero in what follows.

[15] The giving of a name is therefore of significance in the so-called spiritual manifestations. See my paper, 1902, "Occult Phenomena," Collected Papers on Analytical Psychology.

[16] The ancients recognized this demon as συνοπαδός, the companion and follower.

[17] A parallel to these phantasies are the well-known interpretations of the Sella Petri of the pope.

[18] When Freud called attention through his analytic researches to the connection between excrements and gold, many ignorant persons found themselves obliged to ridicule in an airy manner this connection. The mythologists think differently about it. De Gubernatis says that excrement and gold are always associated together. Grimm tells us of the following magic charm: "If one wants money in his house the whole year, one must eat lentils on New Year's Day." This notable connection is explained simply through the physiological fact of the indigestibility of lentils, which appear again in the form of coins. Thus one becomes a mint.

[19] A French father who naturally disagreed with me in regard to this interest in his child mentioned, nevertheless, that when the child speaks of cacao, he always adds "lit"; he means caca-au-lit.

[20] Freud: Jahrbuch, Vol. I, p. 1. Jung: Jahrbuch, Vol. II, p. 33. See third lecture delivered at Clark University, 1909.

[21] I refer to the previous etymologic connection.

[22] Compare Bleuler: Jahrbuch, Vol. III, p. 467.

[23] "Genius and Insanity."

[24] Here again is the connection with antiquity, the infantile past.

[25] This fact is unknown to me. It might be possible that in some way the name of the legendary man who invented the cuneiform char-

acters has been preserved (as, for example, Sinlikiunnini as the poet of the Gilgamesh epic). But I have not succeeded in finding anything of that sort. However, Ashshurbanaplu or Asurbanipal has left behind that marvellous cuneiform library, which was excavated in Kujundschik. Perhaps "Asurubama" has something to do with this name. Further there comes into consideration the name of Aholibamah, which we have met in Part I. The word "Ahamarama" betrays equally some connections with Anah and Aholibamah, those daughters of Cain with the sinful passion for the sons of God. This possibility hints at Chiwantopel as the longed-for son of God. (Did Byron think of the two sister whores, Ohola and Oholiba? Ezeck. xxiii: 4.)

[26] The race does not part with its wandering sun-heroes. Thus it was related of Cagliostro, that he once drove at the same time four white horses out of a city from all the city gates simultaneously (Helios!).

[27] Mysticism.

[28] Agni, the fire, also hides himself at times in a cavern. Therefore he must be brought forth again by generation from the cavity of the female wood. Compare Kuhn: "Herabk. des Feuers."

[29] We = Allah.

[30] The "two-horned." According to the commentaries, this refers to Alexander the Great, who in the Arabian legends plays nearly the same rôle as the German Dietrich von Bern. The "two-horned" refers to the strength of the sun-bull. Alexander is often found upon coins with the horns of Jupiter Ammon. It is a question of identification of the ruler around whom so many legends are clustered, with the sun of spring in the signs of the bull and the ram. It is obvious that humanity had a great need of effacing the personal and human from their heroes, so as finally to make them, through a $\mu\varepsilon\tau\acute{\alpha}\sigma\tau\alpha\sigma\iota\varsigma$ (eclipse), the equal of the sun, that is to say, completely into a libido-symbol. If we thought like Schopenhauer, then we would surely say, Libido-symbol. But if we thought like Goethe, then we would say. Sun; for we exist, because the sun sees us.

[31] Vollers: "Chidher. Archiv für Religionswissenschaft," p. 235, Vol. XII, 1909. This is the work which is my authority on the Koran commentaries.

[32] Here the ascension of Mithra and Christ are closely related. See Part I.

[33] A parallel is found in the Mithra mysteries! See below.

[34] Parallel to this are the conversations of Mohammed with Elias, at which the sacramental bread was served. In the New Testament the awkwardness is restricted to the proposal of Peter. The infantile character of such scenes is shown by similar features, thus by the gigantic stature of Elias in the Koran, and also the tales of the commentary, in which it is stated that Elias and Chidher met each year in Mecca, conversed and shaved each other's heads.

[35] On the contrary, according to Matthew xvii: 11, John the Baptist is to be understood as Elias.

[36] Compare the Kyffhäuser legend.

[37] Vollers: Ibid.

[38] Another account says that Alexander had been in India on the mountain of Adam with his "minister" Chidher.

[39] These mythological equations follow absolutely the rule of dreams, where the dreamer can be resolved into many analogous forms.

[40] "He must grow, but I must waste away."—*John* iii:30.

[41] Cumont: "Textes et Monuments," p. 172.

[42] The parallel between Hercules and Mithra may be drawn even more closely. Like Hercules, Mithra is an excellent archer. Judging from certain monuments, not only the youthful Hercules appears to be threatened by a snake, but also Mithra as a youth. The meaning of the ἄθλος of Hercules (the work) is the same as the Mithraic mystery of the conquering and sacrifice of the bull.

[43] These three scenes are represented in a row on the Klagenfurt monument. Thus the dramatic connection of these must be surmised (Cumont: "Myst. des Mithras").

[44] Also the triple crown.

[45] The Christian sequence is John—Christ, Peter—Pope.

[46] The immortality of Moses is proven by the parallel situation with Elias in the transfiguration.

[47] See Frobenius: "Das Zeitalter des Sonnengottes."

[48] Therefore the fish is the symbol of the "Son of God"; at the same time the fish is also the symbol of the approaching world-cycle.

[49] Riklin: "Wish Fulfilment and Symbolism."

[50] Inman: "Ancient Pagan and Modern Christian Symbolism."

[51] The amniotic membrane(?).

[52] The Etrurian Tages, who sprang from the "freshly ploughed furrow," is also a teacher of wisdom. In the Litaolane myth of the Basutos, there is a description of how a monster devoured all men and left only one woman, who gave birth to a son, the hero, in a stable (instead of a cave: see the etymology of this myth). Before she had arranged a bed for the infant out of the straw, he was already grown and spoke "words of wisdom." The quick growth of the hero, a frequently recurring motive, appears to mean that the birth and apparent childhood of the hero are so extraordinary because his birth really means his rebirth, therefore he becomes very quickly adapted to his hero rôle. Compare below.

[53] Battle of Rê with the night serpent.

[54] Matthew iii:11.

[55] "Das Gilgameshepos in der Weltliteratur," Vol. I, p. 50.

[56] The difference between this and the Mithra sacrifice seems to be extraordinarily significant. The Dadophores are harmless gods of light who do not participate in the sacrifice. The animal is lacking in the sacrifice of Christ. Therefore there are two criminals who suffer the same death. The scene is much more dramatic. The inner connection

of the Dadophores to Mithra, of which I will speak later, allows us to assume the same relation of Christ to the criminals. The scene with Barabbas betrays that Christ is the god of the ending year, who is represented by one of the thieves, while the one of the coming year is free.

[57] For example, the following dedication is found on a monument: D. I. M. (Deo Invicto Mithrae) Cautopati. One discovers sometimes Deo Mithrae Caute or Deo Mithrae Cautopati in a similar alternation as Deo Invicto Mithrae—or sometimes Deo Invicto—or, merely, Invicto. It also appears that the Dadophores are fitted with knife and bow, the attributes of Mithra. From this it is to be concluded that the three figures represent three different states of a single person. Compare Cumont: " Textes et Monuments," p. 208.

[58] Cited by Cumont: " Textes et Monuments," p. 208.

[59] Ibid.

[60] Taurus and Scorpio are the equinoctial signs for the period from 4300 to 2150 B.C. These signs, long since superseded, were retained even in the Christian era.

[61] Under some circumstances, it is also sun and moon.

[62] In order to characterize the individual and the all-soul, the personal and the super-personal, Atman, a verse of the *Shvetâshvatara-Upanishad* (Deussen) makes use of the following comparison:

" Zwei schön beflügelte verbundne Freunde
Umarmen einen und denselben Baum;
Einer von ihnen speist die süsse Beere,
Der andre schaut, nicht essend, nur herab."

(Two closely allied friends, beautifully winged, embrace one and the same tree; One of them eats the sweet berries, the other not eating merely looks downwards.)

[63] Among the elements composing man, in the Mithraic liturgy, fire is especially emphasized as the divine element, and described as τὸ εἰς ἐμὴν κρᾶσιν θεοδώρητον (The divine gift in my composition). Dietrich: Ibid., p. 58.

[64] It is sufficient to point to the loving interest which mankind and also the God of the Old Testament has for the nature of the penis, and how much depends upon it.

[65] The testicles easily count as twins. Therefore in vulgar speech the testicles are called the Siamese twins. (" Anthropophyteia," VII, p. 20. Quoted by Stekel: " Sprache des Traumes," p. 169.)

[66] " Recherches sur le culte, etc., de Vénus," Paris, 1837. Quoted by Inman: " Ancient Pagan and Modern Christian Symbolism," New York, p. 4.

[67] The androgynous element is not to be undervalued in the faces of Adonis, Christ, Dionysus and Mithra, and hints at the bisexuality of the libido. The smooth-shaven face and the feminine clothing of the Catholic priest contain a very old female constituent from the Attis-Cybele cult.

[68] Stekel (" Sprache des Traumes ") has again and again noted the Trinity as a phallic symbol. For example, see p. 27.

[69] Sun's rays = Phalli.

[70] In a Bakairi myth. a woman appears, who has sprung from a corn mortar. In a Zulu myth it is said: A woman is to catch a drop of blood in a vessel, then close the vessel, put it aside for eight months and open it in the ninth month. She follows the advice, opens the vessel in the ninth month, and finds a child in it. (Frobenius: " Das Zeitalter des Sonnengottes " [The Age of the Sun-God], I, p. 237.)

[71] Inman: Ibid., p. 10, Plate IX.

[72] Roscher: " Lexicon," Sp. 2733/4. See section, Men.

[73] A well-known sun animal, frequent as a phallic symbol.

[74] Like Mithra and the Dadophores.

[75] The castration in the service of the mother explains this quotation in a very significant manner: Exod. iv:25: " Then Zipporah took a sharp stone, and cut off her son's foreskin and cast it at his feet and said, Surely, a bloody husband art thou to me." This passage shows what circumcision means.

[76] Gilgamesh, Dionysus, Hercules, Christ, Mithra, and so on.

[77] Compare with this, Graf: " R. Wagner im Fliegenden Holländer: Schriften zur angewandten Seelenkunde."

[78] I have pointed out above, in reference to the Zosimos vision, that the altar meant the uterus, corresponding to the baptismal font.

CHAPTER V

[1] Freud: " Dream Interpretation."

[2] I am indebted to Dr. Abegg in Zürich for the knowledge of Indra and Urvarâ, Domaldi and Râma.

[3] Medieval Christianity also considered the Trinity as dwelling in the womb of the holy Virgin.

[4] " Symbolism," Plate VII.

[5] Another form of the same motive is the Persian idea of the tree of life, which stands in the lake of rain, Vourukasha. The seeds of this tree were mixed with water and by that the fertility of the earth was maintained. " Vendidâd," 5, 57, says: The waters flow " to the lake Vourukasha, down to the tree Hvâpa; there my trees of many kinds all grow. I cause these waters to rain down as food for the pure man, as fodder for the well-born cow. (Impregnation, in terms of the pre-sexual stage.) Another tree of life is the white Haoma, which grows in the spring Ardvîçura, the water of life." Spiegel: " Erân. Alter-tumskunde," I, 465, 467.

[6] Excellent examples of this are given in the work of Rank, " The Myth of the Birth of the Hero," translated by Wm. White.

[7] Shadows probably mean the soul, the nature of which is the same as libido. Compare with this Part I.

[8] But I must mention that Nork (" Realwörterbuch," sub. Theben und Schiff) pleads that Thebes is the ship city; his arguments are much

attacked. From among his arguments I emphasize a quotation from Diodorus (I, 57), according to which Sesostris (whom Nork associates with Xisuthros) had consecrated to the highest god in Thebes a vessel 280 els long. In the dialogue of Lucius (Apuleius: "Metam.," lib. II, 28), the night journey in the sea was used as an erotic figure of speech: "Hac enim sitarchia navigium Veneris indiget sola, ut in nocte pervigili et oleo lucerna et vino calix abundet" (For the ship of Venus needs this provision in order that during the night the lamp may abound with oil and the goblet with wine). The union of the coitus motive with the motive of pregnancy is to be found in the "night journey on the sea" of Osiris, who in his mother's womb copulated with his sister.

⁹ Very illuminating psychologically is the method and the manner in which Jesus treats his mother, when he harshly repels her. Just as strong and intense as this, has the longing for her imago grown in his unconscious. It is surely not an accident that the name Mary accompanies him through life. Compare the utterance of Matthew x:35: "I have come to set a man at variance with his father, a daughter with her mother. He who loves father and mother more than me is not worthy of me." This directly hostile purpose, which calls to mind the legendary rôle of Bertran de Born, is directed against the incestuous bond and compels man to transfer his libido to the Saviour, who, dying, returning into his mother and rising again, is the hero Christ.

¹⁰ Genitals.

¹¹ The horns of the dragon have the following attributes: "They will prey upon woman's flesh and they will burn with fire." The horn, a phallic emblem, is in the unicorn the symbol of the Holy Ghost (Logos). The unicorn is hunted by the archangel Gabriel, and driven into the lap of the Virgin, by which was understood the immaculate conception. But the horns are also sun's rays, therefore the sun-gods are often horned. The sun phallus is the prototype of the horn (sun wheel and phallus wheel), therefore the horn is the symbol of power. Here the horns "burn with fire" and prey upon the flesh; one recognizes in this a representation of the pains of hell where souls were burnt by the fire of the libido (unsatisfied longing). The harlot is "consumed" or burned by unsatisfied longing (libido). Prometheus suffers a similar fate, when the eagle, sun-bird (libido), tears his intestines: one might also say, that he was pierced by the "horn." I refer to the phallic meaning of the spear.

¹² In the Babylonian underworld, for example. The souls have a feathery coat like birds. See the Gilgamesh epic.

¹³ In a fourteenth-century Gospel at Bruges there is a miniature where the "woman" lovely as the mother of God stands with half her body in a dragon.

¹⁴ τὸ ἀρνίον, little ram, diminutive of the obsolete ἀρήν = ram. (In Theophrastus it occurs with the meaning of "young scion.") The related word ἀρνίς designates a festival annually celebrated in honor of Linos, in which the λίνος, the lament called Linos, was sung as a lamentation for Linos, the new-born son of Psamathe and Apollo, torn to pieces by dogs. The mother had exposed her child out of fear of her father Krotopos. But for revenge Apollo sent a dragon, Poine, into Krotopos' land. The oracle of Delphi commanded a yearly lament by women and maidens for the dead Linos. A part of the honor was

given to Psamathe. The Linos lament is, as Herodotus shows (II, 79), identical with the Phœnician, Cyprian and Egyptian custom of the Adonis-(Tammuz) lament. As Herodotus observes, Linos is called Maneros in Egypt. Brugsch points out that Maneros comes from the Egyptian cry of lamentation, *maa-n-chru:* "come to the call." Poine is characterized by her tearing the children from the womb of all mothers. This ensemble of motives is found again in the Apocalypse, xii: 1-5, where it treats of the woman, whose child was threatened by a dragon but was snatched away into the heavens. The child-murder of Herod is an anthropomorphism of this "primitive" idea. The lamb means the son. (See Brugsch: "Die Adonisklage und das Linoslied," Berlin 1852.) Dieterich (Abraxas: "Studien zur Religionsgeschichte des späteren Altertums," 1891) refers for an explanation of this passage to the myth of Apollo and Python, which he reproduces as follows: "To Python, the son of earth, the great dragon, it was prophesied that the son of Leto would kill him; Leto was pregnant by Zeus: but Hera brought it about that she *could give birth only there where the sun did not shine.* When Python saw that Leto was pregnant, he began to pursue her in order to kill her, but Boreas brought Leto to Poseidon. The latter brought her to Ortygia and covered the island with the waves of the sea. When Python did not find Leto, he returned to Parnassus. Leto brought forth upon the island thrown up by Poseidon. The fourth day after the birth, Apollo took revenge and killed the Python. The birth upon the hidden island belongs to the motive of the "night journey on the sea." The typical character of the "island phantasy" has for the first time been correctly perceived by Riklin (1912 *Jahrbuch,* Vol. II, p. 246). A beautiful parallel for this is to be found, together with the necessary incestuous phantasy material, in H. de Vere Stacpool: "The Blue Lagoon." A parallel to "Paul and Virginia."

[15] Revelation xxi: 2: "And the holy city, the new Jerusalem, I saw coming down from the *heaven of God, prepared as a bride adorned for her bridegroom."*

[16] The legend of Saktideva, in Somadeva Bhatta, relates that the hero, after he had escaped from being devoured by a huge fish (terrible mother), finally sees the golden city and marries his beloved princess (Frobenius, p. 175).

[17] In the Apocryphal acts of St. Thomas (2nd century) the church is taken to be the virgin mother-spouse of Christ. In an invocation of the apostle, it is said:

Come, holy name of Christ, thou who art above all names.
Come, power of the highest and greatest mercy,
Come, dispenser of the greatest blessings,
Come, gracious mother.
Come, economy of the masculine.
Come, woman, thou who disclosest the hidden mysteries . . .

In another invocation it is said:

Come, greatest mercy,
Come, spouse (literally community) of the male,
Come, woman, thou who knowest the mystery of the elect,
Come, woman, thou who showest the hidden things
And who revealest the unspeakable things, holy
Dove, thou who bringest forth the twin nestling,
Come, mysterious mother, etc.

F. C. Conybeare: "Die jungfräuliche Kirche und die jungfräuliche Mutter." *Archiv für Religionswissenschaft,* IX, 77. The connection of the church with the mother is not to be doubted, also the conception of the mother as spouse. The virgin is necessarily introduced to hide the incest idea. The "community with the male" points to the motive of the continuous cohabitation. The "twin nestlings" refer to the old legend, that Jesus and Thomas were twins. It plainly expresses the motive of the Dioscuri. Therefore, doubting Thomas had to place his finger in the wound at the side. Zinzendorf has correctly perceived the sexual significance of this symbol that hints at the androgynous nature of the primitive being (the libido). Compare the Persian legend of the twin trees Meschia and Mechiane, as well as the motive of the Dioscuri and the motive of cohabitation.

[18] Compare Freud: "Dream Interpretation." Also Abraham: "Dreams and Myths," pp. 22 f.

[19] Isaiah xlviii: 1. "Hear ye this, O house of Jacob, which are called by the name of Israel and are come forth out of the waters of Judah."

[20] Wirth: "Aus orientalischen Chroniken."—The Greek "Materia" is ὕλη, which means wood and forest; it really means moist, from the Indo-Germanic root *sū* in ὕω, "to make wet, to have it rain"; ὑετός = rain; Iranian *suth* = sap, fruit, birth; Sanscrit *sūrā* = brandy; *sutus* = pregnancy; *sūte, sūyate* = to generate; *sutas* = son; *sūras* = soma; υἱός = son; (Sanscrit, *sūnús;* gothic, *sunus*).

[21] Κοίμημα means cohabitation, κοιμητήριον bedchamber, hence coemeterium = cemetery, enclosed fenced place.

[22] Nork: "Realwörterbuch."

[23] In a myth of Celebes, a dove maiden who was caught in the manner of the swan maiden myth, was called Utahagi after a white hair which grew on its crown and in which there was magic strength. Frobenius, p. 307.

[24] Referring to the phallic symbolism of the finger, see the remarks about the Dactyli, Part II, Chap. I: I mention at this place the following from a Bakairi myth: "Nimagakaniro devoured two finger bones, many of which were in the house, because Oka used them for his arrow heads and killed many Bakairi whose flesh he ate. The woman became pregnant from the finger bone and only from this, not from Oka" (quoted by Frobenius, p. 236).

[25] Further proof for this in Prellwitz: "Griechische Etymologie."

[26] Siecke: "Der Gott Rudra in Rigveda": *Archiv für Religionswissenschaft,* Vol. I, p. 237.

[27] The fig tree is the phallic tree. It is noteworthy that Dionysus planted a fig tree at the entrance to Hades, just as "Phalli" are placed on graves. The cyprus tree consecrated to Aphrodite grew to be entirely a token of death, because it was placed at the door of the house of death.

[28] Therefore the tree at times is also a representation of the sun. A Russian riddle related to me by Dr. Van Ophuijsen reads: "What is the tree which stands in the middle of the village and is visible in

every cottage?" Answer: "The sun and its light." A Norwegian riddle reads:

> "A tree stands on the mountain of Billings,
> It bends over a lake,
> Its branches shine like gold:
> You won't guess that to-day.

In the evening the daughter of the sun collected the golden branches, which had been broken from the wonderful oak.

> Bitterly weeps the little sun
> In the apple orchard.
> From the apple tree has fallen
> The golden apple,
> Do not weep, little sun,
> God will make another
> Of gold, of bronze, of silver."

The picking of the apple from the paradise tree may be compared with the fire theft, the drawing back of the libido from the mother. (See the explanations which follow concerning the specific deed of the hero.)

[29] The relation of the son to the mother was the psychologic basis of many religions. In the Christian legend the relation of the son to the mother is extraordinarily clear. Robertson ("Evangelical Myths") has hit upon the relation of Christ to the Marys, and he conjectures that this relation probably refers to an old myth "where a god of Palestine, perhaps of the name Joshua, appears in the changing relation of lover and son towards a mythical Mary. This is a natural process in the oldest theosophy and one which appears with variations in the myths of Mithra, Adonis, Attis, Osiris and Dionysus, all of whom were brought into relation (or combination) with mother goddesses and who appear either as a consort or a feminine eidolon in so far as the mothers and consorts were identified as occasion offered."

[30] Rank has pointed out a beautiful example of this in the myth of the swan maiden. "Die Lohengrinsage: Schriften zur angewandten Seelenkunde."

[31] Muther ("Geschichte der Malerei," Vol. II) says in the chapter: "The First Spanish Classic": "Tieck once wrote: Sexuality is the great mystery of our being. Sensuality is the first moving wheel in our machinery. It stirs our being and makes it joyous and living. Everything we dream of as beautiful and noble is included here. Sexuality and sensuousness are the spirit of music, of painting and of all art. All wishes of mankind rotate around this center like moths around a burning light. The sense of beauty and the feeling for art are only other expressions of it. They signify nothing more than the impulse of mankind towards expression. I consider devoutness itself as a diverted channel of the sexual desire." Here it is openly declared that one should never forget when judging the ancient ecclesiastic art that the effort to efface the boundaries between earthly and divine love, to blend them into each other imperceptibly, has always been the guiding thought, the strongest factor in the propaganda of the Catholic church.

[32] We will not discuss here the reasons for the strength of the phantasy. But it does not seem difficult to me to imagine what sort of powers are hidden behind the above formula.

[33] Lactantius says: "When all know that it is customary for certain animals to conceive through wind and breath of air, why should any one consider it miraculous for a virgin to be impregnated by the spirit of God?" Robertson: "Evang. Myth.," p. 31.

[34] Therefore the strong emphasis upon affiliation in the New Testament.

[35] The mystic feelings of the nearness of God; the so-called personal inner experience.

[36] The sexual mawkishness is everywhere apparent in the lamb symbolism and the spiritual love-songs to Jesus, the bridegroom of the soul.

[37] Usener: "Der heilige Tychon," 1907.

[38] Compare W. P. Knight: "Worship of Priapus."

[39] Or in the compensating organizations, which appear in the place of religion.

[40] The condition was undoubtedly ideal for early times, where mankind was more infantile in general: and it still is ideal for that part of humanity which is infantile; how large is that part!

[41] Compare Freud: *Jahrbuch,* Vol. III, p. 1.

[42] Here it is not to be forgotten we are moving entirely in the territory of psychology, which in no way is allied to transcendentalism, either in positive or negative relation. It is a question here of a relentless fulfilment of the standpoint of the theory of cognition, established by Kant, not merely for the theory, but, what is more important, for the practice. One should avoid playing with the infantile image of the world, because all this tends only to separate man from his essential and highest ethical goal, moral autonomy. The religious symbol should be retained after the inevitable obliteration of certain antiquated fragments, as postulate or as transcendent theory, and also as taught in precepts, but is to be filled with new meaning according to the demand of the culture of the present day. But this theory must not become for the "adult" a positive creed, an illusion, which causes reality to appear to him in a false light. Just as man is a dual being, having an intellectual and an animal nature, so does he appear to need two forms of reality, the reality of culture, that is, the symbolic transcendent theory, and the reality of nature which corresponds to our conception of the "true reality." In the same measure that the true reality is merely a figurative interpretation of the appreciation of reality, the religious symbolic theory is merely a figurative interpretation of certain endopsychic apperceptions. But one very essential difference is that a transcendental support, independent in duration and condition, is assured to the transubjective reality through the best conceivable guarantees, while for the psychologic phenomena a transcendental support of subjective limitation and weakness must be recognized as a result of compelling empirical data. Therefore true reality is one that is relatively universally valid; the psychologic reality, on the contrary, is merely a functional phenomenon contained in an epoch of human civilization. Thus does it appear to-day from the best informed empirical standpoint. If, however, the psychologic were divested of its character of a biologic epiphenomenon in a manner neither known nor expected by me, and thereby was given the place of a physical entity, then the psychologic reality would be resolved into the true reality; or much more, it would be reversed, because then the

psychologic would lay claim to a greater worth, for the ultimate theory, because of its directness.

[43] " De Isid. et Osir."

[44] Erman: " Aegypten," p. 360.

[45] Here I must again recall that I give to the word "incest" more significance than properly belongs to the term. Just as libido is the onward driving force, so incest is in some manner the backward urge into childhood. For the child, it cannot be spoken of as incest. Only for the adult who possesses a completely formed sexuality does the backward urge become incest, because he is no longer a child but possesses a sexuality which cannot be permitted a regressive application.

[46] Compare Frobenius: " Das Zeitalter des Sonnengottes."

[47] Compare the " nightmare legends " in which the mare is a beautiful woman.

[48] This recalls the phallic columns placed in the temples of Astarte. In fact, according to one version, the wife of the king was named Astarte. This symbol brings to mind the crosses, fittingly called ἐγκόλπια (pregnant crosses), which conceal a secret reliquary.

[49] Spielrein (Jahrbuch, Vol. III, p. 358) points out numerous indications of the motive of dismemberment in a demented patient. Fragments of the most varied things and materials were "cooked" or "burnt." "The ash can become man." The patient saw children dismembered in glass coffins. In addition, the above-mentioned "washing," "cleaning," "cooking" and "burning" has, besides the coitus motive, also the pregnancy motive; the latter probably in a predominating measure.

[50] Later offshoots of this primitive theory of the origin of children are contained in the doctrines of Karma, and the conception of the Mendelian theory of heredity is not far off. One only has to realize that all apperceptions are subjectively conditioned.

[51] Demeter assembled the limbs of the dismembered Dionysus and from them produced the god anew.

[52] Compare Diodorus: III, 62.

[53] Yet to be added is the fact that the cynocephalic Anubis as the restorer of the corpse of Osiris (also genius of the dog star) had a compensatory significance. In this significance he appears upon many sarcophagi. The dog is also a regular companion of the healing Asclepius. The following quotation from Petronius best supports the Creuzer hypothesis (" Sat.," c. 71) : " Valde te rogo, ut secundum pedes statuae meae catellam pingas—ut mihi contingat tuo beneficio post mortem vivere " (I beseech you instantly to fasten beside the feet of my statue a dog, so that because of your beneficence I may attain to life after death). See Nork: Ibid., about dog.)

Moreover, the relation of the dog to the dog-headed Hecate, the goddess of the underworld, hints at its being the symbol of rebirth. She received as Canicula a sacrificial dog to keep away the pest. Her close relation to Artemis as goddess of the moon permits her opposition to fertility. to be glimpsed. Hecate is also the first to bring to Demeter the news of her stolen child (the rôle of Anubis!). Also the goddess of birth Ilithyia received sacrifices of dogs, and Hecate herself is, on occasions, goddess of marriage and birth.

[54] Frobenius (Ibid., p. 393) observes that frequently the gods of fire (sun-heroes) lack a member. He gives the following parallel: "Just as the god wrenches out an arm from the ogre (giant), so does Odysseus pluck out the eye of the noble Polyphemus, whereupon the sun creeps up mysteriously into the sky. Might the fire-making, twisting and wrenching out of the arm be connected?" This question is by this clearly illumined if we assume, corresponding to the train of thought of the ancients, that the wrenching out of the arm is really a castration. (The symbol of the robbery of the force of life.) It is an act corresponding to the Attis castration because of the mother. From this renunciation, which is really a symbolic mother incest, arises the discovery of fire, as previously we have already suspected. Moreover, mention must be made of the fact that to wrench out an arm, means first of all merely "overpowering," and on that account can happen to the hero as well as to his opponent. (Compare, for examples, Frobenius: Ibid., pp. 112, 395.)

[55] Compare especially the description of the cup of Thebes.

[56] Professor Freud has expressed in a personal discussion the idea that a further determinate for the motive of the dissimilar brothers is to be found in the elementary observance towards birth and the after-birth. It is an exotic custom to treat the placenta as a child!

[57] Brugsch: "Religion und Mythologie der alten Aegypter," p. 354.

[58] Ibid., p. 310.

[59] In the conception of Âtman there is a certain fluid quality in so far as he really can be identified with Purusha of the Rigveda. "Purusha covers all the places of the earth, flowing about it ten fingers high."

[60] Brugsch: Ibid., p. 112.

[61] In Thebes, where the chief god is Chnum, the latter represents the breath of the wind in his cosmic component, from which later on "the spirit of God floating over the waters" has developed; the primitive idea of the cosmic parents, who lie pressed together until the son separates them. (Compare the symbolism of Âtman above.)

[62] Brugsch: Ibid., p. 128.

[63] Servian song from Grimm's "Mythology," II, p. 544.

[64] Frobenius: Ibid.

[65] Compare the birth of the Germanic Aschanes, where rock, tree and water are present at the scene of birth. Chidher too was found sitting on the earth, the ground around covered with flowers.

[66] Most singularly even in this quotation, V. 288, the description is found of Sleep sitting high up in a pine tree. "There he sat surrounded by branches covered with thorny leaves, like the singing bird, who by night flutters through the mountains." It appears as if the motive belongs to a hierosgamos. Compare also the magic net with which Hephaestos enfolds Ares and Aphrodite "in flagranti" and kept them for the sport of the gods.

[67] The rite of enchaining the statues of Hercules and the Tyrian Melkarth is related to this also. The Cabiri too were wrapt in coverings. Creuzer: "Symbolik," II, 350.

[68] Fick: "Indogermanisches Wörterbuch," I, p. 132.

[69] Compare the "resounding sun."

[70] The motive of the "striking rocks" belongs also to the motive of devouring (Frobenius: Ibid., p. 405). The hero in his ship must pass between two rocks which strike together. (Similar to the biting door, to the tree trunk which snaps together.) In the passage, generally the tail of the bird is pinched off (or the "poop" of the ship, etc.); the castration motive is once more clearly revealed here, for the castration takes the place of mother incest. The castration is a substitution for coitus. Scheffel employs this idea in his well-known poem: "A herring loved an oyster, etc." The poem ends with the oyster biting off the herring's head for a kiss. The doves which bring Zeus ambrosia have also to pass through the rocks which strike together. The "doves" bring the food of immortality to Zeus by means of incest (entrance into the mother) very similar to Freya's apples (breasts). Frobenius also mentions the rocks or caves which open only at a magic word and are very closely connected with the rocks which strike together. Most illuminating in this respect is a South African myth (Frobenius, p. 407): "One must call the rock by name and cry loudly: Rock Utunjambili, open, so that I may enter." But the rock answers when it will not open to the call. "The rock will not open to children, it will open to the swallows which fly in the air!" The remarkable thing is, that no human power can open the rock, only a formula has that power—or a bird. This wording merely says that the opening of the rock is an undertaking which cannot really be accomplished, but which one wishes to accomplish.

(In Middle High German, to wish is really "to have the power to create something extraordinary.") When a man dies, then only the wish that he might live remains, an unfulfilled wish, a fluttering wish, wherefore souls are birds. The soul is wholly only libido, as is illustrated in many parts of this work; it is "to wish." Thus the helpful bird, who assists the hero in the whale to come again into the light, who opens the rocks, is the wish for rebirth. (For the bird as a wish, see the beautiful painting by Thoma, where the youth longingly stretches out his arms to the birds who pass over his head.)

[71] Grimm: "Mythology," I, p. 474.

[72] In Athens there was a family of Αἰγειρότομοι = hewn from poplars.

[73] Hermann: "Nordische Mythologie," p. 589.

[74] Javanese tribes commonly set up their images of God in an artificial cavity of a tree. This fits in with the "little hole" phantasy of Zinzendorf and his sect. See Pfister: "Frömmigkeit des Grafen von Zinzendorf." In a Persian myth, the white Haoma is a divine tree, growing in the lake Vourukasha, the fish Khar-mâhi circles protectingly around it and defends it against the toad Ahriman. It gives eternal life, children to women, husbands to girls and horses to men. In the Minôkhired the tree is called "the preparer of the corpse" (Spiegel: "Erân. Altertumskunde," II, 115).

[75] Ship of the sun, which accompanies the sun and the soul over the sea of death to the rising.

[76] Brugsch: Ibid., p. 177.

[77] Similarly Isaiah li: 1: ". . . look unto the rock whence ye are hewn, and to the hole of the pit whence ye are digged." Further proof is found

in A. von Löwis of Menar: "Nordkaukasische Steingeburtssagen," *Archiv für Religionswissenschaft*, XIII, p. 509.

[78] Grimm: "Mythology," I, p. 474.

[79] "Das Kreuz Christi. Rel.-hist.-kirchl.-archaeol. Untersuchungen," 1875.

[80] The legend of Seth is found in Jubinal: "Mystères inédits du XV. siècle," Part II, p. 16. Quoted from Zöckler: Ibid., p. 241.

[81] The guilt is as always, whenever possible, thrown upon the mother. The Germanic sacred trees are also under the law of an absolute taboo: no leaf may be taken from them, and nothing may be picked from the ground upon which their shadows fall.

[82] According to the German legend (Grimm: Vol. II, p. 809), the redeeming hero will be born when the tree, which now grows as a weak shoot from the wall, has become large, and when from its wood the cradle can be made in which the hero can be rocked. The formula reads: "A linden shall be planted, which shall bear on high two boughs from the wood of which a " poie " shall be made; the child who will be the first to lie therein is destined to be taken by the sword from life to death, and then salvation will enter in." In the Germanic legends, the appearance of a future event is connected most remarkably with a budding tree. Compare with this the designation of Christ as a " branch " or a " rod."

[83] Herein the motive of the "helpful bird " is apparent. Angels are really birds. Compare the bird clothing of the souls of the underworld, " soul birds." In the sacrificium Mithriacum the messenger of the gods (the " angel ") is a raven, the winged Hermes, etc.

[84] See Frobenius: Ibid.

[85] The close connection between δελφίς = Dolphin and δελφύς = uterus is emphasized. In Delphi there is the cavity in the earth and the Tripod δελφινίς = a delphic table with three feet in the form of a Dolphin). See in the last chapter Melicertes upon the Dolphin and the fiery sacrifice of Melkarth.

[86] See the comprehensive collection of Jones. On the nightmare.

[87] Riklin: "Wish Fulfilment and Symbolism in Fairy Tales."

[88] Laistner: "Das Rätsel der Sphinx."

[89] Freud: *Jahrbuch*, Vol. I, June: "Mental Conflicts in Children ": Collected Papers on Analytical Psychology.

[90] "Epistola de ara ad Noviomagum reperta," p. 25. Quoted by Grimm: "Mythology," Vol. II.

[91] Grimm: Ibid., Vol. II, p. 1041.

[92] Compare with that the horses whose tread causes springs to flow.

[93] Compare Herrmann: "Nord. Myth.," p. 64, and Fick: "Vergleich. Wörterb. d. indogerm. Sprache," Vol. I.

[94] Parallel is the mantic significance of the delphic chasm, Mimir's brook, etc. "Abyss of Wisdom," see last chapter. Hippolytos, with whom

his stepmother was enamoured, was placed after death with the wise nymph, Egeria.

[95] Example in Bertschinger: *Jahrbuch,* Vol. III, Part I.

[96] Compare the exotic myths given by Frobenius ("Zeitalter des Sonnengottes"), where the belly of the whale is clearly the land of death.

[97] One of the fixed peculiarities of the Mar is that he can only get out of the hole, through which he came in. This motive belongs evidently as the projected wish motive in the rebirth myth.

[98] According to Gressmann: "Altorient. Text. und Bild.," Vol. I, p. 4.

[99] Abyss of wisdom, book of wisdom, source of phantasies. See below.

[100] Cleavage of the mother, see Kaineus; also rift, chasm = division of the earth, and so on.

[101] "Schöpfung und Chaos." Göttingen, 1895, p. 30.

[102] Brugsch: Ibid., p. 161.

[103] In a Pyramid text, which depicts the battle of the dead Pharaoh for the dominance of heaven, it reads: Heaven weeps, the stars tremble, the guards of the gods tremble and their servants flee, when they see the king rise as a spirit, as a god, who lives upon his fathers and conquers his mothers." Cited by Dieterich: "Mithrasliturgy," p. 100.

[104] Book II, p. 61.

[105] By Ares, the Egyptian Typhon is probably meant.

[106] In the Polynesian Maui myth, the act of the sun-hero is very plain: he robs his mother of her girdle. The robbery of the veil in myths of the type of the swan maiden has the same significance. In an African myth of Joruba, the sun-hero simply ravishes his mother (Frobenius).

[107] The previously mentioned myth of Halirrhotios, who destroyed himself when he wished to cut down the holy tree of Athens, the Moria, contains the same psychology, also the priestly castration (Attis castration) in the service of the great mother. The ascetic self-torture in Christianity has its origin, as is self-evident, in these sources because the Christian form of symbol means a very intensive regression to the mother incest.

[108] The tearing off from the tree of life is just this sin.

[109] Compare Kuhn: "Herabkunft des Feuers."

[110] Nork: "Wörterbuch s. v. Mistel."

[111] Therefore in England mistletoe boughs were hung up at Christmas. Mistletoe as rod of life. Compare Aigremont: "Volkserotik und Pflanzenwelt."

[112] Just as the tree has the phallic nature as well as a maternal significance, so in myths the demonic old woman (she may be favorable or malicious) often has phallic attributes, for example, a long toe, a long tooth, long lips, long fingers, pendulous breasts, large hands, feet, and so on. This mixture of male and female motive has reference to the fact that the old woman is a libido symbol like the tree, generally determined as maternal. The bisexuality of the libido is expressed in

its clearest form in the idea of the three witches, who collectively possessed but one eye and one tooth. This idea is directly parallel to the dream of a patient, who represented her libido as twins, one of which is a box, the other a bottle-like object, for eye and tooth represent male and female genitals. Relative to eye in this connection, see especially the Egyptian myths: referring to tooth, it is to be observed that Adonis (fecundity) died by a boar's tooth, like Siegfried by Hagen's spear; compare with this the Veronese Priapus, whose phallus was bitten by a snake. Tooth in this sense, like the snake, is a "negative" phallus.

[113] Compare Grimm: Vol. II, Chap. iv, p. 802. The same motive in another application is found in a Low-Saxon legend: Once a young ash tree grew unnoticed in the wood. Each New Year's Eve a white knight upon a white horse rides up to cut down the young shoot. At the same time a black knight arrives and engages him in combat. After a lengthy conflict, the white knight succeeds in overcoming the black knight and the white knight cuts down the young tree. But sometime the white knight will be unsuccessful, then the ash will grow, and when it becomes large enough to allow a horse to be tied under it, then a powerful king will come and a tremendous battle will occur (destruction of the world).

[114] Chantepie de la Saussaye: "Lehrbuch der Religionsgeschichte," Vol. II, p. 185.

[115] Further examples in Frobenius: Ibid., passim.

[116] See Jensen: "Gilgameshepos."

[117] In a Schlesian passionale of the fifteenth century Christ dies on the same tree which was connected with Adam's sin. Cited from Zöckler: Ibid., p. 241.

[118] For example, animal skins were hung on the sacrificial trees and afterwards spears were thrown at them.

[119] "Geschichte der amerikanischen Urreligionen," p. 498.

[120] Stephens: "Central America" (cited by Müller: Ibid., p. 498).

[121] Zöckler: "Das Kreuz Christi," p. 34.

[122] H. H. Bancroft: "Native Races of the Pacific States of North America," II, 506. (Cited by Robertson: "Evang. Myths," p. 139.)

[123] Rossellini: "Monumenti dell' Egitto, etc." Tom. 3. Tav. 23. (Cited by Robertson: Ibid., p. 142.)

[124] Zöckler: Ibid., p. 7. In the representation of the birth of a king in Luxor one sees the following: The logos and messenger of the gods, the bird-headed Thoth, makes known to the maiden Queen Mautmes that she is to give birth to a son. In the following scene, Kneph and Athor hold the Crux ansata to her mouth so that she may be impregnated by this in a spiritual (symbolic) manner. Sharp: "Egyptian Mythology," p. 18. (Cited by Robertson: "Evangelical Myths," p. 43.)

[125] The statues of the phallic Hermes used as boundary stones were often in the form of a cross with the head pointed (W. Payne Knight: "Worship of Priapus," p. 30). In Old English the cross is called rod.

[126] Robertson (Ibid., p. 140) mentions the fact that the Mexican priests and sacrificers clothed themselves in the skin of a slain woman, and

placed themselves with arms stretched out like a cross before the god of war.

[127] "Indian Antiquities," VI, 49.

[128] The primitive Egyptian cross form is meant: T.

[129] Zöckler: Ibid., p. 19. The bud is plainly phallic. See the above-mentioned dream of the young woman.

[130] I am indebted for my information about these researches to Professor Fiechter of Stuttgart.

[131] Zöckler: Ibid., p. 33.

[132] The sacrifice is submerged in the water, that is, in the mother.

[133] Compare later the moon as gathering place of souls (the devouring mother).

[134] Compare here what Abraham has to say in reference to pupilla ("Dreams and Myths").

[135] Retreat of Rê upon the heavenly cow. In a Hindoo rite of purification, the penitent must creep through an artificial cow in order to be born anew.

[136] Schultze: "Psychologie der Naturvölker." Leipzig 1900, p. 338.

[137] Brugsch: Ibid., p. 290.

[138] One need not be amazed at this formula because it is the animal in us, the primitive forces of which appear in religion. In this connection Dieterich's words ("Mithrasliturgie," p. 108) take on an especially important aspect. "The old thoughts come *from below* in new force in the history of religion. The revolution *from below* creates a new life of religion in primitive indestructible forms."

[139] Dispute between Mary and the Cross in R. Morris: "Legends of the Holy Rood." London 1871.

[140] A very beautiful representation of the blood-red sun sinking into the sea.

[141] Jesus appears here as branch and bud in the tree of life. Compare here the interesting reference in Robertson: "Evangelical Myths," p. 51, in regard to "Jesus, the Nazarene," a title which he derives from Nazar or Netzer = branch.

[142] In Greece, the pale of torture, on which the criminal was stretched or punished, was termed ἑκάτη (Hecate), the subterranean mother of death.

[143] Diez: "Etym. Wörterbuch der romanischen Sprachen," p. 90.

CHAPTER VI

[1] Witches easily change themselves into horses, therefore the nail-marks of the horseshoe may be seen upon their hands. The devil rides on witch-horses, priests' cooks are changed after death into horses, etc. Negelein, *Zeitschrift des Vereines fur Volkskunde*, XI, p. 406.

[2] Just so does the mythical ancient king Tahmuraht ride upon Ahriman, the devil.

[3] The she-asses and their foals might belong to the Christian sun myth, because the Zodiacal sign Cancer (Summer solstice) was designated in antiquity as an ass and its young. (Compare Robertson: "Evangelical Myths," p. 19.)

[4] Also a centaur.

[5] Compare the exhaustive presentation of this theme in Jähn's "Ross und Reiter."

[6] Sleipnir is eight-footed.

[7] Negelein: Ibid., p. 412.

[8] Negelein: Ibid., p. 419.

[9] I have since learned of a second exactly similar case.

[10] Preller: "Griech. Mythologie," I, I, p. 432.

[11] See further. examples in Aigremont: "Fuss- und Schuhsymbolik."

[12] Aigremont: Ibid., p. 17.

[13] Negelein: Ibid., p. 386.

[14] Ample proofs of the Centaurs as wind gods are to be found in E. H. Meyer: "Indogermanische Mythen," p. 447.

[15] This is an especial motive, which must have something typical in it. My patient ("Psychology of Dementia Praecox," p. 165) also declared that her horses had "half-moons" under their skin, like "little curls." In the songs of Rudra of the Rigveda, of the boar Rudra it is said that his hair was "wound up in the shape of shells." Indra's body is covered with eyes.

[16] This change results from a world catastrophe. In mythology the verdure and the upward striving of the tree of life signify also the turning-point in the succession of the ages.

[17] Therefore the lion was killed by Samson, who later harvested the honey from the body. The end of summer is the plenteousness of the autumn. It is a close parallel to the sacrificium Mithriacum. For Samson, see Steinthal: "Die Sage von Simson," *Zeitschrift für Völkerpsych.,*" Vol. II.

[18] Philo: "In Genesim," I, 100. (Cited by Cumont: "Textes et Monuments," I, p. 82.)

[19] Spiegel: "Erân. Altertumskunde," Vol. II, p. 193. In the writings ascribed to Zoroaster, Περὶ Φύσεως, the Ananke, the necessity of fate, is represented by the air. Cumont: Ibid., I, p. 87.

[20] Spielrein's patient (*Jahrbuch,* III, p. 394) speaks of horses, who eat men, also exhumed bodies.

[21] Negelein: Ibid., p. 416.

[22] P. Thomas a Villanova Wegener: "Das wunderbare äussere und innere Leben der Dienerin Gottes Anna Catherina Emmerich." Dülmen i. W. 1891.

[23] The heart of the mother of God is pierced by a sword.

[24] Corresponding to the idea in Psalm xi:2, "For lo, the wicked bend their bow, they make ready their arrow upon the string, that they may privily shoot at the upright in heart."

[25] K. E. Neumann: "The Speeches of Gautama Buddha," translated from the German collection of the fragments of Suttanipāto of the Pāli-Kanon. München 1911.

[26] With the same idea of an endogenous pain Theocritus (27, 28) calls the birth throes "Arrows of the Ilithyia." In the sense of a wish the same comparison is found in Jesus Sirach 19:12. "When a word penetrates a fool it is the same as if an arrow pierced his loins." That is to say, it gives him no rest until it is out.

[27] One might be tempted to say that these were merely figuratively expressed coitus scenes. But that would be a little too strong and an unjustifiable accentuation of the material at issue. We cannot forget that the saints have, figuratively, taught the painful domestification of the brute. The result of this, which is the progress of civilization, has also to be recognized as a motive for this action.

[28] Apuleius ("Metam.," Book II, 31) made use of the symbolism of bow and arrow in a very drastic manner, "Ubi primam sagittam saevi Cupidinis in ima praecordia mea delapsam excepi, arcum meum en! Ipse vigor attendit et oppido formido, ne nervus rigoris nimietate rumpatur" (When I pulled out the first arrow of fierce Cupid that had entered into my inmost breast, behold my bow! Its very vigor stretches it and makes me fear lest the string be broken by the excessive tautness).

[29] Thus the plague-bringing Apollo. In Old High German, arrow is called "strala" (strahlen = rays).

[30] Spielrein's patient (Jahrbuch, III, p. 371) has also the idea of the cleavage of the earth in a similar connection. "Iron is used for the purpose of penetrating into the earth. . . . with iron man can . . . create men . . . the earth is split, burst open, man is divided . . . is severed and reunited. In order to make an end of the burial of the living, Jesus Christ calls his disciples to penetrate into the earth."
The motive of "cleavage" is of general significance. The Persian hero Tishtriya, who also appeared as a white horse, opens the rain lake, and thus makes the earth fruitful. He is called Tîr = arrow. He was also represented as feminine, with a bow and arrow. Mithra with his arrow shot the water from the rock, so as to end the drought. The knife is sometimes found stuck in the earth. In Mithraic monuments sometimes it is the sacrificial instrument which kills the bull. (Cumont: Ibid., pp. 115, 116, 165.)

[31] Spielrein's patient also states that she has been shot through by God. (3 shots:) "then came a resurrection of the spirit." This is the symbolism of introversion.

[32] This is also represented mythologically in the legend of Theseus and Peirithoos, who wished to capture the subterranean Proserpina. With this aim they enter a chasm in the earth in the grove Kolonos, in order to get down to the underworld; when they were below they wished to rest, but being enchanted they hung on the rocks, that is to say, they remained fixed in the mother and were therefore lost for the

upperworld. Later Theseus was freed by Hercules (revenge of Horus for Osiris), at which time Hercules appears in the rôle of the death-conquering hero.

[33] This formula applies most directly to dementia praecox.

[34] See Roscher: s. v. Philoktetes, Sp. 2318, 15.

[35] When the Russian sun-hero Oleg stepped on the skull of the slain horse, a serpent came out of it and bit him on the foot. Then he became sick and died. When Indra in the form of Çyena, the falcon, stole the soma drink, Kriçanu, the herdsman, wounded him in his foot with his arrow ("Rigveda," I, 155; IV, 322).   .

[36] Similar to the Lord of the Grail who guards the chalice, the mother symbol. The myth of Philoctetes is taken from a more involved connection, the Hercules myth. Hercules has two mothers, the benevolent Alcmene and the pursuing Hera (Lamia), from whose breast he has absorbed immortality. Hercules conquered Hera's serpent while yet in the cradle; that is to say, conquered the "terrible mother," the Lamia. But from time to time Hera sent to him attacks of madness, in one of which he killed his children (Lamia motive). According to an interesting tradition, this deed occurred at the moment when Hercules refused to perform a great act in the service of Eurystheus. As a result of the refusal, the libido, in readiness for the work, regressed in a typical manner to the unconscious mother-imago, which resulted in madness (as to-day), during which Hercules identifies himself with Lamia (Hera) and murders his own children. The delphic oracle communicates to him the fact that he is named Hercules because he owes his immortal fame to Hera, who through her persecution compelled him to great deeds. It can be seen that "the great deed" really means the conquering of the mother and through her to win immortality. His characteristic weapon, the club, he cuts from the maternal olive tree. Like the sun, he possessed the arrows of Apollo. He conquered the Nemean lion in his cave, which has the signification of "the grave in the mother's womb" (see the end of this chapter). Then follows the combat with the Hydra, the typical battle with the dragon; the complete conquering of the mother. (See below.) Following this, the capture of the Cerynean doe, whom he wounded with an arrow in the foot. This is what generally happens to the hero, but here it is reversed. Hercules showed the captured Erymanthian boar to Eurystheus, whereupon the latter in fear crept into a cask. That is, he died. The Stymphalides, the Cretan bull, and the man-devouring horse of Diomedes are symbols of the devastating powers of death, among which the latter's relation to the mother may be recognized especially. The battle for the precious girdle of the Amazon queen Hippolyte permits us to see once more very clearly the shadow of the mother. Hippolyte is ready to give up the girdle, but Hera, changing herself into the form of Hippolyte, calls the Amazons against Hercules in battle. (Compare Horus, fighting for the head ornament of Isis, about which there is more later. Chap. 7.) The liberation of Hesione results from Hercules journeying downwards with his ship into the belly of the monster, and killing the monster from within after three days labor. (Jonah motive; Christ in the tomb or in hell; the victory over death by creeping into the womb of the mother, and its destruction in the form of the mother. The libido in the form of the beautiful maiden again conquered.) The expedition to Erythia is a parallel to Gilgamesh, also to

Moses in the Koran, whose goal was the confluence of the two seas: it is the journey of the sun to the Western sea, where Hercules discovered the straits of Gibraltar ("to that passage": Faust), and with the ship of Helios set out towards Erythia. There he overcame the gigantic guardian Eurytion (Chumbaba in the Gilgamesh epic, the symbol of the father), then the triune Geryon (a monster of phallic libido symbolism), and at the same time wounded Hera, hastening to the help of Geryon by an arrow shot. Then the robbery of the herd followed. "The treasure attained with difficulty" is here presented in surroundings which make it truly unmistakable. Hercules, like the sun, goes to death, down into the mother (Western sea), but conquers the libido attached to the mother and returns with the wonderful kine; he has won back his libido, his life, the mighty possession. We discover the same thought in the robbery of the golden apples of Hesperides, which are defended by the hundred-headed dragon. The victory over Cerberus is also easily understood as the victory over death by entrance into the mother (underworld). In order to come to his wife Deianira, he has to undergo a terrible battle with a water god, Achelous (with the mother). The ferryman Nessus (a centaur) violates Deianira. With his sun arrows Hercules killed this adversary, but Nessus advised Deianira to preserve his poisoned blood as a love charm. When after the insane murder of Iphitus Delphi denied him the speech of the oracle, he took possession of the sacred tripod. The delphic oracle then compelled him to become a slave of Omphale, who made him like a child. After this Hercules returned home to Deianira, who presented him with the garment poisoned with Nessus' blood (the Isis snake), which immediately clung so closely to his skin that he in vain attempted to tear it off. (The casting of the skin of the aging sun-god; Serpent, as symbol of rejuvenation.) Hercules then ascended the funeral pyre in order to destroy himself by fire like the phœnix, that is to say, to give birth to himself again from his own egg. No one but young Philoctetes dared to sacrifice the god. Therefore Philoctetes received the arrows of the sun and the libido myth was renewed with this Horus.

[87] Apes, also, have an instinctive fear of·snakes.

[88] How much alive are still such primitive associations is shown by Segantini's picture of the two mothers: cow and calf, mother and child in the same stable. From this symbolism the surroundings of the birthplace of the Savior are explained.

[89] The myth of Hippolytos shows very beautifully all the typical parts of the problem: His stepmother Phaedra wantonly falls in love with him. He repulses her, she complains to her husband of violation; the latter implores the water god Poseidon to punish Hippolytos. Then a monster comes out of the sea. Hippolytos' horses shy and drag Hippolytos to death. But he is resuscitated by Aesculapius and is placed by the gods with the wise nymph, Egeria, the counsellor of Numa Pompilius. Thus the wish is fulfilled; from incest, wisdom has come.

[40] Compare Hercules and Omphale.

[41] Compare the reproach of Gilgamesh against Ishtar.

[42] Spielrein's patient is also sick from "a snake bite." *Jahrbuch,* III, p. 385.

[43] The entirely introverted patient of Spielrein uses similar images:

she speaks of "a rigidity of the soul on the cross," of "stone figures" which must be "ransomed."

I call attention here to the fact that the symbolisms mentioned above are striking examples of Silberer's "functional category." They depict the condition of introversion.

⁴⁴ W. Gurlitt says: "The carrying of the bull is one of the difficult ἆθλα (services) which Mithra performed in the service of freeing humanity; "somewhat corresponding, if it is permitted to compare the small with the great, with the carrying of the cross by Christ" (Cumont: "Textes et Monuments," I, 72). Surely it is permissible to compare the two acts.

Man should be past that period when, in true barbaric manner, he haughtily scorned the strange gods, the "dii minorum gentium." But man has not progressed that far, even yet.

⁴⁵ Robertson ("Evangelical Myths," p. 130) gives an interesting contribution to the question of the symbol of the carrying of the cross. Samson carried the "pillars of the gates from Gaza and died between the columns of the temple of the Philistines." Hercules, weighted down by his burden, carried his columns to the place (Gades), where he also died according to the Syrian version of the legend. The columns of Hercules mark the western point where the sun sinks into the sea. In old art he was actually represented carrying the two columns under his arms in such a way that they exactly formed a cross. Here we perhaps have the origin of the myth of Jesus, who carries his own cross to the place of execution. It is worth noting that the three synoptics substitute a man of the name of Simon from Cyrene as bearer of the cross. Cyrene is in Libya, the legendary scene upon which Hercules performed the labor of carrying the columns, as we have seen, and Simon (Simson) is the nearest Greek name-form for Samson, which in Greek might have been read Simson, as in Hebrew. But in Palestine it was Simon, Semo or Sem, actually a name of a god, who represented the old sun-god Semesch, who was identified with Baal, from whose myth the Samson myth has doubtless arisen. The god Simon enjoyed especial honor in Samaria. "The cross of Hercules might well be the sun's wheel, for which the Greeks had the symbol of the cross. The sun's wheel upon the bas-relief in the small metropolis at Athens contains a cross, which is very similar to the Maltese cross." (See Thiele: "Antike Himmelsbilder," 1898, p. 59.)

⁴⁶ The Greek myth of Ixion, who was bound to the "four-spoked wheel," says this almost without disguise. Ixion first murdered his stepfather, but later was absolved from guilt by Zeus and blessed with his favor. But the ingrate attempted to seduce Hera, the mother. Zeus deceived him, however, allowing the goddess of the clouds, Nephele, to assume Hera's form. (From this connection the centaurs have arisen.) Ixion boasted of his deed, but Zeus as a punishment plunged him into the underworld, where he was bound to a wheel continually whirled around by the wind. (Compare the punishment of Francesca da Rimini in Dante and the "penitents" by Segantini.)

⁴⁷ Cited from *Zentralblatt für Psychoanalyse,* Jahrgang II, p. 365.

⁴⁸ The symbolism of death appearing in abundance in dreams has been emphasized by Stekel ("Sprache des Traumes," p. 317).

⁴⁹ Compare the Cassius scene above.

CHAPTER VII

[1] A direct unconstrained expression of sexuality is a natural occurrence and as such neither unbeautiful nor repulsive. The "moral" repression makes sexuality on one side dirty and hypocritical, on the other shameless and obtrusive.

[2] Compare what is said below concerning the motive of fettering.

[3] The sacrilegious assault of Horus upon Isis, at which Plutarch ("De Isis et Osiris") stands aghast; he expresses himself as follows concerning it. "But if any one wishes to assume and maintain that all this has really happened and taken place with respect to blessed and imperishable nature, which for the most part is considered as corresponding to the divine; then, to speak in the words of Aeschylus, 'he must spit out and clean his mouth.'" From this sentence one can form a conception of how the well-intentioned people of ancient society may have condemned the Christian point of view, first the hanged God, then the management of the family, the "foundation" of the state. The psychologist is not surprised.

[4] Compare the typical fate of Theseus and Peirithoos.

[5] Compare the example given for that in Aigremont: "Fuss- und Schuhsymbolik." Also Part I of this book; the foot of the sun in an Armenian folk prayer. Also de Gubernatis: "Die Tiere in der Indo-Germanischen Mythologie," Vol. I, p. 220 ff.

[6] Rohde: "Psyche."

[7] Porphyrius ("De antro nympharum." Quoted by Dieterich: "Mithraslit.," p. 63) says that according to the Mithraic doctrine the souls which pass away at birth are destined for winds, because these souls had taken the breath of the wind into custody and therefore had a similar nature: ψυχαῖς δ' εἰς γένεσιν ἰούσαις καὶ ἀπὸ γενέσεως χωριζομέναις εἰκότως ἔταξαν ἀνέμους διὰ τὸ ἐφέλκεσθαι καὶ αὐτὰς πνεῦμα καὶ οὐσίαν ἔχειν τοιαύτην — (The souls departing at birth and becoming separated, probably become winds because of inhaling their breath and becoming the same substance).

[8] In the Mithraic liturgy the generating breath of the spirit comes from the sun, probably "from the tube of the sun" (see Part I). Corresponding to this idea, in the Rigveda the sun is called the One-footed. Compare with that the Armenian prayer, for the sun to allow its foot to rest upon the face of the suppliant (Abeghian: "Der armenische Volksglaube," 1899, p. 41).

[9] Firmicus Maternus (Mathes., I, 5, 9): "Cui (animo) descensus per orbem solis tribuitur, per orbem vero lunae praeparatur ascensus" (For which soul a descent through the disc of the sun is devised, but the ascent is prepared through the disc of the moon). Lydus ("De mens.," IV, 3) tells us that the hierophant Praetextatus has said that Janus despatches the diviner souls to the lunar fields: τὰς θειοτέρας ψυχὰς ἐπὶ τὴν σεληνικὸν χόρον ἀποπέμπει. Epiphanius (Haeres LXVI, 52): ὅτι ἐκ τῶν ψυχῶν ὁ δίσκος (τῆς σελήνης) ἀποπίμπλαται. Quoted by Cumont: "Textes et Monuments," I, I, p. 40. In exotic myths it is the same with the moon. Frobenius: Ibid., p. 352 ff.

[10] "The Light of Asia, or The Great Renunciation" (Mahâbhinishkramana).

[11] One sees upon corresponding representations how the elephant presses into Maya's head with its trunk.

[12] Rank: "The Myth of the Birth of the Hero," translated by W. White.

[13] The speedy dying of the mother or the separation from the mother belongs to the myth of the hero. In the myth of the swan maiden which Rank has analyzed very beautifully, there is the wish-fulfilling thought, that the swan maiden can fly away again after the birth of the child, because she has then fulfilled her purpose. Man needs the mother only for rebirth.

[14] Indian word for the rustle of the wind in the trees.

[15] Means sound of the waves.

[16] An introjection of the object into the subject in the sense of Ferenczi, the "gegenwurf" or "widerwurf" (Objektum) of the mystics Eckart and Böhme.

[17] Karl Joël ("Seele und Welt," Jena 1912) says (p. 153): "Life does not diminish in artists and prophets, but is enhanced. They are the leaders into the lost Paradise, which now for the first time becomes Paradise through rediscovery. It is no more the old dull unity of life towards which the artist strives and leads, it is the sentient reunion, not the empty but the full unity, not the unity of indifference but the unity of difference." "All life is the raising of the equilibrium and the pulling backwards into equilibrium. Such a return do we find in religion and art."

[18] By the primal experience must be understood that first human differentiation between subject and object, that first conscious placing of object, which is not psychologically conceivable without the presupposition of an inner division of the animal "man" from himself, by which precisely is he separated from nature which is at one with itself.

[19] Crêvecoeur: "Voyage dans la Haute Pensylvanie," I, 362.

[20] The dragons of the Greek (and Swiss) legends live in or near springs or other waters of which they are often the guardians.

[21] Compare the discussion above about the encircling and devouring motive. Water as a hindrance in dreams seems to refer to the mother, longing for the mother instead of positive work. The crossing of water —overcoming of the resistance; that is to say the mother, as a symbol of the longing for inactivity like death or sleep.

[22] Compare also the Attic custom of stuffing a bull in spring, the customs of the Lupercalia, Saturnalia, etc. I have devoted to this motive a separate investigation, therefore I forego further proof.

[23] In the Gilgamesh epic, it is directly said that it is immortality which the hero goes to obtain.

[24] Sepp: "Das Heidentum und dessen Bedeutung für das Christentum," Vol. III, 82.

[25] Compare the symbolism of the arrow above.

[26] This thought is generally organized in the doctrine of pre-existence.

Thus in any case man is his own generator, immortal and a hero, whereby the highest wishes are fulfilled.

[27] Frazer: "Golden Bough," IV, 297.

[28] "Thou seekest the heaviest burden, there findest thou thyself" (Nietzsche: "Zarathustra").

[29] It is an unvarying peculiarity, so to speak, that in the whale-dragon myth, the hero is very hungry in the belly of the monster and begins to cut off pieces from the animal, so as to feed himself. He is in the nourishing mother "in the presexual stage." His next act, in order to free himself, is to make a fire. In a myth of the Eskimos of the Behring Straits, the hero finds a woman in the whale's belly, the soul of the animal, which is feminine (Ibid, p. 85). (Compare Frobenius: Ibid, passim.)

[30] The carrying of the tree played an important part, as is evident from a note in Strabo X, in the cult of Dionysus and Ceres (Demeter).

[31] A text on the Pyramids, which treats of the arrival of the dead Pharaoh in Heaven, depicts how Pharaoh takes possession of the gods in order to assimilate their divine nature, and to become the lord of the gods: "His servants have imprisoned the gods with a chain, they have taken them and dragged them away, they have bound them, they have cut their throats, and taken out their entrails, they have dismembered them and cooked them in hot vessels. And the king consumed their force and ate their souls. The great gods form his breakfast, the medium gods his dinner, the little gods his supper—the king consumes everything that comes in his way. Greedily he devours everything and his magic power becomes greater than all magic power. He becomes the heir of the power, he becomes greater than all heirs, he becomes the lord of heaven, he eats all crowns and all bracelets, he eats the wisdom of every god, etc." (Wiedemann: "Der alte Orient," II, 2, 1900, p. 18). This impossible food, this "Bulimie," strikingly depicts the sexual libido in regression to the presexual material, where the mother (the gods) is not the object of sex but of hunger.

[32] The sacramental sacrifice of Dionysus-Zagreus and the eating of the sacrificial meat produced the "νέος Διόνυσος" the resurrection of the god, as plainly appears from the Cretan fragments of the Euripides' quoted by Dieterich (Ibid., p. 105):

ἀγνὸν δὲ βίον τείνων, ἐξ οὗ
Διὸς Ἰδαίου μύστης γενόμην
καὶ νυκτιπόλου Ζαγρέως βούτας
τοὺς ὠμοφάγους δαῖτας τελέσας.

(Living a blameless life whereby I became an initiate of the Idaean Zeus, I celebrated the carnivorous banquet of Zagreus, the wandering herdsman of the night.)

The mystics took the god into themselves by eating the uncooked meat of the sacrificial animal.

[33] Richter: 14, 14.

[34] Orphic Hymn, 46. Compare Roscher: "Lexicon," sect. on Iakchos.

[35] A close parallel to this is the Japanese myth of Izanagi, who, following his dead spouse into the underworld, implored her to return.

She is ready, but beseeches him, " Do not look at me." Izanagi produces light with his reed, that is to say, with a masculine piece of wood (the fire-boring Phallus), and thus loses his spouse. (Frobenius: Ibid., p. 343.) Mother must be put in the place of spouse. Instead of the mother, the hero produces fire; Hiawatha, maize; Odin, Runes, when he in torment hung on the tree. •

[36] Quoted from De Jong: " Das antike Mysterienwesen." Leiden 1910, p. 22.

[37] A son-lover from the Demeter myth is Iasion, who embraces Demeter upon a thrice-ploughed cornfield. (Bridal couch in the pasture.) For that Iasion was struck by lightning by Zeus (Ovid: " Metam.," IX).

[38] See Cumont: " Textes et Monuments," I, p. 56.

[39] " Mithraslit.," p. 123.

[40] For example upon a Campana relief in Lovatelli (" Antichi monumenti," Roma, 1889, I, IV, Fig. 5). Likewise the Veronese Priapus has a basket filled with phalli.

[41] Compare Grimm: II, IV, p. 899: Either by the caressing or kissing of a dragon or a snake, the fearful animal was changed into a beautiful woman whom the hero wins in this way.

[42] The mother, the earth, is the distributor of nourishment. The mother in presexual material has this meaning. Therefore St. Dominicus was nourished from the breasts of the mother of God. The sun wife, Namaqua, consists of bacon. Compare with this the megalomanic ideas of my patient, who asserted: " I am Germania and Helvetia made exclusively from ' sweet butter ' " (" Psychology of Dementia Praecox ").

[43] Compare the ideas of Nietzsche: " Piercing into one's own pit," etc. In a prayer to Hermes in a London papyrus it is said: ἐλθέ μοι, κύριε Ἑρμῆ, ὡς τὰ βρέφη εἰς τὰς κοιλίας τῶν γυναικῶν (Come to me, Lord Hermes, as the foetus into the womb of the mother). Kenyon: " Greek Papyrus in the British Museum," 1893, p. 116; Pap. CXXII, Z. 2 ff. Cited by Dieterich: Ibid., p. 97.

[44] Compare De Jong: Ibid., p. 22.

[45] The typical grain god of antiquity was Adonis, whose death and resurrection was celebrated annually. He was the son-lover of the mother, for the grain is the son and fructifier of the womb of the earth as Robertson very correctly remarks (" Evangelical Myths," p. 36).

[46] De Jong: Ibid., p. 14.

[47] Faust:

" There whirls the press, like clouds on clouds unfolding,
Then with stretched arm swing high the key thou'rt holding! "

[48] As an example among many, I mention here the Polynesian Rata myth cited by Frobenius: Ibid., pp. 64-66: " With a favorable wind the boat was sailing easily away over the Ocean, when Nganaoa called out one day: ' O Rata, here is a fearful enemy who rises up from the Ocean!' It was an open mussel of huge dimensions. One shell was in front of the boat, the other behind it, and the vessel was directly between. The next moment the horrible mussel would have clapped its shells together and ground the boat and occupants to pieces in its grip.

But Nganaoa was prepared for this possibility. He grasped his long spear and quickly plunged it into the belly of the animal so that the creature, instead of snapping together, at once sank back to the bottom of the sea. After they had escaped from this danger they continued on their way. But after a while the voice of the always watchful Nganaoa was again to be heard. 'O Rata, once more a terrible enemy rushes upwards from the depths of the ocean.' This time it was a mighty octopus, whose gigantic tentacles already surrounded the boat, in order to destroy it. At this critical moment, Nganaoa seized his spear, and plunged it into the head of the octopus. The tentacles sank away limp and the dead monster rose to the surface of the water. Once more they continued on their journey, but a yet greater danger awaited them. One day the valiant Nganaoa called out, 'O Rata, here is a great whale!' The huge jaws were wide open, the lower jaw was already under the boat, and the upper one over it. One moment more and the whale would have devoured them. Now Nganaoa 'the dragon slayer' broke his spear into two parts, and at the moment when the whale was about to devour them, he stuck the two pieces into the jaws of the foe so that he could not close his jaws. Nganaoa quickly sprang into the jaws of the great whale (devouring of the hero) and looked into its belly, and what did he see? There sat both his parents, his father, Tairitokerau, and his mother, Vaiaroa, who had been gulped down into the depths of this monster. The oracle has come true. The voyage has come to its end. Great was the joy of the parents of Nganaoa when they saw their son. They were convinced that their freedom was at hand. And Nganaoa resolved upon revenge. He took one of the two pieces from the jaws of the animal—one was enough to make it impossible for the whale to close his jaws and so keep a passage free for Nganaoa and his parents. He broke this part of the spear in two, in order to use them as wood to produce fire by rubbing. He commanded his father to hold one firmly below, while he himself managed the upper one, until the fire began to glimmer (production of fire). Now when he blew this into flames, he hastened to heat the fatty part (heart) of the belly with the fire. The monster, writhing with pain, sought help swimming to the nearest land (journey in the sea). As soon as he reached the sand-bank (land) father, mother and son walked onto the land through the open jaws of the dying whale (slipping out of the hero)."

[49] In the New Zealand Maui myth (quoted by Frobenius: Ibid., p. 66 ff.) the monster to be conquered is the grandmother Hine-nui-te-po. Maui, the hero, says to the birds who assist him: "My little friends, now when I creep into the jaws of the old woman, you must not laugh, but when I have been in and come out again, from her mouth, then you may greet me with jubilant laughter." Then Maui actually creeps into the mouth of the sleeping old woman.

[50] Published and prepared by Julius v. Negelein, in "Relig. Geschichte." Vers. u. Vorarb. von Dieterich und Wünsch, Vol. XI. Giessen 1912.

[51] Quoted, J. v. Negelein: "Der Traumschlüssel des Jagaddeva," p. 256.

[52] The pine-tree speaks the significant word, "Minne-wawa!"

[53] In a fairy tale, the bird comes to the tree which grows upon the grave of the mother in order to give help.

[54] Roscher: s. "Picus," Sp. 2494, 62. Probably a symbol of rebirth.

[55] The father of Picus is called Sterculus or Sterculius, a name which is clearly derived from stercus = excrementum; he is also said to be the devisor of manure. The primitive creator who also created the mother did so in the manner of infantile creation, which we have previously learned. The supreme god laid an egg, his mother, from which he was again produced—this is an analogous train of thought.

[56] Introversion = to enter the mother; to sink into one's own innerworld, or source of the libido, is symbolized by creeping in, passing through, boring. (Scratching behind the ear = making fire.) Boring into the ear, scratching with the nails, swallowing serpents. Thus the Buddhist legend is understandable. When Gautama had spent the whole day sitting in deep reflection under the sacred tree, at evening he became Buddha, the illumined one.

[57] Compare φαλλός (phallus) above and its etymological connection.

[58] Spielrein's patient received from God three wounds through her head, breast and eye. "Then there came a resurrection of the Spirit" (*Jahrbuch*, III, p. 376).
In the Tibetan myth of Bogda Gesser Khan the sun-hero shoots his arrow into the forehead of the demoniacal old woman, who devours it and spits it up again. In a Calmuc myth, the hero shoots the arrow into the eye emitting rays, which is found on the forehead of the bull. Compare with that the victory of Polyphemus, whose character is signified upon an Attic vase because with it there is also a snake (as symbol of the mother. See the explanation of the sacrificium Mithriacum).

[59] In the form of the father, for Megissogwon is the demon of the west, like Mudjekeewis.

[60] Compare Deussen: "Geschichte der Philosophie," Vol. I, p. 14.

[61] An analogy is Zeus and Athene. In Rigveda 10, 31, the word of prayer becomes a pregnant cow. In Persian it is the "Eye of Ahura"; Babylonian *Nabu:* the word of fate; Persian *vohu mano:* the good thought of the creator God; in Stoic conceptions, Hermes is *logos* or world intellect; in Alexandria the Σοφία, in the Old Testament it is the angel of Jehovah, or the countenance of God. Jacob wrestled with the angel during the night at the ford of Jabbok, after he had crossed the water with all that he possessed. (Night journey on the sea, battle with the night snake, combat at the ford like Hiawatha.) In this combat, Jacob dislocated his thigh. (Motive of the twisting out of the arm. Castration on account of the overpowering of the mother.) This "face" of God was compared in the old Jewish philosophy to the mystic Metatron, the prince of the face of God (Josiah 5, 14), who brings "the prayer to God" and "in whom is the name of God." The Naassens (Ophits) called the Holy Ghost the "first word," the mother of all that lives; the Valentinians comprehended the descending dove of Pneuma as "the word of the mother from above, the Sophia." (Drews: "Christ Myth," I, pp. 16, 22, 80.) In Assyria, Gibil, the fire god, had the rôle of Logos. (Tiele: "Assyr. Gesch." (In Ephrem, the Syrian writer of hymns, John the Baptist says to Christ: "A spark of fire in the air waits for thee over the Jordan. If thou followest it and willst be baptised, then take possession of thyself, wash thyself, for

who has the power to take hold of burning fire with his hands? Thou, who art wholly fire, have mercy upon me." Usener: "Religions-geschichtliche Untersuchungen." Cited by Drews: Ibid., p. 81.

[62] Perhaps the great significance of the name arose from this phantasy.

[63] Grimm mentions the legend that Siegfried was suckled by a doe. (Compare Hiawatha's first deed.)

[64] Compare Grimm's "Mythology." Mime or Mimir is a gigantic being of great wisdom, "a very old Nature God," with whom the Norse gods associate. Later fables make of him a demon and a skilful smith (closest relation to Wieland). Just as Wotan obtained advice from the wise woman (compare the quotation from Julius Cæsar about the German matron), so does Odin go to the brook of Mimir in which wisdom and judgment lie hidden, to the spiritual mother (mother-imago). There he requests a drink (drink of immortality), but no sooner does he receive it than he sacrifices his eye to the well (death of the sun in the sea). The well of Mimir points undoubtedly to the mother significance of Mimir. Thus Mimir gets possession of Odin's other eye. In Mimir, the mother (wise giant) and the embryo (dwarf, subterranean sun, Harpocrates) is condensed; likewise, as mother, he is the source of wisdom and art. ("Mother-imago" therefore may be translated as "phantasy" under certain circumstances.)

[65] The magic sleep is also present in the Homeric celebration of the Hierosgamos. See above.)

[66] This is proved by Siegfried's words:
> "Through furious fire
> To thee have I fared;
> Nor birny nor buckler
> Guarded my breast:
> The flames have broken
> Through to my heart,
> My blood doth bound
> In turbulent streams;
> A raving fire
> Within me is kindled."

[67] The cave dragon is the "terrible mother." In the German legends the maiden to be rescued often appears as a snake or dragon, and must be kissed in this form, through which the dragon is changed into a beautiful woman. A fish's or a serpent's tail is attributed to certain wise women. In the "golden mountain" a king's daughter was be-witched into a snake. In the Oselberg near Dinkelsbühl there lives a snake with a woman's head and a bunch of keys around her neck. (Grimm.)

[68] Faust (II Part):
> Doch im Erstarren such ich nicht mein Heil,
> Das Schaudern ist der Menschheit bestes Teil;
> Wie auch die Welt ihm das Gefühl verteure,
> Ergriffen, fühlt er tief das Ungeheure.

[69] "Etymol. Wörterbuch der deutschen Sprache," sub. Hort.

[70] "Griechische Etymologie," sub. κεύθω.

[71] Pausanias: I, 18, 7.

[72] Rohde: "Psyche," IV. Aufl., Vol. I, p. 214.

[73] J. Maehly: "Die Schlange im Mythus und Kultus der klassischen Völker," 1867.

[74] Duchesne: "Lib. pontifical.," I, S. CIX. Cited by Cumont: "Textes et Monuments," Vol. I, p. 351.

[75] Cited by Cumont: "Textes et Monuments," Vol. I, p. 351.

[76] Like his counterpart, the apocalyptic "son of man," from whose mouth proceeds a "sharp two-edged sword." Rev. i:16. Compare Christ as serpent and the Antichrist seducing the people. Rev. xx: 3. We come across the same motive of the guardian dragon who pierces women, in the myth from Van Diemen's Land: "A horn-back lay in the cavity of a rock, a huge horn-back! The horn-back was large and he had a very long spear. From his cavity he espied the women; he saw them dive into the water, he pieced them with his spear, he killed them, he carried them away. For some time they were to be seen no longer." The monster was then killed by the two heroes. They made fire(!) and brought the women to life again. (Cited by Frobenius: Ibid., p. 77.)

[77] The eyes of the Son of man are like a flame of fire. Rev. i:15.

[78] Cited by Cumont: "Textes et Monuments," I, p. 352.

[79] Compare Roscher: "Lexicon," I, 2, 1885.

[80] The triple form also related to the moon (waxing, full, and waning moon). However, such cosmic relations are primarily projections of metapsychology.

[81] Faust (II Part): The Scene of the mothers: The key belongs to Hecate, προθυραία, as the guardian of Hades, and psychopompic Divinity. Compare Janus, Peter and Aion.

[82] Attribute of the "terrible mother": Ishtar has "tormented the horse with goad and whip and tortured him to death." (Jensen: "Gilgamesh Epic," p. 18.) Also an attribute of Helios.

[83] Phallic symbol of fear.

[84] Murderous weapon as symbol of the fructifying phallus.

[85] Plato has already testified to this as a phallic symbol, as is mentioned above.

[86] Cited by Roscher: I, 2, Sp. 1909.

[87] Compare the symbolism in the hymn to Mary of Melk (12th century).
    "Santa Maria,
        Closed gate
        Opened to God's command—
        Sealed fountain,
        Barred garden,
        Gate of Paradise."

The same symbolism occurs in an erotic verse:
    "Maiden, may I enter with you
        Into your rose garden,
        There, where the little red roses grow,
        Those delicate and tender roses,

With a tree close by,
Whose leaves sway to and fro,
And a cool little brook
Which lies directly beneath it."

[88] Herzog: "Aus dem Asklepieion von Kos." *Archiv für Religionswissenschaft,* Vol. X, H. 2, p. 219 ff.

[89] A Mithraic sanctuary was, when at all possible, a subterranean grotto; often the cavern was merely an artificial one. It is conceivable that the Christian crypts and subterranean churches are of similar meaning.

[90] Compare Schultze: "Die Katakomben," 1882, p. 9.

[91] In the Taurobolia a bull was sacrificed over a grave, in which lay the one to be consecrated. His initiation consisted in being covered with the blood of the sacrifice. Also a regeneration and rebirth, baptism. The baptized one was called *Renatus.*

[92] Additional proof in Herzog: Ibid., p. 224.

[93] Ibid., p. 225.

[94] Indeed sacred serpents were kept for display and other purposes.

[95] Rohde: "Psyche," chap. 1, p. 244.

[96] Vol. I, p. 28.

[97] Fick. Compare "Wörterbuch," I, p. 424.

[98] Compare the stable cleaning of Hercules. The stable, like the cavern, is a place of birth. We find stable and cavern in Mithracism combined with the bull symbolism, as in Christianity. (See Robertson: "Christ and Krishna.") In a Basuto myth, the stable birth also occurs. (Frobenius.) The stable birth belongs to the mythologic animal fable; therefore the legend of the conceptio immaculata, allied to the history of the impregnation of the barren Sarah, appears very early in Egypt as an animal fable. Herodotus, III, 28, relates: "This Apis or Epaphos is a calf whose mother was unable to become impregnated, but the Egyptians said that a ray from heaven fell upon the cow, and from that she brought forth Apis." Apis symbolizes the sun, therefore his signs: upon the forehead a white spot, upon his back a figure of an eagle, upon his tongue a beetle.

[99] According to Philo, the serpent is the most spirited of all animals; its nature is that of fire, the rapidity of its movements is great and this without need of any especial limbs. It has a long life and sheds age, with its skin. Therefore it was inculcated in the mysteries, because it is immortal. (Maehly: "Die Schlange in Mythologie und Kultus der klassischen Völker," 1867, p. 7.)

[100] For example, the St. John of Quinten Matsys (see illustration); also two pictures by an unknown Strassburg master in the Gallery at Strassburg.

[101] "And the woman—having a golden cup in her hand full of abominations and filthiness of her fornication" (Rev. xvii:4). The woman is "drunken with the blood of the saints and with the blood of the martyrs of Jesus": a striking image of the terrible mother (here, cup = genitals). In the Tibetan myth of Bogda Gesser Khan there

is a beetle (treasure attainable with difficulty), which the demoniac old woman guards. Gesser says to her: "Sister, never since I was born have you shown me the beetle my soul." The mother libido is also the soul. It is significant that the old woman desired the hero as a husband. (Frobenius.)

[102] This is also the significance of the mysteries. Their purpose is to lead the useless, regressive incestuous libido over the bridges of symbolism into rational activity, and through that transform the obscure compulsion of the libido working up from the unconscious into social communion and higher moral endeavor.

[103] An excellent example of this is the description of the orgies of the Russian sectarian by Mereschkowski, in his book, "Peter the Great and Alexei." In the cult of the Asiatic Goddesses of love (Anaïtis, Mylitta, etc.), prostitution in the temple was an organized institution. The orgiastic cult of Anâhita (Anaitis) has been preserved in modern sects, with the Ali Illâhîja, the so-called "extinguishers of light"; with the Yezêds and Dushikkurds, who celebrate nocturnal religious orgies which end in a wild sexual debauch, during which incestuous unions also occur. (Spiegel: "Erân. Altertumskunde," II, p. 64.) Further examples are to be found in the valuable work of Stoll ("Das Sexualleben in der Völkerpsychologie," Leipzig 1908).

[104] Concerning the kiss of the snake, compare Grimm, II, p. 809. By this means, a beautiful woman was set free. The sucking refers to the maternal significance of the snake, which exists along with the phallic. It is a coitus act on the presexual stage. Spielrein's insane patient (*Jahrbuch*, III, p. 344) says as follows: "Wine is the blood of Jesus.—The water must be blessed, and was blessed by him. The one buried alive becomes the vineyard. That wine becomes blood—the water is mingled with 'childishness' because God says, 'become like little children.' There is also a spermatic water which can be drunken with blood. That perhaps is the water of Jesus." Here we find a commingling of all the various meanings of the way to win immortality. Wiedemann ("Der alte Orient," II, 2, p. 18; cited by Dieterich: Ibid., p. 101) asserts that it is an Egyptian idea that man draws in the milk of immortality by suckling the breast of a goddess. (Compare with that the myth of Hercules, where the hero attains immortality by a single draw at the breast of Hera.)

[105] From the writings of the sectarian Anton Unternährer: "Geheimes Reskript der bernischen Regierung an die Pfarr- und Statthalterämter," 1821. I owe the knowledge of this fragment to Rev. Dr. O. Pfister.

[106] Nietzsche: "Zarathustra": "And I also give this parable to you: Not a few who wished to drive out the devil from themselves, by that lead themselves into the slough."

[107] Compare the vision of Zosimos.

[108] The significance of the communion ritual as a unio mystica with God is at bottom sexual and very corporeal. The primitive significance of the communion is that of a Hierosgamos. Therefore in the fragment of the Attis mysteries handed down by Firmicus it is said that the mystic eats from the Tympanon, drinks from the Kymbalon, and he confesses: ὑπὸ τὸν παστὸν ὑπέδυον, which means the same as: "I have entered the

bridal chamber." Usener (in Dieterich: Ibid., p. 126) refers to a series of quotations from the patristic literature, of which I mention merely one sentence from the speeches of Proclus of Constantinople: ἡ παστὰς ἐν ᾗ ὁ λόγος ἐνυμφεύσατο τὴν σάρκα (The bridal chamber in which the Logos has espoused the flesh). The church is also to some extent the bridal chamber, where the spirit unites with the flesh, really the Cömeterium. Irenaeus mentions some more of the initiatory customs of certain gnostic sects, which were undoubtedly nothing but spiritual weddings. (Compare Dieterich: Ibid., p. 127 ff.) In the Catholic church, even yet, a Hieros-gamos is celebrated on the installation of a priest. A young maiden there represents the church as bride.

[109] Compare also the phantasies of Felicien Rops: The crucified Priapus.

[110] Compare with that the symbolism in Nietzsche's poem: " Why enticest thou thyself into the paradise of the old serpent? "

[111] " Thus Spake Zarathustra."

[112] Nietzsche himself must have shown at times a certain predilection for loathsome animals. Compare C. A. Bernoulli: " Franz Oberbeck und Friedrich Nietzsche," Vol. I, p. 166.

[113] I recall Nietzsche's dream, which is cited in Part I of this book.

[114] The Germanic myth of Dietrich von Bern, who had fiery breath, belongs to this idea: He was wounded in the forehead by an arrow, a piece of which remained there fixed; from this, he was called the im-mortal. In a similar manner, half of Hrûngnir's wedge-shaped stone fastened itself in Thor's head. See Grimm: "Mythology," I, p. 309.

[115] " Geschichte der Philosophie," Vol. I, p. 181.

[116] Sa tapo atapyata.

[117] The Stoic idea of the creative primal warmth, in which we have already recognized the libido (Part I, Chap. IV), belongs in this con-nection, also the birth of Mithra from a stone, which resulted *solo aestu libidinis* (through the heat of the libido only).

[118] In the accurate prose translation this passage reads: " There Kâma developed from him in the beginning" (Deussen: " Gesch. d. Phil.," Vol. I, p. 123). Kâma is the libido. " The sages found the root of being in the non-being, in the heart, searching with introspection."

[119] " Fame and Eternity."

[120] Grimm: " Mythology," III. The heroes have serpent's eyes, as do the kings: ormr î auga. Sigurdr is called Ormr î Auga.

[121] Nietzsche's

> " In the green light,
> Happiness still plays around the brown abyss.
> His voice grows hoarse,
> His eye flashes verdigris! "

[122] From " The Poverty of the Richest."

[123] Nietzsche's " Fragments of Dionysus-Dithyrambs."

> " Heavy eyes,
> Which seldom love:

> But when they love, it flashes out
> Like a gold mine
> ` Where a dragon guards the treasure of love."

[124] He is pregnant with the sun.

[125] Galatians iii: 27 alludes to this primitive idea: "For as many of you as have been baptized into Christ have *put on* Christ."

[126] Just as is Mânî so is Marsyas a crucified one. (See Robertson: "Evangelical Myths," p. 66.) Both were hung, a punishment which has an unmistakable symbolic value, because the suspension ("to suffer and fear in the torment of suspension") is the symbol of an unfulfilled wish. (See Freud: "The Interpretation of Dreams.") Therefore Christ, Odin, Attis hung on trees (= mother). The Talmudic Jesus ben Pandira (apparently the earliest historic Jesus) suffered a similar death, on the eve of a Passover festival in the reign of Alexander Jannaeus (106-79 B.C.). This Jesus may have been the founder of the "Essenes," a sect (see Robertson: "Evang. Myths," p. 123) which stood in a certain relation to subsequent Christianity. The Jesus ben Stada identified with the preceding Jesus, but removed into the second Christian century, was also hung. Both were first stoned, a punishment which was, so to speak, a bloodless one like hanging. The Christian church, which spills no blood, therefore burned. This may not be without significance for a peculiar ceremony reported from Uganda: "When a king of Uganda wished to live forever, he went to a place in Busiro, where a feast was given by the chiefs. At the feast the Mamba Clan was especially held in honor, and during the festivities a member of this clan was secretly chosen by his fellows, caught by them, and beaten to death with their fists; no stick or other weapon might be used by the men appointed to do the deed. After death, the victim's body was flayed and the skin made into a special whip, etc. After the ceremony of the feast in Busiro, with its strange sacrifice, the king of Uganda was supposed to live forever, but from that day he was never allowed to see his mother again. (Quoted from Frazer: "Golden Bough," Part IV, p. 415.) The sacrifice, which is chosen to purchase everlasting life for another, is here given over to a bloodless death and after that skinned. That this sacrifice has an absolutely unmistakable relation to the mother—as we already know—is corroborated very plainly by Frazer.

[127] Frazer: "Adonis, Attis, Osiris," p. 242.

[128] Frazer: Ibid., p. 246.

[129] Frazer: Ibid., p. 249.

[130] Cited by Dieterich in "Mithrasliturgie," p. 215.

[131] Another attempt at solution seems to be the Dioscuri motive: The sun consists of two brothers similar to each other, the one mortal, the other immortal. This motive is found, as is well known, in the two Açvins, who, however, are not further differentiated. In the Mithraic doctrine, Mithra is the father, Sol the son, and yet both are one as ὁ μέγας θεὸς Ἥλιος Μίθρας. The motive of twins emerges, not infrequently, in dreams. In a dream, where it is related that a woman had given birth to twins, the dreamer found, instead of the expected children, a box and a bottle-like object. Here the twins had male and female significance. This observation hints at a possible significance of the Dioscuri as the sun and its re-bearing mother—daughter(?).

[132] Among the daughters of the desert.

[133] *Zentralblatt für Psychoanalyse,* Vol. II, p. 169.

[134] This problem has frequently been employed in the ancient sun myths. It is especially striking that the lion-killing heroes, Samson and Hercules, are weaponless in the combat. The lion is the symbol of the most intense summer heat, astrologically he is the Domicilium Solis. Steinthal (*Zeitschrift für Völkerpsychologie,* Vol. II, p. 133) reasons about this in a most interesting manner, which I quote word for word:

"When the Sun-god fights against the summer heat, he fights against himself; when he kills it, he kills himself. Most certainly! The Phœnician, Assyrian and Lydian ascribes self-destruction to his sun-god, for he can comprehend the lessening of the sun's heat only as a self-murder. He believed that the sun stood at its highest in the summer and its rays scorched with destroying heat: thus does the god burn himself, but he does not die, only rejuvenates himself.—Also Hercules burns himself, but ascends to Olympus in the flames. This is the contradiction in the pagan gods. They, as forces of nature, are helpful as well as harmful to men. In order to do good and to redeem they must work against themselves. The opposition is dulled, when either of the two sides of the forces of nature is personified in an especial god, or when the power of nature is conceived of as a divine personage; however, each of its two modes of action, the benevolent and the injurious, has an especial symbol. The symbol is always independent, and finally is the god himself; and while originally the god worked against himself, destroyed himself, now symbol fights against symbol, god against god, or the god with the symbol."

Certainly the god fights with himself, with his other self, which we have conceived of under the symbol of mother. The conflict always appears to be the struggle with the father and the conquering of the mother.

[135] The old Etruscan custom of covering the urn of ashes, and the dead buried in the earth, with the shield, is something more than mere chance.

[136] Incest motive.

[137] Compare the idea of the Phœnix in the Apocalypse of Baruch, Part I of this book.

CHAPTER VIII

[1] The kingdom of the mother is the kingdom of the (unconscious) phantasy.

[2] Behind nature stands the mother, in continuation of our earlier discussions and in the foregoing poem of Hölderlin. Here the mother hovers before the poet's mind as a tree, on which the child hangs like a blossom.

[3] Once he called the "stars his brothers." Here I must call to mind the remarks in the first part of this work, especially that mystic identification with the stars: ἐγὼ εἰμι σύμπλανος ὑμῖν ἀστήρ (I am a star who wanders together with you). The separation and differentiation from the mother, the "individuation" creates that transition of the subjective into the objective, that foundation of consciousness. Before this, man was one with the mother. That is to say, with the world as a whole. At that period man did not know the sun as brother. This occurred for

the first time, when after the resulting separation and placing of the object, the libido, regressing to the infantile, perceived in that first state its possibilities and the suspicion of his relationship to the stars forced itself upon him. This occurrence appears not infrequently in the introversion psychoses. A young peasant, an ordinary laboring man, developed an introversion psychosis (Dementia Praecox). His first feelings of illness were shown by a special connection which he felt with the sun and the stars. The stars became full of meaning to him, and the sun suggested ideas to him. This apparently entirely new perception of nature is met with very often in this disease. Another patient began . to understand the language of birds, which brought him messages from his beloved (mother). Compare Siegfried.

[4] The spring belongs to the idea as a whole.

[5] This idea expresses the divine-infantile blessedness, as in Hyperion's " Song of Fate."

> " You wander above there in the light
> Upon soft clouds, blessed genii!
> Shining breezes of the gods
> Stir you gently."

[6] This portion is especially noteworthy. In childhood everything was given him, and man is disinclined to obtain it once more for himself, because it is won only through " toil and compulsion ": even love costs trouble. In childhood the well of the libido gushed forth in bubbling fulness. In later life it involves hard work to even keep the stream flowing for the onward striving life, because with increasing age the stream has a growing inclination to flow back to its source, if effectual mechanisms are not created to hinder this backward movement or at least to organize it. In this connection belongs the generally accepted idea, that love is absolutely spontaneous; only the infantile type of love is something absolutely spontaneous. The love of an adult man allows itself to be purposefully directed. Man can also say " I will love." The heights of culture are conditioned by *the capacity for displacement of the libido.*

[7] Motive of immortality in the fable of the death of Empedocles. Horace: *Deus immortalis haberi—Dum cupit Empedocles ardentem frigidus Aetnam—Insiluit* (Empedocles deliberately threw himself into the glowing Aetna because he wanted to be believed an immortal god).

[8] Compare the beautiful passage in the journey to Hades of Odysseus, where the hero wishes to embrace his mother.

> " But I, thrilled by inner longing,
> Wanted to embrace the soul of my departed mother.
> Three times I endeavored, full of passionate desire for the embrace:
> Three times from my hands she escaped
> Like nocturnal shades and the images of dreams,
> And in my heart sadness grew more intense." (" Odyss.," XI, 204.)

The underworld, hell, is indeed the place of unfulfilled longing. The Tantalus motive is found through all of hell.

[9] Spielrein's patient (*Jahrbuch*, III, p. 345) speaks in connection with the significance of the communion of " the water mixed with childishness; spermatic water, blood and wine." P. 368 she says: " The souls fallen into the water are saved by God, they fall into the deep abyss— The souls were saved by the son of God."

[10] The φάρμακον ἀθανασίας, the drink of Soma, the Haoma of the Persians, might have been made from Ephedra vulgaris. Spiegel: "Erân. Altertumskunde," I, p. 433.

[11] Like the heavenly city in Hauptmann's "Hannele":
"Salvation is a wonderful city,
Where peace and joy never end,
Its houses are marble, its roofs are gold,
But wine flows in silver fountains,
Flowers are strewed upon the white, white streets,
Continually from the towers sound the wedding bells.
Green as May are the battlements, shining with the light of early
    morning.
Giddy with butterflies, crowned with roses.

· · · ·

There below, hand in hand,
The festive people wander through the heavenly land,
The wide, wide sea is filled with red, red wine,
They plunge in with shining bodies!
They plunge into the foam and the splendor,
The clear purple covers them entirely,
And they exulting arise from the flood,
Thus they are washed by Jesus' blood."

[12] Richter: 15, 17.

[13] Prellwitz: "Griech. Etym.," s. σκήπτω.

[14] Of the father.

[15] This was really the purpose of all mysteries. They create symbolisms of death and rebirth for the practical application and education of the infantile libido. As Frazer ("The Golden Bough," I, p. 442) points out, exotic and barbaric peoples have in their initiatory mysteries the same symbolism of death and resurrection, just as Apuleius "Metam.," XI, 23) says of the initiation of Lucius into the Isis mysteries: "Accessi confinium mortis et calcato Proserpinae limine per omnia vectus elementa remeavi" (I have reached the confines of death and trodden the threshold of Proserpina; passing through all the elements, I have returned). Lucius died figuratively (ad instar voluntariae mortis) and was born anew (renatus).

[16] This does not hinder the modern neurasthenic from making work a means of repression and worrying about it.

[17] Compare Genesis xlix:17: "Dan shall be a serpent by the way, an adder in the path, that biteth the horse heels, so that his rider shall fall backward."

[18] Compare with this the Egyptian representation of the Heaven as woman and cow.

[19] Freud: "Formulierungen über die zwei Prinzipien des psychischen Geschehens," 1912 Jahrbuch, p. 1 ff.

[20] This form of question recalls the well-known Indian symbol of the world-bearing animal: an elephant standing upon a tortoise. The elephant has chiefly masculine-phallic significance and the tortoise, like every shell animal, chicfly feminine significance.

[21] *Zentralblatt für Psychoanalyse,* Vol. II, p. 171.

[22] The neurotic Don Juan is no evidence to the contrary. That which the "habitué" understands by love is merely an infirmity and far different from that which love means!

[23] Spiegel: "Erân. Altertumskunde," II, 667.

[24] Freud: "Eine Kindheitserinnerung des Leonardo da Vinci," p. 57: "The almighty, just God and benevolent nature appear to us as a great sublimation of father and mother, rather than revivals and reproductions of the early childish ideas of them. Religiousness leads biologically back to the long-continued helplessness and need of the offspring of man, who, when later he has recognized his real loneliness, and weakness against the great powers of life, feels his condition similar to that of childhood, and seeks to disavow this forlorn state by regressive renewal of the infantile protective powers."

[25] Nietzsche: "Fröhliche Wissenschaft," Aphorism 157. "Mentiri—give heed!—he muses: immediately he will have a lie prepared. This is a stage of culture, upon which whole peoples have stood. One should ponder over what the Romans meant by mentiri!" Actually the Indo-Germanic root *méntis,* men, is the same for mentiri, memini and mens. See Walde: "Lat. Etym.," sub. mendax, memini und mens.

[26] See Freud: *Jahrbuch,* Vol. III, p. 60.

[27] Bundehesh, XV, 27. The bull Sarsaok was sacrificed at the destruction of the world. But Sarsaok was the originator of the race of men: he had brought nine of the fifteen human races upon his back through the sea to the distant points of the compass. The primitive bull of Gayomart has, as we saw above, most undoubtedly female and maternal significance on account of his fertility.

[28] If for Silberer the mythological symbolism is a process of cognition on the mythological stage (*Jahrbuch,* Vol. III, p. 664), then there exists, between this view and mine, only a difference of standpoint, which determines a different manner of expression.

[29] This series of representations begins with the totem meal.

[30] Taurus is astrologically the Domicilium Veneris.

[31] There comes from the library of Asurbanipal an interesting Sumeric-Assyrian fragment (Cuneiform Inscr., I, IV, 26, 6. Quoted by Gressmann: "Altorient. Text. und Bild.," I, p. 101):

> "To the wise man he said:
> A lamb is the substitute for a man.
> He gives a lamb for his life,
> He gives the heads of lambs for the heads of men," etc.

[32] Compare the remarkable account in Pausanias: VI, 17, 9 ff. "While sleeping, the sperma of Zeus has flowed down upon the earth; in time has arisen from this a demon, with double generative organs; that of a man, and that of a woman. They gave him the name of Agdistis. But the gods changed Agdistis and cut off the male organs. Now when the almond tree which sprang forth from this bore ripe fruit, the daughter of the spring, Sangarios, took of the fruit. When she placed it in her bosom, the fruit disappeared at once; but she found herself pregnant. After she had given birth to the child, a goat acted as pro-

tector: when he grew up, he was of superhuman beauty, so that Agdistis fell in love with the boy. His relatives sent the full-grown Attis to Pessinus, in order to marry the king's daughter. The wedding song was beginning when Agdistis appeared and in delirium Attis castrated himself."

[33] Firmicus: "De error. prof. rel.," XXVIII. Quoted by Robertson: "Evang. Myths," p. 136, and Creuzer: "Symbolik," II, 332.

[34] Pentheus, as a hero with a serpent nature; his father was Echion, the adder.

[35] The typical sacrificial death in the Dionysus cult.

[36] In the festival processions they wore women's clothes.

[37] In Bithynia Attis was called πάπας (papa, pope) and Cybele, Mã. In the early Asiatic religions of this mother-goddess, there existed fish worship and prohibition against fish as food for the priests. In the Christian religion, it is noteworthy that the son of Atargatis, identified with Astarte, Cybele, etc., is called Ἰχθύς (Creuzer: "Symbolik," II, 60). Therefore, the anagram of the name of Christ = ΙΗΣΟΥΣ ΧΡΙΣΤΟΣ ΘΕΟΥ ΥΙΟΣ ΣΩΤΗΡ = ΙΧΘΥΣ.

[38] Spiegel: "Erân. Altertumskunde," 2, 76.

[39] A. Nagel: "Der chinesische Küchengott Tsau-kyun." Archiv für Religionswissenschaft, XI, 23 ff.

[40] In Spiegel's "Parsigrammatik," pp. 135, 166.

[41] Porphyrius says: ὡς καὶ ὁ ταῦρος δημιουργὸς ὢν ὁ Μίθρας καὶ γενέσεως δεσπότης (As the bull is the Creator, Mithra is the Lord of birth).

[42] The death of the bull is voluntary and involuntary. When Mithra strangles the bull, a scorpion bites the bull in the testicles (autumn equinox).

[43] Benndorf: "Bildwerke des Lateran Museum," No. 547.

[44] "Textes et Monuments," I, 182.

[45] In another place Cumont speaks of "the sorrowful and almost morbid grace of the features of the hero."

[46] Infantilism is merely the result of the much deeper state of introversion of the Christian in contrast to the other religions.

[47] The libido nature of the sacrificed is unquestionable. In Persia, a ram helped the first people to the first sin, cohabitation: it is also the first animal which they sacrificed (Spiegel: "Erân. Altertumskunde," Vol. I, p. 511). The ram is the same as the paradisical serpent, which was Christ according to the Manichean version. The ancient Meliton of Sardes taught that Christ was a lamb, similar to the ram in the bush, which Abraham sacrificed in place of his son. Here the bush is analogous to the cross (Fragment V, quoted by Robertson: Ibid).

[48] See above. "Blood bridegroom of the mother." From Joshua v:2 we learn that Joshua again instituted the circumcision and redemption of the firstborn: "With this he must have substituted for the sacrifice of children, which earlier it was the custom to offer up to Jehovah, the sacrifice of the male foreskin" (Drews: "Christusmythe," I, p. 47).

[49] See Cumont: Ibid., p. 100.

[50] The Zodiacal sign of the sun's greatest heat.

[51] This solution apparently concerns only the dogmatic symbolism. I merely intimate that this sacrificial death was related to a festival of vegetation or of Spring, from which the religious legend originated. The folk customs contain in variations these same fundamental thoughts. (Compare with that Drews: "Christusmythe," I, p. 37).

[52] A similiar sacrificial death is that of Prometheus. He was chained to a rock. In another version his chains were drawn through a pillar, which hints at the enchainment to a tree. That punishment was his which Christ took upon himself willingly. The fate of Prometheus therefore recalls the misfortune of Theseus and Perithoos, who remain bound to the rock, the chthonic mother. According to Athenaeus, Jupiter commanded Prometheus, after he had freed him, to wear a willow crown and an iron ring, by which his lack of freedom and slavery was symbolically represented. (Phoroneus, who in Argos was worshipped as the bringer of fire, was the son of Melia, the ash, therefore tree-enchained.) Robertson compares the crown of Prometheus to the crown of thorns of Christ. The devout carry crowns in honor of Prometheus, in order to represent the captivity ("Evangelical Myths," p. 126). In this connection, therefore, the crown means the same as the betrothal ring. These are the requisites of the old Hierosgamos with the mother; the crown of thorns (which is of Egyptian derivation according to Athenaeus) has the significance of the painful ascetic betrothal.

[53] The spear wound given by Longinus to Christ is the substitute for the dagger thrust in the Mithraic bull sacrifice: "The jagged tooth of the brazen wedge" was driven through the breast of the enchained and sacrificed Prometheus (Aeschylus: "Prometheus").

[54] Mention must also be made of the fact that North German mythology was acquainted with similar thoughts regarding the fruitfulness of the sacrificial death on the mother: Through hanging on the tree of life, Odin obtained knowledge of the Runes and the inspiring, intoxicating drink which invested him with immortality.

[55] I have refrained in the course of this merely orienting investigating from referring to the countless possibilities of relationship between dream symbolism and the material disclosed in these connections. That is a matter of a special investigation. But I cannot forbear mentioning here a simple dream, the first which a youthful patient brought to me in the beginning of her analysis. "She stands between high walls of snow upon a railroad track with her small brother. A train comes, she runs before it in deadly fear and leaves her brother behind upon the track. She sees him run over, but after the train has passed, the little fellow stands up again uninjured." The meaning of the dream is clear: the inevitable approach of the "impulse." The leaving behind of the little brother is the repressed willingness to accept her destiny. The acceptance is symbolized by the sacrifice of the little brother (the infantile personality) whose apparently certain death becomes, however, a resurrection. Another patient makes use of classical forms: she dreamed of a mighty eagle, which is wounded in beak and neck by an arrow. If we go into the actual transference phantasy (eagle = physician, arrow = erotic wish of the patient), then the material concerning the eagle (winged lion of St. Mark, the past splendor of Venice; beak = remembrances of

certain perverse actions of childhood) leads us to understand the eagle as a composition of infantile memories, which in part are grouped around the father. The eagle, therefore, is an infantile hero who is wounded in a characteristic manner on the phallic point (beak). The dream also says: I renounce the infantile wish, I sacrifice my infantile personality (which is synonymous with: I paralyze it, castrate the father or the physician). In the Mithra mysteries, in the introversion the mystic himself becomes ἀετός, the eagle, this being the highest degree of initiation. The identification with the unconscious libido animal goes very far in this cult, as Augustine relates: " alii autem sicut aves alas percutiunt vocem coracis imitantes, alii vero leonum more fremunt " (Some move the arms like birds the wings, imitating the voice of the raven, some groan like lions).

[56] Miss Miller's snake is green. The snake of my patient is also green. In " Psychology of Dementia Praecox," p. 161, she says: " Then a little green snake came into my mouth; it had the finest, loveliest sense, as if it had human understanding; it wanted to say something to me, almost as if it had wished to kiss me." Spielrein's patient says of the snake: " It is an animal of God, which has such wonderful colors, green, blue and white. The rattlesnake is green; it is very dangerous. The snake can have a human mind, it can have God's judgment; it is a friend of children. It will save those children who are necessary for the preservation of human life " (Jahrbuch, Vol. III, p. 366). Here the phallic meaning is unmistakable. The snake as the transformed prince in the fairy tale has the same meaning. See Riklin: " Wish Fulfilment and Symbolism in Fairy Tales."

[57] A patient had the phantasy that she was a serpent which coiled around the mother and finally crept into her.

[58] The serpent of Epidaurus is, in contrast, endowed with healing power. Similia similibus.

[59] This Bleuler has designated as Ambivalence or ambitendency. Stekel as " Bi-polarity of all psychic phenomena " (" Sprache des Traumes," p. 535).

[60] I am indebted for permission to publish a picture of this statuette to the kindness of the director of the Veronese collection of antiques.

[61] The " Deluge " is of one nature with the serpent. In the Wöluspa it is said that the flood is produced when the Midgard serpent rises up for universal destruction. He is called " Jörmungandr," which means, literally, "the all-pervading wolf." The destroying Fenris wolf has also a connection with the sea. Fen is found in Fensalir (Meersäle), the dwelling of Frigg, and originally meant sea (Frobenius: Ibid., p. 179). In the fairy stories of Red Riding Hood, a wolf is substituted in place of a serpent or fish.

[62] Compare the longing of Hölderlin expressed in his poem " Empedocles." Also the journey to hell of Zarathustra through the crater of the volcano. Death is the entrance into the mother, therefore the Egyptian king, Mykerinos, buried his daughter in a gilded wooden cow. That was the guarantee of rebirth. The cow stood in a state apartment and sacrifices were brought to it. In another apartment near the cow were placed the images of the concubines of Mykerinos (Herodotus, II, p. 129 f).

[63] Kluge: " Deutsche Etymologie."

INDEX